# PLANTATIONS AND OUTDOOR MUSEUMS IN AMERICA'S HISTORIC SOUTH

# PLANTATIONS AND OUTDOOR MUSEUMS IN AMERICA'S HISTORIC SOUTH

Gerald and Patricia Gutek

University of South Carolina Press

Copyright © 1996 University of South Carolina

Published in Columbia, South Carolina, by the
University of South Carolina Press

Manufactured in the United States of America

00 99 98 97 96 5 4 3 2 1

**Library of Congress Cataloging-in-Publication Data**

Gutek, Gerald Lee.
  Plantations and outdoor museums in America's historic South /
Gerald and Patricia Gutek.
    p.    cm.
  ISBN 1-57003-071-5 (pbk.)
  1. Plantations—Southern States—Guidebooks.   2. Outdoor museums—
Southern States—Guidebooks.   3. Historic sites—Southern States—
Guidebooks.   4. Southern States—Guidebooks.   I. Gutek, Patricia,
1941–        II. Title.
F210.G88   1996
917.504'43—dc20                                                 95–38981

# CONTENTS

# PLANTATIONS AND OUTDOOR MUSEUMS IN AMERICA'S HISTORIC SOUTH

# INTRODUCTION

We are both enthusiastic time travelers. Unlike fictional space explorers who travel light years into the future, we travel back in time to recapture and experience what life was like in the past. Our travels have taken us to many of America's historic places, especially to the outdoor museum villages that illustrate, through their buildings and artifacts, life in another place and another time. Our readers' warm reception of our first historical travel guide, *Experiencing America's Past: A Travel Guide to Museum Villages*, encouraged us to explore the historic places of America's South.

The South is to a history buff what Fannie May's or Ghiradelli's is to a chocoholic: there is far too much, rather than too little, from which to choose. For example, during the colonial period, the English colonized Virginia and Maryland, the Spanish colonized Florida, and the French colonized Louisiana and parts of Missouri. Historic sites that focus on colonial times include Williamsburg in Virginia, Historic St. Mary's City in Maryland, the Spanish Quarter and Castillo de San Marcos National Monument in Florida, Acadian Village in Louisiana, and Historic Ste. Genevieve in Missouri.

When the colonies tired of being ruled by England and a revolutionary urge developed among American political figures, Virginia's plantation owners played significant roles in the fight for freedom. Important revolutionary figures included George Washington of Mount Vernon, Thomas Jefferson of Monticello, Patrick Henry of Red Hill, James Monroe of Ash Lawn-Highland, Fielding Lewis (brother-in-law of George Washington) of Kenmore, Benjamin Harrison of Berkeley, and George Mason of Gunston Hall.

The Civil War, fought mainly in the South, affected that region profoundly. We have chosen not to include Civil War battlefields in *Plantations and Outdoor Museums in America's Historic South* because they have been the subject of dozens of well-researched and well-written books. However, the devastating economic effects of the War Between the States on the unique plantation system in the South is clearly evident in the stories of many plantations. In the antebellum period, large plantations generated for their owners great profits on cotton and other crops. These profits, which funded the building of impressive, lavishly furnished mansions, were based on the labor of enslaved African Americans, who received only food and lodging for their work. These workers and their families were, by law, the property of the plantation owners. But the system of slavery and the concept of ownership of human beings were abolished by the Civil War. When the war ended, owners of large agricultural units were faced with severe economic hardship in the cost of labor alone. Scores of these plantations had been looted and burned during the war, and many that remained standing were now neglected and soon fell into disrepair.

Civil War-related sites that we have included are Harpers Ferry National Historical Park in West Virginia, where John Brown made his famous raid that foreshadowed the Civil War; Fort Sumter National Monument in South Carolina, the site of the first engagement of the war; Andersonville National Historic Site in Georgia, which was a prisoner of war camp for Union captives; Appomattox Court House National Historical Park in Virginia, where General Robert E. Lee's Army of Northern Virginia surrendered to General U. S. Grant, thus ending the war; Stratford Hall Plantation, the birthplace of Confederate General Robert E. Lee; Shirley Plantation, where General Robert E. Lee was married; and Arlington House, the Robert E. Lee Memorial in Virginia which was the home of General Robert E. Lee.

We have found that exploring plantations and outdoor museum villages, which depict restored or re-created cross sections of Southern life, is an entertaining way of discovering historical roots and recapturing a sense of life in an earlier time. These visits also make delightful family outings and can provide respites from the noisy routines and urgency of day-to-day life.

This introduction provides an orientation to the various types of plantations and museum villages that you will discover in your journeys through the South.

## OUTDOOR MUSEUMS AND PLANTATIONS

Outdoor museum villages generally consist of collections of original buildings grouped to illustrate the way of life—the society, religion, architecture, industry and occupations, furniture, art, and culture—of a community at a particular time in history. For example, Cades Cove and Mountain Farm Museum in Great Smokey Mountains National Park and the Museum of Appalachia portray the life-style of the mountain people of nineteenth-century Tennessee.

As historical sites, plantations are somewhat like outdoor museum villages in that they are both outdoor and indoor museums. The mansion or main house and the dependency buildings—slave cabins, smokehouse, barns, and stables—formed a living and working unit. Outdoor museum villages portray the lives of the people of a community, while plantations primarily portray the lives of the planter family, with some light shed on the lives of the slaves and other plantation workers who together formed an agricultural unit.

## TYPES OF MUSEUM VILLAGES AND PLANTATIONS

In our historical travels, we have found different types of museum villages and plantations. In order to sort them out, we have devised a few categories that may be helpful to you.

Restored museum villages and plantations are those with original buildings on their original sites. Re-created museum villages are composed of either original buildings or well-researched, contemporary facsimiles assembled on an arbitrary site. Reconstructed museum villages have been rebuilt on their original sites, and though new, reconstructed buildings are copies of the original buildings as determined through historical and archeological research.

In most instances, the buildings of a restored plantation or village have actually been used as residences or work places. Buildings have been restored to their condition when originally constructed, with all later additions and improvements removed. Furnishings include items that belonged to the first residents, if such articles can be found, or similar items that are typical of the period.

A variation is to restore buildings or villages to a later era, when a significant person was in residence or when a significant event occurred there. For example, Harpers Ferry National Historic Park reflects the period of John Brown's raid, and Appomattox Court House National Historical Park has been restored to 1865 when General Lee surrendered the Army of Northern Virginia to General Grant. The Mark Twain Boyhood Home and Museum in Missouri and the Carl Sandburg Home National Historic Site in North Carolina both reflect the time when those famous authors were in residence.

Some restored villages were once the locations of religious societies such as the Shakers, the Moravians, and the Koreshans. These groups, sustained by shared doctrines and beliefs, sought to create communities where they could practice their religion without interference. Examples are Old Salem in Winston-Salem, North Carolina; the Shaker Village at Pleasant Hill in Harrodsburg, Kentucky; and the Koreshan State Historic Site in Estero, Florida.

Another type of outdoor museum village is the re-created one. Here, original historic buildings have been moved to a particular location to re-create a period of time or to preserve a region's historic buildings which were being threatened by neglect. Some of these villages have been developed because the antique collections of particular individuals had outgrown the available space. In studying historical preservation, we often see this pattern: one or two people with a passion for collecting and the financial means and good sense with which to do it leave a valuable legacy for society. Another pattern is that groups of local people who are interested in historic preservation unite their efforts to establish a museum village. Examples are Westville in Georgia, the Antebellum Plantation in Georgia, and the LSU Rural Life Museum in Louisiana.

In some instances, where an actual plantation or village has been completely destroyed, total reconstruction has been done. On the basis of archaeological and historical research, the foundations of the original buildings are located. Historical documents such as drawings, blueprints, and diaries are then used in the design and building of the facsimile structures. Examples of historic reconstruction are Historic St. Mary's City in Maryland and the Tryon Palace Historic Site in North Carolina.

Regardless of their type, the plantation and the outdoor museum village have the advantage of depicting a complete historical environment in relationship to their natural setting. They portray religious, political, cultural, social, and economic life by showing us where people prayed, worked, and lived.

## A VISITOR'S OVERVIEW OF THE HISTORIC VILLAGE

To appreciate a historic plantation or village, be a traveler in space and time rather than a hurried tourist. Allow yourself to become part of the historic-environment experience by taking the time to place your visit in its context.

Many museum villages have visitor centers that provide brochures, maps, exhibits, and guides. Some time spent at the visitor center before you begin your journey through the plantation or village will enhance your overall perspective. If the visitor center has a film or slide presentation, take time to view it. The descriptions in this book also provide background information for your journey into America's Southern heritage.

Most plantations and some museum villages provide guided tours on which a trained historic interpreter will narrate the history, tell you about the people, and describe the art and artifacts of the place that you are visiting. If available, such a tour will further enhance your visit.

After getting a perspective of the plantation or museum village, begin your own personal exploration. Each traveler has his or her own interests, and a historical plantation or village can satisfy all of them. Some travelers may be interested in the style of architecture, while others may be interested in decorative arts and artifacts—the utensils, wall hangings, chinaware, quilts, and furniture. Still others may concentrate on the historic landscaping and gardens, or the life-style of the people.

## USING THE BOOK

The plantations and museum villages described in this book are organized by state. This arrangement will facilitate your planning trips to a number of plantations and museum villages located in the same state.

Each entry for a plantation or outdoor museum village begins with a listing of facts identifying and categorizing the site; the location, mailing address, phone number, operating months and times, and the cost of admission are then provided; and restaurants, shops, facilities, and special features are highlighted. Although we have indicated admission fees, it should be noted that these are subject to change. In our descriptions, we have used the following abbreviations: NR, which signifies that the site is included in the National Register of Historic Places; NHL, which identifies the site or structure as a National Historic Landmark; and HABS, which identifies the structure as being included in the Historic American Building Survey.

To facilitate your travel planning, we have included a "Where to Stay" section that lists accommodations located in the vicinity of each site. These accommodations include resorts, inns, bed-and-breakfast lodgings, motels, and hotels, and campgrounds.

To provide an orientation to the site and its significance, we describe the history of the site and the people who lived there. The history is followed by the "Site Description" section, which includes a description of the buildings, specific rooms, and furnishings.

In the "Festival/Crafts" section can be found special events or activities offered at the particular site. Some visitors may want to plan their visit to coincide with a particular event. For added interest and convenience, we've included brief descriptions of side trips to other points of interest in the vicinity of the plantation or museum village.

# ALABAMA

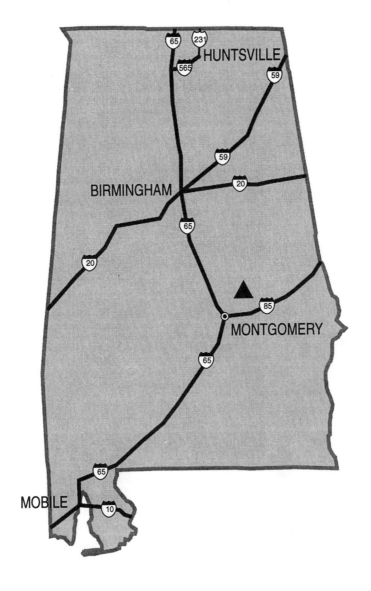

Tuskegee: Tuskegee Institute National Historic Site

# TUSKEGEE INSTITUTE NATIONAL HISTORIC SITE

### African-American college founded in 1881 by Booker T. Washington; NR.

**Address:** 1212 Old Montgomery Rd., PO Drawer 10, Tuskegee Institute, AL 36088

**Telephone:** (205) 727-3200

**Location:** In east central Alabama; the site is on Old Montgomery Rd. (AL Hwy. 126), just outside the city of Tuskegee.

**Open:** 9:00 A.M.–5:00 P.M. daily; closed Thanksgiving, Christmas, and New Year's Days.

**Admission:** Free.

**Shops:** Museum shop in Carver Museum.

**Facilities:** Visitor Orientation Center.

## WHERE TO STAY

**Inns/Bed & Breakfasts:** Crenshaw Guest House, 371 North College St., Auburn AL 36830, (205) 821-1131.

**Motel/Hotels:** Tuskegee Inn, I-85 and Notasulga Hwy., Tuskegee AL 36083, (205) 727-5400. Auburn Conference Center and Motor Lodge, Box 3467, 1577 South College St., Auburn AL 36830, (205) 821-7001. Auburn University Hotel, 241 South College St., Auburn AL 36830, (205) 821-8200, 1-800-228-2876, FAX: (205) 826-8755. Holiday Inn-East, 1185 Eastern Bypass, Montgomery AL 36117, (205) 272-0370, FAX: (205) 270-0339.

**Camping:** Chewalca State Park, PO Box 447, Auburn AL 36831, (205) 887-5621. Baker's Mobile Home and Trailer Campground, US 431 North, Opelika AL 36801, (205) 745-5165. Lazy Lose Ranch, US 431 North, Rt. 3, Opelika AL 36801, (205) 749-9375. Wind Creek State Park, Rt. 2, Box 145, Alexander City AL 35010, (205) 329-0845. Tuskegee National Forest, Rt. 1, Box 457, Tuskegee AL 36083, (205) 727-2652.

## OVERVIEW

Part of Tuskegee Institute, located at Tuskegee University, has been designated a National Historic Site and is a unit of the National Park Service. This Southern college was established by Booker T. Washington in 1881 for the vocational education of African-American students. The historic campus buildings of the post-reconstructionist era were actually constructed by students as part of their industrial training, and represent examples of black architecture.

Washington created the school from virtually nothing; no funds were provided by the Alabama legislature for land, buildings, or equipment. Washington succeeded in persuading many philanthropists such as Andrew Carnegie to donate large sums of money to Tuskegee. In the process, Washington became a powerful figure with national political clout which he used unhesitatingly. His educational philosophy of equipping blacks with agricultural, craft, and occupational skills was severely criticized by contemporary black leaders such as W. E. B. Du Bois, who labeled Washington an accommodationist.

In addition to the historic campus buildings which are still being used by Tuskegee University, visitors can tour the home of Booker T. Washington, called "The Oaks," and Carver Museum, which is named after the famous scientist and Tuskegee faculty member, George Washington Carver.

## HISTORY

Lewis Adams, a former slave, tinsmith, and blacksmith, and George W. Campbell, a former slave holder, banker, and merchant, conceived the idea of Tuskegee Institute. After the Civil War, Adams ran an informal trade school for young black men in his blacksmith shop in Macon County, Alabama. Realizing the need for a facility for teaching trades to African Americans, Adams and Campbell approached the Alabama legislature. In 1881, the legislature passed an act to establish a Negro normal school at Tuskegee with an annual appropriation of $2,000 for teachers' salaries.

Tuskegee Institute officially opened July 4, 1881, with a student population of thirty. Booker T. Washington was named principal of the institute, the mission of which was to teach trades and crafts. Washington had been a student at Virginia's Hampton Institute, a normal and industrial school for teaching and training freed slaves which opened in 1868. Washington was serving as secretary to Colonel Armstrong, Hampton's

Photo by Patricia A. Gutek

**Tuskegee Institute National Historic Site, Tuskegee, Alabama**
On the Tuskegee Institute campus, a statue dedicated to the founder of the late-nineteenth-century African-American college, Booker T. Washington, is inscribed, "He lifted the veil of ignorance from his people and pointed the way to progress through education and industry."

president, at the time the colonel recommended him for the Tuskegee position. The new principal used Hampton as a model for Tuskegee and based his program on Armstrong's philosophy of industrial education.

Initially, Tuskegee's classes were held in the Butler African Methodist Episcopal Zion Church because the Institute itself had no facilities and the Alabama legislature had not appropriated any funds for land or buildings. Washington's exceptional fundraising skills would provide much of the money needed for constructing and running the school. During his tenure, he obtained substantial contributions from John D. Rockefeller, George Eastman, Julia Emery, Henry H. Rogers, and Andrew Carnegie.

Washington's first big problem was to create a campus site. He borrowed $200 from General J. F. B. Marshall, treasurer of Hampton Institute, to purchase a plantation near Tuskegee. Washington then decided that the students would learn construction skills and use them to erect a school building. Washington obtained funds from A. H. Porter of Brooklyn, New York, for the first building. Brick-making became the first trade taught to the students. Appropriately named "Porter Hall," the brick, four-story classroom building was completed in 1883.

Students continued to add campus buildings. Architect Robert R. Taylor, an 1892 graduate of the Massachusetts Institute of Technology and a Tuskegee faculty member, designed most of the buildings and supervised their construction by student laborers.

As well as being engaged in construction, students attended classes in a variety of trades and agriculture. Tuskegee's early curricular offerings included masonry, plastering, carpentry, plumbing, electrical wiring, tinsmithing, blacksmithing, architecture, mechanical drawing, and domestic skills. By 1890, over 700 students were enrolled at the college.

The college founded by Washington reflected his attitudes toward African-American education in the post-Reconstruction era. Washington saw industrial education and the promotion of small business as the avenue for Southern, rural blacks to advance from share-cropping into the middle class. The Tuskegee idea included industrial education, self-help, and black self-sufficiency. Margaret Washington, Booker T. Washington's wife, served as Director of Industries for Girls.

Other contemporary African-American leaders strongly disagreed with Washington's philosophy of education. Many, including W. E. B. Du Bois, advocated traditional college study rather than industrial education for African Americans. Washington was accused of accommodating the white majority at the expense of black civil rights, including voting rights.

Tuskegee became a degree-granting college in 1927 under Washington's successor, Robert Russa Moton.

Washington's fundraising efforts and public speaking took him away from the campus approximately half of each year. His association with presidents, philanthropists, and other prominent Americans turned him into a nationally powerful figure with enormous clout. He headed a politically powerful clique known as the Tuskegee Machine, which made or prevented political appointments and had influential ties with newspapers and magazines.

Booker T. Washington was not the only famous educator at Tuskegee Institute. A faculty member for forty-seven years, the distinguished botanist George Washington Carver was appointed director of the Agricultural Experiment Station in 1896. His scientific reputation was based primarily on his experimental work with improving Southern agricultural crops such as peanuts and sweet potatoes. Carver was born in 1864 in Diamond Grove, Missouri, as a slave owned by Moses and Susan Carver. He was freed by the Civil War. Carver received a Bachelor of Agriculture degree and a Master of Agriculture degree at the State Agricultural College—later renamed Iowa State College—in Ames, Iowa.

## SITE DESCRIPTION

**Tuskegee Institute** remains an educational institution more than 100 years after its founding. Part of the historical appeal of this site is the buildings constructed by students of brick made in the campus brickyard. Another attraction is the spirit and courage of the African Americans who founded and attended this Alabama industrial-education school.

The main campus includes 161 buildings on 268 acres and an academic community of nearly 5,000 students, faculty, and staff. Degrees are awarded in agriculture, architecture, liberal arts, engineering, physical therapy, nursing, and veterinary medicine.

Most of the historic structures are still used as school buildings at Tuskegee. Forty early buildings remain in the campus historic district including **Tantum Hall** (1907), **White Hall** (1910), **Douglass Hall** (1904), **Huntington Hall** (1900), **Carnegie Hall** (1901), **Tompkins Hall** (1910), **Collis P. Huntington Academic Building** (1905), **Mary Scott Cottage** (1897), **Rockefeller Hall** (1903), **Power Plant** (1915), **Emery Dormitories** (1903–1909), **Milbank Agriculture Hall** (1909), and the **Early Hospital Buildings** (1912–1916).

The museum buildings are **The Oaks**, home of Booker T. Washington, and the **George Washington Carver Museum**, which also serves as the site's orientation and information center. The Oaks is a fifteen-room three-story brick house in the Queen Anne style. Built in 1899, it was home to Booker T. Washington, his wife, Margaret Murray Washington, and his three children from his previous two marriages, Portia, Booker T., Jr., and Ernest Davidson.

The Oaks, constructed adjacent to the campus on property owned by Washington, was built of Institute bricks made by students and faculty. The house was restored in 1980 by the National Park Service. A **parlor** and **dining room** are on the first floor. Walls are painted red, and there are dark-stained doors and woodwork in the entry hall. Above the gilded picture molding in first-floor rooms are frieze murals of Europe's countryside and seashore painted in 1908 by European artist E. W. Borman. In the parlor are Portia's piano and the games the family played there, including dominos. The formal dining room, which was used frequently for entertaining, also has a sitting area for after-dinner conversation.

Three bedrooms and **Washington's study** are on the second floor. Furniture in the study includes several pieces built by Institute students as well as hand-carved Oriental items. Walls are decorated with Booker T. Washington's certificate from Hampton Institute, photos of the 1875 graduating class, President Taft, President Roosevelt, Frederick Douglass, Board of Trustees members, the King and Queen of Denmark, and Alexander Pushkin. The third floor with four bedrooms was used as a student dormitory. Washington died at The Oaks in 1915, and Margaret Washington died there in 1925.

The **George Washington Carver Museum** is also the Visitor Orientation Center. The 1915 building, formerly the **laundry**, was established as the George Washington Carver Museum in 1938. On display are Carver's samples of products derived from peanuts, sweet potatoes, sand, and feathers, his vegetable specimens, and his paintings and needlework.

# ARKANSAS

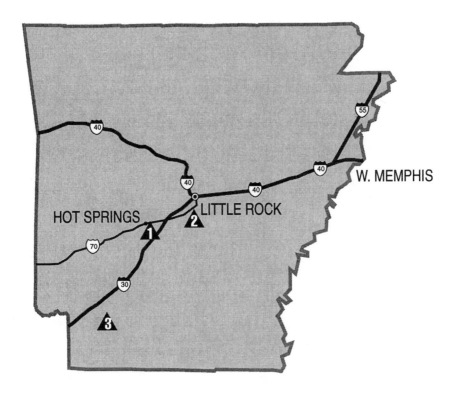

1. Hot Springs: Hot Springs National Park
2. Little Rock: Arkansas Territorial Restoration
3. Washington: Old Washington Historic State Park

# HOT SPRINGS
# NATIONAL PARK

Restored thermal bathhouses in late-nineteenth-century/
early-twentieth-century health and recreational spa;
47 preserved hot springs.

**Address:** PO Box 1860, Hot Springs AR 71902-1860
**Telephone:** (501) 623-1433, (501) 624-3383, TDD: (501) 624-2308
**Location:** In west central Arkansas, 55 miles southwest of Little Rock on
US 70, in the Zig Zag Mountains on the eastern edge of the Oua-
chita Range.
**Open:** Visitor center: 9:00 A.M.–5:00 P.M. daily; closed Thanksgiving,
Christmas, and New Year's Days. Bathhouse tours available year-
round.
**Admission:** National park and visitor center: free. Rates for thermal baths
available at visitor center. Hot Springs Mountain Observation
Tower: adults $2.25, children $1.75.
**Restaurants:** In city of Hot Springs, adjacent to the national park.
**Shops:** Bookstore in Fordyce Bathhouse visitor center.
**Facilities:** Fordyce Bathhouse visitor center with orientation film; thermal
water baths at Buckstaff Bathhouse, Hot Springs Health Spa, and
Libbey Memorial Physical Medicine Center; Swedish massages; hik-
ing trails; picnic areas; camping; Hot Springs Mountain Tower; hy-
drotherapy treatments at the Libbey Memorial Physical Medicine
Center.

## WHERE TO STAY

**Inns/Bed & Breakfasts:** Vintage Comfort Inn, 303 Quapaw Ave., Hot
Springs AR 71901, (501) 623-3258. Williams House Inn, 420 Quapaw Ave., Hot Springs AR 71901, (501) 624-4275.
**Motels/Hotels:** The following hotels have bathhouses which are conces-
sions of Hot Springs National Park. Arlington Resort Hotel and Spa,
Hot Springs National Park AR 71901, (501) 623-7771, 1-800-643-
1502. Downtowner Motor Inn and Baths, 135 Central Ave., Hot

Springs National Park AR 71901, (501) 624-5521. Majestic Resort-Spa, Park and Central Aves., Hot Springs National Park AR 71901, (501) 623-5511, 1-800-643-1504. Park Hilton, One Convention Plaza, PO Box O, Hot Springs National Park AR 71902, (501) 623-6600, 1-800-844-7275.

**Camping:** Hot Springs National Park: Gulpha Gorge Campground, PO Box 1860, Hot Springs AR 71902, (501) 624-3383.

## OVERVIEW

Hot Springs is an unusual national park which preserves forty-seven hot springs along with thermal bathhouses of a nineteenth-century health spa. Hot Springs National Park encompasses about 5,500 acres in the Ouachita Mountain region of Arkansas. A mixture of urbanized and natural property, Hot Springs National Park has campgrounds, hiking trails, mountains, scenic overlooks, and unspoiled landscapes, as well as the elegant thermal bath buildings which comprise Bathhouse Row in the popular resort city of Hot Springs.

One bathhouse, the Fordyce, has been restored as a tour building and visitor's center. Thermal baths, regulated by the National Park Service, are still available in two bathhouses in the park and in four hotels in the city.

Thermal springs, a natural phenomenon that delights and refreshes, are sought by many for their curative powers. Naturally sterile thermal waters with traces of minerals which emerge from the earth at a temperature of 143 degrees are therapeutic, relieving pain and refreshing weary bodies and spirits. Such thermal spas and resorts are popular in Europe, where health seekers come for both cures and respite.

## HISTORY

Stone artifacts found near Hot Springs indicate that the thermal waters were a gathering place for American Indians. Spanish explorers reportedly discovered the hot springs in the mid-sixteenth century, while French trappers and traders found them in the late seventeenth century.

Approximately 850,000 gallons a day flow from forty-seven hot springs grouped at the base of Hot Springs Mountain. Scientists judge that these waters are more than 4,000 years old.

Ever since the hot springs were acquired in the 1803 Louisiana Purchase, the United States government has recognized their special quality and their need for protection and preservation. A year after he negotiated the Louisiana Purchase, a curious President Thomas Jefferson sent an expedition led by William Dunbar and George Hunter to explore the springs.

Their report stirred a great deal of interest and attracted people to the thermal waters.

Four sections of land containing thermal springs were set aside by the federal government as Hot Springs Reservation in 1832. It was the nation's first undertaking to protect a natural resource. In the next half-century, the federal government controlled the springs but allowed private bathhouses to be built. The government even operated a U.S. Free Bathhouse and a Public Health facility for the indigent.

By the early 1910s and 1920s, Hot Springs had become such a popular vacation destination that elegant hotels and bathhouses were built to accommodate health seekers. Pampered guests bathed in luxurious surroundings. Hot Springs became the nation's eighteenth national park in 1921, and the only one with a medical connection.

After World War II, interest in water therapy declined. Between 1962 and 1985, seven of Bathhouse Row's eight bathing establishments closed due to lack of business. Once-elegant Bathhouse Row gradually deteriorated.

In the mid-1980s, the National Park Service became interested in restoring Bathhouse Row and purchased Fordyce Bathhouse. This 1915 Spanish Renaissance Revival-style bathhouse, which operated until 1962, has been restored as a tour building and the park's visitor center. It opened in 1989.

The National Park Service and private businesses are currently cooperating to restore the exterior of other Bathhouse Row structures; the interiors are to be renovated for a variety of adaptive uses.

## SITE DESCRIPTION

Today, there are six operating bathing establishments. Two, the **Hot Springs Health Spa** and **Buckstaff Bathhouse**, are in the national park. The other four bathing facilities are in privately owned city hotels that obtain their thermal water from the park and are permittees of the federal government. As a consequence, their facilities are subject to federal regulation and inspection. National Park personnel caution potential bathers to check with their physicians first, for the baths are not recommended for people with certain health problems.

Water is piped directly from the springs into a reservoir beneath the park's administration building. Initially 143 degrees, it is cooled for bathing by circulating cold water around the thermal water pipes. Water for bathing is maintained at about one hundred degrees.

Bathhouses have stood on Central Avenue for some time, but the eight opulent brick and stucco bathhouses collectively known as **Bathhouse Row** were built between 1911 and 1923. Earlier wooden bathhouses either burned or deteriorated because of shoddy construction or the heavy humidity caused by the springs over which the bathhouses are built.

In the middle of Bathhouse Row is **Fordyce Bathhouse**, a three-story, tan brick Spanish Renaissance Revival-style building with interior courtyards and an ornate copper and glass marquee. Built in 1915 and operated until 1962, it opened in 1989 as the park visitor center. On the first floor of the **Fordyce visitor center** are the orientation movie, the park bookstore, and a historic bathing area. The second and third floors contain exhibit areas and twenty-four restored rooms. All of the women's side and some of the men's side have been re-equipped with steam cabinets, mechano-therapy machinery, tubs, massage tables, sitz tubs, Hubbard tubs, chiropody tools, billiard tables, a beauty parlor, and hydrotherapy equipment. There is a stained-glass skylight depicting Neptune's daughter over the men's bath hall. In the basement are the **Fordyce Spring** and exhibits of the machinery that operated the original elevator and old boilers.

The **Hot Springs Mountain Tower**, a 216-foot structure on Hot Springs Mountain, provides spectacular views of the National Park and the Ouachita Mountains. It has an open-air viewing deck and a glass-enclosed viewing deck.

# ARKANSAS TERRITORIAL RESTORATION

Restoration of Little Rock frontier buildings
dating from Arkansas's territorial and early
statehood period, 1819–1870; NR.

**Address:** 200 East Third St., Little Rock AR 72201-1608
**Telephone:** (501) 324-9351
**Location:** Little Rock, the state capital, is in the center of Arkansas; the
Arkansas Territorial Restoration is in downtown Little Rock.
**Open:** 9:00 A.M.–5:00 P.M. Monday–Saturday; 1:00–5:00 P.M. Sunday;
closed Christmas Eve and Christmas Day, Thanksgiving and New
Year's Days, and Easter.
**Admission:** Adults $2, seniors $1, children $.50. Free admission on first
Sunday of each month.
**Shops:** Craft Shop in visitor center.
**Facilities:** Handicapped accessible; visitor center with orientation film,
Gallery for Arkansas Artists, and Cromwell Hall Historic Gallery.

## WHERE TO STAY

**Inns/Bed & Breakfasts:** The Carriage House, 1700 South Louisiana
St., Little Rock AR 72201, (501) 374-7032. Hotze House, 1619
South Louisiana St., Little Rock AR 72201, (501) 376-6563. Qua-
paw B&B Inn, 1868 South Gaines, Little Rock AR 72201, (501)
376-6873.
**Motels/Hotels:** Holiday Inn-City Center, 617 South Broadway, Little
Rock AR 72201, (501) 376-2071. Capital Hotel, 111 West
Markham St., Little Rock AR 72201, (501) 374-7474. Camelot Ho-
tel, 424 West Markham St., Little Rock AR 72201, (501) 372-4371,
1-800-937-2789. Excelsior Hotel, Markham and Louisiana Sts.,
Little Rock AR 72201, (501) 375-5000, 1-800-527-1745.
**Camping:** Lake Catherine State Park, 1200 Catherine Park Rd., Hot
Springs AR 71913, (501) 844-4176. Petit Jean State Park, Rt. 3, Box
340, Morrilton AR 72110, (501) 727-5441. Maumelle Corps of En-

gineers Campground, Lake Manager, Toad Suck Ferry, Rt. 5, Box 140, Conway AR 72032, (501) 329-2986. Sands RV Park, 8123 Chicot Rd., Little Rock AR 72209, (501) 565-7491. Burns Park Campground, Burns Park, North Little Rock AR 72118, (501) 753-0086. KOA North Little Rock, 7820 Crystal Hill Rd., North Little Rock AR 72118, (501) 758-4598.

## OVERVIEW

Arkansas Territorial Restoration is located on one square block of Little Rock's busy downtown area. As with any historic site in an urban downtown area, it is quite an incongruity amid the modern skyscrapers and heavily traveled thoroughfares.

The territorial period of the city extended from 1821, when the capital was moved here from Arkansas Post, to 1836, when Arkansas achieved statehood. Five early-nineteenth-century furnished houses are shown on guided tours. Red brick and white and beige frame houses are interspersed with flower and herb gardens and red brick paths, while tall magnolia and elm trees provide shade. First-person interpretation, in which costumed interpreters assume the characters of frontier residents, helps bring Arkansas's frontier history to life.

## HISTORY

The state of Arkansas was part of the Louisiana Purchase, that huge portion of land acquired from France by President Thomas Jefferson in 1803. In 1686, Henri de Tonti had established the first semi-permanent French settlement in the lower Mississippi Valley at Arkansas Post.

When it first became part of the United States, Arkansas was in the Missouri Territory. Arkansas became a separate territory in 1819, with its territorial capital at Arkansas Post. In 1821, the capital was moved to Little Rock, which was situated at the territory's geographic center.

The city's name came from a rock outcropping on the Arkansas River used by river travelers to get their bearings. Two miles upstream from the "little rock" was another navigational landmark, a large bare stone face called "big rock." The Arkansas River served as the waterway on which people and goods entered and left Little Rock.

Arkansas was admitted to the Union in 1836, and Little Rock became the state capital. The city's population reached 1,500 by 1840; 3,700 by 1860; 13,000 by 1880, and 38,000 by 1900. As the city's commercial, business, and residential areas expanded, deteriorating structures from the frontier village era were threatened.

Although urban modernization normally wins any battles with preservation, restoration of frontier-era structures by the Works Progress Administration began in 1939. Preservation efforts were led by Louise Loughborough, a descendant of William Fulton, Arkansas's last territorial governor. Arkansas Territorial Restoration, which opened in 1941, is an agency of the Department of Arkansas Heritage.

## SITE DESCRIPTION

In the modern **reception center**, visitors may watch an orientation film about frontier Arkansas, and then visit the **Gallery for Arkansas Artists**, featuring paintings, sculptures, and decorative arts by contemporary artists. The reception center's **Cromwell Hall** has changing historical exhibits of nineteenth-century Arkansas-made crafts, furniture, textiles, glass, and documents. Works by more than 200 Arkansas artisans are sold in the **museum shop**.

**Guided tours** of historic buildings are given hourly, except at noon. A collection of work by artists and craftsmen from the territorial and early statehood period has been used to decorate the museum's houses. A **living-history program** features costumed interpreters who assume the identities of white and African-American residents of Little Rock during the 1830s, 1840s and 1850s and engage visitors in conversation.

The **Hinderliter Grog Shop**, a tavern built in 1827, is the oldest building in Little Rock. Believed to be the only remaining frame building from the city's territorial period, the large, two-story house was originally constructed of oak logs, which were later covered with hand-beaded, red-heart cypress siding.

Owner Jesse Hinderliter operated a grog shop on the first floor. It has a fireplace, cage bar, tables and chairs for card playing, and a beamed ceiling. Today, a bartender welcomes guests as he would have over 150 years ago.

Trunks like those overnight travelers brought to Hinderliter's are stacked in the hallway. Guest bedrooms furnished with rope beds, the family living quarters, and an artist's studio are upstairs.

In an attempt to keep the main house cool and to minimize the danger of fire, Southern kitchens were often separate buildings. The **Hinderliter Kitchen** is a small, white frame building with a brick floor and a walk-in fireplace. The reconstructed kitchen was built in 1939.

The **Brownlee/Noland House** is a small, red brick, Federal-style house built in the 1840s by a Scottish stone mason Robert Brownlee for his brother James. The house, which consists of two rooms and a hall, has a bedroom with a sleigh bed and a parlor with a hand-carved marbleized fire-place. Many furnishings belonged to F. M. Noland, a territorial legislator and author who may have lived in the house in the 1850s.

The **McVicar/Conway House** was moved to its site from a nearby location on the block. The small frame house was built in 1848 for James McVicar, who was both a stonemason and a warden of the state peniten-tiary. Later owners of this house may have included the Conway family, who were politically prominent during the frontier period. The character portrayed today is James McVicar, who is leaving for California to pan gold and is soliciting people to join him. At his side will be his African-American slave, Luther, who has defied the law and in secret learned to read.

Of special importance are the **home and print shop of William Woodruff**, the founder of the *Arkansas Gazette*. Woodruff was indentured as an apprentice to a New York printer, Alden Spooner, in 1810. Freed by Spooner in 1818, Woodruff traveled to Nashville for a job, then to Arkan-sas Post, where he founded the *Arkansas Gazette*. When the capital was moved to Little Rock, Woodruff followed.

The 1824 print shop of the *Arkansas Gazette,* the oldest newspaper west of the Mississippi River until 1992, is a small, two-room building con-taining a printing press, boxes of type, Woodruff's desk, tables, and chairs, and an 1838 map of Arkansas. Docents describe how newspapers were printed on a hand-powered printing press. A time-line exhibit on histori-cal events in both Arkansas and the nation from 1819 to 1861 is illustrated with articles from the *Arkansas Gazette.*

## FESTIVALS/CRAFTS

The **museum shop** in the reception center is an exceptional craft center which carries handmade quilts, jewelry, pottery, wood carvings, bas-kets, rugs, dried flower arrangements, and toys created by over 200 Arkan-sas craftspeople.

The **Crafts and Folk Music Festival** on Mother's Day weekend in May features frontier Arkansas crafts, music, food, and entertainment. The **Christmas Open House**, on the first full weekend in December, fea-tures holiday decorations, traditional Christmas celebrations, music, and food.

## SIDE TRIPS

The restored **Old State House**, the home of state government from 1836 to 1910, is the oldest surviving state capitol structure west of the

Mississippi. The white Greek Revival building has elegantly restored senate and house of representative chambers. Now a museum of Arkansas history, the Old State House contains exhibits that include **First Ladies' gowns, Confederate battle flags**, and six **period rooms**. Open daily. Admission is free. 300 West Markham Street, Little Rock AR 72201. (501) 371-1749.

# OLD WASHINGTON HISTORIC STATE PARK

Restoration of southwestern Arkansas town during
territorial and early statehood periods, 1824–1874; NR.

**Address:** PO Box 98, Washington AR 71862
**Telephone:** (501) 983-2684, (501) 983-2733
**Location:** In southwest Arkansas, about 30 miles northeast of the Texas
border; on AR Hwy. 4, 9 miles northwest of Hope at I-30 exit 30.
**Open:** 8:00 A.M.–5:00 P.M. daily; closed Thanksgiving, Christmas, and New
Year's Days.
**Admission:** Day-passes for all Old Washington sites during guided tours:
adults $9, children ages 6–12 $4.50. "Pioneers, Planters, Printers"
tour or "Living in Town tour": adults $4.50, children ages 6–12
$2.50. "Museum Experience" self-guided tour: adults $3, children
ages 6–12 $1.50.
**Restaurants:** Williams Tavern.
**Shops:** Old Washington Mercantile.
**Facilities:** Visitor center, Southwest Arkansas Regional Archives, guided
tours, special events.

## WHERE TO STAY

**Inns/Bed & Breakfasts:** Old Washington Jail B&B, PO Box 179, Washington AR 71862, (501) 983-2461.
**Motels/Hotels:** Best Western Inn of Hope, I-30 and AR Hwy. 4, Hope AR
71801, (501) 777-9222, FAX: (501) 777-9077. Holiday Inn, I-30
and AR Hwy. 4, Hope AR 71801, (501) 777-8601, FAX: (501) 777-
3142.
**Camping:** Bois d'Arc Lake and Reservoir, Hope AR 71801, (501)
777-3153. Crater of Diamonds State Park, Rt. 1, Box 364, Murfrees-
boro AR 71958, (501) 285-3113. Millwood State Park, Rt. 1, Box
37AB, Ashdown AR 71822, (501) 898-2800. White Oak Lake State
Park, Star Route, Bluff City AR 71722, (501) 685-2748, (501) 685-
2132.

## OVERVIEW

During the Civil War, from 1863 until 1865 while Federal troops occupied Little Rock, Washington served as the Confederate capital of Arkansas. Earlier, the Cherokees had passed through the town in their exodus to Oklahoma. Washington also served as a rendezvous point for volunteers in the Mexican-American War. Due to a series of destructive fires and the fact that it was bypassed by the railroad, the town declined.

Old Washington Historic State Park preserves a number of restored nineteenth-century buildings in the small, living town of Washington. The restored buildings are interspersed with privately owned and occupied residences. Washington retains a mid-nineteenth-century air with quiet streets, huge magnolia trees, spacious lawns, and lovely gardens. Hundreds of daffodils bloom in the spring. The peacefulness of the historic town contributes to one's sense of being in a time warp.

Washington is nine miles northwest of Hope, the birthplace of President William Clinton.

## HISTORY

Old Washington was once a part of the Louisiana Purchase, that great piece of North America claimed by France and eventually sold to the United States in 1803. When the Louisiana Purchase was opened to settlement, homesteaders streamed into the Arkansas Territory. Many traveled on the Southwest Trail, which ran from the Mississippi River across a corner of present-day Missouri, then southwest across Arkansas for almost three hundred miles to the Red River. The town of Washington is located along the Southwest Trail near the Red River.

Because so many settlers traveled on the Southwest Trail, the Reverend William Stevenson, a Methodist preacher, decided to hold revival camp meetings on it. He choose a spot in the southwest corner of the Arkansas Territory which he dubbed the "Ebenezer Campground." In 1819, he built a huge log shed on the side of the hill by the Black Bois d'Arc Creek. The town of Washington developed around Stevenson's campground.

One of the first businesses in Washington was a tavern opened by Elijah Stuart. In 1824, the commissioners of Hempstead County decided to locate the county's permanent seat of justice at the head of the Black Bois d'Arc Creek. The Court of Common Pleas for Hempstead County was held in Elijah Stuart's tavern until 1825, when the hewn-log Hempstead

Courthouse was built. That same year, the Hempstead County commissioners plotted lots in the town they called Washington.

In the early nineteenth century, white settlers were encroaching on the lands occupied by tribes of Native Americans. The conflict was especially intense in the southeastern states. President Andrew Jackson was determined to end the conflict by forcibly relocating the eastern American Indian tribes across the Mississippi River, thus affirming the rights of white settlers to occupy American Indian lands. Some tribes agreed to removal, but many, especially the Cherokee, refused. The Removal Bill of 1830 provided for compulsory removal. Some of the forced marches of tribes passed through Washington on the Southwest Trail. More than 3,000 Choctaws from Mississippi on their way to Oklahoma walked through Washington from 1831 to 1833. Some Washington businessmen obtained government contracts to sell food to these Choctaw and Chickasaw tribes.

Arkansas attracted a growing number of settlers. By 1836, its population had increased sufficiently for it to be admitted as a state.

Because of Washington's proximity to the Texas border, it became a favorite point of entry to Texas, then a part of Mexico. Sam Houston, who wanted to free Texas from Mexican rule, met with Stephen Austin and Jim Bowie at the Washington tavern to plan the Texas Revolt of 1835–1836. Davy Crockett and his men spent several days in Washington in November 1835 before joining Houston's army in Texas.

Washington was a convenient rendezvous point for volunteers in the Mexican-American War, which began in 1846. The first volunteers arrived in late June, and more soldiers kept coming all during the summer and fall, camping in and around Washington.

A story told in Washington is that a town blacksmith, James Black, made the first Bowie knife. It is claimed that in 1831 Jim Bowie asked Black to make a knife he had designed. Bowie had whittled an outline of the knife out of a cigar-box cover. Black made two knives, one according to Bowie's design and one of his own design. Bowie bought Black's design, and Bowie's name became associated with the famous knife. This is just one of several stories of the origin of the Bowie knife.

Washington's most important historic claim is linked to the Civil War when Arkansas joined the Confederate states that had seceded from the Union. After General Frederick Steele's Union forces captured Little Rock in September 1863, many of its residents fled to the southwestern part of the state still held by the Confederates. The attics and basements of every house in Washington were used to shelter women and children. From 1863 to 1865, Washington was the Confederate capital of Arkansas.

Arkansas Governor Harris Flanagan moved to the town, as did the state government. Setting up headquarters in a white frame courthouse, the general assembly and the supreme court continued to function.

Washington became the center of Arkansas's Confederate activities, and its newspaper, the *Washington Telegraph*, was the only rebel newspaper still being published in the state. Some companies in the Confederate army also moved southwest, and the fields near Washington were used for military encampments. The crowded little town also served as Confederate army headquarters for Arkansas.

After the Civil War ended, townspeople began rebuilding their community. Washington was dealt a severe blow in 1874 when the Cairo and Fulton Railroad came to southwest Arkansas, skirting Washington by eight miles to run through the new town of Hope. When a number of businesses were destroyed by a fire that swept through Washington in 1874, many people decided to relocate to Hope. When another fire burned twenty-four businesses in 1883, a similar exodus occurred. Washington's population plummeted.

Recovery efforts by the Foundation for the Restoration of Pioneer Washington began in Washington in 1958. In 1973, the Arkansas State Parks and Tourism Department joined the restoration project, and Old Washington Historic State Park was formed. The Southwest Arkansas Regional Archives, dedicated to collecting and preserving documents and photographs of southwest Arkansas, began in 1978. In 1980, the Ethnic Minority Memorabilia Association was incorporated to preserve and interpret African-American history in the area.

## SITE DESCRIPTION

The **Hempstead County Courthouse**, built in 1874, is the **Old Washington Historic State Park's visitor center**. It served as the county courthouse until 1939 when Hope became the county seat. From 1940 to 1975, it was used as a school. The red brick, two-story Victorian building has the date "1874" written in black iron numbers over its door. The original courtroom has been restored.

**Old Washington** offers a variety of guided tours organized around themes. One such tour is **"Pioneers, Planters, Printers and Merchants Bring Life to Old Washington,"** which interprets Washington's history from 1824 to 1840. **"Living in Town: The Washington Community 1840–1875"** focuses on Washington as a political, social, economic, and professional center of southwest Arkansas. The **"Old Washington Museum Experience" is a self-guided tour of the commercial sites of frontier Washington.

The **Tavern Inn** is a reconstruction of the tavern built by Joshua Morrison in the 1830s. The two-story, white frame building has wide verandas on both the first and second floors. The **first-floor taproom** is a large, bright room with a wooden bar, a fireplace, tables and chairs for card playing, an 1850 reed organ, and a piano. The inn's large detached kitchen has cathedral ceilings and a huge brick fireplace. It is furnished with a large table, a pie safe, a loom, a spinning wheel, and oversized baskets of cotton.

The **blacksmith shop** is a log reconstruction of the business where James Black is said to have made the first Bowie knife. It is a working blacksmith shop with demonstrations by a guide who also retells the Bowie legend.

The most important historic site in Washington is the white frame **courthouse**, which was built in 1836 and was used as the Arkansas Confederate capitol building (1863–1865). On the first floor are original yellow-pine floors, ceilings, paneled walls, and hand-hewn columns. Fireplaces stand at opposite ends of the room. The walls are adorned with portraits of Robert E. Lee, Stonewall Jackson, Bradley Johnson, and General P. G. T. Beauregard.

The **B. W. Edwards Weapons Museum**, housed in a 1925 bank building, displays the guns collected by Edwards. Among the hundreds of foreign and American weapons are rifles, pistols, revolvers, swords, Remingtons, flintlocks, and Bowie knifes. A collection of printing equipment is exhibited in the **Printing Museum**, a 1920 building which had been Washington's post office.

The **Sanders House**, a Greek Revival structure, was built in 1845 by Simon T. Sanders. One of Sanders's daughters, Sarah Virginia, married Augustus H. Garland, who became the governor of Arkansas, U.S. senator, and attorney general under President Cleveland. The house has fifteen-foot ceilings and original cypress floors. Some bedrooms and the dining room can be accessed only from the outside porch.

The **Purdom House**, built around 1850, was the home of Dr. James A. L. Purdom, who practiced medicine until 1866. The restored building houses medical exhibits.

The **Royston Log House**, which was built around 1835, was moved from the Royston Plantation. It is a two-room house built of logs that have been covered by planks. A double-sided fireplace serves both the kitchen and bedroom.

The **Block House**, a Federal-style structure, was built by the Abraham Block family in 1832. The **Royston House** is a Greek Revival house built in 1845 for Grandison D. Royston. A magnolia tree planted in 1839 by Grandison Royston is the largest in Arkansas.

The 1883 **Goodlett Cotton Gin** is one of the few surviving steam-powered gins in the United States. It was built by David M. Goodlett and was used by the Goodlett family until 1966.

The **Williams Tavern Restaurant** was built by John W. Williams in 1832 at Marlbrook, which is seven miles northeast of Washington. Serving now in its new location as the park restaurant, the structure boasts an entry with a cage bar and dining rooms with wooden plank floors, beamed ceilings, and fireplaces.

## FESTIVALS/CRAFTS

The **Jonquil Festival** in March features reenactments and a crafts shows. The **Antique Show and Sale** is held in May. In late October, **Frontier and Founders' Days** features a muzzleloading turkey shoot, music, and a craft show. **Autumn Harvest of Antiques** is held in mid-November. **Christmas and Candlelight**, in December, features strolling carolers, twilight tours, and a special Christmas dinner.

## SIDE TRIPS

Although neither house is open to the public, the **birthplace** and **childhood home of President Bill Clinton** in Hope can be viewed from the exterior. Clinton's grandparents' home, in which his mother lived at the time of his birth, is at 117 South Hervey St. in Hope, Arkansas. His mother's marriage to Mr. Clinton occasioned the family's move to Clinton's childhood home at 321 East 13th St. in Hope. The president attended kindergarten at Miss Marie Purkins's School for Little Folks on East Second St.

# FLORIDA

1. Estero: Koreshan State Historic Site
2. Fort Myers: Thomas Edison Winter Estate
3. Key West: Fort Zachary Taylor State Historic Site
4. St. Augustine: Spanish Quarter and Castillo de San Marcos
    National Monument

# KORESHAN STATE HISTORIC SITE

**Restored early-twentieth-century
Koreshan utopian community; NR.**

**Address:** PO Box 7, Estero FL 33928
**Telephone:** (813) 992-0311
**Location:** In southwestern Florida, on the Gulf Coast south of Fort Myers,
north of Naples; on Corkscrew Rd. at US 41, I-75 exit 19.
**Open:** 8:00 A.M.–5:00 P.M. daily.
**Admission:** State Park: vehicles with maximum of 8 adults and children
over age 6 $3.25; pedestrians and bicyclists $1; ranger-guided tours
$1, minimum of 4 adults.
**Shops:** In park entrance station.
**Facilities:** Guided tours, orientation video, picnic area, nature trail, camp-
ing, canoe rental.

## WHERE TO STAY

**Motels/Hotels:** Ramada Inn Beachfront, 1160 Estero Blvd., Fort Myers
Beach FL 33931, (813) 463-6158, FAX: (813) 765-4240. Comfort
Inn, 9800 Bonita Beach Rd., Bonita Springs FL 33923, (813) 992-
5001, 1-800-221-2222. Days Inn Island Beach Resort, 1130 Estero
Blvd., Fort Myers Beach FL 33931, (813) 463-9759, FAX: (813)
765-4240.
**Camping:** Koreshan State Historic Site, PO Box 7, Estero FL 33928, (813)
992-0311.

## OVERVIEW

Koreshan State Historic Site is a Florida state park which has eleven
restored and preserved structures that belonged to the Koreshans, a late-
nineteenth- and early-twentieth-century utopian community. It is the only
Koreshan site in the country that still contains the physical remains of its
former life.

Koreshanity was a religion founded by Cyrus Read Teed, a New York
physician. Teed had a vision in 1869 in which he was named the messiah.

Subsequently, he tried to attract converts to his religion—which included beliefs in communalism, celibacy, and a number of unusual scientific theories. Teed's theory of the universe, called "Cellular Cosmogony," held that the earth is hollow and that the sun and all life exists inside of the earth.

In 1894, a follower donated 320 acres to the group, which moved ten years later from its headquarters in Chicago to the Florida wilderness where they built a community. After Teed's death in 1908, the number of Koreshans declined so that by 1918, no more than a hundred members remained. The sect gave their land to the state of Florida in 1961. Buildings have been restored to 1904, when the community's population peaked at 200.

## HISTORY

The Koreshan Unity Settlement was established in the Florida wilderness in 1894 by Cyrus Read Teed and his followers. Using the biblical translation of his Christian name, Teed called himself "Koresh" and his religion "Koreshanity." Cyrus was born in Teedsville in Delaware County, New York, in 1839, and grew up near Utica, New York. When he was eleven, he left school for a job on the Erie Canal.

At age twenty, young Teed began studying medicine with his uncle, Dr. Samuel Teed. During the Civil War, he joined the Union army medical service and was attached to a field hospital. He completed his medical studies at New York Eclectic College after the war, graduating in 1868. He then established his own practice in Utica. He was married to Delia M. Row, with whom he had one son.

One night in 1869 when Teed was in his laboratory, he found himself mentally transported from earthly things. He saw a brilliant light which materialized into the form of a beautiful woman who announced that he was to be the new messiah. During this "illumination," as Teed termed it, references were made to reincarnation, immortality, ascendancy to the astral plane, mysteries of life and death, and the relation of man to God. Subsequently, Teed began preaching to his patients while treating them medically—a habit which had a negative impact on his medical practice.

Teed spent the next years in New York trying to make converts and establish a communal home. He was known to be an inspiring speaker. Yet success eluded him until 1886 when he was asked to address the National Association for Mental Health in Chicago, where he received a warm reception. Soon he and a very small band of adherents moved to Chicago and established a communal, celibate society in a large mansion that he called "Beth-Ophra." There, he centered his Guiding Star Publishing

House and the College of Life, which was later renamed the Koreshan University. A number of Chicagoans were attracted to Koreshanity, and in the early 1890s, 126 members were living at Beth-Ophra. Koreshan literature generated by the Guiding Star Publishing House was widely distributed and led to the formation of several other small Koreshan groups throughout the country.

Certain doctrines of Koreshanity—including communalization, abolition of private property, celibacy, and the coming of the millennium—paralleled the religious beliefs of communal groups like the Shakers and the Harmonists of Economy, Pennsylvania. However, Teed's doctrine of Cellular Cosmogony set the Koreshans apart. This theory of the universe holds that the earth—whose surface is concave rather than convex—is a hollow sphere with the sun in the center and with life existing on the inside. The central sun is always half-lit and half-dark, a fact which results in day and night.

Teed was not the first person to postulate a hollow-earth theory which contradicts the Copernican view of astronomy, and he may have been aware of earlier proponents. Captain John Cleves Symmes published a work in 1868 called *A Hollow Globe*, and Jules Verne published a fictionalized version of the hollow earth in 1864.

In 1893, Gustav Damkohler, a German immigrant who was fascinated by Teed's teachings, invited the religious leader to his home in the Estero Bay area of Florida. Teed had been searching for a site for his New Jerusalem, which would be a city of six million people. He found it at Estero, and the Chicago group moved to Florida. The Koreshans were pioneers hacking out habitable space in the Florida wilderness. From the original 320 acres of land that had been donated by Damkohler, they created a settlement which by 1906 had grown to more than thirty-five buildings and 7,000 acres.

The Koreshans conducted scientific experiments to prove that the earth is concave. In 1897, they surveyed a line six miles long on Naples beach, using instruments they called "rectillineators." These instruments, which had been specially designed to project a perfectly straight line, consisted of three twelve-feet-long flat mahogany sections with a crossarm with a brass double T-square. By manipulating the rectillineator and placing a telescope along its axis, they extended a line to a point where the line met the water's surface four miles in the distance. Teed concluded that the earth curves upward and is therefore concave.

Although the population of the Florida settlement never exceeded 200, the prosperous colony had a band, an orchestra, and tropical gardens.

Businesses included a general store, bakery, boat works, water taxi, printing press, sawmill, machine shop, woodworking shop, concrete works, and plant nursery. The Koreshans installed central light and water systems as well as a waste disposal system. Their school was open to those outside their community. They operated the Guiding Star Publishing House, which remained in operation until it was destroyed by fire in 1949. They published a Koreshan newspaper, *The American Eagle,* and a religious magazine, *The Flaming Sword.*

The Koreshans, who led a non-traditional communal celibate life-style, got along well with their neighbors, with one exception. The Kore-shans felt that they were not getting their fair share of road taxes from the county commissioners. Teed inaugurated his own political party, the pro-gressive Liberty Party. As a result of this conflict, Teed was attacked by the town marshal of Fort Myers on October 13, 1906. Many Koreshans felt his injuries were the cause of his death, which occurred on December 22, 1908, despite the fact that Teed had told his people he was immortal. Many waited for him to rise again, but he was eventually buried in a mau-soleum on Estero Island. In 1921, a hurricane blew his tomb into the Gulf of Mexico.

After Teed's death, power struggles over leadership ensued. Some members drifted away, and converts gradually declined. By the 1940s, only a dozen Koreshans remained. Hedwig Michel, the community's leader, was responsible for donating 305 acres of Koreshan property to the state of Florida as a historical site. In 1961, the state accepted this property along with the Koreshan-built structures to be designated as the Koreshan State Historic Site. The last surviving member of the Koreshan Unity, Hedwig Michel, died in 1982.

## Site Description

Although a small number of Koreshans lived at the Florida site until the 1970s, the **Koreshan settlement** has been restored to the 1904–1907 period, when the colony had reached its peak population of 200. At that time, the Chicago community had completed its move to Estero, and Cyrus Teed, the founder, was still alive.

The Koreshans constructed more than seventy-three buildings, some of which were destroyed by fire. The **Art Hall**, also known as the **Music and Art Building**, was built of local pine in 1905. With a seating capacity of 150, it was used for music concerts and plays. An orientation video is shown here, and paintings by Cyrus Teed's son, Douglas, are exhibited.

The **Planetary Court**, built in 1903, is a two-story frame building with a second-story veranda. It housed seven women, who were members of the governing council of the Koreshan unit. Teed and Annie G. Ordway, whom he designated as Victoria Gratia, Pre-Eminent, formed a central duality which ruled the community. Other governmental structures included a Planetary Chamber consisting of seven women, a Stellar Chamber of four men, and a Signet Chamber of six men and six women.

The ovens in the **bakery**, built in 1903–1904, had the capacity to bake more than 500 loaves per day. In addition to supplying the settlement, the bakery sold surplus bread to local people. On the second floor of the building were rooms for visitors.

The **Vesta Newcomb Cottage**, a frame double-pen house, and the **Members Cottage** were used as residences. They were moved to their present location in the 1930s.

The **Founder's House** was built in 1896 and repeatedly modified until Koresh's death in 1908. Part of the building may have been used as a school, for it was also called the **children's house**.

The **Damkohler House**, built in 1892 or 1893, was the home of Gustav Damkohler, the German immigrant who invited Teed to Florida. Damkohler donated his house and 320 acres to the Koreshans. Originally located on the Estero River, the house was moved after Teed's settlement was established.

The **Koreshan Unity General Store** was built during the early 1920s after the Tamiami Trail was opened between Tampa and Miami. The store was a flourishing business. It also was the local post office, a warehouse, and a restaurant. There were rooms for male members called brothers upstairs. There are also the **generator building**, the **small Machine Shop**, the **large machine shop**, and the **Bamboo Landing** on the Estero River. The river was the highway between communities in this wilderness area. Koreshans shipped their excess agricultural products to Fort Myers's markets.

The **Koreshan Museum and Library**, on the east side of US 41, is owned and operated by the Board of Directors of the Koreshan Unity Foundation and includes the **World's College of Life** building. Koreshan archives are housed in the library. A short nature trail leads to the **Anna Lewis house**, a ca. 1930 bungalow that was home to a Koreshan family for many years.

# THOMAS EDISON WINTER ESTATE

Restored 1885 vacation home, laboratory, and tropical
gardens of inventor Thomas Edison, and adjoining
vacation home of Henry Ford; NR.

**Address:** 2350 McGregor Boulevard, Fort Myers FL 33901
**Telephone:** (813) 332-6738
**Location:** Fort Myers is in southwestern Florida, near the Gulf of Mexico,
on the Caloosahatchee River. The Edison and Ford homes are on
McGregor Blvd., which parallels the river.
**Open:** 9:00 A.M.–4:00 P.M. Monday–Saturday; 12:30–4:00 P.M. Sunday.
Closed Thanksgiving and Christmas Days.
**Admission:** Edison house only: adults $8, children $4. Edison/Ford combination: adults $10, children $5.
**Restaurants:** In Fort Myers.
**Shops:** Gift shop.
**Facilities:** Guided tours, tropical gardens, research laboratory, museum;
handicapped accessible.

## WHERE TO STAY

**Inns/Bed & Breakfasts:** Drum House Inn, 2135 McGregor Blvd., Fort
Myers FL 33901, (813) 332-5668, FAX: (813) 337-2355.
**Motels/Hotels:** Hampton Inn, 13000 North Cleveland Ave., Fort Myers
FL 33903, (813) 656-4000, FAX: (813) 656-4000, ext. 305.
Sheraton Harbor Place Hotel, 2500 Edwards Dr., Fort Myers FL
33901, (813) 337-0300, FAX: (813) 337-1530. Fort Myers Travelodge, 2038 West First St., Fort Myers FL 33901, (813) 334-2284,
FAX: (813) 334-2366. Holiday Inn Central, 2431 Cleveland Ave.,
Fort Myers FL 33901, (813) 332-3232, 1-800-998-0466, FAX: (813)
332-0590. Victoria Pier House Inn, 2220 West First St., Fort Myers
FL 33901, (813) 334-3434, FAX: (813) 334-3844.
**Camping:** Up River Campground, 17021 Upriver Dr., North Fort Myers
FL 33917, 1-800-848-1652, (813) 543-3330. Woodsmoke Camping

Photo by Patricia A. Gutek

**Thomas Edison Winter Estate, Fort Myers, Florida**
Visitors (including one of the authors) tour inventor Thomas Edison's Rubber Research Laboratory, built in the mid-1920s in Fort Myers, Florida. For almost half a century, Edison lived and worked at his Florida retreat during the winter.

Resort, 19251 US 41 SE, Fort Myers FL 33908, (800) 231-5053, (813) 267-3456.

## OVERVIEW

Thomas Edison, the inventor, and Henry Ford, the industrialist, are legendary American entrepreneurs whose accomplishments dramatically affected the American life-style. Edison gave Americans the phonograph and incandescent lamps for their homes, and Ford developed an automobile that the average person could afford. These two friends had adjoining winter vacation homes in Fort Myers, Florida. Edison built his home in 1885, while Ford purchased his home in 1916. Both houses—as well as Edison's research laboratory, his fabulous tropical garden, and a museum—are open to the public.

## HISTORY

The inventor Thomas A. Edison took a Florida vacation in the winter of 1884–1885 when he was thirty-seven years old. He found Fort Myers, a village with a population of 349, so appealing that on March 4, 1885, he purchased fourteen acres of land along the Caloosahatchee River, on which he built two houses. He continued to winter there for almost a half-century with his second wife, Mina Miller Edison, whom he had brought to Fort Myers as a bride in 1886.

Thomas Edison was born in Milan, Ohio, in 1847; his family moved to Port Huron, Michigan, in 1854. Thomas had little formal education but was taught at home by his mother, a former teacher. From an early age, Thomas was interested in scientific exploration. When he was ten years old, he set up a chemistry laboratory in his basement. From age eighteen to twenty-three, he worked as a telegraph operator on the Grand Trunk Railway of Ontario, Canada. His first patented invention was the Electrical Vote Recorder, which he offered to sell to Congress in 1868. The offer was refused.

Twenty-two-year-old Edison and a partner, Franklin L. Pope, invented an improved stock ticker, the Universal Stock Ticker, and the Unison device to synchronize stock tickers on a given circuit. In 1871, Edison received $40,000 for these patents, which enabled him to start a business in Newark, New Jersey, manufacturing stock tickers and telegraph instruments.

In 1876, Edison built a research laboratory in Menlo Park, New Jersey, that is considered to be the first laboratory for organized industrial research. Edison concentrated on practical inventions and over the next ten years obtained 420 patents. Experiments on electricity and the incandescent light bulb were conducted there. On December 31, 1879, the inventer gave a public demonstration of his electric lighting system on the streets and in the buildings of Menlo Park. Edison developed the power distribution system which was the supporting network of generators, meters, and wires needed to illuminate the electric light bulb.

The Edison Electrical Light Company was formed in 1878. Over one thousand patents were issued to the prolific scientist who invented the alkaline battery, motion picture camera, phonograph, fluorescent lamp, and electric lamp. In 1887, Edison moved his research laboratory to West Orange, New Jersey, near the home he owned.

In Florida, gardening was one of Edison's hobbies. He loved to collect exotic trees and plants, and friends all over the world sent him unusual seedlings for his tropical gardens. Edison was as serious about horticulture as he was about everything else, and he tried to discover practical new uses for plants.

Edison built a research laboratory on his Fort Myers property in 1884–1885. In the 1920s, Henry Ford wanted to move this historic laboratory to his museum called the Edison Institute in Dearborn, Michigan. The Edison Institute contained both an indoor museum filled with Ford's extraordinary collection of Americana and an outdoor museum of American structures, many of which were connected with famous Americans. In the mid-1920s, a second research laboratory was built at Edison's Fort Myers estate, and the first laboratory was dismantled and shipped by railroad to Michigan.

In his new Fort Myers laboratory, Edison conducted experiments on rubber. He—along with his friends Henry Ford of Ford Motor Company and Harvey Firestone of Firestone Rubber—wanted to find a domestic source of natural rubber so that the United States would no longer be dependent on economically prohibitive rubber imported from the Pacific. After testing 17,000 plants—many of which were growing in his own garden—Edison selected the goldenrod weed with its thick milky sap and high latex content. Through crossbreeding, a strain was developed which grew twelve feet high in a single season. Goldenrod would grow anywhere in the country and could be machine reaped. Edison sent samples to Harvey Firestone, who produced a set of goldenrod rubber tires for Edison's Model T Ford.

Edison died October 18, 1931, at the age of eighty-four. Mrs. Edison gave the estate to the city of Fort Myers in 1947.

Henry Ford was a friend and admirer of Thomas Edison. In 1916, he purchased a winter home in Fort Myers on property adjoining Edison's. The wealthy industrial giant and the innovative genius often talked, fished, and gardened together.

Henry Ford was born July 30, 1863, on his parents' farm in Dearborn, Michigan. When he was sixteen, he worked as a machinist in Detroit. He built his first automobile, the Quadricycle, in a workshop behind his home in Detroit. Although Ford did not invent the automobile, he mechanized the assembly line and mass-produced the automobile, which brought mobility to rural America. As a result of his automobile empire, Ford become one of the wealthiest industrialists in America.

In addition to his automobile empire based on the tremendous success of the Model T, Ford was an avid collector of Americana—tools, vehicles, cars, buildings, furniture, machines, pottery, glassware, textiles, decorative arts, toys, and books. He admired America's people, past, and life-style. He especially liked collecting artifacts associated with his heroes, the greatest of whom was Thomas Edison. His collection of Edisonia included inventions and the remnants of the research and development facility from Menlo Park, New Jersey, which he reconstructed.

After Edison's death, Ford's interest in his Fort Myers property diminished. The city of Fort Myers acquired the Ford estate in 1988.

## SITE DESCRIPTION

For almost half a century, the Edison family spent their winter vacations at their fourteen-acre **Fort Myers estate**. Situated amid tropical gardens along the Caloosahatchee River, their home consisted of two separate houses connected by a colonnade. The houses were among the earliest prefabricated structures in America.

Construction plans were sent to Phillip Nye in Fairfield, Maine, who built the houses in sections. The segments were then transported aboard four schooners to Fort Myers, where the two prefabricated clear-spruce structures were erected in 1885.

In 1906, one house was made the **guest house**, while the kitchen and dining room of the **main house** were converted into two bedrooms with baths. Subsequently, the Edisons ate all their meals in the guest house.

Both of the two-story structures have fourteen-feet-wide porches to protect them from tropical rains. French doors on all sides of the main house open onto the porches. Rooms are light and airy and contain the Edison's Victorian-style furniture. Wicker furniture is in the house and on the porches. In the living room, which is lit by some of Edison's earliest lighting fixtures, is a painting of Mrs. Edison. The brass electrolier lighting fixtures were designed to hold Edison's light bulbs, and no two are alike. The bulbs contain carbon filaments.

Edison brought his own generators to Fort Myers. When the lights were turned on in 1887, the whole town turned out to see this miracle.

A reinforced concrete swimming pool was built in 1910 for the Edison children and guests.

The **Rubber Research Laboratory** was the second laboratory built at Edison's Fort Myers estate. The first one, used by the inventor from the 1880s to the 1920s, is now at Greenfield Village in Dearborn, Michigan, at the immense indoor-outdoor museum of Americana created single-handedly by Henry Ford. A friend and devoted admirer of Edison, Ford purchased, moved, and reassembled many buildings related to Edison's career at Greenfield Village. He asked Edison for permission to move his Fort Myers laboratory to the museum. Edison agreed. Ford and Harvey Firestone funded the construction of another laboratory on the Fort Myers property for a new project. The idea was to identify a plant source of rubber that could be grown in the United States so that the nation would no longer be dependent on expensive imported rubber from the Pacific for its booming automobile industry.

Edison used the cot in the **laboratory office** to take occasional cat-naps during his long hours in the laboratory. The vials, test tubes, racks, machinery, and lab tables used by Edison and his assistants are in the laboratory. Rubber products made from goldenrod latex are displayed.

In the four rooms of the 15,000-square-foot **Museum** are many of Edison's over 1,000 inventions. In addition to the more well-known ones—phonographs, movie projectors, ticker-tape machines, batteries, and light bulbs—many lesser-known inventions are exhibited: hot plates, waffle irons, Christmas lights, talking dolls, electric typewriter balls, mimeographs, electric fans, hair curlers, percolators, and spark plugs. In the family section of the museum are furnishings from the New Jersey home, as well as photographs and paintings. The vehicle display includes the Model T Ford given to Edison by Henry Ford. Although Ford asked Edison to accept new models, Edison refused because he was so fond of his car, which is still in running condition and is driven annually in the **Festival of Lights Parade**.

Thomas Edison was a master horticulturist who developed an outstanding tropical garden on his winter estate. The **gardens** contain hundreds of species of trees and plants from all over the world. Some rare trees are the pachira, or shaving brush tree, the tree of gold from Paraguay, the rain tree from South America, the sloth tree from the West Indies, a huge banyan tree, and coral, sausage, cajeput and mango trees. Flowering shrubs include the yellow elder, chenille plant, angel's trumpet, and powder puff. Wild orchids and flowering vines abound. Underground lighting installed by Edison illuminates the garden at night.

**Memory Garden** is a memorial designed by her friends in honor of Mina Miller Edison. It has a wall of bougainvillea surrounded by a plot of grass with a sundial, a stone bench, and bird sculptures in a reflecting pool.

On the adjoining three-and-one-half-acre property is the **vacation home purchased by Henry Ford** in 1916. It was acquired by the city of Fort Myers in 1988 and has been restored to its appearance during the 1920s. The two-story wooden house has fourteen rooms and wide porches.

## Festivals/Crafts

**Holiday House** is held in early December, when the Edison House is fully decorated with 1920s Christmas decorations, and the extraordinary **Festival of Lights** continues for two weeks in February.

# FORT ZACHARY TAYLOR STATE HISTORIC SITE

Mid-nineteenth-century Civil War seacoast fort; NR, NHL.

**Address:** PO Box 6560, Key West FL 33041
**Telephone:** (305) 292-6713
**Location:** Key West is the southernmost part of the United States, the last of the string of keys south of Miami.
**Open:** Museum: 9:00 A.M.–5:00 P.M. daily. Park: 8:00 A.M.–sunset, daily.
**Admission:** Vehicles: $3.25 plus $.50 per person. Bicyclists and pedestrians: $1.50.
**Restaurants:** Concession stand.
**Facilities:** Guided tours, special events, handicapped-accessible museum, picnic areas, swimming beach, fishing.

## WHERE TO STAY

**Inns/Bed & Breakfasts:** Curry Mansion, 511 Caroline St., Key West FL 33040, 1-800-253-3466, (305) 253-3466. Duval House, 815 Duval St., Key West FL 33040, 1-800-223-8825, (305) 294-1666. Key West B&B, 415 William St., Key West FL 33040, (305) 296-7274.

**Motels/Hotels:** Best Western Hibiscus Motel, 1313 Simonton St., Key West FL 33040, (305) 294-3763. Pier House, One Duval St., Key West FL 33040, 1-800-327-8340, (305) 296-4600. The Reach, 1435 Simonton St., Key West FL 33040, 1-800-874-4118, (305) 296-5000. Holiday Inn LaConcha, 430 Duval St., Key West FL 33040, (305) 296-2991.

**Camping:** Waterfront Campground and Trailer Park, 223 Elizabeth St., Key West FL 33040, (305) 294-5723.

## OVERVIEW

Fort Zachary Taylor, a Florida seacoast fort, played a prominent role in the Civil War. Union troops firing cannons from the huge, heavily armed, red brick fortress disabled and captured hundreds of Confederate supply ships attempting to run the blockade. The confiscated goods retained at the fort were critically needed by the South. In fact, the Confederacy's serious shortage of supplies helped to bring the Civil War to its end.

Built in the mid-nineteenth century off the shore of Key West so that it was completely surrounded by water, the now land-locked Fort Taylor was substantially modified in 1898 during the Spanish-American War. This impressive structure now holds the largest stash of Civil War armaments left in the United States. A Florida state park facility, the fort can be toured. The sixty-acre park also has one of Key West's best beaches, and views from Fort Zachary Taylor are extraordinary.

## HISTORY

During the War of 1812, the British navy successfully blockaded United States east-coast ports. Because the Chesapeake coast was virtually undefended, British forces were able to march into Washington and set fire to the Capitol, the White House, and other government buildings. These humiliating occurrences strengthened U.S. determination to build a chain of fifty seacoast fortifications from Maine to Texas.

In Florida, construction began on a fort to protect the Key West harbor in 1845, the year Florida was admitted to the Union. In 1850, the fort was named for Zachary Taylor, the president of the United States, who died in office earlier that year. Fort Zachary Taylor was completed in 1866. The twenty-one-year project was slowed by adverse weather, bouts of yellow fever among workers, and the difficulty of moving construction materials to the remote location.

Fort Taylor was strategically located next to the Gulf Stream, which served as a shipping lane to New England and Europe. In the 1840s, Key West was the largest and wealthiest city in Florida, due to trade with Cuba and the wrecking industry which developed when large numbers of ships became marooned on Florida's dangerous reefs.

Designed by Major General Joseph G. Totten, the three-story, trapezoidal Key West fort had three sides that faced seaward, while its long side faced land. The fort, completely surrounded by water, was built 1,200 feet offshore. It was connected to land by a wooden causeway, a section of which could be raised during an attack to secure the fort.

The fort was constructed on a solid base of island rock, cypress timbers, and sixteen feet of granite. Five-foot-thick walls made of brick from Pensacola and Virginia rose fifty feet above sea level. In 1854, fifty ten-inch Rodman cannons with a range of three miles were mounted on the finished first tier.

Photo by Patricia A. Gutek

### Fort Zachary Taylor State Historic Site, Key West, Florida

Fort Zachary Taylor is a red brick fort constructed on the Florida coast in the
mid-nineteenth century. During the Civil War, cannon-firing Union troops at
this huge, heavily armed fortress crippled and captured hundreds of Confederate
supply ships attempting to run the blockade.

Sleeping quarters for the troops were on the second and third levels.
Six rooms on the ground level, used as dining rooms and kitchens, were
designed to feed a hundred men each. Forty cisterns were built below Fort
Taylor to collect rain water, the island's only source of drinking water. A
desalinization plant, which could produce 7,000 gallons of fresh water from
sea water daily, was added to the fort in 1861.

On January 13, 1861, at the beginning of the Civil War, Captain
John Brannon occupied Fort Taylor, placing it in Union hands. Brannon
and his men had been working in the unfinished fort, and he requested
permission from Washington to occupy it. Although permission did not
come through until January 30, Brannon had acted on his own decision
seventeen days earlier. Confederate sympathizers in Key West were un-
aware of Brannon's action until it was too late. The fort remained under
Union control throughout the Civil War.

The fort served as an important base of operations for Union Gulf-blocking squadrons. Fort Taylor's powerful cannons were a strong deterrent to blockade-running Confederate ships. Hundreds of Southern supply ships were captured and detained in Key West Harbor. The formidable, well-armed fort was never attacked during the Civil War.

The development of rifled cannon before the end of the Civil War made Fort Taylor and other brick fortresses obsolete because projectiles from rifled cannon could blow holes in brick walls.

Modifications were made to Fort Taylor in 1898 for the Spanish-American War. The top level of the brick was dynamited off to lower it, thus lessening the target area. Modern guns were much heavier and needed more support. Battery Osceola and Battery Adair were mass concrete batteries that were added behind the old Civil War gun rooms. Guns placed on these batteries were forty-seven feet long, weighed over a hundred tons, and shot a thousand-pound, five-foot-long projectile.

In 1947, the army turned Fort Taylor over to the navy. In the mid-1960s, the area around the fort was filled with dredge material from the channel. Now there is a beach in front of the land-locked fort. A moat around the fort has been dug by the Florida Park Service.

In 1968, Howard England, a Navy architect, discovered at Fort Taylor the largest store of Civil War armaments left in the United States. The fort was placed on the National Register of Historic Places in 1971 and designated a National Historic Landmark in 1973. The federal government deeded the fort to the state of Florida in 1976, and it became a state historic site. It opened to the public in 1985.

## SITE DESCRIPTION

**Fort Zachary Taylor State Historic Site** is an eighty-acre Key West park which includes Fort Taylor and its museum, along with an extensive ocean beach. Construction of the original fort began in 1845, and it was still unfinished at the outbreak of the Civil War. However, Union-held Fort Zachary Taylor was used extensively during the Civil War. Serious modifications to the fort were made during the Spanish-American War in 1898. It is the modified fort that one sees today.

Constructed by Howard England, a model of Fort Zachary Taylor as it looked in 1866 is in the **Museum**. Additional models include an 1888 **Non-Disappearing Gun** used during the Spanish-American War, the 15-inch **Rodman Smooth Bolt Cannon**, and the **100 Pounder Parrot Rifle**. Guns, including World War I rifles, are displayed. One exhibit features the types of ammunition used at Fort Taylor from 1854 to 1866; another features historic photographs of the fort.

Guided tours by park personnel leave from the museum at 12:00 noon and 2:00 P.M. daily. Older sections of the fort are made of red brick, while 1898 additions are of reinforced black concrete. The trapezoidal fort has a **Parade Ground** in its center.

**Sally Port**, an arched doorway, was the fort's only entrance and exit prior to the 1898 changes. The mechanism for operating the retractable wooden causeway that connected Fort Taylor to Key West was in the Sally Port. Small rooms on either side of the entrance were for confinement of drunk or disorderly soldiers; stairways on either side led to the troops' sleeping quarters on the second and third levels.

Acquiring fresh water was a serious concern. Rainwater would drain from the top of the fort through cast-iron pipes in the walls, then run through a cistern sand trap to filter out insects and rats. A **cistern sand trap** is displayed in a gun room.

**Gun rooms** were designed to act as wind tunnels to catch air currents. Black powder used in shooting the cannons generated tremendous heat and smoke, and ocean breezes helped flush out the smoke. Temperatures in gun rooms are usually ten to fifteen degrees cooler than other rooms in the fort. Cannons positioned at gun-room windows faced the approach to the Key West harbor. Guns were fired about ten feet above the water level so that they would strike a ship at the waterline.

The fort's four **corner bastions** have high vaulted ceilings. Small guns called "Flank Howitzers" were mounted in the bastions for protection of the fort walls. The southwest and southeast bastions also housed unique sanitary facilities, in which toilets were automatically flushed by the tides.

On an upper level are a ten-inch **Rodman cannon**, which was moved back and forth on metal tracks on the floor, a **300-Pounder Parrot Rifle**, and several **Columbiad cannons**.

**Battery Adair** is a section of the fort built around 1900. It replaced most of the **West Curtain** of the original fort except the exterior wall. It contained four 15-pounder **Rapid Fire Guns** on a masking parapet mount designed to disappear from sight. **Battery Osceola** was built behind the old Civil War gun rooms on the **South Curtain**.

## FESTIVALS/CRAFTS

Modern-day "Union troops" set up camp in the fort to celebrate **Civil War Days** the last weekend in February.

# SPANISH QUARTER AND CASTILLO DE SAN MARCOS NATIONAL MONUMENT

**The Spanish Quarter is a restored and reconstructed eighteenth-century Spanish colonial settlement; NR, NHL, HABS.**
**Castillo de San Marcos NM is a restored seventeenth-century Spanish fort; NR, HABS.**

**Address:** Spanish Quarter: Historic St. Augustine Preservation Board, PO Box 1987, St. Augustine FL 32085. Castillo de San Marcos NM: 1 Castillo Dr., St. Augustine FL 32084.
**Telephone:** Spanish Quarter: (904) 825-6830. Castillo de San Marcos: (904) 829-6506.
**Location:** St. Augustine is on Florida's northeast Atlantic coast, 36 miles south of Jacksonville; both sites are in downtown St. Augustine.
**Open:** Spanish Quarter: 9:00 A.M.–5:00 P.M. daily. Castillo de San Marcos: 8:45 A.M.–4:45 p.m daily. Closed Christmas Day.
**Admission:** Spanish Quarter: adults $5, children ages 6–18 $2.50, families $10. Castillo de San Marcos: adults $2; seniors and children ages 16 and under, free.
**Restaurants:** Many in St. Augustine's historic district.
**Shops:** Spanish Quarter: museum store. Castillo de San Marcos: bookstore.
**Facilities:** Spanish Quarter: orientation center, craft demonstrations. Castillo de San Marcos: ranger talks, cannon-firing demonstrations, tours.

## WHERE TO STAY

**Inns/Bed & Breakfasts:** Kenwood, 38 Marine St., St. Augustine FL 32084, (904) 824-2116. St. Francis, 279 St. George St., St. Augustine FL 32084, (904) 824-6068. Victorian House, 11 Cadiz St., St. Augustine FL 32084, (904) 824-5214

**Motels/Hotels:** Monterey, 16 Avenida Menendez, St. Augustine FL 32084, (904) 824-4482. Days Inn, 2800 Ponce de Leon Blvd., St. Augustine FL 32084, (904) 829-6581. Ramada Inn-Historic Area, 116 San Marco Ave., St. Augustine FL 32084, (904) 824-4352, FAX: (904) 824-2745. Ponce de Leon Resort, 4000 North US 1, St. Augustine FL 32085, (904) 824-2821, 1-800-228-2821, FAX: (904) 829-6108.

**Camping:** Anastasia State Recreation Area, St. Augustine Beach FL 32084, (904) 461-2033. Faver-Dykes State Park, US 1, St. Augustine FL 32085, (904) 794-0997. Ocean Grove Camp Resort, 4225 Hwy. A1A South, St. Augustine FL 32084, (904) 471-3414, 1-800-342-4007. North Beach Camp Resort, 4125 Coastal Hwy., North Beach, St. Augustine FL 32095, (904) 824-1806, 1-800-542-8316.

## OVERVIEW

In the sixteenth century, European nations such as Spain, France, and England extended their empires to North America. In what is now the United States, England and Spain established colonies on the Atlantic coast. Spain claimed territory in the American southwest and Florida. St. Augustine, a city founded in 1565 by Don Pedro Menéndez de Avilés, is part of that Spanish colonial heritage.

The colonial village served as a garrison town charged with protecting Spanish fleets sailing along the Florida coast en route to Spain. After repeated attacks by pirates in the seventeenth century, a huge star-shaped Spanish fort, Castillo de San Marcos, was built. In the early 1700s, St. Augustine became a walled city, one of only three in the United States. Today, the walls are gone, but the fort remains in St. Augustine's harbor.

The Spanish Quarter is a restored and reconstructed Spanish colonial village of the 1700s located within St. Augustine's historic area. Since the town burned many times, the oldest extant buildings are from the eighteenth century. A tourist town, St. Augustine has narrow streets that are lined with privately owned examples of Spanish Colonial architecture, buildings that are used as homes, bed and breakfasts, shops, and restaurants. They are small structures with pastel stucco walls, windows with shutters or wooden grills, intricately carved doors, second-story balconies hanging over the street, and walled courtyards.

## HISTORY

St. Augustine is the oldest permanent European settlement in North American and the nation's oldest continuously occupied city. On September 8, 1565, fifty-two years after Florida's discovery by Ponce de León, Don Pedro Menéndez de Avilés arrived in the Spanish territory with 700 colonists. He named the colony St. Augustine because Florida had first been sighted on St. Augustine's Day, August 28.

The expedition, ordered by King Philip II of Spain, was intended to settle the territory and drive out the French, who had been encroaching on the Spanish claim and threatening Spanish treasure fleets along Florida's shorelines.

Although Menendez was highly successful on both counts, St. Augustine's status as a permanent Spanish colony and military base was constantly challenged. In 1586, Sir Francis Drake pillaged and burned the town, and in 1668, Captain John Davis, a pirate, plundered the homes and killed many people. In 1670, the English settled Charleston in the Carolinas, and England and Spain agreed to respect each other's possessions.

Castillo de San Marcos, St. Augustine's star-shaped stone fortress, was begun in 1672 and took more than twenty years to complete. It was constructed of native shell stone called *coquina* and a cement-like mortar made from shell lime. The white plastered walls are thirty feet high and up to thirteen feet thick.

For fifty days in 1702, Carolinians attacked St. Augustine after destroying Spain's northern missions, but they could not penetrate the fort. The British Carolinians burned the entire city except for the fort and then withdrew. The settlement was rebuilt with stone. To protect the town from future destruction, earthworks and palisades, buttressed at strategic points with redoubts, were built from the Castillo, making St. Augustine a walled city.

Toward the end of the French and Indian Wars, Spain formed an alliance with France against the British. After the British captured Havana, Spain agreed to cede Florida in return for the Havana port. England held St. Augustine for twenty years (1763–1783). During the American Revolution, the Florida outpost remained loyal to England.

A treaty signed by England, France, and Spain in 1783 returned

Photo by Patricia A. Gutek

**Spanish Quarter, St. Augustine, Florida**
The Prince Murat House at 250 St. George Street is an eighteenth-century
Spanish Colonial house built of coquina. One can see this and
other historic dwellings while strolling through the streets of
St. Augustine's historic Spanish Quarter.

Florida to Spain. St. Augustine remained a Spanish possession until July
10, 1821, when Spain ceded Florida to the United States.

In 1836, Seminole Indians attempted to regain control of Florida,
and the Castillo was used by the Americans as a military prison. After the
Seminole War ended in 1842, Florida became the twenty-seventh state in
the Union.

During the Civil War, Florida seceded from the Union; and in 1861,
Confederate troops took possession of the Castillo, a Federal fort. In
March 1862, a Union blockade squadron demanded the surrender of St.
Augustine. The small Confederate garrison withdrew, and the city was oc-
cupied by Union forces for the duration of the war.

After the war, Northern visitors began vacationing in St. Augustine
during the winters. Henry Flagler, a co-founder of Standard Oil Company,

built three luxurious hotels in the Spanish Renaissance style. Although the tourists Flagler attracted brought vitality and income to St. Augustine, older buildings were sacrificed to new construction. Fires in 1887 and 1914 also destroyed many historic buildings.

Castillo de San Marcos was renamed Ft. Marion by the United States. It was decommissioned as an active military installation in 1900. In 1924, the fort was declared a National Monument and was transferred to the National Park Service in 1933.

In 1959, the St. Augustine Historical Restoration and Preservation Commission was established by the Florida legislature. The group, renamed the Historic St. Augustine Preservation Board, has concentrated on preserving and restoring the city's historic section.

## SITE DESCRIPTION

Begin your tour of the **Spanish Quarter** at the **Triay House**, which serves as the orientation center. A reconstruction, the two-room Spanish Colonial home contains exhibits on the discovery of the Spanish colonies. Another exhibit focuses on Spanish Catholicism and includes a display of religious medals and statues or *santos*.

The **Lorenzo Gomez House** is a reconstructed timber-frame house on its original foundation as determined archaeologically. It is typical of those built in the first Spanish period (1565–1763). A modest one-room dwelling, it represents a house occupied in the 1760s by a Spanish infantryman on a small salary. Gomez also operated a trading center in his home in an attempt to supplement his income. He sold or bartered goods like pottery, ropes, and kegs of rum obtained from supply ships.

The **Martin Martinez Gallegos House** is a reconstruction of a two-room tabby house with a walled garden. (Tabby is a type of concrete made from oyster shells and lime.) Among the simple furnishings in the white plastered rooms is a small altar with a candle and a *santos*.

The **blacksmith shop** is a tabby structure. In contrast, the **Bernardo Gonzales House** is constructed of coquina. Gonzales served in the Spanish cavalry.

Filled with children during the eighteenth century, the **Geronimo de Hita Y Salazar House** belonged to a soldier with a large family. Now the house is visited by school children, who are given a chance to try chores the Salazar children performed hundreds of years ago.

Two rooms of the **Antonio de Mesa and Juan Sanchez House** were constructed at the end of the first Spanish period (1565–1763). During the second Spanish period (1783–1821), Juan Sanchez expanded the house

Photo by Patricia A. Gutek

**Castillo de San Marcos National Monument, St. Augustine, Florida**
The central court of Castillo de San Marcos, a seventeenth-century Spanish
fort, is seen from a vaulted storage room that was added in the mid-eighteenth
century. Built of coquina, the massive walls of this 17-x-34-foot room
are strong enough to resist bombardment and to support the
heavy cannons on the ramparts above.

and added a second story. The house is furnished as it would have looked
during the American territorial period (1821–1845).

A **duplex** built during the British period (1763–1783) was lived in
by **Jose Peso de Burgo** and his family from Corsica and the **Francisco Pel-
licer** family from Minorca. A reconstruction, the building now houses the
**museum store**.

Outside the Spanish Quarter but also a project of the Historic St.
Augustine Preservation Board is the **Government House Museum**. Located across from the Plaza, a building on this spot served as the Spanish
governor's office as early as 1598. The present structure was built in 1936
based on a 1764 painting of the former one. Portions of walls built in 1713
have been retained. The museum explores St. Augustine's history from
early native settlements through the European period to the Flagler era.

Exhibits focus on St. Augustine's archaeological findings, early building techniques, religious influences, and the bounty from shipwrecks off the Florida coast. 48 King Street, St. Augustine. (904) 825-5033. Open daily, 10:00 A.M.–4:00 P.M. Admission is charged.

The **Spanish Military Hospital**, 8 Aviles Street, is a reconstruction of the original hospital and pharmacy, Nuestra Señora de Guadalupe, built during the second Spanish period. The building is authentically furnished and equipped with an apothecary shop, a morgue, a doctor's office, an isolation ward, an officers' ward, and an enlisted men's ward. On the second floor is a museum of Florida medical history.

**Castillo de San Marcos National Monument** was begun in 1672 and finished in 1695, replacing a succession of earlier wooden forts. The star-shaped coquina fort is the oldest masonry fortification in the continental United States. Castillo de San Marcos, later known as Fort Marion, was built by American Indians, slaves, and Spanish soldiers. Based on a medieval plan, the fort has thirty-foot walls, a council chamber, officers' quarters, storerooms, dungeons, and watchtowers, and is surrounded by a moat. It was never captured by an enemy.

The **Officers' Quarters** contains exhibits that focus on Spanish sea routes and the military history of the Spanish era, the building of the Castillo, and American Indians who were held at the Castillo during the 1870s and 1880s.

## FESTIVALS/CRAFTS

Eighteenth-century blacksmithing skills are practiced in St. Augustine's **blacksmith shop**, while spinning and weaving are demonstrated in the **Bernardo Gonzales House**. Costumed docents weave on a 1798 double-harness loom.

At Castillo de San Marcos, live **cannon-firing demonstrations**, preceded by a **parade of soldiers** in eighteenth-century Spanish uniforms, attract the attention of many tourists.

## SIDE TRIPS

Also in St. Augustine, the **Gonzalez-Alvarez House** is often referred to as the **Oldest House**. Although its exact date is not known, it is believed to have been built between 1703 and 1727, making it the oldest Spanish residence in the country. It was originally a one-story building with coquina walls and tabby floors. The home of Major Joseph Peavett during the British colonial period (1763–1783), he added a wood-frame second story, a fireplace, and glass windowpanes. 14 St. Francis Street. Open daily. Admission is charged.

Another oldest: the **Old Wooden Schoolhouse** is believed to be the oldest school building in the United States. Records indicate it was built at the end of the first Spanish period, which lasted until 1763. 14 St. George Street. Open daily. Admission is charged.

The Greek Orthodox Church in America has restored **Casa de Avero**, a house dating from the first Spanish period. Now known as **St. Photios Shrine**, it commemorates the first colony of Greeks to arrive in the New World in 1768; Greek Orthodox religious services are conducted here. 41 St. George Street. Open daily.

The **Alcazar Hotel** is one of three Spanish Renaissance-style hotels built by oil magnate Henry Flagler in 1888. It is now occupied by the **Lightner Museum**, which contains the personal collection of O. C. Lightner, founder and publisher of *Hobbies Magazine*. 75 King Street. Open daily. Admission is charged.

The **Ponce de Leon Hotel** has become **Flagler College**; and **Zorayda Castle**, built to resemble the Alhambra, now houses oriental art treasures. 83 King Street. Open daily. Admission is charged.

*Cross and Sword*, an outdoor musical drama about the founding of St. Augustine, is presented in the **St. Augustine Amphitheater**. The play, which was written by Paul Green, is presented from mid-June to late August, 8:30 P.M. nightly, except Sunday. On State Road 3-A1A. (904) 471-1965. Admission is charged.

# GEORGIA

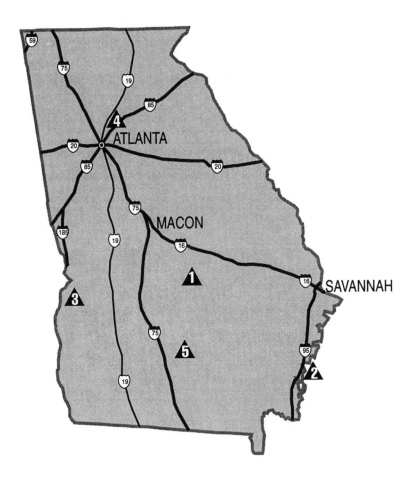

1. Andersonville: Andersonville National Historic Site
2. Jekyll Island: Jekyll Island Museum
3. Lumpkin: Westville
4. Stone Mountain: Antebellum Plantation in Georgia's Stone
    Mountain Park
5. Tifton: Georgia Agrirama

# ANDERSONVILLE NATIONAL HISTORIC SITE

Site of Civil War POW Camp; National Prisoner of War Memorial; National Cemetery; NR.

**Address:** Rt. 1, Box 800, Andersonville GA 31711
**Telephone:** (912) 924-0343
**Location:** In southwestern Georgia, 10 miles northeast of Americus on GA Hwy. 49.
**Open:** 8:00 A.M.–5:00 P.M. daily.
**Admission:** Free.
**Shops:** In the visitor center.
**Facilities:** Self-guided auto-tape tour, commemorative monuments, visitor center and museum, accessible data base of Andersonville prisoners and guards, POW Museum, picnic area.

## WHERE TO STAY

**Inns/Bed & Breakfasts:** New Perry, 800 Main St., Perry GA 31069, (912) 987-1000.
**Motels/Hotels:** Comfort Inn, 1601 16th Ave. East, Cordele GA 31015, (912) 273-2371, FAX (912) 273-2371, ext. 300. Masters Inn, 566 Farmers Market Rd., Cordele GA 31015, (912) 276-1008, 1-800-633-3434. Days Inn, 800 Valley Dr., Perry GA 31069, (912) 987-2142. Windsor Hotel, 125 Lamar, Americus GA 31709, (912) 925-1555, FAX: (912) 924-1555, ext. 113.
**Camping:** Georgia Veterans Memorial State Park, Rt. 3, Cordele GA 31015, (912) 276-2371. Andersonville City Campground, Andersonville GA 31711, (912) 924-2558. Cordele KOA, Rockhouse Rd., Cordele GA 31015, (912) 273-5454. Whitewater Creek Park, Hwy. 128 North, Oglethorpe GA 31068, (912) 472-8171.

## OVERVIEW

Fourteen percent of the 211,400 Union soldiers, sailors, and marines who were captured by the Confederate army and held in prisoner of war camps during the Civil War died in those military prisons. Twenty-nine percent of the Union prisoners held at Andersonville, Georgia, during its fourteen months of active existence, did not survive confinement.

Andersonville prison was an open stockade, essentially a corral, consisting of a sixteen-acre (later expanded to twenty-six acres) field surrounded by a pine-log wall in which as many as 33,000 men at one time were penned. In addition to being extremely overcrowded, the prison provided no shelter; food was inadequate, sanitation was lacking, medical care hopeless, and the water became contaminated.

This field prison, preserved and partially reconstructed by the National Park Service, is a grim reminder of the human toll of war and man's inhumanity to man. The nearby burial ground, where 12,920 prisoners were interred, is a national cemetery. In addition to being a Civil War site, this national historic site is a National Prisoner of War Memorial dedicated to all American prisoners of war.

## HISTORY

The South is filled with reminders of the Civil War. There are battlefields, cemeteries, statues, and monuments. In our book on the historic South, we did not plan to include Civil War sites for several reasons. First, there are enough Civil War sites to fill an entire book, and many such books have already been published. Second, we are not the Civil War experts that many other authors are. Third, we wished to highlight significant historical buildings, i.e., plantations, and collections of historical buildings known as outdoor museum villages, which are our specialty, and typically there are few historical structures at Civil War sites.

Still, there are some places that are so significant historically that we have to break our own rules. Andersonville is one of those sites. While it takes a great deal of imagination to visit a battlefield and envision the stages of the battle fought there, it takes little imagination to see the small field now covered with grass and, with a sickening feeling in your stomach, realize that this was once a fenced, unroofed prison for tens of thousands of Union soldiers, sailors, and marines more than a quarter of whom did not survive. Cattle corrals are less crowded than was this inhumane corral where human beings were penned. No wonder so many men died.

Andersonville Prison, or Camp Sumter which was its official name, was located near a Southwestern Railroad stop known as Anderson Station—the town of twenty people in remote Sumter County, Georgia, that was later named Andersonville. The original "prison" consisted of sixteen and one-half acres in the shape of a parallelogram surrounded by a

Photo by Patricia A. Gutek

**Andersonville National Historic Site, Andersonville, Georgia**
At Andersonville, a Civil War prisoner of war camp held thousands of Union
military men in a sixteen-acre stockade surrounded by a pine-log wall without
any permanent structures. "Shebangs"—shelters the men themselves
constructed out of branches and covered with blankets or clothes—provided
their only protection.

pine-log stockade fifteen feet high. This pen was intended to accommodate a maximum of 10,000 men.

In January 1864, trees were cleared, ditches were dug, and the stockade wall was built. Though this work was not completed until March,
Union prisoners began arriving in late February. In March 1864, Andersonville authorities established a "deadline" inside the pen marked by a
railing about four feet high. Paralleling the palisade, it averaged a distance
of nineteen feet from the stockade. Prisoners were forbidden to enter the
"deadrun," the ground between the deadline and palisade, under penalty
of being shot—hence the name "deadrun."

Initially, there were eight sentry boxes for the prison guards. As the
prison population grew, these were increased to fifty-two. Additional security measures included the building of a second wall around the original

one, three redans, three lunettes, one redoubt, one earthen fort, and a line of rifle pits. Five large field guns were trained on the prison. The number of successful escapes from Andersonville has been estimated at about 300. Most of them were accomplished by prisoners on work details outside the stockade. Men on the inside did attempt to dig escape tunnels out of the camp, but guards discovered most of these efforts.

By June, when the population at Andersonville reached 26,000, the compound was enlarged by ten acres, creating a total of twenty-six and one-half acres. Because of the deadline, only twenty-two acres could actually be occupied by the captured men. During Andersonville's fourteen months as a prisoner of war camp, from February 1864 to May, 1865, it held over 45,000 men. In August, 1864, there were nearly 33,000 prisoners, 2,993 of whom died that month; 127 died on August 23 alone.

The soldiers lived in the open, exposed to the elements. Some constructed shelters called "shebangs," which were raised a few feet off the ground and made of branches covered by a blanket or clothes. Others dug holes or tunnels in which to sleep. Seven months after the camp opened, five dirt-floor barracks, made of rough-cut board sides with clapboard roofs, were built to accommodate 270 men. A month later, five more barracks were added at the opposite end of the prison.

Food was always in short supply. Rations included corn meal, peas, rice, flour, bacon, and syrup, but by the summer of 1864, a prisoner was fed only corn meal and a rare two-ounce ration of spoiled meat. Sanitation was a chronic problem, as was medical attention. Water came from Stockade Branch, a narrow stream that passed under the east and west walls. It became contaminated by bakehouse refuse and from being downstream of Confederate camps. Prisoners made it intolerable by having to use it as a latrine. Some prisoners hand dug wells in an attempt to obtain uncontaminated water.

As if in answer to prayers, in August 1864, after days of torrential rains and flooding, a spring was discovered inside the stockade. Because the spring was within the deadline, a trough was built to funnel the pure water across the deadline so that the men could access it. The grateful prisoners named the spring "Providence Spring" because they believed that the clean water must have been given them through an act of God.

A total of 12,920 Union soldiers died in Andersonville Prison. They died of dysentery, scurvy, starvation, and untreated wounds, and a few were shot by guards. After a prisoner died, his body was carried to the south gate, then brought to the deadhouse, a pole structure with a pine-bough roof fifty yards from the gate. From there, corpses were loaded by work details onto the ration wagon and hauled to the prison graveyard a thousand yards northwest of the south gate. Long, shallow trenches dug by prisoners were three and a half feet deep, seven feet wide, and one or two hundred feet long. Bodies were laid side by side and covered with dirt. A piece of wood etched with the identification number of the deceased, as listed in the hospital register of deaths, was placed on each grave.

The end of Andersonville Prison came with the resumption of prisoner exchanges in March 1865. They had been suspended in October 1863 because both North and South charged each other with abuses of the prisoner exchange agreement. By May 10, 1865, all prisoners had been removed from Andersonville.

A prisoner who was chosen to record prisoners' deaths because of his fine penmanship made his own copy of the list, for he realized how important that information would be to the families of soldiers. After Private Dorence Atwater of the Second New York Cavalry was exchanged in March 1865, he informed the War Department of the existence of his list, which contained more than 10,000 names. He also told Clara Barton, who had been appointed by President Lincoln to deal with the relatives of missing Union prisoners. That list, along with the recovered Confederate record book, made it possible for all but 460 prisoners' graves at Andersonville to be identified. In the summer of 1865, wooden markers were placed on the graves of the 12,920 Andersonville prisoners by an army group that included Atwater, Barton, and three dozen workmen.

Captain Henry Wirz, the interior commandant of Andersonville prison, was convicted by a Federal commission of maltreating and murdering prisoners. He was executed by hanging on November 10, 1865.

Andersonville National Cemetery was established on July 26, 1865. The 12,920 Union soldiers, sailors, and marines who died in the nearby prison camp are interred in sections E, F, H, J, and K along with another 800 Union soldiers who died in hospitals, in other prisoner of war camps, or on Georgia's battlefields. Civil War soldiers comprise the bulk of the over 18,000 veterans buried at Andersonville National Cemetery.

## SITE DESCRIPTION

**Andersonville National Historic Site** is a 475-acre park consisting of a visitor center, a POW Museum, the National Cemetery, and the prison site. Visitor center exhibits are on Andersonville prison, the cemetery, Civil War prisons, and the systems of prisoner exchange and parole used during the Civil War. There is an orientation film.

People whose ancestors might have been connected with Andersonville can access the **visitor center computer data base**, which has information on both prisoners and guards. The **Prisoner of War Museum** contains exhibits and relics relating to war prisoners from the Revolutionary War, World War I, World War II, the Korean War, the Vietnam War, and the Persian Gulf War. Expansion of the visitor center and museums is being planned.

Visitors may walk or drive on their self-guided tours through the cemetery and around the prison camp.

At the prison site, a stone structure has been built over Providence Spring. Several hundred feet of the stockade wall, including the north gate, have been reconstructed. That gruesome line, the deadline, has been rebuilt as well as several examples of shebangs. The sites of several wells and tunnels built by prisoners are marked throughout the prison grounds.

**Several states**—Massachusetts, Ohio, Rhode Island, Wisconsin, Tennessee, and Michigan—have erected **memorials** inside the stockade to honor their military men who perished at Andersonville. Other **monuments** are dedicated to Clara Barton and the Woman's Relief Corps.

Outside of the prison field are the sites of the **bakehouse, dead house, guardhouse, dispensary**, and **hospitals**. A number of earthworks including that of the Star Fort can be viewed.

In 1877, the cemetery's wooden headstones were replaced with marble ones. Row after row of military grave markers look like waves in an ocean. **State monuments** in the cemetery include those from New Jersey, Pennsylvania, Iowa, Connecticut, Minnesota, Maine, Indiana, New York, and Illinois.

## FESTIVALS/CRAFTS

The third weekend of February, a living-history program commemorates the opening of the prison. In May, a **Memorial Day program** in the National Cemetery features military units and guest speakers. On the first weekend in October, a living-history program portrays Union occupation troops at the war's close. An 1865 dedication ceremony of the National Cemetery is performed. Every other year, on odd years, a drama called *The Andersonville Trial* is performed by the Sumter Players in the Park.

## SIDE TRIPS

Also in Sumter County is the small, rural town of **Plains, the home of Jimmy Carter**. The thirty-ninth president of the United States, Carter served in that office from 1977 to 1981. He and his wife, Rosalynn Smith

Carter, are both descendants of families that have lived in Sumter County since the 1700s. Carter's family was involved in peanut farming and operating a seed-and-farm-supply store. Before becoming president, Carter was a naval officer, a state senator, and the governor of Georgia, as well as a participant in the family businesses.

Although in 1987 Congress established the **Jimmy Carter National Historic Site** in Plains, the site is still in the early stages of development. Carter's school and childhood home are part of the historic site, but neither is currently open to the public. A **visitor center** is located in the **railroad depot** that served as Carter's campaign headquarters for the Georgia presidential primaries in 1976 and 1980. An auto tape of the Jimmy Carter related sites is available at the depot. Open daily, 9:00 A.M.–5:00 P.M. Closed Christmas and New Year's Days. (912) 924-0343.

Rosalynn and Jimmy Carter are still residents of Plains, which is located ten miles west of Americus on US 280.

# JEKYLL ISLAND MUSEUM

Restored late-nineteenth-century to mid-twentieth-century winter retreat community of wealthy American industrialists; historic district; NHL, NR.

**Address:** 375 Riverview Dr., Jekyll Island GA 31527
**Telephone:** (912) 635-4036, (912) 635-2119
**Location:** Jekyll Island, one of the barrier islands off the coast of Georgia, is 9 miles from the port city of Brunswick, about 75 miles south of Savannah GA, and 65 miles north of Jacksonville FL. The historic district is located on the western side of the island on the inland waterway.
**Open:** 9:30 A.M.–4:00 P.M. daily; closed Christmas and New Year's Days.
**Admission:** Adults $7, children ages 6–18 $5.
**Restaurants:** Latitude 31 Restaurant (in Jekyll Island Club Hotel, a Radisson Resort).
**Shops:** Museum shop, twelve other shops.
**Facilities:** Museum orientation center, guided tours.

## WHERE TO STAY

**Motels/Hotels:** Jekyll Island Club Hotel, A Radisson Resort, 371 Riverview Dr., Jekyll Island GA 31527, (912) 635-2600, 1-800-333-3333, FAX: (912) 635-2818. Villas by the Sea, 1175 North Beachview Dr., Jekyll Island GA 31527, (912) 635-2521, 1-800-841-6262, FAX: (912) 635-2569. Clarion Resort Buccaneer, 85 South Beachview Dr., Jekyll Island GA 31527, (912) 635-2261, 1-800-253-5955, FAX: (912) 635-3230. Best Western Jekyll Inn, 975 North Beachview Dr., Jekyll Island GA 31527, (912) 635-2531, 1-800-736-1046, FAX: (912) 635-2332. Jekyll Estates, 721 North Beachview Dr., Jekyll Island GA 31527, (912) 635-2256, FAX: (912) 635-2256.
**Camping:** Jekyll Island Campground, North Beachview Dr., Jekyll Island GA 31527, (912) 635-3021. Blythe Island Regional Park Campground, Rt. 6, Box 224, Brunswick GA 31525, (912) 2261-3805, 1-800 343-7855. Golden Isles Campground, Walker Rd., Brunswick GA 31525, (912) 264-3180.

## OVERVIEW

Jekyll Island Club Historic District is the area where some of the world's wealthiest and most powerful families in the years between 1886 and 1942 made their winter home. The Jekyll Island Club, a private club formed by American industrialists, purchased the entire island for $125,000 in 1886. The Jekyll Island Club House was built, followed by private "cottages" whose owners were families named Rockefeller, Pulitzer, Goodyear, Morgan, and Crane.

Now a national landmark and a historic district, the remaining ten "cottages" have been preserved; five have been restored and are open to tourists. The clubhouse is a beautifully restored resort hotel, the Jekyll Island Club Hotel. Walking through the historic district with its elegant club house, architecturally significant mansions, stables, tennis courts, servants' quarters, fragrant flowers, and live oak trees situated on the Jekyll River gives you some feel for the low-key but idyllic life-style enjoyed by club members around the turn of the twentieth century.

Connected to the mainland by a causeway, Jekyll Island is now a year-round resort island with beaches, golf courses, bicycle trails, marinas, and tennis courts, in addition to the restored historic area.

## HISTORY

Before European colonization of North American, Jekyll Island, one of Georgia's barrier islands, was the home of the Guale Indian tribe, who called their island "Ospo." The occupation of Georgia by Native Americans is believed to date from as early as 500 B.C.

Spain claimed the island in 1566. Spanish priests established the Santiago de Ocone (or San Buenaventura) Mission and initiated efforts to convert the natives to Roman Catholicism.

For hundreds of years, Spain, France, and England struggled over possession of North America's southeast coast. Spain controlled Florida, while England controlled the Carolinas. Both countries claimed the land between St. Augustine, Florida, and Charleston, South Carolina.

In 1732, a British charter for all the land between the Savannah and Altamaha Rivers and westward from their headwaters to the Pacific Ocean was granted to a board of trustees by King George II. Georgia was to be a buffer colony and a strategic British military outpost in the unoccupied territory between South Carolina and Florida. In 1732, one of the trustees—James Edward Oglethorpe, a British general and member of

Parliament—and over 100 colonists founded the colony named Georgia in honor of King George II of England.

In 1736, Oglethorpe built a base, Fort Frederica, on Georgia's St. Simons Island, adjacent to Ospo, or Jekyll Island, as it was renamed by Oglethorpe for his friend Sir Joseph Jekyll. The fort and the fortified settlement of Frederica became General Oglethorpe's headquarters for operations against the Spanish in Florida during the Anglo-Spanish conflict. Problems between Great Britain and Spain erupted in 1739 in the War of Jenkins' Ear. In the New World, Spain and England accelerated their conflict in Florida, Georgia, and South Carolina.

Under Oglethorpe's command, troops from Fort Frederica and South Carolina unsuccessfully attacked the Spanish fort, Castillo de San Marcos, at St. Augustine, Florida. Military operations in the Georgia-Florida area culminated in the Battle of Bloody Marsh on St. Simons Island, where Oglethorpe's outnumbered troops defeated a Spanish invasion force on July 7, 1742. This battle ended Spain's threat to Georgia.

A plantation that had been established on Jekyll Island by William Horton, one of Oglethorpe's officers, was destroyed by the Spanish during their retreat from the Battle of Bloody Marsh. Horton rebuilt his plantation in 1746. Cotton, rye, indigo, and sea-island cotton were grown there. Around 1800, the plantation was purchased by a Frenchman, Christophe Poulain du Bignon, who developed a successful cotton plantation using African-American slave laborers. After the Civil War, the du Bignon plantation was no longer economically viable because of the lack of slave labor.

John Eugene du Bignon, a grandson of Christophe Poulain du Bignon, and his brother-in-law, Newton S. Finney, conceived the idea of the island's being used as a private hunting club. Finney, who was a member of New York's powerful Union Club, organized hunting trips on the island for some Union Club members. They were impressed with the island's warm weather, large live oak trees, abundant game, and white beaches. These men formed the 100-member Jekyll Island Club, which purchased the island for $125,000 in 1886. Members included James J. Hill, Marshall Field, William Rockefeller, J. P. Morgan, Joseph Pulitzer, Vincent Astor, and William K. Vanderbilt. The combined wealth of members and their corporations equaled one-sixth of the world's wealth.

Landscape architect Horace W. S. Cleveland was hired to lay out the grounds. Architect Charles A. Alexander designed the Jekyll Island Club House, which was built in 1887. It contained hotel rooms, restaurants, and activity rooms. The club's first season was in 1888. Later, fifteen private cottages were constructed by club members, as well as a six-apartment building. An eight-apartment addition to the club was added in 1901. There was also a church.

The life-style at the Jekyll Island Club was luxurious. All meals, even those for private cottages, were prepared by a large, sophisticated staff in the club house. Chefs and their assistants had been recruited from the finest hotels in the North. Every effort was made to accommodate the needs of guests. The club had its own dairy and a full-time physician. Telephone service to the mainland was established in 1892, golf links were laid out in 1898, and electricity replaced gas lighting in 1903.

Guests arrived by rail, many in their private railroad cars, or by yacht. In addition to hunting, horseback riding was a popular activity. Members brought their own horses, which were stabled on the island. There were also tennis, golf, bicycling, picnicking, and horse and buggy rides.

Several factors contributed to the closing of the club after the 1942 season: the financial problems caused by the Depression's impact on members, the younger generation's preference for European resorts, club management difficulties, and the rationing that was imposed during World War II.

In 1946, the state of Georgia, which wanted to establish a state park on one of its sea islands, condemned the island and confiscated it for public use with the consent of the club, which received a $675,000 settlement. In 1978, the Jekyll Island Club Historic District was designated a National Historic Landmark.

The Jekyll Island Club Historic District is operated by the Jekyll Island Authority Division of Museums and Historic Preservation.

## Site Description

**Jekyll Island Museum** encompasses the 240-acre **Jekyll Island Club Historic District**, its remaining preserved cottages, club house, and support buildings, as well as a collection of decorative arts, historical photographs, and documents related to the club era which are displayed in the restored houses. Particularly noteworthy at Jekyll Island Museum are the quality and variety of late-nineteenth- and early-twentieth-century American architecture.

The **orientation center** of the Jekyll Island Museum is located in the **stables**, built in 1897 to house the horses and carriages shipped to Jekyll each year. The exterior of the Stables was restored in 1984–1985. An orientation film recounts the history of the island.

Of the fifteen original cottages, ten remain. Guided tours via trams take visitors to five cottages and **Faith Chapel**. The **Clubhouse** and the **Sans Souci Apartments** are hotel facilities operated by Radisson.

The **du Bignon Cottage** (ca. 1884) was built for John Eugene du Bignon. The cream-colored Queen Anne-style house with brown trim and green shutters has a wrap-around porch on the first floor as well as a second-floor porch. Rooms, decorated in the Victorian style, have been restored to their appearance in the 1896 to 1917 period.

**Indian Mound Cottage** (ca. 1892), a shingle-style cottage, was originally built for inventor Gordon McKay in 1892. In 1904, it was purchased by William Rockefeller, who made substantial additions and changes. Rockefeller added the *porte cochere*, built dormer windows on the north and south sides, and extended the living room and the second-floor bedroom to form a large rounded bay. Restoration, including landscaping, has been to 1917.

**Mistletoe Cottage** (ca. 1900) was designed by Charles Alling Gifford for Henry Kirke Porter, a locomotive manufacturer and a U.S. representative from Pennsylvania. In the 1920s, it was purchased by John Claflin. Mistletoe is a Dutch Colonial Revival house with tidewater cypress-shingle siding and a gambrel roof. The interior is used for museum exhibits.

**Villa Ospo** is a Spanish Colonial Revival cottage designed by John Russell Pope in 1927 for Walter Jennings, a director of Standard Oil. Architectural features include a red-tiled, low-pitched roof, arches, carved doors, casement windows, and wrought-iron decorations.

**Crane Cottage** is an Italianate villa designed by David Adler for Richard T. Crane, Jr., of Chicago, whose father founded a plumbing-fixture business. Built in 1917, the large house has seventeen bathrooms.

**Faith Chapel**, a non-denominational chapel built in 1904, has been restored to its 1921 appearance. The interior of the cypress-shingle church also features cypress shingles, six carved animal heads, and stained-glass windows by Tiffany and D. Maitland Armstrong.

The 1906 **Goodyear Cottage** was built for Frank Henry Goodyear, a lumber baron from Buffalo, New York. It is used as a gallery for regional and southeastern artists.

The **Hollybourne Cottage** was designed by William Day for Charles Stewart Maurice in 1890. Maurice was a partner in the Union Bridge Company, and the house incorporates bridge-building techniques in its support structure. It is the only cottage built of tabby, a local building material made of crushed oyster shells, lime, water, and sand.

Other cottages in the historic district which have been preserved and may be viewed from the outside include the 1890 **infirmary**, and the 1896 **Moss Cottage**.

The **Club House**, designed by Chicago architect Charles A. Alexander and built in 1887, is a Queen Anne building with wrap-around porches, towers, and an asymmetrical plan. It has been restored and modi-fied for use as a hotel. Also used as a hotel is the **Sans Souci**, a three-story, six-apartment shingle building built by five members in 1896.

The **Jekyll wharf** was built in 1886 as a private wharf for club mem-bers' yachts. Members and their guests were met at the wharf by horse-drawn carriages which took them to the club house.

## SIDE TRIPS

**Fort Frederica National Monument** is an archaeological site main-tained and preserved by the U.S. Department of the Interior's National Park Service on St. Simons Island at the location of the eighteenth-cen-tury military garrison and town.

Fort Frederica was established by General Oglethorpe in 1736. Three years later, the town of Frederica was enclosed with a ten-feet-high cedar-stake fence surrounded by a moat because of the threat of a Spanish invasion. The military fortification **Fort St. Simons**, constructed on the southern tip of the island, was square-shaped and commanded river ap-proaches to the town. It was occupied by the 630 British soldiers in the Forty-second Regiment of Foot, who arrived in 1738.

In June 1740, General Oglethorpe led troops from Georgia and South Carolina in an attack on Castillo de San Marcos, the Spanish fort at St. Augustine, Florida. After shelling the town and fort for three weeks, the British troops withdrew in defeat.

In retaliation, St. Simons Island was attacked by 2,000 Spanish troops commanded by St. Augustine's governor, Manuel de Montiano, in July 1742. After capturing Fort St. Simons, which had been abandoned by the British, Spanish troops marched within one and one-half miles of Fre-derica. Oglethorpe and his men were able to repel the Spanish Grenadiers, who withdrew and thus ended the last Spanish threat to Georgia. The Battle of Bloody Marsh was fought on July 17, 1742.

Fort Frederica's Forty-second Regiment was relocated in 1749, and in 1758, most of the buildings in the town burned. Frederica was never rebuilt. Today, archaeological excavations have exposed some of the ruins of the fort and the town. A **visitor center** presents an orientation movie and exhibits; tourists may visit the historic area.

The Fort Frederica Monument is open daily, 8:00 A.M.–5:00 P.M. Ad-mission is charged. Rt. 9, Box 286-C, St. Simons Island GA 31522-9710. (912) 638-3639.

# WESTVILLE

Re-created mid-nineteenth-century
Georgian antebellum farming community.

**Address:** PO Box 1850, Lumpkin GA 31815
**Telephone:** (912) 838-6310
**Location:** In southwestern Georgia, 35 miles south of Columbus, at the intersection of US 27 and GA Hwy. 27.
**Open:** 10:00 A.M.–5:00 P.M. Tuesday–Saturday; 1:00–5:00 P.M. Sunday. Closed Mondays, Thanksgiving, Christmas, and New Year's Days, and early January.
**Admission:** Adults $6, senior citizens $5, students $3, children under age 5 free.
**Restaurants:** Snacks available in village kitchens; restaurants in town of Lumpkin.
**Shops:** Handicrafts and reproduction items in Randle-Morton Store.
**Facilities:** Picnic area, mule-drawn wagon rides, special events, partially handicapped accessible.

## WHERE TO STAY

**Inns/Bed & Breakfasts:** The Cottage Inn, PO Box 488, Hwy. 49 North, Americus GA 31709, (912) 924-6680. Merriwood Country Inn, Rt. 6, Box 60, Americus GA 31709, (912) 924-4992.
**Motels/Hotels:** Windsor Hotel, 104 Windsor Ave., Americus GA 31709, (912) 924-1555, FAX: (912) 924-1555. Sheraton Airport, 5351 Simons Blvd., Columbus GA 31904, (706) 327-6868, FAX: (706) 327-0041. La Quinta-Midtown, 3201 Macon Rd., Columbus GA 31906, (706) 568-1740, FAX: (706) 569-7434.
**Camping:** Stewart County Campground, Trotmon Rd., Lumpkin GA 31815, (912) 838-6769. Florence Marina State Park, GA Hwy. 39C and GA Hwy. 39, Florence GA 31815, (912) 838-4244.

## OVERVIEW

Westville, a re-created museum village, depicts daily life in pre-industrial Georgia during the 1850s. More than thirty buildings have been relocated, and restored, to form a typical mid-nineteenth-century west

Georgia town. Westville never existed in Georgia's historical past; it is a re-created town which functions as an outdoor museum. Preservation of the crafts of 1850 is one of the primary goals of this museum village. Visitors witness the life-style of a Southern town 150 years ago as docents practice appropriate crafts and perform appropriate chores. Westville has one of the largest displays of mid-nineteenth-century Georgia-made decorative art. Vegetable and flower gardens throughout the village bloom with plants popular in the nineteenth century.

## HISTORY

West Georgia was originally inhabited by Native American tribes, including the Mississippian, from 800 to 1400 A.D., who left two large mound systems: Rood and Singer-Moye. From 1400 to 1836, the Muskogean or Creek culture dominated. Pioneers were eager to settle the land, and the Treaties of Indian Springs opened west Georgia for non-native settlement in 1827. The last native culture, the Lower Creeks, sold their land to the state and moved west. West Georgia land was distributed by a lottery open to legal residents of the United States held in May 1827. Each lot was 202½ acres. Lumpkin is in Stewart County, one of the west Georgia counties settled at that time. By 1850, Stewart County's population was over 16,000, almost half of whom were enslaved African Americans.

Westville is named for Colonel John Word West, a historian who served as acting president of North Georgia College. The village developed from the 1966 purchase of his private collection of historic buildings and artifacts. After a fifty-acre site in Lumpkin was donated for the museum, the process of moving buildings to Westville began in 1968. The museum village opened to the public on April 2, 1970. It is a project of Westville Historic Handicrafts, Inc., a nonprofit educational corporation.

## SITE DESCRIPTION

Westville is a fifteen-block town encompassing fifty-eight acres with more than thirty restored buildings. One of the first buildings you'll see after passing through the village gates is **Stewart County Academy** (1832), with its collection of period textbooks. Academies were generally private educational institutions for students in their teens. Unlike the New England states, Southern states did not establish common or public schools until after the Civil War.

The **Grimes-Feagin House** (1842), from Stewart County, is a one-story Greek Revival cottage. It was built by John Grimes for his son-in-law,

Henry Feagin. Doll-making and quilting are demonstrated by village craftspeople here.

The **McDonald House** (1843 and 1859) was the home of Scotsman Edward McDonald, a man of wealth and social status. Originally, it was a modest two-room house to which two front parlors and a second floor was added. Now, the impressive Greek Revival mansion has a two-story portico with six columns. It is furnished with mid-nineteenth-century Empire-style pieces, including an ornate square piano, elaborate bedroom wardrobes, a hand-carved rosewood bed, and an oversized dining-room table. The Empire style (which takes its name from the second French Empire) is more elaborate than the earlier Federal style and was popular with wealthy Americans.

**Chattahoochee County Courthouse,** a two-story frame building, was the seat of county government. Built in 1854, it was used until 1975, and much of its furnishings and woodwork are original. President Jimmy Carter's great-grandfather and grandfather served as county officials in this building. Southern political life centered in the county, in contrast with the town government prevalent in New England. Today, the courthouse is the home of Westville's educational programs.

The **Bryan House** (1831) was built in Stewart County by Loverd Bryan, a wealthy cotton-gin operator. The two-story frame house is in the "plantation plain" style (the Southern term for the "I-frame" style) with Federal influences. This style was popular in the South from 1750 to 1950. Inside, a craftsperson spins cotton yarn and weaves fabric on a loom. Across from the Bryan House is an 1850 cotton press and a gin house. The **Bagley Gin House** was built in the 1840s. This cotton gin, which is mule-driven, has an adjacent cotton-screw press for baling cotton after it has been ginned. The cotton gin, invented by Eli Whitney in 1793, was essential to the Southern economy. Before its invention, little cotton was produced in the United States because the process of separating the fiber from the seeds by hand was too time-consuming. The mechanical efficiency of the gin helped to make cotton "king" in the American South. Westville's gin is one of the few remaining in the United States.

The **Doctor's Office** (1845) was built by Dr. William Lewis Paullin of Fort Gaines. It displays medical and dental instruments. Physicians in small towns and rural areas were general practitioners and often among the few college graduates in a community.

Many early settlers in Stewart County were farmers, and the **Patterson-Marrett Farmhouse and Farm** represent their life-style. The rambling two-story log house has a dog-trot, which is an open breezeway between two separate wings under one roof. It was built in South Carolina in 1850. The farmhouse **kitchen** was built separately from the main house to minimize the threat of fire. Displayed in the large open fireplace are iron frying pans, ovens, pots, and other utensils; there is also a brick oven in the chimney that was used for baking. Near the farmhouse are the **mule barn, whiskey still, sugar-cane mill**, and **syrup kettle**. The fields are planted with sugar cane, and there are **vegetable, herb, and flower gardens** as well as fruit trees growing near the house.

The **Yellow Creek Camp Meeting Tabernacle**, built in 1840 in Hall County, is a large, open structure with a roof supported by twelve-inch-square hand-hewn beams. It contains a pulpit and benches. The camp meeting, peculiar to the South and the frontier, was a social event as well as a religious revival that attracted widely scattered families. Lasting anywhere from three to ten days, camp meetings were characterized by highly emotional reactions to the preaching of the minister.

The **Singer House**, built in Lumpkin in 1838, was once the home and shoemaking shop of Johann Singer. Perhaps because his family of eleven children outgrew their quarters, the cobbler built a separate shop next to his home in 1839. The two-story building had the shop on the first floor and sleeping accommodations for Singer's apprentices upstairs. Singer family furnishings include a cradle and a small spinning wheel brought from Germany.

The **Moye Whitehouse** (1840) is an excellently proportioned cottage of Greek Revival influence. It was moved from its original location on a 3,000-acre plantation near Cuthbert. The **West House** (1850) was the residence of Colonel John Word West's grandparents.

## FESTIVAL/CRAFTS

One of the major purposes of Westville is to keep alive and to demonstrate the crafts of early pre-industrial America. Among the shops where crafts are demonstrated are the **blacksmith shop**, the **cabinetmaker's shop** (1836), and the **shoemaker's shop** (1838). The **pottery shop, pug mill,** and **kiln** comprise an example of a jug factory, where churns, jars, pitchers, and other items were made. Craft items are sold at the **Randle-Morton Store**.

Special events at Westville include a **Dulcimer Festival** and a **Storytelling Festival** in March, a **Spring Festival**, a **May Day celebration**, an **1836 Encampment** in May, an old-fashioned **Independence Day Celebration**, the **Fair of 1850** in the fall, and **Yuletide Season** in December.

## SIDE TRIPS

In the town of Lumpkin, visit the **Bedingfield Inn,** located on the town square. Built in 1836, it is a restored stagecoach inn. Open 1:00–5:00 P.M. Wednesday–Sunday. Admission is charged.

# ANTEBELLUM PLANTATION IN GEORGIA'S STONE MOUNTAIN PARK

Re-created antebellum cotton plantation.

**Address:** PO Box 778, Stone Mountain GA 30086
**Telephone:** (404) 498-5600
**Location:** 16 miles east of Atlanta on US 78.
**Open:** 10:00 A.M.–9:00 P.M. daily in summer; 10:00 A.M.–5:30 P.M. daily for the rest of the year.
**Admission:** Adults $3.00, children ages 3–11 $2.00.
**Restaurants:** In Stone Mountain Park: Memorial Depot Chicken Restaurant, Whistle Stop Barbecue, Memorial Plaza Deli, snack bars.
**Shops:** Gift shop in the General Store.

## WHERE TO STAY

**Inns/Bed & Breakfasts:** Stone Mountain Inn, PO Box 771, Stone Mountain GA 30086, (404) 469-3311.
**Camping:** Georgia's Stone Mountain Park, PO Box 778, Stone Mountain GA 30086, (404) 498-5701.

## OVERVIEW

The Antebellum Plantation is a re-created cotton plantation that was formed by moving original pre-Civil War Georgia buildings to Stone Mountain Park. It provides an excellent overview of the Georgia cotton planter's society and life-style. Plantation structures were painstakingly researched, carefully restored, and then furnished with authentic period pieces.

Georgia's Stone Mountain Park offers a wide range of entertainment and attractions such as the Confederate Memorial Carving of three equestrian figures—Confederate President Jefferson Davis and Generals Robert E. Lee and Stonewall Jackson—a Swiss-made cable-car skylift, a steam train, the Antique Auto and Music Museum, a paddle-wheel riverboat, and the Water Works Beach Complex, as well as golfing, boating, and fishing. While enjoying these many features of the park, we concentrated on the Park's Antebellum Plantation of the 1800s.

## HISTORY

The Southern plantation, an agricultural estate often consisting of hundreds of acres, became a feature of economic and social life for the region's landowning elite. The plantation system was supported by slaves who were either seized in Africa and forcibly transported to the United States or born in the Caribbean and the South. These people constituted the bulk of the plantation system's labor force. In 1790, there were about 650,000 slaves in the South. On the eve of the Civil War in 1860, the slave population had increased to more than four million.

Supported by slavery, the plantation economy rested on the production and sale of a single cash-crop such as cotton, tobacco, or rice, which was sold in the North or exported to Europe. Patterned after these large agricultural units, Stone Mountain's Antebellum Plantation depicts a cotton-producing plantation.

The South's slave system established social and economic relationships not only between whites and blacks but also among whites. The larger the plantation and the more slaves a planter owned, the higher his status and power. Among whites, the large planters dominated social, economic, and political life before the Civil War. Non-slaveowners, often small farmers, ranked much lower in social and economic status. The owner of a plantation such as the Antebellum Plantation, who possessed many acres of land and many slaves, would have been at the top of Georgia's social structure.

Only a minority of whites in the South, estimated to be twenty-five percent in 1860, owned slaves. Other Southern whites—business and professional people in towns and the owners of small farms—owned few or no slaves. Planters who owned twenty or more slaves were an even smaller group, estimated at twelve percent of all slave owners. Given these statistics, the owner of the Antebellum Plantation would have been a member of a small, elite group. Yet despite their small number, such planters were a very powerful force who controlled the politics and set the style of life throughout the South.

To be economically profitable, the plantation had to be efficiently managed. A successful owner needed to employ an overseer, or manager, to help run the plantation. It was the overseer who supervised the work in the fields. Since it was he who dealt directly with the field slaves, his kindness or cruelty had a direct impact on their lives. The owner's family most likely dealt only with a few house servants, drivers, and craftsmen.

Some plantation owners imitated the English gentry by gracious living, hosting large social events, balls, and parties. As the code of "Planter Chivalry" evolved, sons were expected to follow their father's life-style. While they might enter politics or the military, they were to avoid business. Daughters, expected to become the mistresses of plantations, were educated to play the piano, speak French, and dress in the latest Parisian fashions.

The plantation system has to be seen from the standpoint of the slaves as well as that of the owners and overseers. By the mid-nineteenth century, Northern abolitionists were condemning slavery as the "South's peculiar institution." Since slaves were regarded as property rather than persons with rights, they had no legal protection. Although some planters might be paternalistic, slaves were often controlled by force and the constant threat of breaking up their families by selling off its members.

Slaves on a plantation were divided into domestic or house servants, craftsmen such as carpenters or smithies, and field hands. On the plantation itself, the social hierarchy consisted of the plantation owner and his family at the top, and next, the manager or overseer who ran the day-to-day operations of the enterprise. In some cases, he might be followed by a tutor, who instructed the family's children and served as secretary to the owner. Next in the hierarchy were the domestic or household servants—the butler, valet, and maids. The domestic staff was followed in status by the drivers, craftsmen, and artisans. At the bottom of the social and economic structure but also its foundation were the field hands, who planted and harvested the crops and cared for the livestock.

The plantation system was a unique feature of Southern life until slavery was ended by the Civil War, Lincoln's Emancipation Proclamation, and the Thirteenth Amendment to the Constitution.

The history of the Antebellum Planation at Georgia's Stone Mountain Park began with the efforts of the Stone Mountain Memorial Association to create a plantation complex to illustrate how a wealthy Georgia family lived in the period between 1820 and 1860. The task of identifying the buildings that would constitute the plantation and selecting the antiques with which they would be furnished was entrusted to Ms. Christie McWhorter, a widely recognized expert in the field. An outstanding feature of restoration is the use of authentic period pieces and antiques. The Antebellum Plantation opened on April 6, 1963.

## SITE DESCRIPTION

Today, the visitor to the **Antebellum Plantation** at Georgia's Stone Mountain Park can experience the South's plantation past by touring an assemblage of buildings that represent a pre-Civil War Georgia plantation. Begin your tour at the **country store**, constructed in 1830 in Orange, Georgia. Originally a general store and post office, today the restored store is well-stocked with souvenirs and gifts.

The **overseer's house**, or **Kingston House**, originally the manor house of the Bryan Allen plantation at Kingston, Georgia, dates from 1845. The house, constructed in the late Federal architectural style, features tapered octagonal columns and overhead timbers of hand-hewn Georgia heart pine. Most of its Palladian windows still contain their original handmade glass. In the parlor, furnishings include an early American Jacobean wing chair, a mahogany Queen Anne tilt-top table, a cherry Sheraton chest, black wrought-iron candle stands, and an American Empire-style walnut clock. The **dining room** contains a Chippendale drop-leaf table set with Cauldon chinaware and deer-horn knives and forks, a walnut corner cabinet, and a grandfather clock. The **master bedroom** features a maple and pine bed, a Sheraton chest, and a Pennsylvania Dutch blue blanket chest. Other rooms are the **child's bedroom**, with children's furniture and toys, **the keeping room**, and **the birthing room**.

The **smokehouse**, a cabin-like structure, was used to cure hams, pork, and bacon which were smoked over a slow-burning hickory fire. Nearby is a covered **well**.

**Mammy's Cabin**, originally Dr. Chapman Powell's office, was built in 1826 on a Cherokee Indian trail located in what is now the north Atlanta area. Dr. Powell (1798–1870), one of DeKalb County's pioneer physicians, used the cabin as a home, office, and drug store. Its hand-hewn logs are "keyed" or locked in place to provide extra strength for the structure. In 1864, General William T. Sherman's Union soldiers commandeered the cabin as a first-aid station during the siege of Atlanta. At Stone Mountain, the building called "Mammy's Cabin" is furnished as a slave dwelling. However, it is a more elaborate dwelling than many slave houses of the period. For example, it has a large stone fireplace and a plank floor rather than a simple dirt floor. It also is furnished more extensively than typical slave cabins of the period. Among its furnishings are an iron foot tub, a bed, smoothing irons and cooking pots, a work table, and ironstone dishes.

The **Thornton House** was built by Thomas Redman Thornton in the 1790s at Union Point near Greensboro in Greene County, Georgia. It is believed to be one of Georgia's oldest restored buildings. The wooden frame home was designed in the cottage architectural style popular among early settlers in the South's piedmont regions. Among the house's features are its simple entrance stoop and the twin chimneys on the north side connected by a "pent" or warming closet, which has inside and outside doors. Food, brought from the cook house to the pent, was kept warm until served. Another interesting feature is the nogging construction—a combination of wood framing and brick masonry—visible in the closet under the stairway.

The Thornton House is entered through large "coffin" doors, so called because their width allowed a coffin to be carried into the house. Noteworthy antique furnishings in the **entry** are a lantern chandelier, ladder-back chairs, and a Queen Anne-style console table. The **parlor**, accessed from the entry and furnished with eighteenth-century swag curtains and Bokhara carpeting, contains a Georgia-made cellaret of pine and boxwood, an eight-legged Sheraton-style sofa, a cherry tea table, and period jars and candle sticks. The **dining room** contains a large dining table, applewood chairs, a mahogany sideboard, and china pieces. The **master bedroom** is furnished with a bed, chairs, and a spinning wheel—all crafted in Georgia. A stairway leads upstairs to the **children's and guests' bedrooms**, which are furnished with eighteenth-century pieces. The house's **gardens**, in period horticultural design, feature formally trimmed boxwood, as well as herbs, flowers, and vegetables.

The **slave cabins**, built between 1825 and 1840, originally were located at the Graves Plantation at Covington, Georgia. Simple clapboard frame buildings, they are covered with hand-cut shingles, or shakes. Although a plantation of the size represented by the Antebellum Plantation would have had many similar cabins, the two preserved here represent typical slave habitations. Slave cabins were generally furnished with simple handmade furniture such as a bed, table, chairs, and cots. The locations of the cabins of particular slaves usually depended upon their work assignments. Domestic servants often had better cabins which were nearer the manor house than field workers.

The **barn complex** includes several functional buildings related to the work of the plantation. The barn, built around 1800 in Calhoun, Georgia, is constructed of square-hewn timbers, keyed to provide added structural stability. The barn includes stables for horses and cows, a hay loft for storing fodder, and storage spaces for tools, equipment, grain, and supplies. The barn also contains a cotton gin.

The **cribs**, built around 1800, were used for crop storage. The **coach house**, a feature of large plantations, built in the style of the 1800s, housed carriages and drivers. The **smokehouse**, built between 1825 and 1845, was originally located at the Graves Plantation in Covington, Georgia. An unusual feature is its hand-hewn salt bin. The **necessary house**, a privy or outhouse, was moved to the site from Talbottom, Georgia.

The **kitchen garden** and the **cook house** were also features of the typical plantation. To reduce the possibility of fire and keep the manor house cooler in the summer heat, slaves prepared food in the separate kitchen. The food was then brought to the manor house, where it was kept in the warming kitchen until served. Today, the kitchen, with its large cooking fireplace and preparation table, is stocked with authentic period utensils such as a wooden butter churn, wooden bowls, a meat grinder, an apple peeler, variously shaped cookie cutters, a large waffle iron, ladles, pots, pans, and dishes. The kitchen garden produced vegetables and herbs used by the plantation family.

As was true of large plantations throughout the south, the **manor house**, occupied by the planter and his family, was the plantation's focal point. The Antebellum Plantation's manor house, originally the **Dickey House**, was built around 1850 near Dickey, Georgia. The builder and first occupant of the house was Charles Davis, who married Agnes Nelson Dickey, daughter of Thomas Edwin Dickey, a leading Georgia planter. Descendants of the original owners lived in the house until it was moved to Stone Mountain Park in 1961.

The manor house, a fine example of neoclassical architecture, represents the home of a prosperous Georgia cotton planter of the nineteenth century. A large structure that covers 6,250 square feet, the house contains fourteen rooms. Its twin outside stairways represent welcoming arms, and its columns are constructed of handmade curved bricks. The house has Palladian arches over the front and music-room doors. Illustrating the decor and furniture used by wealthy planters, the manor house has been furnished with antiques from the seventeenth, eighteenth, and early-nineteenth centuries.

The house's spacious **entrance hall**, which leads to several rooms, is illuminated by a large hanging lantern and is furnished in the style of the second French Empire. The life-style of the planter class is illustrated by the ladies' and the gentlemen's parlors. After formal dinners, the ladies and gentlemen retired to separate rooms for conversation, coffee, and liquors. The **ladies' parlor**, decorated in Empire style, is furnished with Roman toga-style draperies and has a Regency table and chairs, a mahogany plantation desk, a large American Empire-style gold-leaf mirror, a Duncan Phyfe lyre, and a Federal-period sofa. The **gentlemen's parlor** is appointed with a mahogany tea table, a large drop-front secretary, and a camelback sofa.

In the **dining room**, the large, Federal-style drop-leaf banquet table is set with china and silverware, as though in preparation for a formal dinner. The room's prominent Empire mirror permitted the hostess unobtrusively to observe the needs of her guests, who were seated on English hand-carved chairs around the massive table. The cabinet in the room is stocked with Coalport china.

Food was brought from the **cook house** to the manor's **warming kitchen**, where it was kept warm until served. The warming kitchen, with a large fireplace, is furnished with pine work-tables, cooking utensils, serving dishes, and a large walnut corner cabinet. The **children's dining room**, next to the warming kitchen, is where the family's youngsters took their meals. The **summer dining room**, where the family took their informal meals, is furnished with a Sheraton sectional dining table set with ironstone china, early Queen Anne chairs, a Hepplewhite console table, a pine Welsh hutch, a Chippendale china cupboard and a Queen Anne sideboard.

French Empire, American Empire, and English furnishings decorate the **drawing room**. Illuminated by an elegant hand-cut English crystal chandelier, it is furnished with a large Sheraton sofa, Queen Anne chairs, a drop-leaf Pembroke table, and a rare French Empire harp.

The **master bedroom** is appointed with a mahogany Federal Regency tester bed with carved posts, a trundle bed that could be pulled out for small children, a mahogany step table, a Chippendale drop-front desk, and a Queen Anne tilt-top table. Entered from the master bedroom is the dressing room used by the planter and his wife. The **dressing room** is furnished with an oak folding rack, clothing and shoes of the period, an American Empire-style Trumeau mirror, a traveling trunk, an English mahogany wash table, and an Oxford hip bath.

The **son's bedroom** is furnished with an American Empire bed, early American mahogany cheval mirror, a Windsor arm chair, a sleepy hollow rocker, and an eighteenth-century washstand. The **daughter's room** contains Regency fiddle-grained mahogany chairs, a Sheraton four-poster bed, a walnut dressing table, a French Pocono clock, a Victorian Lincoln rocker, and a wooden traveling trunk.

A bedroom called the **mother-in-law room** contains an Empire four-poster bed with maple posts and pine headboard, a pine traveling trunk, a three-legged pine console, a ladder-back rocker with lap quilt, and a late Victorian chest. There is an attractively designed **formal garden with a gazebo**. In the gazebo is a Roman-appearing statue of George Washington wearing a toga.

The **plantation office** was the place where the planter and the overseer transacted business. The building now serves as the office of the Georgia Chapter of the United Daughters of the Confederacy.

## FESTIVALS/CRAFTS

Georgia's **Stone Mountain Park** features many special events such as the **Old South Celebration** in April, **Springfest** in May, **Fantastic Fourth** in July, the **Yellow Daisy Festival** in September, the **Scottish Festival and Highland Games** in October, and the **Holiday Celebration** in December.

# GEORGIA AGRIRAMA

Re-created late-nineteenth-century southern Georgia rural village, farmsteads, and industrial sites.

**Address:** PO Box Q, Tifton GA 31793
**Telephone:** (912) 386-3344
**Location:** In south central Georgia, 60 miles north of the Florida line; I-75 exit 20.
**Open:** 9:00 A.M.–5:00 P.M. Tuesday–Saturday; 12:30–5:00 P.M. Sunday. Closed Thanksgiving Day, the three days prior to Christmas, and Christmas and New Year's Days.
**Admission:** Adults $6, seniors $5, children ages 4–18 $3, families $15.
**Restaurants:** Concession stand, drug store.
**Shops:** Country Store, Junction Leather.
**Facilities:** Special events, visitor center.

## WHERE TO STAY

**Inns/Bed & Breakfasts:** Hummingbird's Perch (5 miles north of I-75 exit 23), Tifton GA 31794, (912) 382-5431. Myon B&B (3 miles east of I-75 exit 19), Tifton GA 31794, (912) 382-0959.
**Motels/Hotels:** Comfort Inn, 1104 King Rd. (I-75 exit 19), Tifton GA 31794, 1-800-223-5234, (912) 382-4410. Day's Inn, 1008 West 2nd St. and I-75, Tifton GA 31794, 1-800-882-7210. Quality Inn, I-75 and 2nd St., Tifton GA 31794, 1-800-833-4154, (912) 386-2100. Holiday Inn, I-75 and US 82 West, Tifton GA 31794, (912) 382-6687. Hampton Inn, I-75 and US 82, Tifton GA 31794, 1-800-892-2753, (912) 382-8800.
**Camping:** Reed Bingham State Park (6 miles west of Adel, off GA Hwy. 37), Adel GA 31620, (912) 896-3551. Covered Wagon Campground (I-75 exit 17), Tifton GA 31794, (912) 382-9700. South Georgia RV Park (I-75 exit 16), Tifton GA 31794, (912) 386-8441.

## OVERVIEW

Georgia Agrirama is a Georgia living-history museum presenting a re-created rural town and farmsteads from 1870 to 1910. Thirty-five original structures from the wire-grass region of Georgia have been relocated to the ninety-five acre site. Structures have been restored and furnished with period furniture and artifacts.

The four areas of this outdoor museum are a traditional farm community of the 1870s, a progressive farmstead of the 1890s, an industrial-sites complex, and a rural town.

## HISTORY

Pioneers settled in Georgia's pine belt in the 1820s, purchasing land for as little as twenty-five cents to one dollar per acre. Some brought large herds of livestock; the thick wire grass growing amid the pine trees was good for grazing.

Because of the difficulty of clearing the virgin yellow-pine forest, farmers often cultivated only enough acres to grow crops for their families. By 1870, there were many farmers who practiced subsistence agriculture and ranged large herds of livestock.

Towards the end of the nineteenth century, rural industrialization began to impact the isolated area. The lumbering industry built sawmills and began clearing the pine forests. The naval stores industry also developed.

Railroads such as the Brunswick and Albany and the Macon and Brunswick began moving into the wire-grass region between 1865 and 1876. Railroad trains moved industrial products to the markets, and railroad towns became commercial centers. The population of rural southern Georgia grew with the influx of industrial workers. Merchants and professionals arrived to serve growing towns.

As the turpentine and timber industries depleted the vast stands of virgin yellow pines, commercial agriculture developed on the cleared land. Instead of subsistence farming, farmers planted cash crops, especially cotton. Although most farmers were still self-sufficient, those who planted only cotton relied on merchants for their food.

During the period represented by Georgia Agrirama, 1870–1910, the "new South" evolved. Following the War Between the States and Reconstruction, Georgia, like other Southern states, underwent agricultural and industrial renewal. This museum village allows visitors to compare and contrast aspects of late-nineteenth-century Southern farming and small-scale industry. This ninety-five-acre outdoor museum, consisting of thirty-five restored southern Georgia buildings, opened in July 1976.

## SITE DESCRIPTION

Georgia Agrirama's distinctive features are a traditional farm community of the 1870s, a progressive farmstead of the 1890s, an industrial sites complex, and a rural small town. Exhibits and demonstrations are staffed by interpreters attired in period costumes.

The **visitor center complex**, housed in an 1850 log cabin built by James C. Sumner in the northwest part of Tift County, includes **Junction Leather**, a leather crafts shop; the **concession stand**, in a farm commissary building from Hat, Georgia; the **Opry Shelter**, based on a traditional tabernacle in Ashburn and now the site of the Wiregrass Opry and music variety programs; and the **Country Store**, in a reconstructed brick cotton-warehouse.

Georgia Agrirama's **Traditional Farmstead** represents an 1870s subsistence farm on which cattle, sheep, and hogs were raised. The **Clark Cabin** (1886) is a single-pen log structure with two shed rooms that was moved from Crosland. Its mud and stick chimney is especially interesting. A separate kitchen/dining room is connected to the house by a walkway. The primitive furnishings are typical of the late frontier domestic environment.

The **Progressive Farmstead** of the 1890s features a large farming area with barns, farm animals, and outbuildings. Its **farmhouse** (1896) was built by Allen Gibbs in Worth County. Typical of Southern farmhouses of the late 1890s, it features the posts, railings, and steep roof of the Victorian era. Noteworthy is the **dogtrot**, a breezeway running through the center of the house, and the **traveler's room** on the front porch, which was used by drummers (peddlers) and circuit riders (preachers).

Also in the Progressive Farmstead are the reconstructed **cane mill, syrup shed**, and **syrup house**, which contain exhibits on syrup production. After the juice was extracted from the cane by crushing, it was boiled to produce syrup. The cane syrup was then stored in jars and cans in the syrup house.

The **smokehouse** was used for curing and smoking shoulders, sides, hams, and sausages. The smoking of meat was a usual feature of Southern food preparation.

The farmstead's **barn** is a reconstruction of an 1889 Miller County barn. The **seed-cotton house**, which protected the newly picked seed cotton, came from the town of Hat. There are also a chicken house, corncrib, tack room, and hog pen, dating from the 1880s and 1890s.

Vegetables, herbs, and fruits now grown in the gardens and fields of both the traditional and progressive farms are typical of those found a century ago. Sugar cane, melons, corn, peanuts, and cotton were all important agricultural products in the wire-grass region.

Churches and schools were important aspects of Georgia's rural communities. At the Agrirama, the church, known as the **Wesley Chapel**, was constructed in 1882 in Dougherty County. Pulpit, pews, and railings are all original; the windows have large panes of hand-poured glass. The **Sand Hill School House** was built near Ty Ty around 1895 by Johnnie Gibbs. The one-room school has a teacher's desk, pupil's desks of various sizes, recitation benches, and a pot-bellied wood-burning stove.

The **Gristmill** (1879) was built by Barney Kearce and moved from Warwick in Worth County. It was used to grind corn into meal and grits. The **miller's house**, which represents the home of a gristmiller, was built by Benjamin and Mary Elizabeth Cravey in 1877 in Turner County. The **blacksmith shop**, a re-created building, is the scene of smithing demonstrations.

Economic development in late-nineteenth-century southern Georgia revolved around forest industries and the railroads. At the **sawmill**, a Deloach circular saw, powered by a 25-horsepower Atlas steam engine, was capable of cutting 10,000 board-feet per day. It took a crew of ten to operate.

The **turpentine still** represents an important enterprise in rural Georgia, the distilling of turpentine from resin, which was readily available from plentiful pine forests. The resin was boiled in a large copper pot; the steam passed through a condensing coil and distilled as turpentine, leaving rosin in the pot. Rosin had many uses including waterproofing and caulking ships and making cosmetics and paper sizing. Nearby is the **cooper's shed**, where the barrels used to ship rosin were made.

The **commissary**, built in 1889, was operated by Toombs Taylor Morgan in Dooly County. Commissaries were built by employers near isolated sawmill or turpentine camps to provide workers with food and supplies. At these company stores, expenditures were deducted from laborer's wages.

The turn-of-the-century **depot** was moved from Montezuma. It originally belonged to the Atlanta, Birmingham and Atlantic Railroad. The prefabricated building was shipped by train and reassembled on location.

Merchant and professional buildings are found in the museum's rural village. The **print shop** features an 1888 Whitlock press. Also in the print shop is the **telephone exchange**. Independent telephone companies provided telephone service to the area by 1900.

The **doctor's office** (early 1870s) displays the instruments of a small-town physician. The **variety works** is a wood-working business which produced furniture, doors, sashes, and decorative trim and moldings. Along with dispensing medicines, the **drug store's soda fountain** was a powerful attraction. Coca-cola floats are still sold there.

The **cotton-gin warehouse**, a re-created building, contains an 1896 Lummus cotton gin and rotating double-bale press that is powered by a Frick 110-horsepower steam engine. The gin is operated during the late fall ginning season.

The **Tift-Willingham House** was built in 1887 by Captain Henry Harding Tift who came from Mystic, Connecticut. The town of Tifton developed around the sawmill built by Tift in 1872. The spacious two-story Victorian house is obviously the home of a wealthy family.

## FESTIVAL/CRAFTS

On selected Saturday nights during the spring and summer, country, bluegrass, and gospel music, and clogging performances are given at the **Wiregrass Opry**.

Special events include **Winter Homecoming** in February, the **Folk Life Festival and Fiddlers' Jamboree** in late April, the **Turpentine Still Firing** in late May, the **Old-Fashioned Independence Day Celebration** in July, the **Labor Day County Fair of 1896** in September, **Cotton Ginning** in October, the **Historical Political Rally** in mid-October, the **Cane Grinding Parties** in November, and **Victorian Christmas** in December.

# KENTUCKY

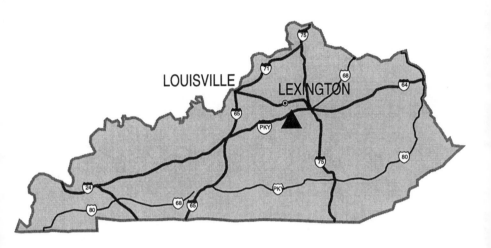

Harrodsburg: Shaker Village of Pleasant Hill

# SHAKER VILLAGE OF PLEASANT HILL

## Restoration of a nineteenth-century Shaker community; NR, NHL.

**Address:** 3500 Lexington Rd., Harrodsburg KY 40330
**Telephone:** (606) 734-5411
**Location:** In central Kentucky, 25 miles southwest of Lexington and 7 miles northeast of Harrodsburg, on US 68.
**Open:** Mid-March–November, 9:30 A.M.–5:00 P.M. daily. Some exhibition buildings are closed December–mid-March.
**Admission:** Village: adults $8.50, students ages 12–17 $4, children ages 6–11 $2, family (2 adults, unlimited number of children) $20. River-boat: adults $5.50, students ages 12–17 $3.50, children ages 6–11 $2. Combination village/boat: adults $11.50, students ages 12–17 $6, children ages 6–11 $3, family $27.50.
**Restaurants:** Trustees' Office Restaurant (reservations essential); Summer Kitchen in West Family Dwelling.
**Shops:** Post Office craft shop, Carpenters' Shop craft shop.
**Facilities:** Paddle-wheel riverboat rides, craft demonstrations, conference facilities, music and dance programs, winter weekends, special events, overnight accommodations in historic buildings.

## WHERE TO STAY

**Inns/Bed & Breakfasts:** Shaker Inn at Pleasant Hill (80 rooms in 15 original Shaker buildings), 3500 Lexington Rd., Harrodsburg KY 40330, (606) 734-5411 (reservations essential).
**Motels/Hotels:** Best Western, 1680 Danville Rd., Harrodsburg KY 40330, (606) 734-9431.
**Camping:** Chimney Rock Campground, Harrodsburg KY 40330, (606) 748-5252. My Old Kentucky Home State Park, Bardstown KY 40004, (502) 348-3502. Pioneer Playhouse Campground, Danville KY 40422, (606) 236-2747.

## OVERVIEW

One of two Shaker communities in the South, both of which are in Kentucky, Shaker Village of Pleasant Hill re-creates aspects of the life-style of the American communal religious group who lived there for more than a century. Celebrated today for their simple, functionally designed yet exquisite furniture and their serenely restored historic sites, the Shakers were some 17,000 Americans who in the years between the American Revolution and the Civil War practiced a religion based on Christian beliefs, celibacy, exuberant worship services, sexual equality of religious leadership, pacifism, and a communal economy.

Though there are no longer Shaker brothers and sisters at Pleasant Hill, the Shaker spirit permeates the site today. Picturesquely situated in Kentucky bluegrass country, the museum village is surrounded by 2,700 acres of rolling fields edged in stacked flagstone fences. An evening mist often envelopes the site contributing to its aura of separation from the modern world. First-time visitors to Pleasant Hill are struck by a sense of harmony in everything they see, from the orderliness of the setting to the pleasing proportions of buildings, the elegant simplicity of the furniture, and the utilitarianism of the plain tools. White picket fences, stone walkways, lanterns hung on posts, and guides in Shaker costumes add to the sense of rural serenity.

Shaker Village at Pleasant Hill is one of our favorite restorations. Set in lovely bluegrass countryside, the buildings are original and architecturally impressive. The group of people who lived here is fascinating. The Shaker furniture is authentic, and the collection large and varied. The site is of medium size and do-able without courting exhaustion, the guides knowledgeable, and the craft stores well-stocked. Lodging and dining rooms retain a historically authentic atmosphere.

There are eighty guest rooms in fifteen original Shaker buildings. Even though these buildings are restored to nineteenth-century standards, the guest rooms are heated and air-conditioned, and have their own bathrooms. They are furnished with reproduction Shaker rockers, beds, desks, and handwoven rugs.

The dining rooms are in the Trustees' House. Meals are moderately priced, and the Shaker and Kentucky recipes showcase American cuisine at its finest: fresh foods properly prepared and beautifully served. No alcohol is sold.

# History

The term "Shaker" is an informal name applied to members of a Christian sect who called themselves the United Society of Believers in Christ's Second Appearing. The United Society was founded by Ann Lee, a native of Manchester, England. Prior to founding her own religious movement, Ann Lee had been a member of a group of dissident English Quakers led by Jane and James Wardley, whose worship was characterized by revivalistic activities including shaking, shouting, and speaking in tongues—thus, Shaking Quakers.

Ann Lee gradually developed her own distinctive faith, which centered in the belief that lust is the basis of evil and that celibacy is necessary for true religious life and salvation. When she assumed the spiritual leadership of the thirty-member Wardley group in 1770, she was addressed as "Mother."

When James Whittaker, one of the English Shakers, had a vision prophesying the widespread growth of the Shaker Church in America, Mother Ann too became convinced of the need to transplant Shakerism to the New World. She and eight followers sailed from England to New York Harbor in 1774. After a few years occupied by the struggle to survive in revolutionary America, the small group, based at Niskayuna, New York, near Albany, began to attract converts.

In 1781, Mother Ann undertook missionary trips in the northeast which resulted in rapid growth for the Shakers. For the remainder of the eighteenth century, the Shakers concentrated their religious and missionary activities in New York and New England. Shaker communities were established in New York, Massachusetts, Connecticut, New Hampshire, and Maine. Confirming the accuracy of the Whittaker vision, Shaker membership in America would reach 17,000 in its nineteen communities. Not until 1805 did the Shaker missionaries head west. In the early 1800s, seven Shaker communities were established in Ohio, Indiana, and Kentucky.

Shaker communities usually began with missionaries' holding worship services for local people in the home of a sympathizer or believer. Later, when there were enough believers to form a family, a communal site was agreed on. Members donated their money and property and sold their possessions to buy land, which would be held in common ownership.

On January 1, 1805, three Shaker missionaries from New Lebanon, New York, traveled 1,200 miles to Kentucky. They had heard about the

Great Kentucky Revival, in which a wave of camp meetings had reawakened religious sentiments among thousands of people. After making some converts, the Shaker group gathered on Shawnee Run, a few miles from Harrodsburg.

Two years later, in 1807, a permanent settlement was established on the elevation that came to be called "Pleasant Hill." In January 1809, two elders and two eldresses were sent from Union Village in Ohio to form the first ministry. In 1809, the first building in the village, the first Centre Family Dwelling, now known as the Farm Deacon's Shop, was built. Of the 270 buildings erected over the ensuing century, 30 remain today.

The Shakers were active craftspeople. They produced brooms, cooper's wares, weaving implements, shoes, woolen goods, pressed cheese, medicinal products, seeds, and herbs. By 1816, they had begun to make trading trips to New Orleans to sell their surplus goods.

By 1820, Pleasant Hill's membership had increased to nearly 500. During the course of the century, 1,500 Shakers lived in this prosperous community. Their landholdings reached approximately 4,000 acres, and they grew wheat, rye, oats, flax, Indian corn, broomcorn, and potatoes. There were also extensive fruit orchards.

Like other Shaker communities founded by Mother Ann Lee, these Kentuckians believed in confession of sin, celibacy, communal ownership of property, withdrawal from the world, and equality of sexes and races. Since they believed work was a form of worship, they strove for efficiency, quality, and simplicity in all their endeavors. Their furniture and tools were made to be functional and simple, without unnecessary adornment. They were responsible for many labor-saving inventions and for the first municipal water system in Kentucky.

The Society was divided into five communal families, each numbering from 50 to 100 members and governed by two elders and two eldresses. Each family was a semi-autonomous unit, with its own dwelling, shops, barns, fields, and orchards.

During the late 1850s, Pleasant Hill, like the other Shaker communities, began to experience the effects of the Industrial Revolution. Mass-produced items turned out on factory assembly lines were cheaper than the Shaker-made handicrafts. As their markets declined, so did Pleasant Hill's prosperity.

Along with a declining economy, the Kentucky Shakers faced the sectional issues generated by the Civil War. Although a border state with many Southern sympathizers, Kentucky remained loyal to the Union. The Shakers were pacifists and refused to fight. Elder Frederick Evans of Mount

Lebanon persuaded President Abraham Lincoln to exempt Shakers on religious grounds. The Pleasant Hill Shakers, like their brothers and sisters elsewhere, generously fed, housed, and nursed both the Confederate and the Union troops who marched through their village. This impartiality angered their neighbors, who were also intolerant of the Shaker practice of buying and freeing slaves and accepting them into full membership in the Society. The Shakers' stores of food, cattle, horses, wagons, and flatboats were often confiscated by the military.

In 1898, the Trustees' Office and hundreds of acres were sold. By 1900, three of the families had disbanded, and their vacant buildings were rented out. On September 12, 1910, the last of the property was sold, and the Society—four brothers and eight sisters—was dissolved. Between 1910 and 1960, the property was redivided and resold. The buildings, used for various purposes (including a bus station), were neglected, and two were destroyed by fire.

In 1961, a group of people led by Earl D. Wallace of Lexington decided to restore Pleasant Hill. They formed a nonprofit educational corporation known as Shakertown at Pleasant Hill, Inc. James L. Cogar, a former curator of Colonial Williamsburg, became Pleasant Hill's first president, and the village opened to the public in the spring of 1968.

Cogar is responsible for restoring the thirty original buildings according to the principle of adaptive use. The three functional uses are exhibitions that tell the story of the life and customs of the Shaker society; education by means of seminars, symposia, and conferences; and hospitality, dining, and overnight accommodations. Pleasant Hill is the only museum village in which all overnight accommodations for guests are in restored buildings.

## SITE DESCRIPTION

Begin your self-guided tour at the **Centre Family Dwelling**. The Centre, or First, Family was the highest rank according to the spirituality of the members and was given the place of honor nearest the meetinghouse. The T-shaped Centre Family Dwelling was started in 1824 and completed in 1834. Master architect and carpenter Micajah Burnett laid out the plan of the village and designed the buildings, including this one.

The symmetry of the double doorways and two inside stairways to separate the men's quarters from the women's, along with the utter simplicity of the wide halls, white walls, high ceilings, arched doorways, wood trim, and plain wooden floors, contribute to the beauty of this outstanding building.

Burnett's design was based on the style of the early New England Shaker building, with elements of Federal classicism. The roof has square gabled ends and three massive chimneys. There are forty rooms in this four-story Kentucky limestone building, the largest erected at Pleasant Hill. It housed one hundred Shakers and is now the major exhibition building.

All rooms contain authentic Shaker furniture from the early nineteenth century, much of it made at Pleasant Hill. There are a kitchen complete with cooking utensils, a dining room, a meeting room, an infirmary, and simply-furnished sleeping rooms.

The **Meetinghouse** was the spiritual center of the community. The one at Pleasant Hill was built in 1820 and has the double doorways typical of Shaker architecture. The white frame building rests on a heavy limestone foundation. Roof and ceilings are supported by a series of interlocking cantilever-type trusses and overhead studdings and rafters; this construction made it possible to have a meeting room large enough to accommodate all the worshipers.

The **Farm Deacon's Shop**, built in 1809, was the first permanent structure in the village. Originally the dwelling house of the Centre Family, it was used as a tavern after 1817 and, finally, as an office for the farm deacons. The two-foot-thick walls of this two-and-a-half-story structure are built of white limestone quarried from cliffs along the nearby Kentucky River. The ash floors are original. Artifacts relating to the Shakers' herb industry are displayed on the first floor; the second floor is used for guest lodgings.

In 1833, Micajah Burnett devised a water system that provided every house and barn in the village with running water. The yellow frame **Water House** contains the machinery and tanks for the first public waterworks in Kentucky.

Next to the water house is the small **Brethren's Bath House**, built in 1860. Each family was a self-sufficient unit with its own large dwelling for eating and sleeping; a craft shop for women; separate bathhouses for men, women, boys, and girls; a washhouse; and various other outbuildings.

On the first floor of the **East Family Brethren's Shop** (1845), a broom-maker works in his fully equipped shop. Across the hall, a carpenter uses traditional tools. The **East Family Sisters' Shop** (1855) houses spinning and weaving demonstrations on the first floor. The second floor of each shop now accommodates overnight guests.

The **Trustees' Office**, built in 1839 by Micajah Burnett, is one of the finest examples of Shaker architecture extant. It was used by the Shakers to conduct business with the outside world and to house and feed guests. Trustees were the people appointed to transact that business. The building is of flemish-bond brick and has a single front door. As you enter it, you'll be struck by the impressive twin spiral staircases.

Today, the first floor is used as a restaurant and a registration office for overnight guests. Upstairs, there are lodging rooms. The trundle beds for children are a delight.

Coopering demonstrations are conducted in the **Cooper's Shop**, which was remodeled in 1847. The **East Family Wash House** has its original cauldrons and parts of their washing apparatus. The 1848 **Post Office** and the 1815 **Carpenters' Shop** are craft shops which sell many Shaker reproductions and Kentucky crafts. A **Research Library** is in the 1859 **Preserve Shop**, where Shaker sisters prepared jars of sweetmeats. The 1875 **Scale House** and the 1840 **Drying House** are currently undergoing restoration.

Pleasant Hill has two gardens: the **kitchen garden** by the Trustees' Office and the **herb garden** by the Centre Family Dwelling. You will also want to stroll over to the peaceful **Shaker graveyard**.

## FESTIVALS/CRAFTS

Special events at Shaker Village include demonstrations of **flax working, beehive-oven baking, silk culturing, candle dipping, vegetal dyeing, basketry, cider-making,** and **hearth cooking.** There are also programs on **Shaker songs.**

You can take a one-hour ride on a **paddle-wheel riverboat, the** *Dixie Belle*, from May through October. The rides on the Kentucky River leave from **Shaker Landing**, east of the village entrance.

## SIDE TRIPS

**Shakertown at South Union** is the site of the other Shaker community in Kentucky. It was founded in 1807 and disbanded in 1922. Eleven of its original 175 buildings still stand, though all but four are in private hands.

The 1824 **Centre Family Dwelling** has been restored and is now a museum of Shaker furniture, photographs, and artifacts. The **Smoke and Milk House** has butter- and cheese-making equipment and wooden dairy tools. The 1869 nearby **Shaker Tavern** is used as a restaurant and a bed-and-breakfast. A 1917 **Shaker Store and Post Office** is on Hwy. 73, several miles from the Centre FamilyDwelling museum.

Shakertown at South Union is located in southwestern Kentucky, on US 68-80, ten miles west of Bowling Green. South Union KY 42283. (502) 542-4167.

**Ashland** is the restored estate of Henry Clay, early-nineteenth-century U.S. senator, speaker of the House of Representatives, secretary of state under John Quincy Adams, and three-time (in 1824, 1832 and 1844) unsuccessful presidential candidate. He represented Kentucky in Congress for almost forty years.

Ashland was Henry Clay's home from 1811 until his death in 1852. The estate remained in the Clay family for four generations—from 1806, when it was purchased by Henry Clay, until his great-granddaughter's death in 1948.

Ashland is not the 1805 house that Henry Clay lived in. Because of structural defects, the 1805 house was razed in 1857 and reconstructed on its original foundation. The Italianate house has twenty rooms and contains many Clay possessions and memorabilia. Twenty wooded acres remain of the original 600. In addition to the house, which may be toured, the property consists of twenty acres of lawn, a formal garden, icehouses, and a smokehouse. Open year round. Admission is charged. Richmond Rd. at Sycamore Rd., Lexington KY 40502. (606) 266-8581.

# LOUISIANA

1. Baton Rouge: LSU Rural Life Museum
2. Great River Road Plantations between Baton Rouge and New Orleans
    Darrow: Houmas House
            Tezcuco Plantation
    Destrehan: Destrehan Plantation
    Reserve: San Francisco Plantation House
    Vacherie: Oak Alley
    White Castle: Nottoway Plantation
3. Lafayette: Acadian Village
4. Lafayette: Vermilionville
5. New Iberia: Shadows-on-the-Teche
6. St. Francisville: Oakley House, Audubon State Park
                Rosedown Plantation and Gardens
7. St. Martinville: Longfellow-Evangeline State Commemorative Area

# LSU RURAL LIFE MUSEUM

### Re-creation of a nineteenth-century Louisiana working plantation.

**Address:** Museum entrance: Essen Lane at I-10, Burden Research Plantation, Baton Rouge LA 70808. Mailing address: 4600 Essen Lane, Baton Rouge LA 70809.

**Telephone:** (504) 765-2437, FAX: (504) 765-2639

**Location:** Baton Rouge is in southeast Louisiana, 80 miles northwest of New Orleans; the museum entrance is at the intersection of I-10 and Essen Lane.

**Open:** Year-round, 8:30 A.M.–4:00 P.M. Monday–Friday. Also open Saturday, 9:30 A.M.–4:00 P.M., and Sunday, 1:00–4:00 P.M., March through October. Closed on some university holidays.

**Admission:** Adults and children ages 12 and older $3, children ages 5–11 $2.

**Facilities:** Group tours.

### WHERE TO STAY

**Inns/Bed & Breakfasts:** Nottoway Plantation, PO Box 160, White Castle LA 70808, (504) 545-2730, FAX: (504) 545-8632. Pointe Coupee, 401 Richey St., New Roads LA 70760, (504) 6388254, 1-800-832-7412.

**Motels/Hotels:** Hampton Inn, 4646 Constitution Ave., Baton Rouge LA 70808, (504) 926-9990, FAX: (504) 923-3007. Crown Sterling Suites, 4914 Constitution Ave., Baton Rouge LA 70808, (504) 924-6566, FAX: (504) 387-1111, ext. 7647. Residence Inn by Marriott, 5522 Corporate Blvd., Baton Rouge LA 70808, (504) 927-5630, FAX: (504) 926-2317. Sheraton Baton Rouge, 4728 Constitution St., Baton Rouge LA 70898, (504) 925-2244, FAX: (504) 927-6925. Wilson Inn, 3045 Valley Creek, Baton Rouge LA 70808, (504) 923-3377.

**Camping:** Baton Rouge KOA Campground, 7628 Vincent Rd., Denham Springs LA 70726, (504) 664-7281. Knight's RV Park, 14740 Florida Blvd., Baton Rouge LA 70819, (504) 275-0679.

### OVERVIEW

Louisiana State University's Rural Life Museum focuses on the culture, life-style, and skills of nineteenth-century Louisiana plantation workers. Plantations, which are large Southern farms, have been glamorized and romanticized in the movies. Much attention has been paid to the life-style of the owners, who occupied the big house. However, the majority of plantation workers, both black and white, were hard-working farm laborers whose life-style was anything but glamorous.

Nineteenth-century rural homes and workshops have been relocated to Louisiana State University's Burden Research Plantation. These historic buildings typify the architecture found on a southern Louisiana working plantation of that era. Artifacts in the buildings date from the pre-industrial age. LSU has done a fine job of selection, presentation, and historical interpretation at this museum complex.

## HISTORY

During the eighteenth and nineteenth centuries, indigo, tobacco, sugar cane, and cotton were cultivated on plantations in Louisiana's Mississippi Valley. Large numbers of people worked the fields, harvested the crops, and plied the crafts necessary to the plantation's economic success.

A folk museum to preserve aspects of the material culture from Louisiana's pre-industrial era was conceived about 1970 by Steele Burden, Ione Burden, and Cecil G. Taylor, all of whom were connected to LSU. The museum was to focus on Louisiana's rural heritage in an era when its settlers depended on the land and the water for their livelihood.

The Rural Life Museum is located on the Burden Research Plantation, a 430-acre agricultural research experiment station owned by LSU. Formerly the Windrush Plantation, the land was donated to the university by the Burden Foundation.

## SITE DESCRIPTION

The **Rural Life Museum** is divided into three areas. The **Barn** holds collections of Louisiana artifacts related to cotton, as well as bathroom fixtures, washing implements, textiles, vehicles, blacksmithing tools, woodworking tools, entertainment, lumbering, wildlife, hunting and trapping, the Civil War, Native American artifacts, steam-operated machines, and the state's history. Exhibits cover Louisiana residents from the earliest American Indian civilizations to pre-industrial times.

The **plantation** consists of homes and shops related to farming and the laborers who made up the farming community. One essential building was the Commissary or **general store**, which was built between 1830 and 1835 as a storeroom on the Welham Plantation in St. James Parish. Con-

Photo by Patricia A. Gutek

**LSU Rural Life Museum, Baton Rouge, Louisiana**
A collection of Louisiana-pottery whisky jugs and food-storage jars is displayed
in the Barn Museum at Louisiana State University's Rural Life Museum.
Exhibited are artifacts relating to Louisiana and its residents from Native
Americans to the pre-industrial population.

verted into a general store in 1880, its position on the banks of the Mississippi facilitated supplies being loaded directly from river steamboats.

Also from the Welham Plantation is the **overseer's house**, which dates to about 1835. An early 1800s construction method, *briquette entre poteaux* (brick between posts), can be seen on the exposed front wall of the house.

A second *briquette-entre-poteaux* structure is the **kitchen**, built around 1855 on Bagatelle Plantation in Union. Kitchens were often built separately because of the heat and the danger of fire. The kitchen has a brick floor and a large fireplace in which the cooking was done.

The **sick house**, from Welham Plantation, was a slave cabin built in the 1830s. Plantation communities usually did not have a doctor, so the sick were often nursed by the wife of the overseer or plantation owner. One room of the house was used as a treatment room, while the other served as the infirmary. The seriously ill were kept in the infirmary, which has three rope beds with poles for mosquito netting.

The **1835 schoolhouse** served only the children of the white overseers and neighboring farmers. Plantation owners' children were privately tutored and African-American slave children were not formally educated.

The **blacksmith's shop** was reconstructed using the 1835 frame of a blacksmith's shop from Welham Plantation. Inside are blacksmith tools and a fully operational forge.

Several simple frame **slave cabins**, furnished with almost nothing but a bed, indicate the rudimentary life-style of the plantation's slave laborers. Entire families lived in these little houses, which were occupied by tenant farmers and sharecroppers after the Civil War.

The 1880 **cane grinder** and the reproduction **sugarhouse** illustrate the process of manufacturing sugar. Implements indicate that the open-kettle method of making sugar, which came from the West Indies, was employed. The **grist mill** is a reproduction of the animal-powered mechanism used to grind corn.

The **Folk Architecture** exhibit features structures built according to the guidelines of tradition and custom by and for the people who occupied them. Most of Louisiana's structures before the twentieth century would fall into that category.

A **country church** built in 1870 in Convent, Louisiana, served the College Grove Baptist congregation. A structure that is an extremely simple version of the Gothic Revival style, its pews and altar are original. Windows are plain glass which have been painted red and white to resemble stained glass. Now used as a religious museum, it holds articles from a number of faiths. Across the road from the church is a simulated cemetery, with grave markers from various parts of Louisiana.

The **pioneer's cabin** was built in 1810 in Sunny Hill, Washington Parish, of heart-pine logs that were planed smooth and pegged together. Its one room has a fireplace and is furnished with a bed, pie safe, and desk. There is a loft upstairs and a corncrib outside.

A reproduction, **Acadian House** is based on houses using the *bousillage* construction techniques of Acadian settlers in southern Louisiana. The outside stairway to the second-floor sleeping area is typical of Acadian-style homes. The gabled roof covers the house as well as the detached kitchen, which is separated by a open porch. Furnishings include a prayer stand, an item which attests to the strong religious fervor of the Acadians.

Two other examples of folk architecture are the dogtrot house, and the shotgun house. The **dogtrot house**, built in 1870 in the Kisatchie Forest west of Alexandria, consists of two self-contained rooms or cabins under one roof with an open space between them. Wooden frame chimneys packed with red clay and pine straw stand at each end of the house.

The **shotgun house** takes its name from the arrangement of its rooms, which are one behind another. From the Bayou Goula area, this house is typical of those built for share croppers after Reconstruction.

Adjacent to the museum are the **Windrush Gardens**, designed by Steele Burden, which may be toured. Within the complex are an All-American Rose Testing Garden, an annuals garden, an herb garden, nature trails, and wooded areas.

## SIDE TRIPS

A historic ship, a steamboat, and the Old State Capitol are among the attractions at **Riverfront Park** in Baton Rouge's downtown area on the banks of the Mississippi River. The **USS *Kidd*,** a World War II destroyer, may be toured Tuesday–Sunday. Admission is charged. (504) 342-1942. Take a cruise on the Mississippi aboard the ***Samuel Clemens* steamboat.** April–August, daily; the rest of year, Wednesday–Sunday. Admission is charged. (504) 381-9606. The 1849 **Old State Capitol**, whose architectural excesses nearly sent Mark Twain into apoplexy, is again open for touring after a recent restoration and the installation of exhibits.

# GREAT RIVER ROAD PLANTATIONS BETWEEN BATON ROUGE AND NEW ORLEANS

## WHERE TO STAY

**Inns/Bed & Breakfasts:** Tezcuco Plantation, 3138 Highway 44, Darrow LA 70725, (504) 562-3929, FAX: (504) 562-3923. Nottoway Plantation Inn, PO Box 160, White Castle LA 70788, (504) 545-2730, (504) 545-2409. Oak Alley Plantation Inn, 3645 LA Hwy. 18, Vacherie LA 70090, (504) 265-2151.

**Motels/Hotels:** Holiday Inn-New Orleans Airport, 2929 Williams Blvd., Kenner LA 70062, (504) 467-5611, FAX: (504) 469-4915. Ramada Inn, 2610 Williams Blvd., Kenner LA 70062, (504) 466-1401, ext. 570. Hilton-New Orleans Airport, 901 Airline Hwy., Kenner LA 70063, (504) 469-5000, FAX: (504) 466-5473.

**Camping:** Bayou Segnette State Park, Westwego LA 70053, (504) 436-1107. Baton Rouge KOA Campground, 7628 Vincent Dr., Denham Springs LA 70726, (504) 664-7281. Knight's RV Park, 14740 Florida Blvd., Baton Rouge LA 70819, (504) 275-0679. Jude Travel Park of New Orleans 7400 Chef Menteur Hwy., New Orleans LA 70126, 1-800-523-2196. Parc D'Orleans, 7676 Chef Menteur Hwy., New Orleans LA 70126, (504) 241-3167.

## OVERVIEW

Louisiana's **Great River Road** extends along both sides of the Mississippi River from Baton Rouge to New Orleans. Because rivers rather than roads were used for transportation and shipping agricultural products to markets, plantations were established on property near the Mississippi River. Large, prosperous sugar-cane plantations operated with black slave labor to produce profits that enabled the planters and their families to enjoy a luxurious life-style. This included attractive landscapes and gardens, with homes that were designed by prominent architects on a scale large enough for entertaining and were filled with fine furnishings and decorations. Houses faced the river, since guests usually arrived by boat.

Plantation culture was permanently disrupted by the human and economic devastation of the Civil War, and by the emancipation of slaves and its attendant elimination of enforced farm labor. Many plantation houses were burned during that war. Fortunately, some fine examples of plantation architecture have not only survived but have been beautifully restored and are now open to the public. They provide a glimpse of an earlier American life-style that developed in the South along the banks of the Mississippi River.

On both sides of the Mississippi River from Baton Rouge to New Orleans are six of these plantations, which can be visited one after the other. Veering from our usual format, we have lumped these River Road plantations together with a single "Where to Stay" section. Traveling south from Baton Rouge to New Orleans, one will first see Nottoway Plantation on the west side of the river; Houmas House Plantation and Tezcuco Plantation are next, on the east side of the river; then, one will see Oak Alley Plantation, which is on the west side, and San Francisco Plantation and Destrehan Plantation on the east side.

In addition to being house museums, several of the plantations have overnight accommodations, and some have fine restaurants. These historic inns offer exceptional accommodations enhanced by well-landscaped grounds and gardens. A good way to soak up the atmosphere of the antebellum South, they are reminiscent of the fine country inns of Great Britain.

# HOUMAS HOUSE

Restored 1840 Greek Revival mansion.

**Address:** 40136 Hwy. 942 Burnside, Darrow LA 70725
**Telephone:** (504) 473-7841
**Location:** Near the Mississippi River, on Rt. 942, near Burnside.
**Open:** February–October, 10:00 A.M.–5:00 P.M. daily; November–January, 10:00 A.M.–4:00 P.M. daily. Closed Thanksgiving, Christmas, and New Year's Days.
**Admission:** Adults $7, students ages 13–17 $5, children ages 6–12 $3.50.
**Shops:** Gift shop.
**Facilities:** Guided tours, gardens.

## HISTORY

Houmas House stands on land originally acquired from the Houmas tribe of American Indians by Maurice Conway and Alexandre Latil in the late eighteenth century. Latil built a four-room dwelling there. A later owner, Daniel Clark, sold it to General Wade Hampton in 1812. Hampton's daughter, Caroline, and her husband, John Smith Preston, built Houmas House, a Greek Revival mansion, in 1840. Latil's house was preserved and was later attached to the rear of their mansion. Caroline Hampton Preston was from Columbia, South Carolina, and traveled there for the birth of each of her eight children.

The owner who succeeded the Prestons managed to accomplish an overwhelming task—saving Houmas House from destruction during the Civil War. As so well dramatized in *Gone with the Wind*, many plantation houses were burned or badly damaged. John Burnside, an Irishman, purchased 12,000-acre Houmas Plantation from the Prestons for one million dollars in 1858. Burnside increased his acreage to 20,000, most of which was planted in sugar cane, and built four mills to process the cane. He became the foremost sugar producer in America. When General Benjamin Butler tried to occupy Houmas House, Burnside successfully argued immunity as a British subject.

Houmas Plantation thrived after the war under Colonel William Porcher Miles, but after Miles's death in 1899, most of the land was sold. The house was neglected and began to decay. In 1940, Houmas House and its remaining grounds were purchased from the Miles family by Dr. George

B. Crozat, who embarked on an enormous project to restore the house to the 1840s. The gardens have also been brought back to life.

Houmas House was the setting for the movie *Hush, Hush, Sweet Charlotte*, starring Bette Davis, Olivia de Haviland, and Joseph Cotten.

## SITE DESCRIPTION

**Houmas House** is a classic two-and-one-half-story Greek Revival house built in 1840. The brick house covered with white stucco is surrounded on three sides by Doric columns and has first- and second-floor galleries, dormers, and a glass belvedere on the roof. It is connected to the original late-eighteenth-century four-room dwelling in the rear by means of an arched carriage way. There are twenty rooms and thirteen fireplaces. Although the furniture is not original to the house, it is an outstanding collection of mid-nineteenth-century Louisiana furniture, including twenty-two armoires. Some pieces are from the Crozat family's home in New Orleans.

The kitchen and informal dining rooms are part of the eighteenth-century four-room house. Their original dirt floors have been replaced with tile. Wooden ceilings show exposed rafters. In the large fireplace in the **kitchen** is a collection of copper cooking utensils. Blue-willow china is stored in a glass-front cupboard. The long work-table is made of cypress, and the case clock is from the 1700s. The informal **dining room** has a large fireplace, a corner cabinet, a buffet, Hitchcock chairs, and a candelabrum, which was a gift from Bette Davis.

In the **entrance hall** of the mansion is a remarkable three-story spiral staircase as well as a Louisiana tall clock and a statue of Eve, which is original to the house.

The **parlor** has green Victorian couches and marble-topped tables. The formal **dining room** has thirteen-foot ceilings, a marble fireplace, a mahogany table, twin tables with petticoat mirrors, 100-year-old Normandy lace curtains, and a few pieces of original Houmas House china.

The **guest bedroom** has a mahogany four-poster bed, an armoire, a writing table, and a dresser. In the hallway on the second floor are five armoires and several trunks, maps of early North America, a print of the battle of New Orleans, and a French country clock.

The **master bedroom** has a solid mahogany four-poster bed, two matching armoires, a marble fireplace, and Louisiana slat-back chairs from the seventeenth century. The **children's room** contains a rocking chair covered with horsehide.

On each side of the mansion are brick, two-story hexagonal *garcon-nieres*, which were used as **bachelor quarters** and for guests. A sitting room is downstairs and a bedroom is above.

In the gardens surrounding the house are **Carrara marble statues** of the "Four Seasons," thirty-foot high magnolia trees, and live oaks—at least one of which is over 200 years old and measures twenty-five feet in circumference. Steamboats still occasionally tie up at the plantation's riverside landing.

# TEZCUCO PLANTATION

### Restored 1855 Louisiana-style raised cottage.

**Address:** 3138 Highway 44, Darrow LA 70725
**Telephone:** (504) 562-3929, FAX: (504) 562-3923
**Location:** Darrow is in southeastern Louisiana, 60 miles west of New Orleans and 30 miles southeast of Baton Rouge; I-10 exit 179, LA Hwy. 44 South.
**Open:** 9:00 A.M.–5:00 P.M. daily; closed Thanksgiving, Christmas, and New Year's Days.
**Admission:** Adults $5.50, seniors and teens $4.50, children ages 4–12 $2.75.
**Restaurants:** Tezcuco Plantation Restaurant.
**Shops:** Gift and antique shop.
**Facilities:** Overnight accommodations in former slave cabins; a Civil War Museum; an African-American Museum; guided tours; grounds are handicapped accessible.

## HISTORY

Tezcuco's plantation house is a cypress and brick Louisiana-style raised cottage built between 1850 and 1855 by Benjamin Tureaud, son of Augustin Tureaud and Elizabeth Bringier. Tureaud married his cousin Aglae Bringier; she was the daughter of Michel Douradou Bringier, the owner of the l'Hermitage plantation.

Tureaud, a veteran of the Mexican wars, named his plantation *Tezcuco*, an Aztec word meaning "resting place." Tezcuco is also the name of a lake near Mexico, where Montezuma took refuge from the Spanish conquistador Cortez. Tureaud obtained from swamps on his land the cypress used in constructing his house. The bricks were made on the plantation by slaves.

The house was originally restored by Dr. and Mrs. Robert H. Potts, Jr., in 1950. Restoration was continued by General and Mrs. O. J. Daigle.

## SITE DESCRIPTION

One of Louisiana's Great River Road plantations, **Tezcuco Plantation** has a restored 1855 **plantation house**, a chapel, a Civil War museum, a commissary museum, and bed-and-breakfast facilities in former slave dwellings. The grounds include majestic live oaks, formal gardens, and brick paths.

The plantation house is a raised cottage with Greek Revival influences. Its galleries are trimmed with wrought-iron in a grapevine pattern. Although small by planation-house standards, the house boasts front corner rooms that are twenty-five feet square with sixteen-foot ceilings.

Interior decoration is elaborate, with detailed plaster ceiling cornices and center rosettes. Interior doors and window sashes have retained their original hand-painted false graining, called *faux bois*. The house is furnished with antiques that include an 1860 Rosewood piano, a half tester bed, Meissen porcelains, and Prudence Mallard furniture.

Other buildings on the plantation include a **blacksmith shop** with old farm implements, a **commissary museum** with old store items, and a **carriage house**.

# DESTREHAN PLANTATION

Oldest intact plantation house in lower Mississippi Valley.

**Address:** 13034 River Rd., PO Box 5, Destrehan LA 70047
**Telephone:** (504) 764-9315, (504) 764-9345
**Location:** In southeast Louisiana, 8 miles west of New Orleans International Airport; on Louisiana's River Rd., along the Mississippi River; I-310 Destrehan exit.
**Open:** 9:30 A.M.–4:00 P.M. daily; closed major holidays.
**Admission:** Adults $6, teens $3, children ages 5–12 $2.
**Shops:** Gift Shoppe.
**Facilities:** Partially handicapped accessible.

## HISTORY

Built in 1787, Destrehan is believed to be the oldest documented plantation house left intact in the lower Mississippi Valley. It was built, according to the contract, by "Charles, a free mullato" between 1787 and 1790 for Robin de Logny, a Frenchman whose descendants occupied it for the next 120 years. Initially, most of the plantations 6,000 acres were planted in indigo, but in the early 1800s, sugar cane became the dominant crop.

After Robin de Logny's death in 1792, the property passed to his son, Pierre. In 1802, Pierre's daughter, Celeste, and her husband, Jean Noel Destrehan, made their home at the plantation. Jean Noel Destrehan was a member of a wealthy and prominent family. His father was the royal treasurer for the Louisiana colony. His brother-in-law and guardian, Etienne de Bore, was the first mayor of New Orleans.

Jean Noel, who was active politically, helped to write the first state constitution and served in the Louisiana senate. Celeste and Jean Noel had fourteen children. Cramped for space, they added wings to the house in 1810. They also changed the plantation's major crop from indigo to sugar cane.

After Celeste's and Jean Noel's deaths in 1823 and 1824, the plantation was purchased by their youngest daughter, Zelia, and her husband, Stephen Henderson. A Scotsman and a millionaire, Henderson was thirty years older than Zelia, yet he outlived her by eight years. In a controversial will, he stipulated freeing his slaves, and converting the plantation to a manufacturing complex run by the freed slaves, or paying the freed slave's passage back to Africa. The Henderson family contested the will, and these provisions were never implemented.

In 1839, the estate was purchased by another daughter of Celeste and Jean Noel—Louise, and her husband, Judge Pierre Rost. The Rosts changed the French Colonial house to the then-popular Greek Revival style. During the Civil War, Judge Rost became a Confederate ambassador to Europe, and while the family was out of the country, the Union army seized their home. The Freedman's Bureau placed over 700 newly freed slaves and their families on the Rost Plantation while they were learning trades.

When Judge Rost returned from Europe in 1866, he demanded and received the return of his home, in which he died in 1868. In 1877, the house was purchased by his son, Judge Emile Rost, the last descendant to live there. In 1910, Emile Rost sold Destrehan Plantation to the Destrehan Planting and Manufacturing Company. Four years later, it was sold to the Mexican Petroleum Company. The former sugar-cane plantation was now home to a major oil refinery, and the mansion was used in a variety of ways. In 1958, the current owner of the refinery, the American Oil Company, tore down the refinery and virtually abandoned the site. The house was neglected and vandalized over the next twelve years. In 1971, Amoco donated the house, with a new roof and four acres of land, to the River Road Historical Society, a nonprofit group formed to save and restore the antebellum home. The plantation house was opened to the public after restoration was complete. Continuing its support, in 1990 Amoco donated funds to install a sprinkler system and again replace the roof; in 1992, the company donated an additional 12.8 acres of land surrounding the house.

## SITE DESCRIPTION

**Destrehan Plantation House** has gone through a number of changes since it was constructed over 200 years ago. The directions given to the builder, Charles, by planter Robin de Logny, were to construct a "house of sixty feet in length, by 35 feet raised 10 feet on brick piers with a surrounding gallery of 12 feet, 5 chimneys and the roof full over the body of the building."

In 1810, Celeste and Jean Noel Destrehan added wings on either side of the house. Around 1830, the current owners, Louise and Pierre Rost, decided to change the appearance of the house to the then-popular Greek Revival style. Doors and windows were replaced. The original thin columns were changed to full-length ones of plastered brick. The back gallery was enclosed to make an entrance foyer.

Photo by Patricia A. Gutek

### Destrehan Plantation, Destrehan, Louisiana

The oldest intact plantation house in the lower Mississippi Valley, Destrehan Plantation House was built in 1787 for Robin de Logny and was occupied by his descendants until 1910. Its Greek Revival appearance dates from remodeling projects in 1810 and 1830.

The house now seen on the guided tour retains its nineteenth-century changes. All of the damage done through years of neglect has been repaired. Although the first floor has been made handicapped accessible, the second floor has not. However, the River Road Historical Society is making a commendable effort to solve the problem: they have decided to reproduce two cisterns which originally stood at the rear of the house and to use one of them to house an elevator that would bring handicapped visitors to the upper level.

A **Fall Festival** is held the second weekend of November.

# SAN FRANCISCO PLANTATION HOUSE

Restored antebellum "Steamboat Gothic"
plantation house; NR, NHL.

**Address:** Drawer AX, Reserve LA 70084
**Telephone:** (504) 535-2341
**Location:** Reserve is in southeast Louisiana, 35 miles west of New Orleans;
San Francisco Plantation is 3 miles west of Reserve on LA Hwy. 44.
**Open:** 10:00 A.M.–4:00 P.M. daily; closed Easter, Thanksgiving, Christmas,
and New Year's Days, and Mardi Gras Day (Shrove Tuesday)
**Admission:** Adults $7, students ages 12–17 $4, children ages 6–11 $2.75.
**Shops:** Gift shop.
**Facilities:** Partially handicapped accessible.

## HISTORY

San Francisco Plantation House is an elaborate version of a raised
Creole-style design that novelist Frances Parkinson Keyes dubbed "Steamboat Gothic." It was built by Edmond Bozonier Marmillion between 1853
and 1856 on a sugar-cane plantation he had purchased in 1830 from Elisee
Rillieux, a free man of color. Although there had been a house on the
property, a levee break in 1852 is thought to have destroyed it and thus to
have created the need for a new home.

When construction started on the plantation house, Edmond
Marmillion was a widower with two sons, a third son having died the previous year. Edmond died in 1856, the year that his new home was completed. His older son, Antoine Valsin, then took over management of the
estate. Valsin was married to Louise von Seybold, who was from Munich,
Germany; they had three daughters.

The unusual name "San Francisco" is thought to have derived from
Valsin Marmillion's comment about the high cost of decorating his home.
Because of the extraordinary expenses, he declared he was *sans fruscins*,
"without a penny." This phrase evolved into "St. Frusquin," so that when
Louise Marmillion sold the property in 1879 after her husband's death, the
new owner, Achille D. Bougere, called it "San Francisco."

The distinctive, ornate Creole-style structure was the inspiration for novelist Frances Parkinson Keyes's *Steamboat Gothic*, which uses the plantation house as the setting for a story about a fictional family.

San Francisco Plantation House was passed through other hands, and some modernization occurred. In 1973, the plantation was purchased by Energy Corporation of Louisiana as the site for an oil refinery. But at the urging of Frederick B. Ingram, chairman of the corporation, the building and seven acres of land were donated to the San Francisco Plantation Foundation. Restoration of the mansion to its 1860 appearance began in 1975 and was completed in 1977.

## SITE DESCRIPTION

Incongruously surrounded by oil tanks and refineries, **San Francisco Plantation House** is a galleried brick and frame three-story building in the old Creole style. In the elaborate "Steamboat Gothic" design, the house has exterior details that include Italianate brackets, Corinthian columns, Gothic Revival dormer windows, shutters, intricately carved porch railings on two levels, and a louvered attic. It is cream-colored, with sky-blue shutters and trim.

Standing on brick piers, the house has a raised first floor. The main entrance and the living and sleeping areas are on the main floor, while the brick-floored ground level has only the **dining room** and **service rooms**, which include a **wine cellar**, a **china pantry**, a **food storage room**, and a **billiard room**. San Francisco Plantation House has been restored to the way it appeared in the 1860s, when the mansion was decorated and occupied by Valsin and Louise Marmillion. Furniture displayed was not family-owned but was selected on the basis of detailed inventories of the house's contents. The Marmillion family's furnishings were sold with the house to the Bougeres in 1879. When the Bougeres sold San Francisco in 1905, they took this furniture to their new home, which was subsequently destroyed by fire.

Without hallways, rooms open to each other. Decorating characteristics include vividly painted walls, grained woodwork and doors, faux marble fireplaces, patterned carpeting, and elaborate painted ceilings. Victorian furniture, draperies, and light fixtures are used throughout.

On the main floor are the **main entrance hall and reception area**. The **upriver drawing room** has light purple walls, and a ceiling and frieze adorned with flowers, birds, jewels, and scrolls. The rosewood furniture is in the style of John Henry Belter. French doors lead to the **gallery**.

Doors in the **downriver drawing room** sport designs representing the four seasons. In the center of the **boudoir**'s ceiling design of trellis with leaves against the sky are three cherubs with adult faces on infant bodies. The daybed, draped with blue silk taffeta, is a fine example of New Orleans rosewood furniture.

A small green **sitting room** was sometimes used as a dining room for the children. The **girls' bedroom** has deep red walls and chintz window and bed coverings. Mosquito nets encase the beds. The back **loggia** is an open area where the children often played games.

On either side of the house are cisterns on one-story-high brick foundations, each capped by Moorish-style domes. They look like windmills without blades. Rain water from the roof is collected in these cisterns for drinking and washing.

# OAK ALLEY

## 1839 Greek Revival mansion; NHL.

**Address:** 3645 LA Hwy. 18, Vacherie LA 70090
**Telephone:** (504) 265-2151, FAX: (504) 265-7035
**Location:** Great River Rd. between New Orleans and Baton Rouge.
**Open:** March–October, 9:00 A.M.–5:30 P.M. daily; November–February, 9:00 A.M.–5:00 P.M. daily. Closed Thanksgiving, Christmas and New Year's Days.
**Admission:** Adults $6.50, students ages 13–18 $3.50, children ages 6–12 $2.
**Restaurants:** Oak Alley Plantation Restaurant.
**Shops:** Gift shop.
**Facilities:** Guided tours; overnight accommodations in 1880 cabins; mansion is available for rental for private functions; open-air pavilions also available for rental.

## HISTORY

Oak Alley Plantation House was built in 1837–1839 by Jacques Telesphore Roman on the site of a small cabin built by a French settler in the early 1700s. This early settler also planted two rows of twenty-eight live oaks eighty feet apart that reached from the house to the Mississippi River. Now forming a dense canopy over the road, they create a dramatic entrance to Oak Alley Plantation.

Jacques Telesphore Roman was the youngest son of Jacques Etienne Roman and Marie Louise Patin. His brother, Andre Beinvenu Roman, was governor of Louisiana. In 1834, Telesphore married Celina Pilie. In 1836, Telesphone purchased the plantation from his brother-in-law, Francois Gabriel Valcour Aime, a wealthy sugar-cane planter. Gilbert Joseph Pilie, Telesphore's father-in-law, was the architect and George Swainy was the master builder.

Designed in the Greek Revival style, the two-and-one-half-story brick house was built of materials found or manufactured on the property-with the exception of the marble for the floors and fireplaces, and the slate for the roof. The mansion has twenty-eight brick columns, each measuring eight feet in circumference; sixteen-inch walls; fifteen-foot ceilings; and a veranda that extends thirteen feet. Though the house was originally named *Bon Sejour* (good rest), the towering oaks caused it to be commonly called "Oak Alley."

Although Oak Alley was not destroyed during the Civil War, the Roman family's fortunes plummeted, and they were forced to sell their plantation at auction. John Armstrong bought it in 1866 for less than $33,000. In 1881, Oak Alley Plantation was sold to Antoine Sobral, who lived there until 1905. Over time, the house deteriorated. Josephine and Andrew Stewart purchased it in 1925 and began extensive repair and restoration work. On Josephine Stewart's death, the house was acquired by a nonprofit foundation created by Mrs. Stewart, which operates it today.

## SITE DESCRIPTION

**Oak Alley** is much better known for its rows of ancient live oaks than for its architecture. The quarter-mile, arched canopy-shaded approach to the plantation is stunning and seems to evoke the feel of plantation life in the South. Like the other plantation houses, Oak Alley faces the river, but the tunnel of trees no longer extends to the river.

Oak Alley is a two-and-one-half-story Greek Revival-style house with twenty-eight Doric columns, the same number as those famous live oak trees. There are galleries on the first and second floors. Stressing architectural balance, the house is seventy feet square. A chimney and three dormer windows are on each side of the hipped roof which has a balustraded belvedere at its peak. The brick house is covered with plaster tinted a pale pink.

Oval, fanlighted doorways, with wide, side sunlights, are at each end of the hallways that run through the house on both floors. The Stewarts furnished the house with antiques.

A number of 1880–1890 outbuildings on the property have been converted to bed and breakfast accommodations.

# NOTTOWAY PLANTATION

### 1859 Greek Revival plantation house; largest plantation house in the South.

**Address:** PO Box 160, White Castle LA 70788
**Telephone:** (504) 545-2730, (504) 545-2409
**Location:** 18 miles south of Baton Rouge on the west bank of the Mississippi River.
**Open:** 9:00 A.M.–5:00 P.M. daily; closed Christmas Day.
**Admission:** Adults $8, children $3.
**Restaurants:** Randolph Hall.
**Shops:** Gift shop.
**Facilities:** Guided tours, overnight accommodations in 13 guest rooms.

## HISTORY

John Hampden Randolph, the builder of Nottoway Plantation House, was a member of the prominent Randolph family of Virginia. Born in Virginia, he moved first to Woodville, Mississippi, and then, in 1841, to Iberville Parish, Louisiana. He planted sugar cane on land seven miles inland from the Mississippi River, but eventually purchased acreage that extended the Randolph property to the river. By 1859, John Randolph owned 7,000 acres of farm property and between 800 and 1,000 African-American slaves.

John Randolph hired Henry Howard, a New Orleans architect, to design his house, which took a decade to build (1849–1859). A mixture of Italianate and Greek Revival styles, the massive house has sixty-four rooms and 53,000 square feet. Fifty-seven people were on the original household staff, including grooms and gardeners. The Randolphs had eleven children, three boys and eight girls, which may have been a factor in the size of the dwelling.

Randolph named the mansion "Nottoway" for a river and a county in Virginia, though it was commonly referred to as the "White Castle." Constructed on the eve of the Civil War, the house was spared destruction—on the orders, it is said, of a Northern gunboat officer who had been a guest of the Randolphs there. Union troops did camp on Nottoway's grounds, however, and confiscated livestock and weapons.

Although Nottoway was never flooded, six and one-half acres in front of the house have been lost to the river. A thirty-five-foot levee was built by the Army Corps of Engineers to prevent further erosion.

Nottoway passed out of the family when Mrs. Randolph sold it in 1889. Restoration was begun by Arlin Dease, and the house was opened to the public in the early 1980s. In addition to being a historic plantation house, Nottoway is now a very special inn and restaurant.

## SITE DESCRIPTION

Guided tours are given of only a portion of the huge Southern "White Castle." **Nottoway Plantation House** is a white, three-story Greek Revival and Italianate mansion with twenty-two Corinthian columns and first- and second-floor galleries. The 53,000-square-foot house has 64 rooms, 200 windows, 16 fireplaces, 165 doors, 6 inner staircases, and 26 closets. Ceilings are 15½ feet high; doors are 11 feet high; and there are cypress floors throughout. The mansion was built with hot running water, porcelain water closets, gas lighting, and coal fireplaces. The house was constructed on a twelve-foot graduated brick foundation.

In addition to its size, the most impressive aspect of Nottoway is its elegant, white, sixty-five-foot **grand ballroom**, in which six of the eight Randolph daughters were married. Located in the formal curved wing of the mansion, this bright room has many windows that extend to the floor and are draped with white lace curtains. Even the floor is painted white. In addition to elaborate frieze work, there are matching crystal chandeliers, and curved arches with columns.

The **dining room** is painted peach, has two chandeliers and a camellia motif in its frieze work. The mahogany table was made in Natchez, Mississippi, in 1845 and has a Victorian silver centerpiece on it.

In the **gentlemen's study**, the windows are adorned with dark green velvet draperies with gold fringe trim patterned after the draperies made famous by Scarlett O'Hara. John Randolph conducted business here.

The **music room** is a sunny yellow room with a marble fireplace and an Aubusson rug. Instruments include a pianoforte, a harp, and a melodian.

The **wicker room** is a summery room furnished with white wicker chairs and tables.

On the second floor is a large **central hall** with doors at either end. Hanging in the hall are a portrait of the Randolphs and two children, and an enormous painting of Nottoway. There is elaborate original frieze work around the ceiling and in the center medallion. The frieze work was

molded of a combination of mud, clay, plaster, Spanish moss, and horsehair.

The **Randolph suite** in the rounded wing has curved walls. It contains a sitting room and bedroom with a half tester bed and a large armoire.
On the second floor of the square wing are the bedrooms of the Randolph
daughters. On the third floor is the **ancestral hall**, where portraits of ancestors were hung.

# ACADIAN VILLAGE

Re-created village and folk life
museum of Acadian culture.

**Address:** Acadian Village, 200 Greenleaf Dr., Lafayette LA 70506
**Telephone:** (318) 981-2364, 1-800-962-9133
**Location:** South of Lafayette. Access the Acadian Village from I-10 exit
97, south on LA Hwy. 93 to Ridge Rd., turn right onto Ridge Rd.
and then left onto H. Mouton Rd.; or from I-10 exit 100, south on
Ambassador Caffery Rd., turn right onto Ridge Rd., then left onto
H. Mounton Rd. Coming from south of Lafayette, take Hwy. 90 to
Hwy. 90 West, turn left onto Hwy. 93, then right onto Ridge Rd.,
and left onto H. Mounton Rd.
**Open:** 10:00 A.M.–5:00 P.M. daily; closed major holidays.
**Admission:** Adults $5.50, seniors $4.50, children ages 6–14 $2.50.
**Shops:** Gift shop in General Store.

## WHERE TO STAY

**Inns/Bed & Breakfasts:** Bois des Chenes Inn, 388 North Sterling, Lafayette LA 70501, (318) 233-7816. Hotel Catillo Inn, 220 Place
d'Evangeline, 220 Evangeline Blvd., St. Martinville LA 70582,
(318) 394-4010. Maison Marceline, 442 East Main St., New Iberia
LA 70560, (318) 364-5922. Nottoway Plantation and Inn, Hwy. 1,
PO Box 160, White Castle LA 70788, (504) 545-2730.
**Motels/Hotels:** Acadian Motel, 120 North University Ave., Lafayette LA
70506, (318) 234-3268. Acadian Village Inn, I-49 North, exit Ser-
vice Rd. 282, Carencro LA 70520, (318) 896-0316. Best Western
Motor Inn, 108 Frontage Rd., Lafayette LA 70501, (318) 233-2090.
Comfort Inn of Lafayette, 1421 Southeast Evangeline Thruway,
Lafayette LA 70501, (318) 232-9000. Friendship Inn, 707 Frontage
Rd., Lafayette LA 70501, (318) 235-4591. Holiday Inn-North, US
167 North at I-10, Lafayette LA 70509, (318) 233-0003. Holiday
Inn-South, US 90 East, Lafayette LA 70508, (318) 234-8521.
Howard Johnson's, 1421 Evangeline Thruway, Lafayette LA 70501,
(318) 234-8321. LaFayette Inn, 2615 Cameron St., Lafayette LA
70506, (318) 235-9442.

**Acadian Village, Lafayette, Louisiana**

Found at this outdoor folk-life museum village of Acadian heritage and culture is New Hope Chapel, or Chapelle du Nouvel Espoir—a replica of an 1850 Louisiana Roman Catholic chapel. French Acadians, expelled from eastern Canada in 1755 by the British, brought their devotion to Catholicism with them to the bayous of Louisiana.

Photo by Patricia A. Gutek

**Camping:** Acadian Village Campground, 200 Greenleaf Dr., Lafayette LA 70506, (318) 981-2489. Acadiana Park Campground, 1201 East Alexander, Lafayette LA 70501, (318) 234-3838. Cajun Station Campground, St. Martinville Hwy. 96, Breaux Bridge LA 70517, (318) 837-6286. KOA Kampground, Exit 97 off I-10 near Scott, Scott LA 70583, (318) 235-2739.

## OVERVIEW

An outdoor folk-life museum village of Acadian heritage and culture during the nineteenth century makes Acadian Village an ideal setting to learn about the region's culture and life-style. The re-created village consists of well-restored nineteenth-century homes and buildings of Acadian architecture which were moved to the ten-acre woodland and garden setting, and furnished with native Louisiana antiques.

Acadian Village provides visitors with the opportunity to experience the feel of the Acadian past and the Cajun present. Located in Lafayette, it is in the center of southern Louisiana Cajun bayou country.

## HISTORY

Southern Louisiana's Creole and Acadian/Cajun population have their roots in France, though their ancestors have been in North America for more than 300 years. Decades of civil and religious conflict, famine, and epidemics drove French peasants from France's Centre-Ouest provinces of Poitou, Aunis, Angoumois, and Saintonge to immigrate to Maritime Canada, now the provinces of Nova Scotia and New Brunswick. Between 1632 and 1654, French colonists sailed to a proprietary colony operated by the Company of New France, which Samuel Champlain had founded for France in 1604. It was named *La Cadie*, which is a Micmac word meaning "land of plenty." Later the colony came to be called *l'Acadie*, or "Acadia." Thus, its settlers are known as Acadians.

In eastern Canada, the Acadians developed a distinctive society based on their geographic isolation and frontier mentality, their common French origins and language, social solidarity, and a strong extended-kinship system. As a result of ongoing strife between France and England, Acadia became a British colony. When the Acadians were ordered to take an oath of allegiance to the British crown, the fiercely independent French-speaking Acadians refused. Consequently, in 1755, they were expelled by the British from Acadia, renamed Nova Scotia by the British, where they had lived for a hundred years.

The exodus of the Acadians was called the "Grand Derangement." The expelled Acadians were dispersed to the English middle colonies, France, and the French Antilles. Families were broken up. No compensation was made for the farms, houses, and other possessions they had to leave behind. Many deportees died en route, and the destitute survivors found only hardship and misery. In an effort to reunite their families and reestablish their life-style, the Acadians looked to Louisiana, a sparsely settled French colony now under Spanish rule. Eventually, many found their way to southern Louisiana, arriving between 1765 and 1785. The Spanish government welcomed the industrious, anti-British settlers and supplied them with modest amounts of land, tools, and food.

The French explorer Robert Cavelier de La Salle had claimed all the North American land drained by the Mississippi for France in 1682. A small number of French colonists migrated to Louisiana in the early eighteenth century. Their descendants, those born in Louisiana, were called "Creoles," a term that meant "homegrown, not imported, and adapted to the environment."

Class differences separated the two French groups in Louisiana. The Acadians were peasant farmers, while the French Creoles had developed large farms and plantations on which they used captured Africans as slave workers. African slaves who were born in Louisiana were called "Creole slaves."

Louisiana was sold to the United States in 1803. Several states were carved out of the Louisiana Purchase. When the state of Louisiana was defined, it lumped together the southern, French-occupied parishes with the northern, English-speaking parishes, although the two parts of the state had little in common culturally. Gradually, Louisiana Acadians came to be called "Cajuns," a corruption of the term "Acadian."

In southern Louisiana, Acadians settled near the waterways, the rivers, and bayous, including the Mississippi River. Strip villages developed along the riverbanks. Other Cajun settlements were in Louisiana's swamps and marshes and on its prairies. Many Cajuns operated small farms, fished, and hunted. Travel was by waterway rather than road. The Acadians intermarried with their Louisiana neighbors who included Houmas, Chitimachas, and Attakapas Indians; German Alsatians; Spanish; Anglo-Americans; Irish; and Scots.

Because of the remoteness of the bayou area, residents had little contact with the larger American culture. The Acadians maintained a separate culture even during the Civil War. Their high desertion rate indicated their lack of commitment to the South's cause. They continued to speak

French, the language used in their schools. Their values were family, the Catholic religion, hard work, and the joy of life that is evident in their frequent celebrations with distinctive food and music.

The Cajun subculture managed to stay intact until about 1900, when several factors speeded up its Americanization. Discovery of oil in 1901 brought in outsiders and created salaried jobs and a cash economy. The Education Act of 1916 made English mandatory in the schools. Roads, railroads, communications, and commercial and tourist facilities have all impacted the area and its people. The Cajun culture still exists today in Southern Louisiana, but with adaptations to modern times.

Serving as a cultural and educational center, Acadian Village was established as a project of the Lafayette Association for Retarded Citizens. A unique feature of Acadian Village is the training and employment that it provides for handicapped persons as grounds keepers, janitors, and retail store workers. Products made by handicapped persons at the village and the New Hope Sheltered Workshop can be purchased in the Village General Store.

## SITE DESCRIPTION

Tours are conducted in both English and French.

The **general store—Le Magasin General**—is a replica built on site in 1976. Made of old red cypress and Louisiana long leaf pine, it is an example of the *briquette entre poteaux* (bricks between posts) style of construction. The visible exposed wiring is typical of the kind of wiring used when electricity first came to rural Louisiana. Between 1860 and 1900, stores like the old country store were the main social centers of many small rural communities.

**Aurelie Bernard House—La Maison Aurelie Bernard**—was constructed in St. Martinville and is the village's oldest structure. The section on the left, built in 1800, contains an exhibit on Cajun music, instruments, and tools; the section on the right was added in 1840. As you enter the addition, you will see Robert Dafford's large painting of the Acadian diaspora from their homes in Nova Scotia in Canada in 1755. The painting in the small rear room depicts their arrival and settling along the Louisiana bayous in 1764–1766. The house contains shadow boxes containing religious objects. Notice the insulation, called *bousillage entre poteaux* (mud between posts), a mixture of Spanish moss and mud.

The **Thibodeaux House—La Maison Thibodeaux**—was built around 1820 in the Breaux Bridge area. Constructed of rot- and insect-resistant cypress, the structure stands on pre-cut beams and posts that were marked with roman numerals for efficient assembly. Typical houses of the period, like the Thibodeaux House, consisted of a large central room (the *salle*) and a master bedroom (the *chambre*), with a smaller bedroom attached. The parents' bedroom contains a bed with a moss mattress. It was customary for young daughters of the family to sleep in a small rear "cabinet" room, the daughters' room, accessible only through the parents' room. The cabinet room contains an interesting leather chair and a *petit armoire*. The boys slept in the loft (the *garconniere*), accessed directly by an outside staircase. An open porch (the *galerie*) provided a shaded, open-air place for rest and relaxation. Since the Spanish had levied a tax on interior staircases, the Cajuns evaded its assessment by building exterior ones.

The **LeBlanc House—La Maison LeBlanc**—was built between 1821 and 1856 near Youngsville and is the birthplace of the Acadian favorite son, State Senator Dudley J. LeBlanc (1894–1971). Author of *The True Story of the Acadians* and *The Acadian Miracle*, LeBlanc was a supporter of the preservation of Cajun local history. He became famous nationally during the 1950s for his patent vitamin tonic, Hadacol. Containing twelve percent alcohol, Hadacol was a popular, widely advertized patent medicine allegedly potent in curing a variety of ills. The house has exhibits on the life and times of LeBlanc, known as "Couzan Dud," Longfellow's heroine Evangeline, and the city of Lafayette.

The **St. John House—La Maison Saint Jean**—was built around 1840 from salvaged cypress timbers; its original location was on St. John Street in Lafayette. Once the home of a local dentist, it has been restored as a schoolhouse. Included in the school exhibit are old textbooks, ink wells, lunch pails, an old stove and an unusual three seat desk. Acadians were originally indifferent to schooling, which they felt would remove children from their native culture. When Louisiana began to enforce compulsory school attendance in 1916, Acadian children, too, were enrolled in schools.

The **Blacksmith Shop—La Forge**—is a replica built on site from weathered cypress boards; it exhibits a smithy's anvil, forge, bellows, tongs, pincers, hammers, and other tools.

The **Billeaud House—La Maison Billeaud**—is an antebellum structure that was built on the Billeaud sugar plantation to house slaves serving as domestic servants. It has been restored as a spinning and weaving cottage that illustrates the Acadians' production and use of homespun cloth woven from white and brown cotton and their use of natural dyes. One loom is more than 150 years old.

New Hope Chapel—Chapelle du Nouvel Espoir—is a replica of an 1850 chapel which was built with the support of the Knights of Columbus. The chapel's cypress-wood ceiling is held up by pegs. The floor is made of Louisiana longleaf pine that is about 200 years old. There is only one original pew, which is 150 years old. The rest are copies. The Stations of the Cross were hand-carved by a local sculptor, Lester Duhon. The main altar originally was in St. Anne's Church in Youngsville.

The **Castille Home—La Maison Castille**—is the village's historic landmark. Built around 1860, it was the home of the Dorsene Castille family in Breaux Bridge. The house was occupied by descendants of Dorsene Castille until 1971. The cypress mantels have a carved emblem which contains a fish, the Christian symbol for a long and happy life, and a rosette, called a "progression," which signifies a large and prosperous family. The kitchen is particularly interesting for its fireplace, wood mantel, and large carved wooden bowls. In the bedroom is a large mahogany four-poster bed with mosquito netting, often a necessity in bayou country.

The **Doctor's Museum** contains a physician's office with an examination office and examination table, medical charts, and nineteenth-century medical instruments.

## SIDE TRIPS

**Lafayette**, called the capital of French Louisiana, and its surrounding area are rich repositories of Acadian history and culture. For detailed information on tours, places to visit, and special events, contact the Lafayette Convention and Visitor's Commission, PO Box 52066, Lafayette 70505. (318) 232-3737.

**Lafayette Museum** exhibits local historical artifacts and furnishings. 1122 Lafayette St, Lafayette LA 70505. (318) 234-2208. The **Henry Wadsworth Longfellow Monument** in Saloom Office Park features sculptures of Evangeline and Gabriel by artist George Rodrique. 100 Asma Blvd., Lafayette LA 70505.

# VERMILIONVILLE

Re-creation of Cajun and Creole culture in a southern
Louisiana bayou village, 1765–1890.

**Address:** 1600 Surrey St., Lafayette LA 70501
**Telephone:** (318) 233-4077, 1-800-99-BAYOU
**Location:** Lafayette is in south central Louisiana. Vermilionville is 4 miles
south of the I-10 and I-49 intersection.
**Open:** 9:00 A.M.–5:00 P.M. daily; closed Christmas and New Year's Days.
**Admission:** Adults $8, seniors $6.50, children ages 6–18 $5.
**Restaurants:** La Cuisine de Maman, Le Quartier Creole (Food Quarters),
bakery.
**Shops:** La Boutique in the visitor center.
**Facilities:** Visitor center, cooking school, handicapped accessible; craft
demonstrations, band and dance performances, special events, the-
ater productions.

## WHERE TO STAY

**Motels/Hotels:** Quality Inn, 1605 North University, Lafayette LA 70501,
(318) 232-6131, FAX: (318) 232-6285. Hotel Acadiana, 1801 West
Pinhook Rd., Lafayette LA 70508, (318) 233-8120, 1-800-826-8386.
Ramada Inn-Airport, 2501 Southeast Evangeline Thruway, Lafayette LA 70508, (318) 234-8521, FAX: (318) 232-5764.
**Camping:** Lake Fausse Pointe State Park, St. Martinville LA 70582, (318)
229-4764. KOA Lafayette, Rt. 2, Box 261, Scott LA 70583, (318)
235-2739. Harry Smith Lodge and RV Park, PO Box 448, Broussard
LA 70518, (318) 837-6286.

## OVERVIEW

Southern Louisiana bayou culture is the focus of Vermilionville,
which is a living-history museum of Cajun and Creole folklife on the
banks of Bayou Vermilion. In addition to a re-created village of historic
structures furnished with authentic artifacts, Vermilionville features Cajun
and Creole music, crafts, and food.

Louisiana was a seventeenth-century French colony in North America.
The two French groups who settled on the rivers and bayous of Southern

Louisiana developed a distinctive culture based on their French heritage and their adaptation to frontier life along the remote, subtropical waterways. Even today, in this age of homogenized American culture, contemporary Cajun culture is unique. Yet the French ancestors of these Louisianans have been in North American for over 300 years, the Acadians having lived in maritime Canada for 100 years before coming to Louisiana, and the Creole group descendants of original French colonists in Louisiana.

## HISTORY

For the history of Louisiana's Acadians, see Acadian Village, Lafayette, LA.

In 1984, the Lafayette Parish Bayou Vermilion District was created to establish a living-history museum depicting the life-styles and cultures of the Cajuns, Creoles and others who settled the Attakapas District of South Central Louisiana between 1765 and 1890. Vermilionville, a nonprofit museum, opened in 1990 on a twenty-two-acre site in Lafayette's Beaver Park. Vermilionville was an earlier name of the city which was renamed Lafayette one hundred years ago.

## SITE DESCRIPTION

**Vermilionville** is organized into three sections: the Festive Area, the Folklife Area, and the Living-history area.

The **Festive Area** contains replicas of buildings typically found on a Creole plantation. The **visitor center**, or **Bienvenue Chez Nous Autres**, is modeled after a Creole plantation house. An orientation film is shown here. A plantation overseer's house is occupied by the **restaurant La Cuisine de Maman**, while the **Food Quarters**, or **Le Quartier Creole**, is in plantation slave quarters. The **Performance Center**, based on the design of a cotton gin, is used for dance demonstrations, daily band performances, plays, and lectures. There are also a **bakery** and a **cooking school** featuring authentic Cajun and Creole recipes.

The **Folklife Area** contains a re-created village of restored historic buildings from southern Louisiana, along with some re-created structures. Most Cajun houses are small, frame structures built on stilts with steep pitched roofs, and front and back porches. The style of architecture that evolved in southern Louisiana was based on the environment. Raising a house on tree stumps or bricks prevented flooding. Steep roofs allowed the frequent rains to run off rapidly. Roofed porches provided cooler air, shade, and a place to socialize.

Photo by Patricia A. Gutek

**Vermilionville, Lafayette, Louisiana**
Vermilionville's bi-lingual entrance sign reveals the French roots of the Cajun and Creole people, whose culture is the focus here. The museum, located on the banks of Bayou Vermilion, re-creates a southern Louisiana bayou village from about 1765 to 1890.

**Beau Bassin**, a two-room house that blends Creole and American Greek Revival styles, was built around 1840 in the Carencro area of Lafayette Parish by the children of Louis Arceneux.

**Le Magasin**, a replica of an early Acadian barn, is used for water-related crafts including boat building, decoy carving, and net- and trap-making. **L'Academie de Vermilionville** is a replica of an 1890s schoolhouse. Children are often taught French songs or given a history lesson here. Woodworking is done in **La Maison Mouton**, a reconstruction of an 1810 four-room house. Behind the house is **La Forge**, a working blacksmith shop where many of the woodworker's tools were made.

**La Maison Acadienne** was built in 1860 as a two-family, or double-pen cabane, slave cabin near Carencro. Later, it was used as a school for the grandchildren of Jean Mounton, the founder of the city of Vermilionville. It has not been completely restored but is left as a work-in-progress to display construction techniques. **La Maison Boucvalt**, built in the late nineteenth century in Opelousas, is a four-room white frame house with a center chimney. An unusual feature of the 1803 **La Maison Buller** from Ville Platte is its stranger's room, a bedroom used by travelers, which did not connect to any other room in the house.

**La Chapelle des Attakapas** is a replica church based on the eighteenth-century Catholic churches at Pointe Coupee and St. Martinville. Inside the simple church are a white wooden altar, wooden pews, and black, wrought-iron chandeliers. The priest's house, called **Le Presbytere**, was known as Maison La Grange when it was built in Grand Coteau in 1840. The simply furnished house has a bed, a kneeler for praying, religious pictures, a desk, and a small fireplace.

**Fausee Pointe**, the living-history area, is the Amand Broussard farmstead, which includes a farmhouse, a kitchen, a barn, a garden, and farm animals. The 1790 **Broussard House** belonged to the wealthy cattle rancher and his family of fourteen children. Construction methods used in this house include *colombage* and *bousillage*. There are four rooms downstairs and a dormitory upstairs. Mattresses are filled with moss.

Costumed docents perform everyday chores done by the Broussard family 200 years ago. They cook, tend gardens, feed animals, and speak as if they were living a century or two ago. Many tour guides and craftspeople are bilingual Cajuns.

## FESTIVALS/CRAFTS

Costumed craftspeople demonstrate **spinning, dyeing, weaving, quilting, broom-making, woodworking, basketry, musical instrument-making, toy-making, furniture-making, candle-making, soap-making, decoy carving, chair caning**, and **homebuilding and renovation**. Craftspeople also fashion rosaries from seeds and ropes from horsehair.

Special events at Vermilionville include **Cajun and Creole weddings, baptisms, Mardi Gras festivities, Christmas, Bastille Day, Native American Rendezvous**, and **plays** performed by the village's own theater group.

## SIDE TRIPS

The **Acadian Cultural Center**, a feature of the Acadian unit of Jean Lafitte National Historical Park and Preserve, includes museum exhibits, a bookstore, and a theater with a film on the Acadian people.

Also in the Acadian unit is the **Prairie Acadian Cultural Center** in Eunice, and the **Wetlands Acadian Cultural Center** in Thibodaux.

# SHADOWS-ON-THE-TECHE

Restored mid-nineteenth-century plantation house and historic gardens; NR, NHL, HABS.

**Address:** 317 East Main St., PO Box 9703, New Iberia LA 70562
**Telephone:** (318) 369-6446, FAX: (318) 365-5213
**Location:** New Iberia is in south central Louisiana, 20 miles south of Lafayette; from I-10 exit 103A, south on US 90 to LA Hwy. 14 East.
**Open:** 9:00 A.M.–4:30 P.M. daily; closed Thanksgiving, Christmas and New Year's Days.
**Admission:** Adults $6, children ages 6–11 $3.
**Restaurants:** None on site but several cafes within two blocks of museum.
**Shops:** Museum Shop.
**Facilities:** Guided tours, gardens, special events, children's programs, workshops; handicapped accessible.

## WHERE TO STAY

**Inns/Bed & Breakfasts:** Le Rosier, 314 East Main St., New Iberia LA 70560, (318) 367-5306. Maison Nadine, 423 Charles St., New Iberia LA 70560, (318) 364-6198. La Maison du Teche, 417 East Main St., New Iberia LA 70560, (318) 367-9456. Pourtos House, 4018 Old Jeanerette Rd., New Iberia LA 70560, (318) 367-7045. Old Castillo Hotel, 220 Evangeline Blvd., St. Martinville LA 70582, (318) 394-4010, 1-800-621-3017.
**Motels/Hotels:** Holiday Inn, 2801 Center St., New Iberia LA 70560, (318) 367-1201, FAX: (318) 367-1201, ext. 194. Best Western, 2700 Center St., New Iberia LA 70560, (318) 364-3030, FAX: (318) 367-5311.
**Camping:** Lake Fausse Pointe State Park, Rt. 5, Box 5648, St. Martinville LA 70582, (318) 229-4764. Belmont Campground, New Iberia LA 70562, (318) 364-6020. Frenchman's Wilderness, P.O. Box 646, Henderson Station, Breaux Bridge LA 70517, (318) 228-2616.

## OVERVIEW

Shadows-on-the-Teche is an antebellum plantation lived in by four generations of the Weeks family, sugar-cane plantation owners. A National Trust for Historic Preservation property, the Shadows, which has been restored to the 1830–1860 period, is interpreted to reflect domestic life on a south Louisiana plantation before the Civil War. Extensive twentieth-century gardens with flowering shrubs and ancient live oaks have also been restored and invite a stroll.

## HISTORY

Shadows-on-the-Teche Plantation House was built between 1831 and 1834 on Bayou Teche for David Weeks, his wife Mary Clara Conrad Weeks, and their six children. However, David Weeks never lived in the house. He died in the summer of 1834 in New Haven, Connecticut, after traveling to Yale Medical College seeking a cure for a persistent illness.

David Weeks, whose family was English in origin, made his fortune from half a dozen southwestern Louisiana sugar-cane plantations, which he operated with slave labor. The more than 150 acres at Shadow-on-the-Teche was used as a farm which produced potatoes, cabbage, turnips, and other vegetables for the household and the other plantation residents.

After she was widowed, Mary Weeks married Judge John Moore, a U.S. congressman from Louisiana, who lived in the house until 1867. In late 1863, during the Civil War, the Shadows was used as a headquarters for Union troops under the command of General William B. Franklin. During that occupation, when the family was living on the second floor of the house, Mary Weeks Moore died.

The house remained in the Weeks family for four generations. The last owner was William Weeks Hall, a great-grandson of the builder, who lived in the Shadows from 1922 until his death in 1958. He left the property to the National Trust for Historic Preservation, who restored it to its 1830s appearance. It was opened to the public in 1961.

Restoration was aided by the extensive documentation of the site. There are 17,000 documents in the Weeks Family Papers collection, as well as historic photographs. Archaeological investigations and microscopic paint analysis also provided valuable information.

## SITE DESCRIPTION

**Shadows-on-the-Teche** is an impressive two-and-one-half-story coral red brick structure with green shutters and eight white Tuscan columns across the front. Designed for a hot and humid environment, the house has doors facing doors and windows facing windows for cross ventilation. First- and second-floor galleries provide outdoor shaded areas. Construction was primarily by African-American slaves. Bricks were made

Photo by Patricia A. Gutek

### Shadows-on-the-Teche, New Iberia, Louisiana

Massive columns lend both support and grace to the antebellum house built in Louisiana in the early 1830s by David Weeks and lived in by four generations of the Weeks family. In the mid-twentieth century, the plantation house was acquired by the National Trust for Historic Preservation, who restored it and its gardens to the mid-nineteenth century.

locally of clay taken from the banks of the bayou. Cypress for doors and woodwork was cut from nearby swamps, and window glass and hardware were brought by steamboats from New Orleans. The mansion is a combination of classical or Anglo-American elements with a French Colonial floor plan.

Shadows-on-the Teche has been restored to the 1830–1860 period and reflects the domestic life-style of a nineteenth-century southern Louisiana plantation owner. A French Colonial floor plan shaped like a "U" has three rooms across the front on two floors, and two small rooms on either side at the back. On the first and second floors, there are no interior hallways, closets, or staircases; the stairs are on the outside. On the first floor are the dining room, pantry, and guest bedroom. The **family quarters** upstairs include the parlor, the boys' bedroom, the girls' bedroom, the master bedroom, and the sitting room. Many of the furnishings belonged to the Weeks family.

The formal **Victorian parlor** has reproduction buff-on-buff damask-look wallpaper, a marble fireplace mantel, a gilt-bronze candle-lit chandelier, and elaborate plaster molding around the ceiling. Furniture is mahogany with horsehair upholstery. Green silk fringed damask curtains adorn the windows. Oil portraits of three of the Weeks children, William, Frances and Alfred, painted around 1845 by John Bordley hang on the walls.

The **dining room**, also a formal room, was used primarily for entertaining guests. It has a marble floor, a cut-glass chandelier, mahogany American Empire-style sideboard, French porcelain china, and Bohemian glassware.

The utilitarian **pantry** nearby was used by servants to warm food carried in from the outside kitchen. Functional furniture includes a cypress table that once stood in the detached kitchen.

The **downstairs bedroom** is furnished as an art studio, patterned after the studio which belonged to Weeks Hall.

On the second floor, the **master bedroom** has a mahogany bed with draperies, a very large mahogany armoire, and a marbleized wooden fireplace.

In the **girls' bedroom** is a portrait of Lily Weeks at the age of eight. The dress she wears in the portrait is displayed. The **boys' bedroom** contains a student's desk which may have come from the plantation's schoolhouse. Children were educated by tutors until they were sent away to school. The Weeks boys attended college in Virginia, while the girls attended school in Baton Rouge and in Georgetown in Washington DC.

The **sitting room** is probably where the family ate their meals. The bookcase was purchased by David Weeks. Notice the Weeks's family Bible.

The **gardens** are especially beautiful from the galleries. In the 1920s, William Weeks Hall designed and installed a significant and evocative landscape based on "the bones" of earlier landscape layers. Most of his design is still intact. The National Trust is in the process of rehabilitating this twentieth-century landscape, which involves replacing design elements lost in the last thirty years. More azaleas will be planted, and the camellia garden will be restored. Live oaks, wisteria, and bamboo hedges will be replaced.

Although the outbuildings on the property have disappeared, outlines of the slaves' cabins and kitchen will be laid in stone on the ground to indicate where they once stood.

An administrative/educational facility adjacent to the historic site features changing exhibits.

## SIDE TRIPS

**Avery Island** is the home of Tabasco Pepper Sauce, that hot sauce that is an ingredient in Cajun and Creole cooking. The sauce is made from Capsicum pepper plants by the McIlhenny Company, which was founded by Edmund McIlhenny. Tours of the **Tabasco Pepper Sauce Factory** are conducted Monday–Friday, 9:00 A.M.–4:00 P.M., and Saturday, 9:00 A.M.–noon. McIlhenny Company, Avery Island LA 70513. 1-800-634-9599, (318) 365-8173.

Also on Avery Island is the 200-acre **Jungle Gardens and Bird City** that is filled with tropical plants and water birds, particularly the Snowy Egret. Open daily, 9:00 A.M.–5:00 P.M. Admission is charged.

# OAKLEY HOUSE, AUDUBON STATE PARK

### West Indies-style 1799 house in which Audubon worked as a tutor and painted 36 bird illustrations; 100-acre state park.

**Address:** Audubon State Commemorative Area, PO Box 546, St. Francisville LA 70775
**Telephone:** (504) 635-3739
**Location:** 25 miles north of Baton Rouge, in West Feliciana Parish, on LA Hwy. 965, near St. Francisville.
**Open:** 9:00 A.M.–5:00 P.M. daily; closed Thanksgiving, Christmas, and New Year's Days.
**Admission:** Adults 13-61 $2.
**Facilities:** 100-acre state park, picnic area, nature trail.

## WHERE TO STAY

See entry for Rosedown Plantation and Gardens.

## OVERVIEW

In addition to its plantation cultural heritage, Feliciana is proud of a former resident, John James Audubon. The artist-naturalist painted over eighty of his *Birds of America* series while living in the parish in the 1820s. In 1821, he was hired by the owners of Oakley Plantation to tutor their daughter. Though that job lasted only four months, Lucy Bakewell Audubon, the artist's wife, taught at another Feliciana plantation, Beech Woods, for eight years beginning in 1823. Lucy maintained the family while John pursued his enormous task of painting all of America's birds.

The state of Louisiana has restored Oakley Plantation, in which John James Audubon tutored Eliza Pirrie. The 100-acre Commemorative Area has interpreted the 1799 West Indies-style house to reflect the 1820s, when Audubon was in residence. In addition to the house, there are a separate kitchen, a barn, two slave cabins, and a formal garden.

**Oakley House, Audubon State Park, St. Francisville, Louisiana**
A first-edition Audubon print of the wild turkey hangs above a mantel in the
1799 West Indies-style Oakley House. John James Audubon, the artist and
naturalist, resided in this house in 1821 while employed by the family as an art
tutor. Audubon completed thirty-six bird illustrations while living here.

Photo by Patricia A. Gutek

## HISTORY

The history of Oakley House is intertwined with the life of one of America's great artists and naturalists. John James Audubon (1785–1851) is known for his monumental work *The Birds of America*. For years, Audubon traveled throughout the American wilderness on his quest to identify and paint all the birds of America. After shooting the birds, he brought them to his studio for measurement. Specimens were placed in characteristic poses to be painted. Audubon depicted them in their actual sizes. Many of his illustrations also portray the behavior and natural habitats of the birds.

Audubon was born in Haiti and grew up in France on the coast of Brittany, where he received drawing instruction. He came to the United States in 1803 to avoid conscription in Napoleon's army and to manage his father's estate near Philadelphia. Three years later, he settled permanently in this country. He married Lucy Bakewell and was the father of two sons, Victor and John. After failing at a number of commercial ventures, the artist declared bankruptcy in 1819. Soon afterward, he decided to devote his life to his bird project while his wife supported the family by teaching.

In October 1820, Audubon traveled to New Orleans, Louisiana, to commence his ambitious project. Louisiana's Mississippi Valley lies on the migratory route of birds from Canada to Mexico, which made it a rich resource for the bird illustrator.

In mid-1821, Audubon was hired as a tutor to Eliza Pirrie, the daughter of Lucy Alston Gray and James Pirrie of Oakley Plantation, located in Feliciana. Audubon and his assistant, Joseph Mason, a boy of thirteen employed to paint backgrounds and settings for the birds, were given room and board at Oakley. Audubon also received a monthly fee of sixty dollars and was to have half of his time free to collect specimens and paint.

The arrangement with the Pirries lasted only four months before Audubon was asked to leave. He went to New Orleans, taking with him the thirty-six bird pictures he had painted at Oakley.

Oakley was built by James Pirrie, a Scotsman, on land that had been a 1770 land grant to Ruffin Gray. On Gray's death, the property was inherited by his widow, Lucy, who subsequently married James Pirrie. The simple West Indies-style house was occupied by Pirrie family descendants until 1944. The state of Louisiana acquired the property in 1947 and restored the house and grounds. Now a state park, the 100-acre tract is in the Audubon State Commemorative Area.

## SITE DESCRIPTION

**Oakley Plantation House** was built around 1799 and is less lavish than many later Louisiana plantations. This West Indies-style house, ideal in Louisiana's tropical climate, is a rectangular, frame, two-and-one-half-story structure built over a high basement. A full-width two-story front porch with jalousies on each level is supported by ground-floor brick piers. A similar porch without jalousies is at the rear of the house. There is a brick ground floor. Two front first-story entrances each have a transom. An exterior stairway is on the first-floor gallery. The interior of the house is one and one-half rooms deep and two rooms wide.

The house has been restored to the 1820s, when Audubon lived with the Pirries, and furnishings reflect the late Federal period. A number of first-edition Audubon prints are displayed. In the **entry room**, used as a plantation office, hangs a print of an American redstart. Other Audubon prints include the wild turkey, flamingo, swamp sparrow, and spoonbill.

The rose-colored **morning room**, on the second floor, has a portrait of Eliza Pirrie. Eliza's room has a large four-poster bed covered with mosquito netting.

Audubon shared a modest room off the parlor with Joseph Mason. Too small for more than a daybed and two small tables, the room contains such items as eyeglasses, quill pens, drawing material, a snake skin, and a bird's nest.

A restored **formal garden** near the house has roses, crepe myrtles, and moss-draped oaks.

A large detached **kitchen** was reconstructed on its original foundation around the chimney, which still was standing. One room was used as a laundry and contains baskets, an ironing board, and pottery. Cooking was done in the kitchen's large brick fireplace. Displayed are cast iron pots, a work table, and a vegetable drying rack. A loom and spinning wheels are in the weaving room.

A **barn** contains farm equipment, saddles, and carriages. There are also two **slave cabins**, one of which is furnished.

# ROSEDOWN PLANTATION AND GARDENS

**Restored 1835 Greek Revival mansion and nineteenth-century formal gardens.**

**Address:** 12501 Hwy. 10, St. Francisville LA 70775
**Telephone:** (504) 635-3332
**Location:** East of St. Francisville on LA Hwy. 10.
**Open:** March–October, 9:00 A.M.–5:00 P.M. daily; November–February, 10 A.M.–4:00 P.M. daily.
**Admission:** Adults $10.00, children 4–12 $4.00.
**Facilities:** Reception center, guided tours, formal gardens, overnight accommodations.

## WHERE TO STAY

**Inns/Bed & Breakfasts:** Rosedown Plantation, 12501 Hwy. 10, St. Francisville LA 70775, (504) 635-3332. Barrow House, PO Box 1461, 524 Royal St., St. Francisville LA 70775, (504) 635-4791. Wolf Schlesinger House-St. Francisville Inn, Drawer 1369, 118 North Commerce, St. Francisville LA 70775, (504) 635-6502, 1-800-488-6502.
**Camping:** Cajun Country Campground, Rebelle Lane, Baton Rouge LA 70819, (504) 383-8554.

## OVERVIEW

Rosedown Plantation is located in the historic town of St. Francisville. This picturesque town of two thousand people has an abundance of nineteenth-century architecture. St. Francisville is a part of Feliciana which includes East and West Feliciana Parishes. These parishes extend thirty miles north of Baton Rouge on the Mississippi River's eastern bank.

In colonial times, Feliciana was owned by Spain. It was not included in the Louisiana Purchase. Settlers came from eastern-seaboard colonies. In 1810, these people rebelled against Spanish rule and formed a short-lived independent republic.

Photo by Patricia A. Gutek

**Rosedown Plantation and Gardens, St. Francisville, Louisiana**
European-style formal gardens designed 150 years ago by Martha Turnbull have
been restored. The 1835 Greek Revival plantation house,
built in Feliciana on the banks of the Mississippi River,
was occupied by Turnbull descendants until recent times.

Cotton and sugar-cane plantations dotted the area. Rosedown is a
classic Southern plantation house, approached through an avenue of live
oaks. The 1835 Louisiana Greek Revival mansion was built by Daniel and
Martha Turnbull, who owned a 3,500-acre cotton, sugar-cane and indigo
plantation. Martha Turnbull developed notable European-style gardens.
Occupied by Turnbull descendants until 1956, the mansion as well as the
nineteenth-century gardens has been restored.

## HISTORY

Rosedown Plantation was built in 1835 by Daniel Turnbull, an En-
glishman, and his wife, Martha Hilliard Barrow, on property that had originally been a 1779 Spanish land grant to John Mills, one of the founders of
St. Francisville. The Turnbulls raised cotton, sugar cane, and indigo on
their 3,500 acres. Their plantation house is a 1835 Louisiana Georgian

mansion with two 1840s stucco-covered brick Greek Revival wings, and a bedroom wing that was added to the rear of the house in 1859.

Daniel and Martha Turnbull toured Europe and returned laden with art, tapestries, chandeliers, and furnishings for their new home. Their visits to Europe's famous formal gardens, including the one at Versailles, inspired Martha, who was interested in horticulture, to develop extensive gardens at Rosedown.

The Turnbulls had two sons and a daughter, Sarah, who married James Pierre Bowman and had ten children. As happened at other plantations in the South, the Civil War caused severe economic disruption at Rosedown. Daniel died in 1861, but Martha, Sarah, and her family remained on the plantation, worked the fields, and paid off their debts. For over 120 years, until 1956, the house was occupied by the Turnbull and Bowman families.

The house and gardens were restored in the 1950s by Catherine Fondren Underwood. Her family continues to manage the plantation, which was opened to the public in 1964.

## SITE DESCRIPTION

Entrance to **Rosedown** is through an alley of 175-year-old live oak trees with gardens on either side.

Rosedown is a two-and-one-half-story Louisiana Greek Revival mansion of white-painted cypress built in 1835. Across the front are double galleries as well as six sets of hand-hewn cypress Doric columns. Two Greek Revival wings, of brick covered with stucco, were added in the 1840s, and a bedroom wing was added to the rear of the house in 1859.

Front doors on both the first and second floors have Georgian fanlights and sidelights of leaded glass. Ceilings in the house are over fourteen feet high. There are eleven fireplaces. Many of the cypress floors are covered with Aubussan carpets. Eighty-five percent of the original furniture remained in the house when purchased by the Underwoods.

In the **parlor**, original pieces include a walnut parlor set upholstered in red velvet and a desk. Two large walnut secretaries made in France and filled with books are in the **library**.

In the **dining room** are portraits of Daniel and Martha Turnbull by Thomas Sully. A shoofly fan hangs over the dining-room table, and there is an Italian marble fireplace.

The **master bedroom**, in the north addition, has a massive Gothic bedroom suite designed as a gift for Henry Clay to be used in the White House. When Clay lost his bid for the presidency in 1844, the Turnbulls purchased the elaborately carved rosewood tester bed, made by Crawford Riddle of Philadelphia, as well as the armoire, dresser, chair, and floor mirror in the set. The ceilings in this addition are higher than those in the rest of the house in order to accommodate the Clay poster bed.

There are two Havell copper plates of Audubon prints as well as several Audubon prints in the **upstairs front hall**, which was used as a sitting room. One of the **bedrooms** is furnished with an armoire and four-poster bed made by master cabinetmaker Prudent Mallard of New Orleans. In another bedroom is a mahogany swan cradle.

Rosedown's twenty-eight-acre garden is viewed as one of the most important historic gardens in the nation. In the nineteenth century, some of the first azaleas and camellias to be planted in the South were at Rosedown. Other late nineteenth-century gardens were influenced by the design of the Rosedown gardens. In the **formal gardens** are winding paths, marble statues, fountains, original tool and hot houses, other outbuildings, two herb gardens, an arboretum, and a natural century-old camellia arboretum.

# LONGFELLOW-EVANGELINE STATE COMMEMORATIVE AREA

State park with a 1790 Acadian house and an 1815 plantation complex; commemorates French-speaking cultures of Bayou Teche; NR, NHL.

**Address:** 1200 North Main St., St. Martinville LA 70582
**Telephone:** (318) 394-3754
**Location:** On LA Hwy. 31, in St. Martinville, on the banks of Bayou Teche.
**Open:** 9:00 A.M.–5:00 P.M. daily; closed Thanksgiving, Christmas, and New Year's Days.
**Admission:** Adults $2, children free.
**Shops:** Gift shop in Interpretive Center.
**Facilities:** Interpretive center, picnic area, amphitheater, boat launch.

## WHERE TO STAY

**Inns/Bed & Breakfasts:** Old Castillo Hotel, 220 Evangeline Blvd., St. Martinville LA 70582, (318) 394-4010, 1-800-621-3017.
**Motels/Hotels:** Days Inn, 1620 North University, Lafayette LA 70506, (318) 237-8880, FAX: (318) 235-1386.
**Camping:** KOA of Lafayette, Inc., Rt. 2, Box 261, Scott LA 70583, (318) 235-2739. Acadiana Parks Campground, Alexander Avenue, Lafayette LA 70502, (318) 234-3838.

## OVERVIEW

Longfellow-Evangeline State Commemorative Area is a historic site in a 157-acre state park which features three main exhibit areas: a ca. 1790 Acadian Cabin, an interpretative center housing several multimedia exhibits, and the ca. 1815 Olivier Plantation Complex.

The site is named for both Henry Wadsworth Longfellow and one of his poems, *Evangeline,* to signify the importance of that epic-length poem to the Bayou Teche region of Louisiana.

Love, romance, history, and broken hearts are intertwined in the legend of Evangeline, the fictional heroine of Longfellow's 1847 narrative poem. French Canadian lovers, cruelly separated by French and English political conflicts, spend their lives in a futile search for each other. Their quest ends with a deathbed reunion in the Bayou Teche/St. Martinsville area.

Longfellow's popular poem drew attention to the plight of the Acadians, the French-speaking people who had lived in Nova Scotia, Canada, for one hundred years before the French and Indian Wars pitted the French against the British. When the Acadians refused to swear allegiance to either side, they were deported as prisoners of war and shipped to multiple locations.

## HISTORY

Henry Wadsworth Longfellow's *Evangeline* tells the story of eighteenth-century lovers named Evangeline and Gabriel. French descendants, they lived in what is now Nova Scotia, Canada, but was in the eighteenth century called Acadia. After the French and Indian Wars between the British and French, and the resulting deportation of the Acadians, Evangeline searches for years for her lover. Eventually despairing of ever finding him, she enters a convent. Years later, as a nun nursing the sick, she discovers Gabriel, who is dying. They have a brief reunion before his death.

After having lived in Canada for a hundred years, the Acadians considered themselves a separate people—that is, Acadians, who were neither French nor British, though both France and Britain had governed them. (France deeded Acadia to England in the 1713 Treaty of Utrecht.) In 1755, during the last phase of the French and Indian Wars between the British and the French, those Acadians or French Canadians who refused to swear allegiance to either side were perceived as a threat and were expelled from Acadia. Following several guerrilla-type offensives against the British, Acadians were collected and deported as prisoners of war. Acadians were shipped to several different locations. Their houses were burned, and their livestock was confiscated. Some deportees were loaded onto ships and sent to English colonies along the Atlantic coast. Others traveled to the West Indies and from there to Louisiana, a French colony. Families and friends were separated.

St. Martinville, which was settled about 1760, became the refuge for many displaced Acadians who were attracted to French-speaking Louisiana. Though the territory was owned by Spain, many French-speaking people remained. Upon arrival in New Orleans, groups of Acadians were issued the basic supplies for survival and granted tracts of land in areas needing settlement. Refugees from the French Revolution also came to the town. A number of natural disasters around the time of the Civil War sent the town into decline.

The property became the first park of the Louisiana State Parks system in 1934.

## SITE DESCRIPTION

The state of Louisiana has acknowledged the importance of Longfellow's poem *Evangeline* as a popular history of the Acadian people in Louisiana by declaring a 157-acre site and its structures as the **Longfellow-Evangeline State Commemorative Area**. The park, located on the banks on Bayou Teche, focuses on the French-speaking cultures that settled in the Bayou Teche region prior to the Civil War.

The 1790 one-room **Acadian Cabin** is typical of houses lived in by the relocated Acadians. It is simply furnished with primitive Louisiana pieces. Adjacent to the cabin is a **vegetable garden**.

The land in the state park was first used as a *vacherie*, or cattle ranch, and later used as a indigo plantation. Plantations in the Bayou Teche area were usually owned by Creoles, descendants of French and Spanish settlers. The Pierre Olivier family bought land in the region around 1790. The plantation house was begun about 1815 by Pierre Olivier, and additions were made about 1840 by his son, Charles. It has been furnished to reflect the plantation's most prosperous period, 1840–1850.

The **Olivier Plantation House** is a French Caribbean-style structure built of native materials. The ground floor of the two-and-one-half-story raised cottage is constructed of sun-baked brick made of mud from Bayou Teche. Walls are fourteen inches thick. The upper floors are made of *bousillage*, a mud-and-moss mixture, and are covered with cypress clapboarding. The rectangular house has a front two-story gallery with brick piers at ground level and frame posts at the second level. There is a two-story partially enclosed gallery at the rear of the house.

On the ground level are the **storage room, work room, dining room**, and **plantation office**. The main level houses a **drawing room**, a **salon** or parlor, and **two bedrooms**.

Outbuildings include an 1840 **kitchen**, a reconstructed **blacksmith shop**, and a **barn**, which was relocated. Small stands of brown cotton, indigo, and sugar cane are grown seasonally. There is a **vegetable and herb garden** nearby as well as a **formal garden**.

At the **visitor center**, exhibits focus on the history, culture, and lifestyles of the Acadian and Creole people of the area. Maps indicate routes taken by Acadians to Louisiana. One exhibit is on Acadian architectural styles. Weaving looms are displayed, for weaving is a traditional Acadian craft. Other items displayed include pottery, tools, lace, and embroidery.

## SIDE TRIPS

Also in St. Martinville stands the **Evangeline Oak** on Port St. at the Bayou Teche landing. A statue of Evangeline stands next to **Saint Martin de Tours Catholic Church**, which was built in 1832, although an earlier church was established in 1765.

# MARYLAND

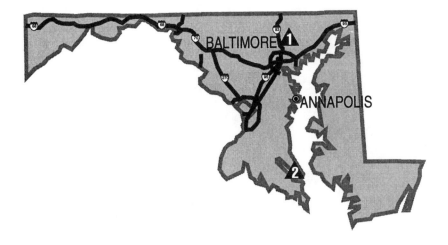

1. St. Mary's City: Historic St. Mary's City
2. Towson: Hampton National Historic Site

# HISTORIC ST. MARY'S CITY

Reconstruction of seventeenth-century
English colonial town; capital of the province
of Maryland 1634–1695; NR, NHL.

**Address:** Box 39, St. Mary's City MD 20686
**Telephone:** (301) 862-0990, 1-800-SMC-1634
**Location:** In southern Maryland, about 2 hours south of Washington and Baltimore, on MD Hwy. 5, south of Lexington Park.
**Open:** Late March through November, 10:00 A.M.–5:00 P.M. Wednesday–Sunday. Visitor center: year-round, 10:00 A.M.–5:00 P.M. Wednesday–Sunday. Closed Thanksgiving, Christmas, and New Year's Days.
**Admission:** Adults $6.50; seniors, college students, and students ages 13–18 $6; children ages 6–12 $3.25.
**Restaurants:** Farthing's Kitchen.
**Shops:** Historic St. Mary's City Gift Shop in visitor center.
**Facilities:** Visitor center with orientation film, walking trails, partially handicapped accessible.

## WHERE TO STAY

**Motels/Hotels:** Belvedere Motor Inn, 60 Main St., Lexington Park MD 20653, (301) 863-6666, 1-800-428-2871, FAX: (301) 863-6666, ext. 144. Patuxent Inn, Box 778, Lexington Park MD 20653, (301) 862-4100, FAX: (301) 862-4673. Super 8, 9290 Three Notch Rd., California MD 20619, (301) 862-9822, 1-800-800-8000
**Camping:** Point Lookout State Park, Star Rt., Box 48, Scotland MD 20687, (301) 872-5688. Dennis Point Maria and Campground, Drayden MD 20630, (301) 994-2288. La Grande Estate Camping Resort, Rt. 1, Box 118A, Leonardtown MD 20650, (301) 475-8550. Take It Easy Ranch, Callaway MD 20620, (301) 994-0494, (301) 994-2726.

## OVERVIEW

Historic St. Mary's City is an outdoor museum at the site of Maryland's first permanent English settlement, founded in 1634. St. Mary's City was the capital of the province of Maryland from 1634 until 1695, when Annapolis became the capital. This distinctive colony was conceived by its proprietor, Lord Baltimore, as a North American refuge for English Roman Catholics. Separation of church and state and toleration of citizens' private religious beliefs were founding principles. Though Maryland's experiment in religious toleration was overturned in 1689, separation of church and state would be an important provision of the United States Constitution.

Although the buildings in St. Mary's City were burned, torn down, or fell down in the early 1700s, no other construction occurred at this site. Consequently, St. Mary's City remained a buried seventeenth-century townsite. On the basis of historical records and archaeological work on the original buildings' foundations, however, the Old State House, the *Maryland Dove*, William Farthing's Ordinary, the planter's house, freedman's cottage, and the barns have been reconstructed on their original sites. Archaeological work continues in Chapel Field, site of the first Catholic church in Britain's North American colonies.

## HISTORY

Maryland was one of the thirteen original colonies; St. Mary's City was that state's first capital. The fourth permanent English settlement in North America, St. Mary's City was preceded by Jamestown, Plymouth, and Massachusetts Bay. The Maryland land grant was held by George Calvert, Lord Baltimore, who was a Catholic. Both Catholics and Protestants were among the first settlers who arrived in Maryland in 1634.

Sir George Calvert was named Baron of Baltimore in 1625 by King James I, whom he had served as a secretary of state. Calvert's public career ended when he announced his Roman Catholicism. At that time, Catholics could not hold state office in England. After an attempt at colonization in Newfoundland, Lord Baltimore appealed to King Charles I and was granted a tract of land in the Northern Chesapeake, north of Virginia. In addition to colonizing the land, Baltimore intended to establish a refuge for English Catholics, who could not legally practice their religion in their own country.

Needing wealthy gentlemen to share the enormous expenses associated with colonization, Lord Baltimore intended to transfer to his colony the English manor plan with its feudal system of lords and peasants. To attract investors, the new gentry were promised large parcels of land, provincial office, titles of honor, partnership roles in the colony's trade, and other privileges. He was unable to recruit sufficient numbers of Catholics

Photo by Patricia A. Gutek

## Historic St. Mary's City, St. Mary's City, Maryland

St. Mary's City, founded in 1634, was the capital of the Province of Maryland from 1634 to 1695. The "Farthing's Ordinary" sign indicates that the building is an inn, a necessity for travelers to this seventeenth-century English colonial town. The inn has been reconstructed on its original site.

to migrate to Maryland, however, and was forced to include many Protestants among the colonizers. Calvert realized that religious tolerance would be essential in Maryland to prevent differences between Catholics and Protestants from disrupting the civil order.

Because George Calvert died before he could accomplish his goals in Maryland, the task then passed to his son, Cecil Calvert, the second Lord Baltimore, who named the region of the grant "Maryland."

St. Mary's City was founded by 140 people who in 1633 sailed from England on an expedition led by Leonard Calvert, Cecil's brother. Maryland's investors included Catholic landed gentry, Jesuit priests, and Lord Baltimore himself. They paid for the passages of people, many of whom were Protestant, who would work for a time as indentured servants in repayment.

In March 1634, two ships carrying the colonists, the *Ark* and the

*Dove*, sailed into the Chesapeake Bay and up the Potomac River, landing at Maryland's St. Clement's Island. Leonard Calvert and a small group of men chose a Yaocomico village south of St. Clement's on the St. Mary's River as their permanent settlement. The advantage of the site was that the Yaocomico Indians, who were hunters and farmers, had already cleared the land so that spring planting could be started immediately. The Englishmen struck a deal with the Native Americans to surrender half of their village site immediately and the remainder over the coming year in exchange for hatchets, hoes, and cloth.

When Calvert returned to St. Clement's Island on March 25, 1634, with the news, the priests offered a mass of thanksgiving. Two days later, the settlers unloaded the ships and moved ashore. The Maryland party took over the land in the names of King Charles I and Lord Baltimore. Leonard Calvert named the place "Saint Maries" in honor of the Virgin Mary.

The new settlers built a fort in anticipation of trouble with the Native Americans, but relationships with them were peaceful. The Yaocomico tribe supplied the English with corn and fish, and taught them to make corn bread and hominy. Next, housing was built; wood was plentiful. About 500 more settlers arrived over the next eight-year period, but malaria and dysentery took a heavy toll so that the population of St. Mary's in 1642 was between 340 and 390, most of whom were young men. Although some people arrived in family units, most did not, and there were few women for the young men to marry.

As in other English colonies, there were problems with leadership, inadequate funding, insufficient labor forces, and disease. Investors had anticipated quick profits from a fur trade, which did not materialize, and from trading voyages made by the *Dove*, which was lost at sea on its return trip to England. However, the rich soil lent itself to agriculture which became the primary industry.

Tobacco was the major crop. By 1639, Maryland exported 100,000 pounds of tobacco. As soon as indentured servants paid off their debts and were free, they purchased their own land, leaving large landowners with inadequate labor forces. Soon, owner-operated plantations became more prevalent than large plantations worked by laborers and tenants who were in short supply. In the 1650s, African slaves were brought to Maryland to work in the tobacco fields. By the 1690s, slaves in Maryland outnumbered indentured servants and hired free men.

Since the tobacco economy necessitated shipping the crop by water, settlers were scattered along the waterways, which acted like highways, rather than clustered in a town. A town center did not develop until the 1660s, when public buildings, inns, and stables were built. St. Mary's City had been Maryland's capital for sixty-one years when, in 1695, the capital was moved to Annapolis. By 1720, the structures that comprised St. Mary's City had disappeared.

The Toleration Act of 1649 formalized the religious tolerance which had been practiced from the beginning in the colony founded jointly by Catholics and Protestants. The act promised freedom of worship and assembly to all who professed belief in the Holy Trinity. For sixty years, Anglicans, Catholics, Quakers, Labadists, and Presbyterians freely practiced their own faiths and shared political power. At this time, Maryland was the only colony that extended toleration to Catholics.

Separation of church and state and religious tolerance ended after a Protestant rebellion against Lord Baltimore's authority in 1689. Catholics were barred from holding political office or publicly practicing their faith. All residents, regardless of religion, were obliged to pay taxes to support the Church of England. In 1704, the Maryland Assembly passed a law closing all Catholic churches and schools. Religious toleration and separation of church and state were not restored in Maryland until 1776.

Beginning in 1934, archaeologists uncovered the foundations of several structures in St. Mary's City. Since then, buildings have been reconstructed on the basis of historical records and archaeological evidence.

## SITE DESCRIPTION

Start your tour of this 800-acre outdoor museum at the **visitor center**. After viewing the orientation film, examine objects uncovered by **archaeological excavation** at St. Mary's City. On display are pipe stems, cannon fragments, armor, brick, eating utensils, stoneware, tools, rosaries, and glass. An exhibit corridor connecting the visitor center to the site of the original town center is planned. One area, called "Encountering," deals with the contact between Native Americans and European settlers. Interactive exhibits and a reconstructed American Indian longhouse are featured. Other areas are devoted to the themes of "Worshiping," "Settling and Growing," "Building," "Working and Playing," "Governing," and "Trade and Travel."

Because archaeological studies precede the reconstruction of early-eighteenth-century buildings, rebuilding the city has been painstaking and slow. Archaeological excavation of St. Maries Chapel site—which dates from about 1634–1645, the earliest period of Maryland's settlement—has revealed two seventeenth-century Catholic chapels. A wooden Catholic

chapel, in existence by 1638, was burned in 1645 during a Protestant rebellion. The second chapel, believed to have been built by the Jesuits
about 1667, was a massive cross-shaped brick building. This **Chapel Field**
is viewed as the founding site of the American Catholic Church.

A major exhibit area, **Governor's Field**, includes the *Maryland
Dove*, a square-rigged replica of the 1630s ship that transported supplies for
the first settlers from England. This type of merchant vessel transported
trading goods between the Old World and the New.

The reconstructed **State House of 1676** is a Jacobean-style brick
building built in 1934 about 100 yards from its original foundation, which
is located under the Trinity Church graveyard. Maryland's first public
building was two and one-half stories—complete with stair tower, porch,
and tile roof. The **assembly room** and **provincial court** were on the first
floor, while the **committee room, council chamber**, and **secretary's office**
were on the second floor. The attic was used to store muskets and powder.
Copies of paintings of Charles, George, and Cecil Calvert hang in the assembly room. Trials drawn from colonial records are reenacted by costumed interpreters on summer weekends.

**Farthing's Ordinary** is a re-created seventeenth-century inn. Inns
were necessary in St. Mary's City because people came to the capital to
attend sessions of the courts and conduct business.

Also on the historic townlands are the **Margaret Brent Memorial
Garden and Gazebo.** Nearby, archaeologists have identified the sites of
Governor Leonard Calvert's 1635 Country House, Smith's Ordinary,
Cordea's Hope, lawyer's offices, Van Severingen's Lodging House and
Pope's Fort.

The **Godiah Spray Tobacco Plantation**, a working farm of the 1660s,
is a re-created tobacco plantation. The **planter's dwelling house** is an English-style frame house with clapboard exterior, glass windows, plaster
walls, a brick fireplace, pit-sawn flooring and paneling, and oak doors with
iron hinges and latches. The **tenant house** is a small, one-room building
with a dirt floor and a wattle-and-daub chimney. **Tobacco barns** are covered with unpainted hand-split clapboards and have steeply pitched roofs.
There are a **hen house**, a **hog pen**, a **cow pen**, and **gardens**. Living-history
demonstrations are conducted here in which costumed interpreters play
the roles of historic figures who lived in early St. Maries City. They perform domestic and agricultural chores while conversing with visitors in
seventeenth-century English.

Nearby is **Trinity Episcopal Churchyard** (1829), site of the original

State House and the **Leonard Calvert Monument** (1890), and **St. Mary's College of Maryland** (1839).

## FESTIVALS/CRAFTS

Special events include **Maryland Days Weekend** in late March, **Charter Days** in mid-June, **Grand Militia Muster** in late October, **Tidewater Archaeology Dig** at the end of July, **Maritime Heritage Weekend** in May, **American Indian Culture Day** in early October, **Madrigals and Carols** in late November, and **Christmas Madrigal Evenings** in early December.

## SIDE TRIPS

**St. Clement's Island Potomac River Museum** at Colton's Point has exhibits on the local history and prehistory of Maryland. St. Clement's Island is the landing site of Maryland's first English settlers in March 1634. Picnic area, excursion boat, fishing. Open daily from late March through September; and Wednesday–Sunday, from October through late March. Admission is free. On MD Hwy. 242, Colton Point. (301) 769-2222.

**Sotterley Plantation** is a working plantation which dates to about 1717. The mansion has a Chinese Chippendale staircase. Grounds include **English country gardens**. Open June through October, Tuesday–Sunday. Admission is charged. Off Rt. 245 near Hollywood. (301) 373-2280.

# HAMPTON NATIONAL HISTORIC SITE

Eighteenth-century plantation occupied by
the Ridgely family from 1745 to 1948;
outstanding 1790 Georgian mansion.

**Address:** 535 Hampton Lane, Towson MD 21286
**Telephone:** (410) 962-0688
**Location:** About 3 miles north of Baltimore; via Baltimore Beltline, I-695
exit 27B (Providence Rd. north to Hampton Lane) or exit 28 North
(Dulaney Valley Rd. to Hampton Lane).
**Open:** 9:00 A.M.–5:00 P.M. daily; closed Thanksgiving, Christmas, and New
Year's Days.
**Admission:** Free.
**Restaurants:** Tearoom in mansion, 11:30 A.M.–3:00 P.M. Tuesday–Sunday;
closed Monday.
**Shops:** Gift Shop in mansion.
**Facilities:** Guided tours of mansion; self-guided tours of grounds, stables,
gardens, and farm site.

## WHERE TO STAY

**Inns/Bed & Breakfasts:** Barn House, 13710 Cripplegate Rd., Phoenix MD
21131, (301) 527-0873.
**Motels/Hotels:** Sheraton, 903 Dulaney Valley Rd., I-695 exit 27A, Towson MD 21204, (410) 321-7400, FAX: (410) 296-9534. Days Inn
Baltimore East, 8801 Loch Raven Blvd., Towson MD 21204, (410)
882-0900, FAX: (410) 882-4176. Holiday Inn-North, 8712 Loch
Raven Blvd., Towson MD 21204, (301) 823-8750.
**Camping:** Morris Meadows Recreation Farm, I-83, exit 36, Freeland MD
21053, (301) 329-6636.

## OVERVIEW

Hampton National Historic Site preserves a remarkable late-eighteenth-century Georgian mansion that was home to seven generations of

Photo by Patricia A. Gutek

**Hampton National Historic Site, Towson, Maryland**
Hampton's 1790 Georgian mansion was home to seven generations of the
Ridgelys, a prominent Maryland family. The elegant five-part residence was
once the centerpiece of a 24,000-acre planation.

the Ridgely family. The prominent Maryland family acquired its wealth
through iron-making, mercantile interests, and agriculture. While the land
was once a prosperous 24,000-acre Southern plantation with hundreds of
slaves comprising the bulk of its labor force, the historic site property now
consists of sixty-two acres. The house has been well restored and furnished.
In addition to the mansion, there are restored formal gardens as well as
natural landscaping. Many outstanding trees adorn the property, including
several which are state champions. Although more than twenty dependency buildings remain, they are not open for viewing.

## History

A portrait by the early-nineteenth-century American artist Thomas
Sully was instrumental in preserving the mansion at Hampton as a Na-
tional Historic Site. Sully's 1818 painting of Eliza Eichelberger Ridgely,
*The Lady with a Harp*, hung in Hampton's great hall for over a century.

Wishing to acquire significant works by Sully for the National Gallery of Art, its director, David Finley, traveled to Hampton in 1945 to negotiate the purchase of that painting from John Ridgely, Jr. During his visit, Finley learned of Ridgely's concern for the preservation of the fine Georgian mansion since the upkeep of the house, grounds, and outbuildings had become increasingly difficult.

Through Finley's intervention, the Avalon Foundation, a Mellon family trust, purchased the property and gave it to the National Park Service. The purchase price for the mansion, some of its furnishings, and 43.29 acres was $46,000. Ridgely agreed to this incredibly low price because of the importance he placed on preserving his home as a museum open to the public.

The late-eighteenth-century house, an outstanding example of Georgian architecture, is considered extremely important in the history of American architecture. The Hampton acquisition marked the first time that the National Park Service acquired a historic property based on its significance as a piece of architecture rather than for its historic connection to a person or event.

Captain Charles Ridgely constructed Hampton between 1783 and 1790 on property he received from his father, Colonel Charles Ridgely. Colonel Ridgely was born in Maryland in 1702. His grandfather, Robert Ridgely, was a barrister who came to Maryland from England around 1634. Robert served as clerk of the Maryland Council, deputy secretary of the province, and acting attorney general.

Colonel Ridgely purchased what was called the Northampton tract—1,500 acres with houses, outhouses, tobacco barns, stables, gardens, and orchards— from Ann Hill and her sons, Henry and Clement, for 600 pounds sterling on April 2, 1745. Colonel Ridgely owned other Maryland property totaling at least 8,000 acres.

Between 1760 and 1762, on a 100-acre tract just north of Northampton, Colonel Ridgely established an ironworks: the Northampton Furnace and Forges, which operated until 1829. Originally, the company was a three-way partnership among Colonel Ridgely and his sons, John and Charles. Ironworks sprung up in the area because iron ore was easily mined there. Large quantities of wood and limestone along with water power, all of which were necessary for the production of bar and pig iron, were available nearby.

The younger Charles Ridgely spent the years from 1755 to 1763 at sea, first as a supercargo on one of his father's ships and later as the captain of several ships. The elder Ridgely enticed his son home from the sea to

manage the ironworks by deeding him 2,000 acres of land, including a major portion of Northampton. Captain Ridgely acquired his brother John's
third of the iron business after John's death in 1771.

The Northampton Furnace and Forges employed many workers including slaves, indentured servants, convict laborers, artisans, tradesmen,
and even British prisoners during the Revolutionary War. Captain Ridgely's management of the ironworks was immensely successful as demand for
iron accelerated during the Revolutionary War. Military contract profits
enabled Captain Ridgely to buy up additional land and ironworks. In addition to being an ironmaster, Ridgely was involved with local politics and
bred horses. As his wealth and position grew, so did his desire for a house
that would reflect the position of a Maryland country gentlemen.

The five-part Georgian mansion, which was probably designed by
Captain Ridgely, was begun in 1783 and finished in 1790, the year he died.
Because he and his wife, Rebecca, had no children, Charles Ridgely Carnan, a nephew, inherited the estate on the condition that he change his
last name to Ridgely, which he did.

The renamed Charles Carnan Ridgely was a politician who served as
governor of Maryland from 1815 to 1819. Governor Ridgely also managed
the diverse agricultural interests of his vast estate, became sole owner of
the Hampton ironworks, and was one of the foremost racers and breeders
of thoroughbred horses in America. He completed the work on Hampton's
formal gardens and extensive landscaping. He was a very wealthy man
with huge property holdings and over 300 slaves, most of whom he set free
in his will.

Governor Ridgely's estate was divided among his eleven children,
who reached adulthood after his death in 1829. John Carnan Ridgely was
the son who inherited the mansion and approximately 4,000 surrounding
acres. John's second wife, Eliza Eichelberger Ridgely—the daughter of
Nicholas Greenbury Ridgely who was not a relative—was the beautiful
young woman with the harp in the Sully portrait commissioned by her father in 1818, ten years before she married John Carnan Ridgely. Eliza updated the furnishings of the house and also improved the gardens.
Plumbing, gas light, central heating were added. Slaves, whom John had
purchased or inherited from both his first and second wives' families, were
used to run the plantation until 1864, when servants were hired.

The fourth of the six generations that owned Hampton was John and
Eliza's son, Charles, who inherited Hampton in 1867 and died in 1872.
Next, Hampton passed to John—the son of Charles and his wife, Marga-
retta Sophia Howard Ridgely—who inherited the estate at age twenty-one

and retained title until his death at age eighty-seven in 1938. During this time, the fortunes of the Hampton estate declined, and some acreage was sold to developers. In 1938, the sixth and last master, John Ridgely, Jr., inherited the estate. It was he who sold Hampton to the Avalon Foundation in 1948.

The Society for the Preservation of Maryland Antiquities served as the custodian of Hampton National Historic Site for more than thirty years. Later, two acres of land, two racing stables, and the Hampton cemetery were added to the site. In 1979, the National Park Service assumed full responsibility for the site. An additional fourteen-acre farm property was purchased in 1980 from the heirs of John Ridgely, Jr.

## SITE DESCRIPTION

This small national historic site is an overlooked gem on the plantation circuit. Its especially fine **Georgian mansion, family furnishings, formal gardens, landscaped grounds and dependencies** reflect the economic and social life-style of an early Maryland family from the American Revolution era to the mid-twentieth century. On sixty-two acres, the setting and views of the rolling Maryland hills are idyllic.

**Hampton** is a three-story, 28,000-square-foot, thirty-four-room Georgian house built of locally quarried fieldstone. It is covered with a slightly pink stucco, the color the result of iron bearing sand used in the stucco. Built between 1783 and 1790 by both slaves and hired artisans, the mansion was originally named Hampton Hall. The Georgian-style house was probably designed by Charles Ridgely rather than an architect. Its Georgian design follows the balanced five-part plan: a main house, two flanking wings, with hyphens or enclosed passages connecting the wings to the central structure. Evidence of the lack of an architect's expertise is the oversized cupola.

The first floor of the main house has a large central receiving area with a pair of rooms on each side which open onto the hall. Called the **great hall**, the 51-x-21-foot central hall spans the depth of the house, extending from the carriage entrance to the garden entrance, and has neither staircase nor fireplace. The great hall was used for parties, balls, receptions, and large dinners. It also served as a family portrait gallery, and still does today. A copy of Sully's *The Lady with the Harp*, the portrait of Eliza Ridgely, dominates one wall. There is a set of ca. 1810 painted Baltimore chairs and benches in the hall; each piece is individually decorated with different botanical specimens.

Rooms on the first floor have been restored to a variety of time periods to reflect the 160 years that seven generations occupied the mansion. About seventy percent of the furnishings in the house belonged to the Ridgely family.

The **family parlor** is decorated in Federal style, and dates to about 1790 when the house was built. Furnishings in this informal family room include a Baltimore mahogany gaming table, an American walnut tea table, and an Baltimore mahogany tall-case clock.

The **dining room** has been restored to 1815–1829, when it was decorated by Charles Carnan Ridgely. It is painted a vivid Prussian blue and the elaborate window hangings are blue and yellow. The porcelain is French, and the silver is embossed with the family crest. The vividly colored patterned woolen Brussels carpet was handwoven in England.

The **drawing room** appears as it was decorated by John and Eliza Ridgely after 1832 when they ordered a suite of painted furniture from John Finlay of Baltimore. The drawing room suite included fourteen black and gold hollow-back framed chairs, a sofa with gilt swans, one pier table, and one centre table. The gilt and cut-glass English chandelier originally used candles and was converted to gas around 1850. The house did not have electricity until 1929.

The **music room**, decorated in the Victorian style, is indicative of occupancy during the late nineteenth century. There are a large square ca. 1872 Steinway piano, Eliza's 1817 painted and gilded harp, made in London, and her music stand. Among the family portraits in the room is an 1860 John Carlin portrait of John and Eliza's four grandsons fishing in a pond. Three of the boys are in dresses. An 1820 three-quarter length portrait of Charles Carnan Ridgely is another Sully copy; the original was donated to the National Gallery of Art by the Ridgely family.

The **east wing** was the original kitchen. Now a small tearoom, it retains its original fireplace and oven. The **west wing**, which was the original laundry, now houses a gift shop.

The six bedrooms on the second floor were primarily for adults, while the ten bedrooms on the third floor were for children. The third floor is not open for viewing. The **master bedroom** has a bed draped with opulent bed hangings, a secretary desk, a huge trunk which belonged to Governor Ridgely, and a child's crib or playpen that belonged to Betsey Patterson Bonaparte, wife of Jerome and sister-in-law of Napoleon. The **principal guest bedchamber** has two large four-poster beds and a traveling bathtub.

Of equal importance to the house are the **surrounding grounds**. Natural landscaping was used on the north side of the house. In this English landscape park-style, carefully planned vistas and tree plantings are intended to have a natural look. The view from the north facade of the mansion looks across a sweeping lawn to distant Maryland hills. On the south side of the house were formal terraced gardens. Construction of the parterres, or formal geometric gardens, was begun in 1800 under the supervision of William Booth. Eliza Ridgely was an avid gardener who expanded and improved the gardens. An irrigation system supplied the gardens with water. In 1880, there were over 20,000 bedding plants and 4,000 roses in over 275 beds. By the end of the nineteenth-century, the Ridgelys were unable to support their lavish life-style, and all but one of the parterres were allowed to return to grass.

**Four parterres** on two terraces have been restored to their appearance prior to 1830. Each parterre has boxwood perimeters. **Parterres I and II** are planted with ground covers, and interplanted with spring bulbs. On the second terrace, **parterres III and IV** feature Heritage Roses.

Hampton National Historic Site is noted for its special collection of **mature trees**. The tulip tree and the purple European beech on the north lawn were planted around 1825. On the south lawn are three gnarled catalpas and one cedar that are nearly 200 years old. The mid-nineteenth-century cedar of Lebanon planted by Eliza Ridgely is the state champion, as is the saucer magnolia tree, planted in the 1820s. The pecan tree is 115 feet tall.

Although there are outbuildings including slave quarters on the site, most of the buildings are closed, with the exception of an equestrian exhibit in the 1803 **upper stable**.

## SIDE TRIPS

**Ladew Topiary Gardens** is a twenty-two-acre site with fifteen flower gardens, a house, and trees and shrubs trimmed into ornamental shapes. Open mid-April through October, 10 A.M.–4:00 P.M. Tuesday–Friday, and 12:00 noon–5:00 P.M. Saturday and Sunday. Admission is charged. 3535 Jarrettsville Pike, Monkton MD 21111. (410) 557-9570.

# MISSISSIPPI

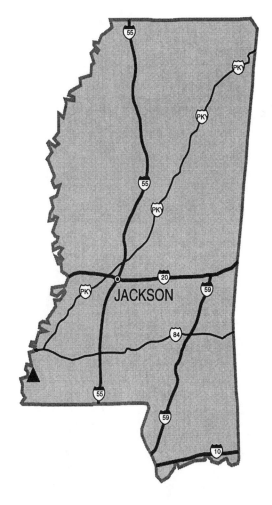

Natchez: Melrose Estate, Natchez National
    Historical Park

# MELROSE ESTATE, NATCHEZ NATIONAL HISTORICAL PARK

**Restored Natchez estate with ca. 1847 Greek Revival house and outbuildings; NR, NHL, HABS.**

**Address:** One Melrose-Montebello Parkway, Natchez MS 39121; or Superintendent, Natchez National Historical Park, PO Box 1208, Natchez MS 39121
**Telephone:** (601) 442-7047
**Location:** Natchez is in southwestern Mississippi, on the Mississippi River.
**Open:** 9:00 A.M.–4:00 P.M. daily.
**Admission:** Adults $4, seniors $2, children ages 6–17 $2.
**Shops:** Bookstore.
**Facilities:** 80-acre property with 1847 mansion, original outbuildings, and formal gardens; visitor center.

## WHERE TO STAY

**Inns/Bed & Breakfasts:** The Briars, 31 Irving Lane, Natchez MS 39120, (601) 446-9654, 1-800-634-1818. Dunleith, 84 Homochitto St., Natchez MS 39120, (601) 446-8500, 1-800-433-2445. Monmouth, 36 Melrose Ave., Natchez MS 39120, (601) 442-5852, 1-800-828-4531, FAX: (601) 446-7762
**Motels/Hotels:** Howard Johnson Lodge, US 61 North, Natchez MS 39120, (601) 442-1691, 1-800-654-2000. Scottish Inn, 40 Seargent Prentiss Dr., Natchez MS 39120, (601) 442-9141.
**Camping:** Natchez State Park, US 61, 230 B Wickcliff Rd., Natchez MS 39120, (601) 442-2658. Traceway Campground, 1113 US 61 North, Natchez MS 39120, (601) 445-8279.

## OVERVIEW

One of three units of newly created (1988) Natchez National Historical Park, Melrose Estate focuses on the life-style of a cotton planter in the era before the Civil War when cotton was king. During the first half of the nineteenth century, the rich soils of the lower Mississippi River Valley produced good yields of cotton per acre. With African Americans providing the labor, the nearby Mississippi River affording easy access to markets, and the demand for cotton remaining strong and consistent, profits for cotton planters were enormous. Natchez was the city on the Mississippi River where many wealthy cotton planters built opulent homes and pursued extravagant life-styles.

Melrose Estate was built in Natchez in 1847 by lawyer and plantation-owner John Thompson McMurran. It was owned by only three Mississippi families before being purchased by the National Park Service in 1990. The Greek Revival mansion has never been altered architecturally and contains much of its original furniture. Six original outbuildings are also still on the eighty-acre property. Melrose Estate presents a remarkably well preserved home of a Natchez cotton planter.

## HISTORY

John Thompson McMurran and his wife, Mary Louisa Turner, built a home on 132 acres several miles east of Natchez in 1847. Their Greek Revival mansion was designed by Jacob Byers.

John McMurran was born in Franklin County, Pennsylvania, in 1801. He studied law in Chillicothe, Ohio, with his uncle, who was a Chillicothe judge. McMurran moved to Port Gibson, Mississippi, in 1823 and by late 1825 was practicing law in Natchez. In 1826, he joined the law firm of John Anthony Quitman, whom he had met in Ohio, and William B. Griffith, and became a partner the next year.

On January 11, 1831, he married Mary Louisa Turner, the daughter of Edward Turner, former state attorney general, speaker of the Mississippi house of representatives, and state supreme court justice. They had three children, the oldest of whom died before age three.

Mary Louisa's parents gave the young couple "Holly Hedges," a house and lot in Natchez which became their home, and "Hope Farm," a 654-acre plantation. Now a prosperous lawyer and plantation owner, John McMurran was appointed secretary of the bar of Natchez in 1832 and was elected a member of the Mississippi house of representatives in 1835.

In 1841, the McMurrans purchased property for a new home in an area east of Natchez where other prominent plantation owners were building large, extravagant homes. The Greek Revival house was completed in 1847 and was named "Melrose" after the Scottish abbey in Sir Walter Scott's *Lay of the Last Minstrel*. Fine contemporary, American-made pieces were used to furnish the house. The McMurrans usually spent hot summers in the East or in Europe and the winters at Melrose. Nineteen slaves maintained the estate.

From Melrose, McMurran managed the cotton plantations he continued to acquire in Mississippi, Louisiana, and Arkansas, as well as the 300 slaves he owned. His fortunes continued to rise until the Civil War years. Because Union troops controlled the Mississippi River, McMurran was unable to ship his cotton to market. Many of his slaves ran away or were impressed into the Union army.

Although their economic condition began improving around 1864, the McMurran family suffered several tragedies. Their only daughter, Mary Elizabeth McMurran Connar, died in 1864; two of her children died shortly thereafter.

In December 1865, the McMurrans sold Melrose and its furnishings to Elizabeth and George Davis. Except for two caretakers, the house was unoccupied until 1901, when a Davis grandson, George Kelly, and his wife, Ethel Moore, inherited the house and began to use it part of the year. In 1910, they became full-time residents, and Mrs. Kelly lived there until her death in 1975. Melrose was purchased in 1976 by Mr. and Mrs. John Callon, who did a great deal of restoration. They sold it to the National Park Service in 1990.

A McMurran inventory of 1865 and a Davis inventory of 1883 confirmed that most of the furnishings in Melrose were original. These inventories, which proved invaluable in restoring the house to the McMurran era, also helped determine the original fabrics, wall coverings, and carpet designs used in the house. Restoration focuses on the opulent life-style of the nineteenth-century Natchez planters in along the Mississippi.

Melrose Estate is one of three units comprising Natchez National Historical Park, which was established to depict Natchez's legacy, from its roots as an outpost of the old Southwest to the symbolic capital of the Cotton Kingdom. The other units are the William Johnson House Complex, which, though now awaiting restoration, will highlight the life of a free African American in Natchez, and the Fort Rosalie Site, the ruins of an early-eighteenth-century French fortress which protected an agricultural settlement.

## SITE DESCRIPTION

Begin your tour at the **visitor center** located in an outbuilding behind the mansion. **Melrose Estate** consists of a eighty-acre site with a two-story Greek Revival brick mansion designed by Jacob Byers in 1847, as well as a half dozen dependencies.

**Melrose**, one of Natchez's most harmonious examples of Greek Revival architecture, has an entry portico featuring four unfluted Doric columns supporting a classical pediment. Fluted Ionic columns frame the front door. At the rear of the house is a two-story colonnaded gallery. A widow's walk, a raised roof-deck with balustrade, sits on the hipped roof.

The house was designed to reflect the taste and wealth of Natchez gentry. From the front to the rear door is a twenty-one foot expanse encompassing the **entrance foyer** and **first-floor center hall**. The **drawing room, parlor**, and **library** form another continuous space across the length of the house when pocket doors between the rooms are opened. Ceilings are fifteen feet high on the first floor and thirteen feet high on the second floor.

Rare original hemp floor cloths have remained in the foyer and first-floor center hall since they were installed in 1845. The design in the hall resembles a twelve-color Brussels carpet, while in the foyer is a grey and white Italian marble pattern. It took workers two and one-half years to restore the floor cloths, which were covered with layers of shellac.

The McMurrans decorated their new home with the finest contemporary furniture available in mid-nineteenth-century America. In the **foyer** are pier tables attributed to Anthony G. Quervelle of Philadelphia. Other notable furnishings are the Rococo Revival furniture and brocatelle draperies in the **drawing room**, the marble-top pillar-and-scroll center table made by Joseph Meeks, and the mahogany sideboard signed by Charles White of Philadelphia. Above the dining room table is a mahogany punkah fan, which was swung to keep flies and mosquitos away. Around the table are ten side chairs and two Gothic-style arm chairs. Throughout the house are mid-nineteenth-century lighting devices.

At the rear of the house are a pair of **two-story brick dependencies**, one of which had a kitchen on the first floor and slave quarters above. It now serves as the visitor center.

Approximately twenty enslaved African Americans worked at Melrose, as cooks, nurses, laundresses, butlers, coachmen, groundsmen, and gardeners. Melrose's reconstructed slave quarters consist of long, multiroom, raised-frame structures, one of which is open. One room is furnished.

Other outbuildings include a **smokehouse, slave privy, stable, and carriage house**. A **formal garden** contains flower beds of various shapes and sizes.

## SIDE TRIPS

**Natchez** is famous for the hundreds of fine **antebellum homes**. Many of these privately owned and occupied homes open their doors for tours during the city's two very popular annual pilgrimages, in the spring and the fall. **Natchez Pilgrimage Tours**, Canal at State St., PO Box 347, Natchez 39121. (601) 446-6631, 1-800-647-6742. For information, contact the Natchez Convention and Visitor Bureau, PO Box 1485, Natchez MS 39121. (601) 446-6345, 1-800-647-6724.

The city of Natchez is at the southern terminus of **Natchez Trace Parkway**, a modern 445-mile parkway constructed by the National Park Service along an early 1800s trail. This trail extended from the Mississippi River near Natchez through Alabama to present-day Tennessee, and was used by hunters, Native Americans, and French, Spanish, and American settlers. Along the Trace are **hiking and nature trails, picnic areas**, and **public campgrounds**, as well as **historical exhibits** on the Old Trace and American Indians. There are two restored historic structures. **Mount Locust**, a 1779 Mississippi inn, and an 1837 **Rocky Springs church**. Superintendent, Natchez Trace Parkway, RR. 1, NT-143, Tupelo MS 38801. (601) 842-1572.

# MISSOURI

1. Arrow Rock: Arrow Rock State Historic Site
2. Hannibal: Mark Twain Boyhood Home and Museum
3. Ste. Genevieve: Historic Ste. Genevieve

# ARROW ROCK STATE HISTORIC SITE

Nineteenth-century frontier town which was a supply base for the Santa Fe Trail; NHL, NR.

**Address:** PO Box 1, Arrow Rock MO 65320
**Telephone:** (816) 837-3330, (816) 837-3231
**Location:** In central Missouri, 140 miles west of St. Louis, 86 miles east of Kansas City; on Hwy. 41, 13 miles north of I-70.
**Open:** June–August: daily. April, May, September, and October: weekends.
**Admission:** Adults $3, children $1.
**Restaurants:** The Old Tavern, Evergreen Restaurant, The Old Schoolhouse Café.
**Shops:** Antique shops, craft shops.
**Facilities:** Visitor center, slide show, guided tours.

## WHERE TO STAY

**Inns/Bed & Breakfasts:** Arrow Rock: Borgman's B&B, Van Buren St., (816) 837-3350. Cedar Grove B&B, Hwy. 41, (816) 837-3441. Miss Nelle's B&B, Main St., (816) 837-3280. DownOver B&B Inn, Main St., (816) 837-3280.
**Camping:** Arrow Rock State Historic Park, PO Box 1, Arrow Rock MO 65320, (816) 837-3330.

## OVERVIEW

For a town with a population of eighty, Arrow Rock certainly has its act together. In addition to nine or ten well-restored nineteenth-century buildings which can be seen on guided tours, there are a new visitors' center with an orientation film and historical exhibits, a good restaurant in the restored tavern, several charming bed-and-breakfasts, fine antique stores, a summer theater, several other shops and restaurants, and a campground. Arrow Rock is a jewel of a town in a picturesque rural setting, and though its eighty residents must all be dynamic people, the atmosphere is slow and sleepy.

Once upon a time, Arrow Rock's population was closer to 1,000. That was in the first half of the nineteenth century, when the town served as an eastern terminus for the Santa Fe Trail. Wagon trains would assemble at this Missouri site to prepare for their months-long journey to Santa Fe. These were business trips taken by traders looking for profits, not treks westward by pioneers looking for new land to settle. Food, water, wagons, guns, livestock, and clothing were needed for the round-trip as well as the commodities that would be traded for gold, silver, furs, and animals in New Mexico. Seeing a good business opportunity, merchants settled in Arrow Rock to supply goods and necessities for the wagon trains of the traders.

## HISTORY

It was ease of crossing the Missouri River in the vicinity of the high rocky cliff that drew Native Americans, explorers, and traders to this Missouri site. Arrow Rock, named for its rocky cliff whose flint was used to make arrowheads, was initially the site of an American Indian crossing. The explorer Captain William Clark crossed the river at Arrow Rock in 1808 when heading toward what is now Jackson County, Missouri, to establish Fort Osage, the first United States outpost in the Louisiana Purchase. When conditions got too dangerous at Fort Osage during the War of 1812, Clark, then governor of the Missouri Territory, directed George Sibley, the American Indian factor at Fort Osage, to establish a blockhouse and trading post for the Great and Little Osage Indians at Arrow Rock. The two-story log fort was abandoned in 1814.

When Clark's expedition originally stopped at Arrow Rock, the explorer indicated that the Missouri River was confined within a bed of 200 yards at the site of the large cliff. It was this advantageous location which accounted for the town's becoming a supply depot for the wagon trains on the Santa Fe Trail. In 1811, Henry Becknell established a ferry at Arrow Rock which would remain in operation until 1927. Trading expeditions to the far west on what would become the Santa Fe Trail were begun by Henry's brother, William Becknell, in 1821.

Santa Fe was located in northern New Spain and, until the nineteenth century, Spain retained a monopoly on all trade within its territory. That meant that goods destined for Santa Fe had to be shipped from Spain to Mexico, and then brought overland in wagons on the El Camino Real from Mexico City to Santa Fe, a distance of 1,600 miles. Because Spanish goods were expensive and scarce, residents of Santa Fe were eager for American manufactured goods. However, the Spanish refused foreigners entry into New Spain and stopped all attempts at foreign trade.

Photo by Patricia A. Gutek

**Arrow Rock State Historic Site, Arrow Rock, Missouri**
Arrow Rock was a frontier town on the Missouri River that became a supply
base for traders traveling along the Santa Fe Trail. Merchants settled in Arrow
Rock to sell goods and necessities for the wagon trains. In the restored Huston
Store are nineteenth-century products, including barrels, jugs, and jars.

When Mexico won independence from Spain in 1821, the opportunity for Americans to do business in Santa Fe opened up. The trail that traders blazed from Missouri to Santa Fe was called the "Santa Fe Trail." They carried goods 900 miles to the Southwest and returned laden with gold, silver, furs, mules, and other livestock. Their enormous profits attracted more men who assembled huge quantities of trade goods transported in long wagon trains west to Santa Fe. Items carried to Santa Fe included broadcloth, muslin, taffeta, calico, linen, velveteen, clothing, buttons, buckles, handkerchiefs, razors, razor strops, writing paper, needles, thread, thimbles, scissors, pots, pans, coffee mills, knives, drills, shovels, hoes, axes, and tools.

Because the arrow rock on the Missouri River was frequently the gathering place for these expeditions, business people settled at the spot to supply the needs of the wagon caravans. In addition to selling trade goods in New Mexico, the caravans often sold off their wagons and oxen, because the volume of goods returning to Missouri was considerably less than going out and there was no profit in hauling back empty wagons. The fact that every year, the wagon trains going out had to again purchase mules, horses, and wagons meant a ready market for Missouri's stockmen and vehicle manufacturers.

Trading expeditions on the Santa Fe Trail continued from the early 1820s to the mid-1840s. In 1843, President Santa Anna of Mexico placed an embargo on all commerce between Missouri and Santa Fe. Trading resumed, though not at previous levels, in 1846 during the Mexican War when the United States invaded New Mexico. New Mexico became American territory as a result of the Mexican War.

Supply and demand eventually affected trading between Missouri and Santa Fe. A continuing supply of goods had been delivered to a relatively fixed market, and demand had eroded greatly by the mid-1840s.

In the 1850s, United States Army outposts which were established throughout the Southwest to protect white settlers from American Indian attacks became steady customers of the Santa Fe traders, who furnished the soldiers with food, animals, and supplies. During the Civil War, however, army troops were posted elsewhere, and wagon trains again fell prey to American Indian attacks.

The most disruptive factor in trading between Missouri and Santa Fe was the establishment of the railroad in the southwestern United States. In 1880, the Atchison, Topeka, and Santa Fe Railroad reached Santa Fe providing an easier and cheaper means of transporting goods and making wagon trains obsolete.

Settlement in the Missouri Territory began after the War of 1812, when the fear of American Indian attacks subsided. The first settlers in the Arrow Rock area were from Kentucky, Tennessee, and Virginia. A town was platted in 1829 and named New Philadelphia; the town's name was changed to Arrow Rock in 1833. More and more settlers moved into central Missouri. Building materials, furniture, and clothing needed by these frontier people were sent by steamboat on the Missouri to Arrow Rock. Between the Santa Fe trade caravans and the influx of settlers in the region, Arrow Rock became an active business center.

Among the town's prominent citizens was Dr. John Sappington, the physician who discovered quinine to be an effective treatment of malaria. Another prominent family, the Marmadukes, produced two governors of Missouri. A noted frontier artist, George Caleb Bingham, whose paintings depicted life in the mid-nineteenth century, had a home in Arrow Rock. Bingham also painted portraits of men and women in many of the surrounding Missouri counties.

Although Missouri, one of the border states, officially remained in the Union during the Civil War, many of its citizens had recently migrated from Southern states and chose to fight for the Confederacy. Because of Arrow Rock's many Southern sympathizers, martial law was imposed on the town during the war.

After the Civil War, in 1873, the town was hit by a disastrous fire. A second serious fire struck Arrow Rock's business district in 1901, dealing yet another serious blow to the declining town. Railroads had made the Santa Fe trail obsolete, the frontier had moved westward, and major highways bypassed the town. Arrow Rock's citizens moved on to more prosperous areas, leaving a community with a weakened economy and dwindling population behind.

In the early 1920s, preservationists became involved in restoring the historic town. The Missouri legislature purchased the tavern in 1923, and the Missouri Daughters of the American Revolution restored and furnished it. Arrow Rock State Park was established in 1926. Friends of Arrow Rock, Inc., was founded in 1959 and began restoring buildings. Still other structures have been restored by the Missouri State Park Department. In 1964, the village of Arrow Rock was designated a National Historic Landmark.

## SITE DESCRIPTION

**Arrow Rock** is a small historic community, four blocks long and eight blocks deep, where restored nineteenth-century buildings blend with the living town. Well-maintained white frame and red-brick buildings surrounded by large yards with flower gardens line the streets. Stores on Main Street open to a canopied boardwalk.

Two guided tours are given by the Friends of Arrow Rock. You may go on either one or both. Start at the **Arrow Rock State Historic Site Interpretive Center**, where an audiovisual program on Arrow Rock is shown, and exhibits on local, state, and national history are displayed. One exhibit features a large wall map of the Santa Fe Trail, while another focuses on European colonization in North America.

Visit the **Old Tavern** on Main Street, even if you're not on a tour; several rooms on the first floor are used as a restaurant. Adjacent to the **dining rooms** is the restored **nineteenth-century kitchen** with a large fireplace and a variety of cooking utensils. There is also a **parlor** on the first floor with a mother's rocker. The brick, Federal-style tavern was built in 1834 by Judge Joseph Huston to accommodate travelers heading west. In 1840, Huston added the store on the first floor. The restored **Huston Store**, shown on the tour along with the second floor, is filled with nineteenth-century goods. Upstairs are **travelers' rooms** with straw mattresses and linsey-woolsey coverlets, and family bedrooms. Both **parents' and children's rooms** are furnished with mid-nineteenth-century four-poster beds, secretaries, chests, and wardrobes. A **ballroom** on the second floor was used for large gatherings such as town meetings.

Famous American portrait, genre, and landscape painter **George Caleb Bingham** built a brick **Federal-style house** in Arrow Rock in 1837, where he lived intermittently until 1845. The house had only two rooms, a parlor and a bedroom, with a separate kitchen in back. Bingham spent most of his life in Missouri and produced portraits of many people in the counties surrounding Arrow Rock. He also sketched scenes of frontier life, political gatherings and the Missouri River. Bingham's easel is displayed in the house, and his paintings can be seen at several locations in Arrow Rock.

Both the **gun shop and home of gunsmith John P. Sites, Jr.**, have been restored. Sites was a Virginian whose family moved to Missouri when he was thirteen years old. He worked as an apprentice in his father's gunsmith shop in Boonville. In 1844, Sites and his wife moved to Arrow Rock, where he opened the gunsmith shop he was to operate for almost sixty years. The busy gunsmith's customers came from the Santa Fe Trail wagon trains. Sites's business included making and repairing rifles and pistols, as well as selling powder, lead, buckshot. and percussion caps. The shop is a simple, two-story brick building with the gun shop on the first floor. The narrow shop displays original equipment with which Sites made rifle barrels and stocks. Sites's guns, most of which ended up in the West, are rare and highly prized. In the shop are three Sites rifles, one pistol, and one anti-thief gun, as well as a collection of antique firearms.

The Sites moved into a brick Victorian cottage next to the shop in 1866. On the first floor are a wallpapered parlor with a piano and an 1886 music box, a dining room, and a kitchen with a cast-iron stove and a pie safe.

The **Sappington Memorial Building** is a museum dedicated to the career of Dr. John Sappington, whose most notable achievement was discovering that quinine was an effective cure for malaria. Malaria, with its chills and fever, was prevalent in the river-bottom lands and swamps of the Missouri frontier. Sappington, who lived from 1776 to 1856, and his sons began manufacturing quinine pills in the early 1830s. Salesmen on horseback sold the pills throughout the midwest. In 1844, Sappington published the *Theory and Treatment of Fever*. Exhibits in the Memorial Building relate to malaria and Sappington's life.

The small **court house** is a log structure with walnut siding built in the 1830s and used as the Saline County Courthouse from 1839 to 1840. One of George Caleb Bingham's best-known paintings, *County Elections*, has this courthouse as its setting.

The **Hall House** is a four-room house built in 1846 by Matthew Hall for his family of five children. Also on the tour are the **I.O.O.F. Hall**, which has print-shop equipment in it, and the 1872 **Christian Church**. The **doctors' museum** contains equipment typical of an 1830s medical office including a wheel chair, a dental chair, and casts.

The **Arrow Rock Lyceum**, the state's oldest professional regional theater, is housed in the 1872 Baptist Church. Plays are presented throughout the summer.

## FESTIVALS/CRAFTS

On summer weekends in Arrow Rock, **craftspeople** demonstrate broom-making, chair caning, wheat weaving, stained-glass making, spinning and dyeing, herb gardening, candle-making, woodworking, and weaving.

The **Art and Antique Fair** is held the third weekend of May. The **Crafts Festival**—featuring quilting, gunsmithing, basket weaving, and chair caning—is held the second weekend of October.

# MARK TWAIN BOYHOOD HOME AND MUSEUM

Restored mid-nineteenth-century childhood home
of author Samuel Clemens; NR, NHL.

**Address:** 208 Hill Street, Hannibal MO 63401
**Telephone:** (314) 221-9010
**Location:** In northeast Missouri, on the Mississippi River, which divides
Missouri and Illinois, about 90 miles north of St. Louis.
**Open:** Memorial Day through Labor Day, 8:00 A.M.–6:00 p.m. daily. Sep-
tember, October, April, and May, 8:00 A.M.–5:00 p.m. daily. Novem-
ber, December, and March, 9:00 A.M.–4:00 p.m. daily. January and
February, 10:00 A.M.–4:00 p.m. daily. Closed Thanksgiving, Christ-
mas, and New Year's Days.
**Admission:** Adults $4, children ages 6–12 $2.
**Restaurants:** In Hannibal.
**Shops:** Museum shop in Mark Twain Museum.
**Facilities:** Visitor center with audiovisual program; partially handicapped
accessible.

## WHERE TO STAY

**Inns/Bed & Breakfasts:** Fifth Street Mansion, 213 South Fifth St., Hannibal MO 63401, (314) 221-0445, 1-800-874-5661. Queen Anne's
Grace, 313 North Fifth St., Hannibal MO 63401, (314) 248-0756.
Garth Woodside Mansion, Rt. 1, Hannibal MO 63401, (314) 221-
2789. Riverfront Inn, 111 Bird St., Hannibal MO 63401, (314) 221-
6662, 1-800-882-4890.
**Motels/Hotels:** Holiday Inn, 4141 Market St., Hannibal MO 63401, (314)
221-6610, FAX: (314) 221-3840. Hannibal House Motor Inn, 3603
McMasters Ave., Hannibal MO 63401, (314) 221-7950. Best Western Hotel Clemens, 401 North Third St., Hannibal MO 63401,
(314) 248-1150.
**Camping:** Bayview Campers Park, PO Box 22, Hannibal MO 63401, (314)
221-6589, 1-800-729-6580. Injun Joe Campground, Rt. 3, New Lon-

**Mark Twain Boyhood Home and Museum, Hannibal, Missouri**
The Mark Twain boyhood home is a white frame two-story house in Hannibal, Missouri, a Mississippi River Town. Samuel Clemens—author of *The Adventures of Tom Sawyer* and *The Adventures of Huckleberry Finn* under the pseudonym of Mark Twain—spent his youth here. Also pictured is the fence that Tom Sawyer's story made famous and a bridge over the nearby Mississippi.

gon MO 63459, (314) 985-3581, (314) 985-9491. Mark Twain Cave Park, PO Box 913, Hannibal MO 63401, (314) 221-1656, 1-800-527-0304.

## OVERVIEW

Hannibal, Missouri; the Mississippi River; and Tom Sawyer, Huck Finn, and Becky Thatcher are all inexorably linked—thanks to the classic works of Mark Twain. Hannibal, Missouri, has become a place of pilgrimage for millions of Twain's readers who want to visit the river town where Huck, Tom, and Becky shared their adventures. Hannibal is no longer the sleepy river town described by Twain, but some of that atmosphere has been recaptured due to the careful restoration of buildings that are represented in the stories.

Under the pseudonym Mark Twain, Samuel Clemens wrote popular semi-autobiographical novels about his carefree life as a youngster in Hannibal, Missouri, a small town on the Mississippi River. In Hannibal, only a block from the Mississippi, are the restored frame house in which he grew up, complete with whitewashed fence; his father's law office; the Pilaster House/Grant's Drug Store, where the Clemens family lived briefly; and the Mark Twain Museum and Museum Annex.

## HISTORY

Samuel Langhorne Clemens was born November 30, 1835, in Florida, Missouri. He was the sixth child and fourth son of John Marshall Clemens and Jane Lampton Clemens. In 1839, John and Jane Clemens and their five surviving children moved thirty-five miles east to Hannibal, the town on the Mississippi River where Samuel lived from the age of four to seventeen.

In 1835, Hannibal was a small pioneer village with fewer than 100 residents. Five years later, the population of the Mississippi River town reached over 1,000. In the era before the railroad, Hannibal was a growing port city with steamboats arriving at the city dock to unload cargo and pick up freight for St. Louis and then New Orleans. These steamboats provided a great deal of excitement for town residents, but most especially, for the children. Showboats brought music, plays, dancing, minstrel shows, and vaudeville to Hannibal. The navigation season was usually from March through November. During the winter months, people would ice skate on the frozen river; horses and buggies could be driven across the river to Illinois.

Judge John Marshall Clemens, Samuel's father, was a lawyer who had been admitted to the bar prior to coming to Hannibal and had been named judge in the Monroe County Court while living in Florida, Missouri. He built a modest two-story frame house at 206 Hill Street for his family in 1844 when Samuel was about nine years old. As a small child, Samuel had been in poor health and was kept indoors under the caring eye of his mother. At nine, he appeared to recover completely. He then was free to play outdoors with the other children in Hannibal who swam in the swimming hole, explored caves, climbed hills, hung around the city dock when a steamboat docked, and got into mischief. Samuel Clemens attended a private or "select" school which charged $.25 per week for each student.

In 1847, when Samuel was twelve, his father died. Shortly before his death, the Clemens family had been forced to move across the street to Pilaster House above Grant's Drug Store because a friend had defaulted on a loan that Judge Clemens had guaranteed with his home. After her husband's death, Mrs. Clemens was able to recoup financially and resume residence in the family home.

At age thirteen, Clemens left school and was apprenticed to Joseph Ament to learn the printing trade. Two years later, he began working for his brother Orion as a printer and editorial assistant. Doing stories for Orion's newspaper, Samuel Clemens found he enjoyed writing. In 1853, at age seventeen, Samuel left Hannibal to become a journeyman printer in St. Louis. That year, his brother Orion moved his printing business to Iowa and took his mother and brother with him. This ended the Clemens family's residence in Hannibal, Missouri.

Still drawn by the fascination of the Mississippi River, Clemens apprenticed himself to a river pilot and was himself licensed in that capacity in 1858. He remained on the river until the start of the Civil War in 1861 disrupted commercial river traffic. Clemens's pen name, "Mark Twain," is a river term which means two fathoms or twelve feet when the depth of water for a boat is being sounded. "Mark twain" means that it is safe to navigate.

Samuel Clemens worked as a newspaper reporter for a variety of newspapers both in the west and the east. In 1870, he married Olivia Langdon, and they had four children, one of whom died in infancy and two who died in their twenties. Their daughter, Clara Clemens, who lived to the age of 88, had one daughter, Clemens's only grandchild. Because she died without having children, there are no direct descendants of Samuel Clemens.

Eventually, Clemens started traveling, lecturing, and writing books. *The Innocents Abroad* was published in 1869, *The Adventures of Tom Sawyer* was published in 1876, and *The Adventures of Huckleberry Finn* in 1885. Well-known and loved as a humorist and local-colorist, Clemens wrote twenty-eight books, in addition to publishing short stories, letters, and sketches. He died in 1910.

Characters in the Tom Sawyer and Huck Finn books were based on childhood friends or adults Clemens knew in Hannibal. Clemens's mother was the model for Aunt Polly, and the author used himself as the model for Tom Sawyer. Becky Thatcher was based on Anna Laura Hawkins, who lived across the street, and Huckleberry Finn was based on Tom Blankenship, who lived half a block from Samuel. Many of the children's escapades that are described by Twain actually happened. Settings in the books are in or near Hannibal.

The Mark Twain Boyhood Home is a white frame two-story house at 206 Hill Street. As originally constructed, it had four rooms upstairs and three down. After the Clemens family left Hannibal, it became a rental property. Rooms on the back of the house were removed in the 1880s. The dilapidated house was threatened with demolition in 1911 but was saved by George Mahan, who renovated the building and then gave it to the city of Hannibal. Opened to the public in 1937, Twain's boyhood home was toured by more than six million people between that year and 1984. This traffic caused so great a degree of damage to the house that, in 1985, a structural engineer declared it unsafe for visitors.

In 1991, a major restoration of the Twain boyhood home was undertaken, based on archeological research, paint analysis, and dating of wood samples. The foundation, which had been inadequate when built, was improved, and back rooms that had been torn off were rebuilt. Shutters were removed, and windows were replaced with hand-blown glass ones, like those originally there. The house is now restored to its appearance when Samuel Clemens and his family lived there.

## SITE DESCRIPTION

Red-brick streets and nineteenth-century buildings in **Hannibal's historic area** draw one back to the era of Samuel Clemens's carefree childhood. Tours begin at the **Museum Annex**, where an audiovisual presentation focuses on life in Hannibal in the 1840s and 1850s.

The **Mark Twain Boyhood Home** is a two-story, plain white frame house with the legendary whitewashed fence next to it. There are three rooms downstairs and four upstairs. Although most furnishings in the house did not belong to the Clemens family, they are of that period and are similar to those that the family owned.

On the first floor are a parlor, dining room and kitchen. The **parlor** and **dining room** are painted a deep orange, their original color according to an analysis of paint chips and plaster. The **kitchen**, reconstructed in 1991, has a brick fireplace, wood floors, a wooden table and chairs, and a rocking chair.

The four upstairs rooms are the **parents' front bedroom** with a sewing table in front of the window, the **middle bedroom** used by Samuel's sister, the boys' room in the back, and a small storage room. The **boys' rear bedroom**, which Samuel shared with his younger brother Henry, had, like the kitchen, been torn off the house and was reconstructed during the 1991 restoration. The simply furnished room has whitewashed walls, a rag rug on a wood floor, a trundle bed, a dresser, and a chair. Like Tom Sawyer,

Samuel had a spy glass for checking out town activities; it and his piggy bank are on his bed.

The **Mark Twain Museum** is a stone building constructed in the mid 1930s by the Federal Works Progress Administration. Items in the museum include the desk on which *The Adventures of Tom Sawyer* was written, a pilot wheel from a riverboat, one of the white suits in which Twain was always pictured in later years, several busts of Twain, first editions of his books, and copies of *Tom Sawyer* and *Huck Finn* in more than fifty languages. Norman Rockwell paintings used for editions of *Tom Sawyer* and *Huckleberry Finn* are displayed.

Recently, restoration began on the **Sonnenburg Building** on Main Street. This two-story nineteenth-century commercial building will serve as a new Mark Twain Museum.

**Grant's Drug Store** is on the first floor of the 1839 Greek Revival-style **Pilaster House**, across the street from the Clemens home. The Clemens family was given refuge upstairs by the Grants in 1846, when serious financial problems caused them to lose their house. In 1847, Judge John Clemens died here in an upstairs bedroom.

The **John M. Clemens Law Office**, next to Pilaster House, was originally located at 112 Bird Street. It was nearing collapse before it was rescued and moved to 205 Hill Street. It has been restored as it looked when Judge Clemens worked there.

Although not part of the restoration, the **home of Laura Hawkins**— on whom Becky Thatcher was modeled—is on Hill Street. A bookstore is on the first floor, and the upstairs rooms where Laura lived may be toured.

## FESTIVALS/CRAFTS

The **Mississippi River Art Fair** is held in the historic district on Memorial Day weekend. **National Tom Sawyer Days** on the 4th of July weekend feature a fence-painting contest and a frog-jumping competition. The **Autumn Historic Folklife Festival**, held the third weekend of October, features artisans demonstrating the crafts of the mid-1800s, musicians playing traditional music, and food cooked over wood fires.

Cruise along the Mississippi River on an old fashioned steamboat. The *Mark Twain* offers one-hour cruises and dinner cruises daily from May through October. (314) 221-3222, 1-800-621-2322. Admission is charged.

# HISTORIC STE. GENEVIEVE

Eighteenth-century French community;
NR, NHL, HABS.

**Address:** Tourist Information Office, 66 South Main St., Ste. Genevieve
MO 63670
**Telephone:** (314) 883-7097
**Location:** Ste. Genevieve is in east central Missouri, near the Mississippi
River, 60 miles south of St. Louis, 4 miles east of I-55.
**Open:** Ste. Genevieve Museum: April–November, 9:00–11:00 A.M. and
12:00 noon–4:00 p.m. daily; November–April, 12:00 noon–4:00
p.m. daily. Guibourd-Valle House: April–October 10:00 A.M.–5:00
p.m. daily; November–March, 10:00 A.M.–4:00 p.m. Thursday–
Monday. Felix Valle State Historic Site: 10:00 A.M.–4:00 p.m.
Monday–Saturday; 12:00 noon–5:00 p.m. Sunday. Bolduc House
and Bolduc-Le Meilleur House: April–November, 10 A.M.–4:00 p.m.
Monday–Saturday, 11:00 A.M.–5:00 p.m. Sunday.
**Admission:** Ste. Genevieve Museum: adults $1.25, children $.50. Guibourd Valle House, Felix Valle SHS, and Bolduc House: adults $2,
children ages 6–12 $1. Bolduc Le Meilleur House: adults $.50, chil-
dren ages 6–12 $.25
**Restaurants:** In town: Hotel Ste. Genevieve, Main and Merchant Sts.;
Lucretia's Restaurant, 242 Merchant St.; Inn Ste. Gemme Beauvais,
78 North Main St.; Old Brick House Restaurant, Third and Market
Sts.; Anvil Restaurant, 46 South Third St.; Sirrosm, 261 Merchant
St.
**Shops:** Gift shop in the Tourist Information Office, many antique and
craft shops in town.
**Facilities:** Tourist Information Center, museum, French colonial museum
houses, historic district.

## WHERE TO STAY

**Inns/Bed & Breakfasts:** Main Street Inn, 221 North Main St., Ste.
Genevieve MO 63670, (314) 883-9199. Southern Hotel, 146 South
Third St., Ste. Genevieve MO 63670, (314) 883-3493. Inn Ste.
Gemme Beauvais, 78 North Main St., Ste. Genevieve MO 63670,

(314) 883-5744. Hotel Ste. Genevieve, Main and Merchant Sts., Ste. Genevieve MO 63670, (314) 883-3562. The Creole House, 339 St. Mary's Rd., Ste. Genevieve MO 63670, 1-800-275-6041, (314) 883-7171. Belle Rive, 406 North Third St., Ste. Genevieve MO 63670, (314) 883-3830. Steiger Haus, 1021 Market St., Ste. Genevieve MO 63670, (314) 883-5881. Pecan Corner, 406 Jefferson St., Ste. Genevieve MO 63670, (314) 883-9398.

**Motels/Hotels:** Econolodge, I-55 Ozora exit, Ste. Genevieve MO 63670, (314) 543-2272. Triangle Inn, Hwy. 61, Ste. Genevieve MO 63670, (314) 883-7191.

**Camping:** River's Edge RV Park, North Main St., Ste. Genevieve MO 63670, (314) 883-5881. Hawn State Park, Hwy. 144, Weingarten MO 63670, (314) 883-3603. Saint Francois State Park, Bonne Terre MO 63628, (314) 358-2173. Mark Twain National Forest, Potosi Ranger District, Bonne Terre MO 63628, (314) 325-4233. Washington State Park, DeSoto MO 63020, (314) 586-2995.

## OVERVIEW

Mississippi River floods during the summer of 1993 did millions of dollars in damage to property in Iowa, Illinois, and Missouri. In the endangered areas in Illinois and Missouri were the rare remnants of historic French colonial settlements. Although France was one of the European colonial powers in North America, few traces of French colonies outside of those in Louisiana remain.

Fortunately, the historic early-eighteenth-century town of Ste. Genevieve survived the floods, though it did suffer some damage. Prized for its French Colonial architecture, the living community of under 5,000 contains several restored museum houses as well as a museum. This Missouri hamlet exudes the charm of a small European village. Eighteenth-century French wooden structures stand beside early-nineteenth-century German stone buildings. Thirty-one privately owned structures built in the 1700s and another fifty built before 1825 contribute to a strong sense of the past.

## HISTORY

In the Mississippi River Valley, a pre-Columbian society erected a 6-square-mile city with a population of 40,000. This location at the hub of inland rivers allowed community members to control an enormous trade network. The society flourished from approximately 700 to 1300 A.D. It eventually vanished after erecting an estimated 120 large mysterious earthen mounds, over 60 of which still exist. Although some mounds were burial sites, most of them were ceremonial.

Centuries later, when Europeans arrived, the Mississippi River Valley was populated by American Indian tribes. The French explorers Jacques Marquette and Louis Joliet traveled on inland rivers during an expedition commissioned by Governor Frontenac of New France (Canada) in 1673. In succeeding years, settlers from Canada, including missionary priests and fur traders, followed. French colonies in Illinois Country were established before 1700 and in the early 1700s along a fifty mile strip of land on the east side of the Mississippi River at Cahokia, Kaskaskia, Fort de Chartres, Prairie du Rocher, and St. Phillippe.

Founded in approximately 1735, Le Vieux Village de Ste. Genevieve was an offshoot of these older French communities on the eastern side of the Mississippi. The town's original residents were either farmers or fur and lead traders who traveled by boat to the markets in New Orleans. Francois Phillipe Renault, a French agent of the Company of the West who was based near Fort Chartres, mined lead as early as 1720 on the west side of the Mississippi River. By 1725, he was bringing smelted lead for shipment down river from Ste. Genevieve.

Ste. Genevieve claims to be the first permanent European settlement west of the Mississippi River in Illinois Country, a division of the Louisiana Territory which extended north to Wisconsin, east to Vincennes, and west to the Missouri River. When the French settled Ste. Genevieve, the area was inhabited by the Peoria Indians.

France surrendered final control of its North American empire after its defeat in the French and Indian Wars in 1763. According to the terms of the Treaty of Paris, Canada and the Illinois Country east of the Mississippi River were ceded to Great Britain, while the Illinois Country west of the Mississippi went to Spain. To escape British occupation, a number of French people from eastern Illinois fled across the river to Ste. Genevieve, where they were welcomed by Spanish colonial authorities.

Originally, Le Vieux Village de Ste. Genevieve was situated on the Mississippi floodplain several miles below its present site. Serious flooding in the 1780s forced the abandonment of the old town. A new town was built on higher ground between two branches of the Gabouri Creek. The town plan included a town square and church at the center and a neat grid plan which conformed to Spanish regulations for the layout of colonial towns.

Ste. Genevieve prospered as a center for agriculture, fur trading, and salt processing on Saline Creek, and as a shipping point for the lead mines in the Ozark hills. Spanish governance had little impact on the French settlement, which kept its traditional language and customs. The town became American territory as a result of the Louisiana Purchase in 1803. American commerce and trade brought rapid change to the town. Near the end of the eighteenth century, English-speaking settlers began moving into the community. In the 1830s, German immigrants settled near Ste. Genevieve, moving into the town after the Civil War.

More recently, the small country town was bypassed by major highways and railroad lines. It was not an important port like neighboring French colonial St. Louis. Therefore, Ste. Genevieve's older buildings were not razed to make way for the kind of expansion and progress that occurred in St. Louis, which now has no surviving French Colonial buildings. Preservation occurs, it seems, only when progress doesn't. In 1935, the Department of the Interior recognized the importance of Ste. Genevieve in the Historic American Building Survey, and, in 1976, the National Register designated its downtown as a Historic District.

## SITE DESCRIPTION

Soak up the atmosphere on a leisurely stroll through this European-style village. Information about this repository of rare French Colonial architecture can be found at the **Great River Road Interpretive Center**, 66 South Main St., which has an orientation movie, gift shop, and exhibits on local history. Maps for self-guided tours of Ste. Genevieve can be obtained here.

The **Ste. Genevieve Museum**, at Merchant St. and Dubourg Square, exhibits rare documents including Spanish land grants, artifacts from the Saline Creek Salt Works, and a scale model of the Mississippi River Railroad transfer boat.

The French architectural style in the Mississippi Valley featured walls of vertical logs either set in the ground (*poteaux en terre*) or set into a sill on a stone foundation (*poteaux sur sole*), and hewn wood truss systems supporting the steeply pitched roofs that extend beyond the walls to form galleries on two to four sides.

An example of *poteaux sur sole* (posts on a sill) is the restored **Bolduc House**, a large rectangular structure consisting of two large rooms separated by a central hall, though the building was built as a one-room house in 1770. It is the only house known to have been moved from Le Vieux Village to the new town after the flood of 1784. Simply furnished rooms have wide plank wooden floors and white stucco walls. French Canadian furnishings include an armoire damaged by the flood, a cherry-wood side board, a reading chair, a hutch table with a removable top, and a fiddle baby cradle. A **separate stone kitchen and bakehouse** are at the rear of the house because of the danger of fire. It is surrounded by a stockade fence.

The **Bolduc-Le Meilleur House** was built in 1820 by a grandson-in-law of Louis Bolduc. Architecturally, it combines French and American styles. It has front and back galleries. Nineteenth-century furnishings include a Federal mirror, a horsehair couch, and hitchcock chairs.

The **Guibourd Valle House** (1784), built by Jacques Jean Rene Guibourd, is noted for its French Colonial architectural style. It is an example of *poteaux-sur-sole* vertical log construction. Its attic contains great Norman trusses of hand-hewn oak beams secured by wooden pegs. Nine-light casement windows are original. The house was restored by Jules Felix Valle, a great-great-grandson of Jean Baptiste Valle. Many of the French-Canadian furnishings are family heirlooms. An attractive **flower garden** enhances the house.

The **Felix Valle House State Historic Site**, Merchant and Second Streets, was built in 1818 by Jacob Philipson, a Philadelphia merchant. The stone structure was designed as a Federal-style store and residence. In 1824, the house was sold to Jean Baptiste Valle, the village's last civil commandant. Valle's son, Felix, lived in the house until his death in 1877. The Valle House has been restored to the early 1800s, the period after the Louisiana Purchase by the United States. In the commercial side of the house was the Menard and Valle store; goods were obtained through trading with Native Americans from Missouri and Arkansas. Shelves of the store are stocked with merchandise of the period. In the house, the floors, windows, and parlor fireplace are original. Furnishings are American Empire.

The **Amoureau, Beauvais,** and **Bequette-Ribeau Houses,** which were probably built in 1770 as farmhouses away from the village, were not affected by the flood. They are the only three examples of the French Colonial style of architecture called *poteaux en terre* (posts in the ground). They have vertical logs cut from red cedar, wood that has withstood insects and rot for over two centuries. These houses may be viewed from the exterior.

Visit **Ste. Genevieve's Catholic Church**, which is an 1876 brick Gothic Revival building. The first Catholic church, a *poteaux-en-terre* structure built in the old town in 1794, was moved to the new town and enlarged. In 1830, a stone church was built over the foundation of the log church, and the present brick church was built over the foundation of the stone church.

## Festivals/Crafts

**Jour de Fete**, held the second weekend in August, celebrates the town's French and German heritage. Weekend activities include craft demonstrations, an arts and crafts fair, music, and dancing.

## Side Trips

To extend your French colonial tour: cross the Mississippi River into Illinois and visit these sites.

**Fort de Chartres State Historic Site** is the location of a stone fort built in the 1750s by the French colonial administration. Abandoned in 1771, the fort has been partially reconstructed. Also at the site are the archaeological remains of a earlier wooden French fort. A very popular annual **Rendezvous** is held the first weekend in June. Open 9:00 A.M.–5:00 p.m. daily. Rt. 2, Prairie du Rocher IL 62277. (618) 284-7230.

The **Pierre Menard Home** was constructed for Illinois's first lieutenant governor, Pierre Menard. The 1802 French Colonial mansion has been restored and furnished with many items that belonged to the Menard family. Open 9:00 A.M.–5:00 p.m. daily. Rt. 1, Box 58, Ellis Grove IL 62241. (618) 859-3031.

**Cahokia Courthouse**, constructed in 1737, was built as a residence using the *poteaux-sur-sole* style. Purchased by the Common Pleas Court in 1793, the building was the center for political and judicial activity in the Northwest Territory until 1814. Open 9:00 A.M.–5:00 p.m. daily. First and Elm Sts., Cahokia IL 62206. (618) 332-1782.

Archaeological remains and earthworks of the French colonial **Fort Kaskaskia**, built in 1760, are all that remain at **Fort Kaskaskia State Park**. Open 6:00 A.M.–10 p.m. daily. Rt. 1, Box 63, Ellis Grove IL 62241. (618) 859-3741.

**Cahokia Mounds**, where sixty earthen mounds built by a pre-Columbian society are preserved, has been designated a World Heritage Site. These large ceremonial mounds were used to support temples and residences for the elite. **Monks Mound** is the largest prehistoric mound north of Mexico. Archaeological excavations have partially uncovered remains of four circular sun calendars constructed about 1000 A.D. Museum and Interpretive Center. In Collinsville, across the river from St. Louis, Missouri. Open 9:00 A.M.–5:00 p.m. daily. PO Box 681, Collinsville IL 62234. (618) 346-5160.

# NORTH CAROLINA

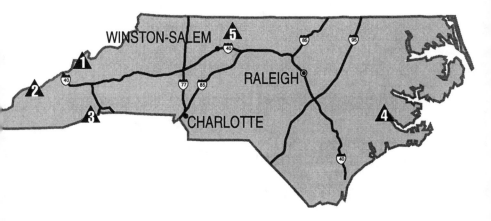

1. Asheville: Biltmore Estate
2. Cherokee: Oconaluftee Indian Village
3. Flat Rock: Carl Sandburg Home National Historic Site
4. New Bern: Tryon Palace Historic Sites and Gardens
5. Winston-Salem: Old Salem

# BILTMORE ESTATE

### 250-room 1895 French Renaissance-style chateau on an 8,000-acre estate, built by George Vanderbilt; NR, NHL.

**Address:** One North Pack Square, Asheville NC 28801

**Telephone:** 1-800-543-2961

**Location:** Asheville is near the Great Smoky Mountains of western North Carolina; Biltmore Estate is on US 25, off I-40, exit 50 or 50B, in Asheville.

**Open:** 9:00 A.M.–5:00 P.M. daily; closed Thanksgiving, Christmas, and New Years Days.

**Admission:** House tour: adults $24.95, students ages 10–15 $18.75.

**Restaurants:** Deerpark Restaurant, Stable Café, Winery Café.

**Shops:** Gatehouse Gift Shop, Winery Gift Shop, Carriage House Gift Shop, The Bookbinder, The Confectionery, The Toymaker.

**Facilities:** Extensive gardens on 8,000-acre estate, winery, guided tours, audio cassettes, special events.

## WHERE TO STAY

**Inns/Bed & Breakfasts:** Grove Park Inn and Country Club, 290 Macon Ave., Asheville NC 28804, (704) 252-2711.

**Motels/Hotels:** Haywood Park Hotel, 1 Battery Park Ave., Asheville NC 28801, (704) 252-2522. Asheville Airport Holiday Inn, I-26 and Airport Rd., Asheville NC 28732, (704) 684-1213. Best Western of Asheville, 501 Tunnel Rd., Asheville NC 28805, (704) 298-5562. Forest Manor Motor Lodge, 866 Hendersonville Rd., Asheville NC 28803, (704) 274-3531. Great Smokies Hilton, 1 Hilton Dr., Asheville NC 28806, (704) 254-3211.

**Camping:** Pisgah National Forest: Lake Powhatan Recreation Area or North Mills River Recreation Area, (704) 877-3265. Bear Creek RV Park and Campground, 81 South Bear Creek Rd., Asheville NC 28806, (704) 253-0798.

## OVERVIEW

The largest house in the country and surely one of the most opulent, the Biltmore House is an American palace built by a grandson of wealthy industrialist Commodore Cornelius Vanderbilt. Vanderbilt represents the nation's equivalent of royalty. In 1895, George W. Vanderbilt built a 250-room mansion on a country estate which grew to 125,000 acres in the scenic mountains of North Carolina. No expense was spared in building, decorating, or landscaping the property named Biltmore.

The 100-year-old French Renaissance-style chateau designed by Richard Morris Hunt remains in the family. The current owner is William Amherst Vanderbilt Cecil, a grandson of George W. Vanderbilt, who is responsible for its outstanding state of preservation. The mansion is filled with European paintings, wall hangings and tapestries, and exceptional antique furnishings. The formal gardens and grounds are the design of Frederick Law Olmsted, America's premiere landscape architect. Allow all day to visit the Biltmore House.

## HISTORY

Like many others, George Washington Vanderbilt (1862–1914) was attracted to Asheville for its scenic location near western North Carolina's Great Smoky and Blue Ridge Mountains. When he was visiting Asheville in 1887, George Vanderbilt, grandson of Commodore Cornelius Vanderbilt, decided to build a European-style country estate in the area.

The Vanderbilts were one of America's wealthiest families. Cornelius Vanderbilt, already a multimillionaire when he entered the railroad business, built a massive family fortune. In 1867, Vanderbilt took control of the New York Central Railroad. He expanded the railroad until it operated over 45,000 miles of tracks. Like other industrialists of the post-Civil War era, Vanderbilt left a legacy that allowed his family to enjoy the luxuries of the "Gilded Age" long after his death in 1877.

In 1888, George Vanderbilt, determined to realize his dream of a North Carolina estate, began purchasing land above the French Broad River. By the turn of the century, he owned 125,000 acres. Vanderbilt employed Richard Morris Hunt, the noted architect, to design a mansion that was to be patterned after the Renaissance-style chateaux found in France's Loire Valley. Hunt, who had designed homes for America's rich and famous, was familiar with the opulent tastes of the wealthy "captains of industry." Although built in the Renaissance style, Vanderbilt's house was designed to incorporate new technological innovations such as central heating, mechanical refrigeration, electric lights, and electric appliances.

Construction began in 1890. It would take five years for the assembled army of architects, engineers, stonecutters, masons, wood-workers, engineers, carpenters, decorators, and craftsmen to construct Biltmore

House. Hunt made a worldwide search for the finest building materials. Tons of marble were imported from Italy. Train-loads of pale gray limestone for the exterior were brought from Indiana. Materials were transported by a temporary railroad from Biltmore Village to the construction site. Brick and tile kilns and a woodworking mill were erected on the grounds.

Completed in 1895, Biltmore House, a giant 175,000-square-foot mansion of 250 rooms, was the largest private home in the United States—a distinction it still enjoys. The name "Biltmore" combines "Bildt," the name of the Dutch village where the Vanderbilts originated, and the Old English term *more*, meaning "rolling hills."

To furnish his mansion, Vanderbilt and Hunt traveled throughout Europe, searching for antiques, art treasures, and other artifacts. Vanderbilt, an eclectic collector, did not furnish the house in any one style. Among his acquisitions were tapestries that once belonged to France's Cardinal Richelieu and a gaming table and set of ivory chessmen once owned by Napoleon Bonaparte.

The period from 1895 when the house was finished until George Vanderbilt's death in 1914 has been called by various names—the "late Victorian-Edwardian Era," the "Era of Conspicuous Consumption," or in Edith Wharton's words, "The Age of Innocence." It was an era marked by a great economic chasm between America's wealthiest families and its mass of poor, many of whom were immigrants. For the Vanderbilts and their guests at Biltmore House, the age represented an opulent and elegant life-style, marked by lavish entertaining. The Vanderbilts' guests, many of whom were the social elite of New York City, would travel by train to the Carolina mountains to enjoy the hospitality of Biltmore. During the Christmas and New Year's holidays, they enjoyed riding, hunting, fox chasing, and quail shooting.

Biltmore Estate was also the workplace of a staff of eighty domestic servants. In this "Upstairs-Downstairs" society, the wealthy enjoyed a luxurious life and the servants worked in the estate's kitchens, laundries, and pantries to make that life-style possible.

The Vanderbilt estate, which originally encompassed 125,000 acres, involved some individuals who were pioneers in their field. Among them were the well-known landscape architect Frederick Law Olmsted and the innovative conservationist and forester Gifford Pinchot. Olmsted, who designed New York's Central Park, was employed to design Biltmore Estate's gardens. Pinchot, who would be Theodore Roosevelt's chief of forestry, helped to shape the timberland surrounding the estate.

George Vanderbilt died in 1914 at age fifty-two. His only child, Cornelia, inherited the house, while much of his forested land was sold to the government and is now part of Pisgah National Forest. In 1930, certain sections of the house were opened to the public. Cornelia's son, William Amherst Vanderbilt Cecil, assumed management of the estate in 1960. Today, it is a self-supporting, private historic site whose house and 8,000 acres can be enjoyed by the public.

## SITE DESCRIPTION

Visitors enter Biltmore Estate through the **lodge gate**, an arch of stucco, bricks, and tiles made on the estate. **Biltmore House** is reached by a three-mile road bordered by fast-flowing streams, wooded ravines, and fern-fringed pools. A tour of the house including the upstairs and downstairs is self-guided. Admission includes the **gardens** and the **winery**, where free wine tasting is offered. A separate **"Behind the Scenes" tour** is also available. Uniformed hosts provide directions and answer questions.

Tours begin at the central front entrance. The **entrance hall** on the main floor contains bronzes by Antoine Louis Bayre (1796–1875). The **Winter Garden**, a sunken marble conservatory which features a domed skylight supported by Gothic-style vaulting, displays flowers and plants from the estate's gardens and greenhouse. Its central fountain is the work of Karl Bitter, a Viennese sculptor.

The massive **billiard room**, part of the **bachelor's wing**, has oaken walls decorated with theatrical and sporting prints and hunting trophies. Its billiard tables were specially designed for the room. Concealed doors lead to smoking and gun rooms, seen at the end of the tour, where the gentlemen retired after dinner for cigars, brandy, and conversation.

The 3,000-square-foot **banquet hall**, with its 70-feet-high vaulted ceilings, is a 72-x-42-foot expanse. It is decorated with five large sixteenth-century Flemish tapestries that recount the story of Vulcan and Venus. Its dining table seats 64 persons. A central feature of the hall is the triple fireplace wall.

The **breakfast room** has walls of Spanish leather above red marble. The fireplace is framed with jasperware tiles made by the Josiah Wedgwood Company. The **morning salon** contains the small chess table and antique chess set that once belonged to Napoleon Bonaparte. The **music room** contains a large Albrecht Dürer engraving. By the fireplace is a rare set of white Meissen Apostles by sculptor Johann Joachim Kändler.

The **tapestry gallery** features three sixteenth-century Brussels tapestries depicting the "Triumph of Virtue over Vice." There are also Vanderbilt family portraits by John Singer Sargent. The two-story baroque-design **library** has a painted canvas ceiling attributed to Giovanni Antonio Pellegrini, which was moved from a Venetian palace. The carved walnut-paneled library houses about half of Mr. Vanderbilt's collection of over 20,000 books.

The **grand staircase** leads to the second floor. Next are the **Louis XVI bedroom**, and the **living hall** used for informal gatherings. **Mr. Vanderbilt's bedroom**, furnished in eighteenth- and nineteenth-century Mediterranean style, overlooks Mount Pisgah. Other rooms are the **oak sitting room** with Jacobean furnishings, **Mrs. Vanderbilt's room**, and a series of guest rooms.

Some **third-floor rooms** are open to the public. Among them are Mrs. Vanderbilt's **personal maid's quarters** and a **sitting room** for the upstairs servants. The third-floor **living hall** is also open, as are four more bedrooms on that floor.

The tour continues downstairs behind the Grand Staircase and through a corridor that leads to a variety of recreational areas available to the Vanderbilt's guests. The **Halloween Room** is so named because its walls were painted in 1926 by houseguests preparing for a Halloween dance. Next is the **bowling alley**, which was installed by Brunswick-Balke-Collendere Company in 1895. Bowling balls were made of wood. There is an indoor **swimming pool** along with individual **dressing rooms** and a **gymnasium** containing exercise machines, parallel bars, and other small equipment.

Life **downstairs** among the servants is shown in the house's service rooms. Provisions were stored in the **canning pantry, housekeeper's pantry**, and **vegetable pantry**. Nearby are the **servants' bedrooms**, simply decorated with iron beds, wash stands, and rocking chairs. Separate halls of bedrooms were provided for each sex and rank of servant, ranging from the senior staff—which included the chef, butler, housekeeper, personal valet, and lady's maid—to the more lowly servants such as the scullery maid, the footman, and the page.

The degree to which food preparation was specialized in the large mansion is shown by the variety of kitchens such as the **main kitchen**, the **rotisserie kitchen**, and the **pastry kitchen**. Electric and hand-operated dumbwaiters transported trays of prepared food from the **kitchen pantry** to the dining rooms upstairs. The large walk-in refrigerators, cooled by circulating ammonia gas, were innovations of the period.

The **servants' hall** is where the staff relaxed between chores. There are several staff **dining halls**.

The **laundry complex** is located at the foot and to the left of the stairwell. The largest room contains a barrel washer, a water extractor, tubs with wringers, and an ironing mangle. The **drying room** contains drying racks and coils.

The master plan for the estate grounds, developed by Frederick Law Olmsted, includes a number of gardens. The **shrub garden** has extensive plantings of Chinese holly, Japanese cut-lead maples, and native American dogwoods and azaleas. The **walled garden** features espaliered flowering fruit trees, perennial borders, and pattern beds of annuals. The **rose garden** contains 3,000 bushes of a wide range of varieties. In the **azalea garden** is one of the most complete collections of native American azaleas in the country. The **greenhouse** is used to grow tropical and subtropical plants.

The **Biltmore Estate Winery**, added in 1985, is located in the estate's old dairy. A self-guided tour and free wine tastings of Biltmore's award-winning European-style wines are available.

## FESTIVALS/CRAFTS

The **Festival of the Flowers** is held each spring, and **Christmas at Biltmore** and **candlelight tours** are featured in winter. Biltmore celebrates its centennial in 1995 with a variety of special activities.

## SIDE TRIPS

For fine native crafts, visit the **Folk Art Center** of the Southern Highland Handicraft Guild, Blue Ridge Pkwy. at Milepost 382, 5 miles north of US 70. (704) 298-7928. Open daily, 9:00 A.M.–5:00 P.M.

**Thomas Wolfe Memorial State Historic Site** is located at 48 Spruce St. in Asheville. The writer's boyhood home is open April–October, 9:00 A.M.–5:00 P.M. Monday–Saturday, and 1:00–5:00 P.M. Sunday; November–March, 10:00 A.M.–4:00 P.M. Tuesday–Saturday, and 1:00–4:00 P.M. Sunday. (704) 253-8304.

Of scenic and recreational interest are the **Great Smoky Mountains National Park** and the **Blue Ridge Parkway**.

# OCONALUFTEE INDIAN VILLAGE

### Re-creation of a 1750 Cherokee settlement.

**Address:** PO Box 398, US 441 North, Cherokee NC 28719
**Telephone:** (704) 497-2315, (704) 497-2111
**Location:** In southwestern North Carolina, on the Cherokee Indian Reservation, adjacent to Great Smoky Mountains National Park, off US 441 North.
**Open:** May 15–October 25, 9:00 A.M.–5:30 P.M. daily.
**Admission:** Adults $8, children ages 6–13 $4.
**Restaurants:** Snack bar.
**Shops:** Qualla Arts and Crafts Mutual is located nearby.
**Facilities:** Guided tours, craft demonstrations, arboretum, extensive gardens, nature trail.

## WHERE TO STAY

**Motels/Hotels:** Boundary Tree Cottages and Lodge, Cherokee NC 28719, (704) 497-2155. Pageant Hills Motel, PO Box 172, Cherokee NC 28719, (704) 497-5371, 1-800-255-5371. Best Western Great Smokies Inn, Box 1809, US 441 North at Acquoni Rd., Cherokee NC 28719, (704) 497-2020. Cool Waters, PO Box 950, US 19, Cherokee NC 28719, (704) 497-3855, FAX: (704) 497-3855. Craig's, PO Box 1047, US 19, Cherokee NC 28719, (704) 497-3821. Pioneer, PO Box 397, US 19, Cherokee NC 28719, (704) 497-2435.

**Camping:** Great Smoky Mountains National Park, Gatlinburg TN 37738, 1-800-365-CAMP. Riverside Campground, PO Box 58, Cherokee NC 28719, (704) 497-9311. Irene's Campground, Cherokee NC 28719, (704) 497-7245. KOA Campground, Cherokee NC 28719, (704) 497-9711.

## OVERVIEW

The focus of Oconaluftee Indian Village is Cherokee culture during the period of European colonization of North America. A re-creation of the Native American life-style in the Appalachian region around 1750, the village is not an original historic site. However, the Cherokee people occupied this region for centuries.

Cherokee and most other Native American tribes were continually pushed west by European pioneers who settled on land that had been occupied by these tribes for centuries. Most American Indian reservations are in the western half of the United States. The Cherokee also faced forced removal from their homeland in North Carolina to what was designated as Indian Territory in Oklahoma. Unable to combat the removal legally, thousands of Cherokee reluctantly walked 800 miles west in 1838. Those who refused to go hid in the mountains. Through a series of successful legal maneuvers, they were eventually recognized as citizens of North Carolina. Oconaluftee Indian Village is staffed by the Eastern Band of the Cherokee, descendants of those Cherokee who escaped removal to Indian Territory.

## HISTORY

Cherokee lived in the southern Appalachians—occupying land that would become North and South Carolina, Virginia, Tennessee, Georgia, and Alabama—for several centuries before the Spanish explorer Hernando de Soto sighted them in 1540. This prosperous, nonmigratory tribe was composed of hunters, fishers, traders, artists, and farmers who grew corn, beans, squash, melons, and tobacco. They were also warriors who defended their lands against encroachment by other Native American tribes and, by the late 1700s, white settlers. The Cherokee suffered many losses from these battles, but lost even more of their people to smallpox, introduced by whites.

In an attempt to prevent further war, the Cherokee tribe in 1820 established the Cherokee Nation, a republican form of government with a thirty-two member unicameral legislature. The nation was divided into eight districts that sent representatives to the Cherokee National Legislature at New Echota, Georgia. During this period, the Cherokee also became a literate people. Sequoyah, a native of Tennessee who was half white and half Cherokee, invented and developed a complete Cherokee alphabet called a "syllabary." After twelve years of work, Sequoyah isolated eighty-six Cherokee syllables and assigned a character to each one. This resulted in widespread literacy among the Cherokee. The Western and Eastern Bands of the Cherokee began to communicate with each other in writing. A national newspaper, the *Cherokee Phoenix*, with columns in English and Cherokee was published by the tribe at its capital of New Echota, Georgia.

**Oconaluftee Indian Village, Cherokee, North Carolina**
An artifact used by the Cherokee Indians in sacred ceremonies is displayed in
the Squareground, a small outdoor amphitheater. The Oconaluftee Indian
Village, a re-created Cherokee village dating to about 1750, is located in a
forested cove in the Great Smoky Mountains where Native Americans camped
thousands of years ago.

Photo by Patricia A. Gutek

As a result of Sequoyah's work, the Cherokee adopted a written constitution and code of law in 1828. This constitution, which declared the tribe a sovereign and independent nation, angered the people of Georgia, in whose state the Cherokee capital was located. Georgia opposed the notion of an independent nation within their state boundaries. Relations between the Cherokee and Georgians deteriorated further when the discovery of gold on the edge of Cherokee territory led to ten thousand people staking mining claims in Georgia. Dispossessed tribes had no legal recourse because Native Americans were not allowed to testify against white persons in Georgia's courts.

The developments in Georgia fueled the efforts of the federal government, under President Andrew Jackson, to have Native Americans removed from eastern lands and relocated in Indian Territory. Most of the Cherokee vigorously opposed removal, but Elias Boudinot and Major Ridge, two Cherokee who favored it, signed the Treaty of New Echota in December 1835. The terms of the treaty specified that in exchange for all Cherokee land east of the Mississippi, the tribe would receive millions of acres of land in Indian Territory which would not be under state or territorial jurisdiction, and five million dollars. Further, all Cherokee must emigrate beyond the Mississippi River within two years.

When the Cherokee who opposed removal did not leave voluntarily, General Winfield Scott and U.S. Army units were dispatched to force their removal. In 1838, Scott placed seventeen thousand Cherokee in hastily built stockades. After the first group left by boat, Cherokee chieftains asked to lead the remainder of their people overland. Under an agreement negotiated with the Cherokee chief, John Ross, General Scott permitted Cherokee leaders to take charge of the emigration, which began in October of 1838. Thirteen thousand Cherokee began an 800-mile overland march on the route that came to be called the "Trail of Tears." This grueling march, which lasted all winter and ended in Oklahoma in March 1839, resulted in the deaths of four thousand Cherokee.

Approximately 1,100 North Carolina Cherokee avoided removal by hiding out in the Smoky Mountains. Aided by Colonel William Holland Thomas, a white trader who became their legal advisor, the Cherokee tried to take advantage of a treaty provision that allowed them to stay in their home state if they became citizens. In 1866, North Carolina finally recognized the Cherokee's right to permanent residency. Thomas had purchased 50,000 acres for the Cherokee in his name because it was illegal for the Native Americans to own land. Title reverted to the Native Americans when they paid Thomas.

In 1876, the Cherokee, having acquired even more land, were granted final title to the 65,000-acre Qualla Boundary. In 1889, the tribe incorporated as the Eastern Band of Cherokee Indians. They live in western North Carolina in the communally held Qualla Boundary, which is a tribal-owned preserve, not a reservation held in trust by the federal government. The Cherokee language is now dying out, due in part to intermarriage. It is taught in the Cherokee schools as a foreign language.

In 1952, the Cherokee Historical Association, a nonprofit organization, was formed to perpetuate the history and traditions of the Cherokee. Oconaluftee Indian Village, a re-creation of an early-eighteenth-century Cherokee community, was originated by the Tsali Institute for Cherokee Indian Research, an Association-sponsored technical organization centered in the anthropology departments of the Universities of Tennessee, North Carolina, and Georgia.

## SITE DESCRIPTION

The **Oconaluftee Indian Village**, located in a forested cove where Native Americans camped thousands of years ago, is a 30-acre site surrounded by a palisade of locust posts. There are five structures: **three 1750 dwellings, one sixteenth-century dwelling**, and a **council house**. Cherokee men and women wearing traditional dress work at their crafts throughout the village.

After a brief orientation, a guide leads a tour group to a **beadwork demonstration**. Using the same type of imported Venetian beads introduced by white traders to create sashes worn by chiefs, craftswomen decorate clothing with scroll work and make belts with solid work.

Down the winding, shaded path are **potters** making pottery with local clay. Coil and ball methods are explained by the guide; no potter's wheel is used. The construction of **blowguns** from green river cane is also demonstrated. Particularly interesting is the **basket-weaving demonstration**, in which original Cherokee designs and native dyes and materials are used. Members of the tribe grind corn, make arrowheads, and carve wooden masks, tomahawks, and various tools.

The process of making a **Cherokee canoe** is slow and laborious; the interior of a yellow poplar tree trunk is burned out with hot coals. These long-lasting dugouts, which could transport ten to twelve people, were communally owned.

In **finger weaving**, the weaver manipulates up to forty-eight threads without using a loom of any kind. Belts, straps, and other decorative items are made in this manner.

The Eastern Band of Cherokee were not migratory; they lived in houses, not tepees or wigwams. A small stucco-like house is representative of a **sixteenth-century Cherokee home**, the time predating the arrival of Europeans in this region. Its walls are made from woven river cane cut into strips and tightly interlaced with small saplings, then covered with a plaster of river clay. There are no windows, chimneys, or doors; a fire burns in the center of the dirt floor.

The **1750 houses** are built of logs with mud chinking. They have fireplaces, chimneys, and earthen floors. In one of these eighteenth-century log cabins, the animal skins hanging on the walls emphasize Cherokee hunting abilities.

The **squareground**, a small outdoor amphitheater with its seats divided into seven sections, is a ceremonial ground. In the sand-floored center is a tree stump with an umbrella top covered with branches; this is where sacred ceremonies, which could last several days, were performed. Drums, tom-toms, and rattles were used in these religious rituals. Masks were worn by lead dancers to identify the type of dance—for example, a bear mask for a hunt dance. Dances were performed by groups, rather than solo. The size of a squareground depended on the size of the village.

Religious, civil, and marriage ceremonies were performed in a seven-sided wooden building known as a **council house**. The sacred fire of the Cherokee was kept here, and once a year, all fires in the village were relighted from it. The walls are of woven oak splints covered with clay. The roof is conical, with a hole in the peak to allow for smoke to escape. The sand-floored structure has seven sets of risers, one for each Cherokee clan. Marriage within a clan was forbidden. A husband joined his wife's clan, and children belonged to their mother's clan.

Adjacent to the village is the **Cherokee Botanical Garden and Nature Trail**, where more than 150 species of plants native to the Great Smokies are grown.

## FESTIVALS/CRAFTS

The Cherokee Historical Association sponsors *Unto These Hills*, an outdoor dramatization of the Cherokee story beginning with the arrival of de Soto in 1540 and culminating with the removal of most Cherokee on the infamous Trail of Tears to the West. This stirring drama, performed by Cherokee descendants, is presented from mid-June through late August at 8:30 P.M. nightly (except Sunday). Admission is charged. Box 398, US 441 North, Cherokee 28719. (704) 497-2111.

**Qualla Arts and Crafts Mutual, Inc.**, is an Native American arts and crafts cooperative which sells outstanding traditional crafts, including handmade baskets and jewelry. Box 277, at US 441 North and Drama Rd., Cherokee NC 28719. (704) 497-3103.

## SIDE TRIPS

The modern **Museum of the Cherokee Indian** is located on US 441 and Drama Rd. In its collection are clothing, wooden masks, handwoven baskets, pottery, and stone weapons. In six mini-theaters, multimedia slide and tape shows trace the story of the Cherokee tribe from ancient times to the present. A special display is devoted to Sequoyah, the inventer of the Cherokee alphabet. Open from September to mid-June, 9:00 A.M.–5:00 P.M. daily, and from mid-June through August, 9:00 A.M.–8:00 P.M. daily. PO Box 1599, Cherokee NC 28719. (704) 497-34381. Admission is charged.

At the entrance to Great Smokey Mountains National Park, which is the most heavily visited national park in the East, the **city of Cherokee** is a tourist town with numerous gift shops, miniature golf courses, wax museums, and amusement lands.

# CARL SANDBURG HOME NATIONAL HISTORIC SITE

**Home of American poet and author Carl Sandburg for the last twenty-two years of his life.**

**Address:** 1928 Little River Road, Flat Rock NC 28731-9766
**Telephone:** (704) 693-4178
**Location:** In the Blue Ridge Mountains of western North Carolina, Flat Rock is 26 miles south of Asheville and 3 miles south of Hendersonville, on Little River Rd. near US 25.
**Open:** 9:00 A.M.–5:00 P.M. daily; closed Christmas Day.
**Admission:** House tour: adults (ages 17 and older) $2. Grounds only: free.
**Shops:** Bookstore.
**Facilities:** Orientation film, guided tours, handicapped accessible, hiking trails.

## WHERE TO STAY

**Inns/Bed & Breakfasts:** Woodfield Inn, US 25, Flat Rock NC 28731, (704) 693-6016, 1-800-533-6016. Mill House Lodge, PO Box 309, Flat Rock NC 28731-0309, (704) 693-6077. Waverly Inn, 783 North Main St., Hendersonville NC 28792, (704) 693-9193, 1-800-537-8195. Echo Mountain Inn, 2849 Laurel Park Hwy., Hendersonville NC 28739, (704) 693-9626. Claddagh Inn, 755 North Main St., Hendersonville NC 28792, (704) 697-7778, 1-800-225-4700, FAX: (704) 697-8664.

**Motels/Hotels:** Comfort Inn, 206 Mitchell Dr., Hendersonville NC 28792, (704) 693-8800. Hampton Inn, 155 Sugarloaf Rd., Hendersonville NC 28792, (704) 697-2333, FAX: (704) 693-5280. Holiday Inn, 201 Sugarloaf Rd., Hendersonville NC 28792, (704) 692-7231, FAX: (704) 693-9905. Days Inn, 110 Orr's Camp Road, Hendersonville NC 28792, (704) 697-5999.

**Camping:** Little River Camping Resort, Brevard NC 28712, (704) 877-4475. Davidson River Campground, Pisgah National Forest, Brevard

Photo by Patricia A. Gutek

### Carl Sandburg Home National Historic Site, Flat Rock, North Carolina

Connemara is the 240-acre retreat and goat farm in western North Carolina's Blue Ridge Mountains where the poet and author Carl Sandburg lived from 1945 till his death in 1967. While Carl wrote, his wife, Lilian Steichen Sandburg, tended her prize-winning dairy goats and managed the farm.

NC 28712, (704) 877-3265. Holmes State Forest, Crab Creek Rd., Rt. 4, Box 308, Hendersonville NC 28792, (704) 692-0100.

## OVERVIEW

Connemara, the home of Carl Sandburg for the last twenty-two years of his life, is a literary shrine. Visitors come to see where and how one of America's favorite writers lived, and they are not disappointed. Sandburg's house—which became a National Historic Site in 1968, only a year after the author's death—is filled with Sandburg himself: his typewriter, books, guitar, clothes, photographs, records, and furniture. You can sense his presence everywhere.

In the foothills of western North Carolina's Blue Ridge Mountains, Connemara was the Sandburg family's 240-acre retreat and goat farm. In this rural setting, Carl wrote, and his wife, Lilian Steichen Sandburg, raised prize-winning dairy goats and managed the farm. Their three daughters and two grandchildren lived with them. The property has not been restored as much as it has been "left," complete with furnishings and artifacts, just as it was when Carl Sandburg was alive. A guided tour of the house is given, while the rest of the farm can be enjoyed on a self-guided tour.

## HISTORY

Carl Sandburg was born January 6, 1878, in Galesburg, Illinois, to August and Clara Sandberg, who were Swedish immigrants. His father took the name Sandberg after arriving in the United States in 1869 at approximately age twenty-three, though his actual surname was probably Danielsson, or Sturm, or Johnson. August and Clara's children changed the spelling of their surname from Sandberg to Sandburg, and the rest of the family followed. August Sandberg was a hard-working man who labored in the Chicago, Burlington & Quincy Railroad blacksmith shop, who could read Swedish but not English, and who never learned to write his own name. Carl's mother was Clara Mathilda Anderson, who was born in 1850 and came to the United States in 1873.

Carl quit school after eighth grade and worked at a series of jobs, including delivering milk. He was a restless young man who was looking for adventure and opportunity. At age nineteen, he hopped on a freight car headed west and led the life of a hobo for the next several months. During the Spanish-American War, twenty-year-old Sandburg enlisted in the Sixth Infantry Regiment of Illinois Volunteers, in which he served for six months—mostly in Puerto Rico. After this military stint, he returned to Galesburg and enrolled in Lombard College. During his college years, he served as Lombard's reporter for the *Galesburg Evening Mail* and began writing poetry. He left college without graduating in spring 1902.

Sandburg's first book of prose and poems, *In Reckless Ecstasy,* was published in December 1904 by Asgard Press, operated by his former Lombard professor Philip Green Wright. Carl moved to Chicago in 1906, where he wrote, lectured, and supported himself with a series of jobs in publishing. He was interested in socialism, the subject of many of his lectures. Sandburg met Lilian Steichen, whom he called "Paula," at a socialist meeting in Milwaukee in December 1907; the couple married on June 15, 1908. They had three daughters—Margaret, Janet, and Helga.

Lilian's parents were from Luxembourg. Her brother Edward Steichen was a famous American photographer. Carl Sandburg and Edward Steichen became very good friends; Sandburg wrote his brother-in-law's biography, *Steichen the Photographer.*

After his marriage, Carl lectured and worked for a series of magazines and newspapers in Chicago and Milwaukee, writing news items, columns, and editorials. In 1917, he began a thirteen-year career at Chicago's *Daily News,* with which he continued to be associated till the 1940s. From mid-1918 to mid-1919, he was a foreign correspondent in Sweden for the Newspaper Enterprise Association. In addition to being a newspaperman, Sandburg was a poet, a biographer of Abraham Lincoln, a collector of folk songs, and an author of children's stories.

The Sandburg family lived in Chicago and its western suburbs from 1911 to 1928, when they moved to Harbert, Michigan. They built a large frame two-and-one-half-story house situated on a Lake Michigan sand dune. Here, Mrs. Sandburg began raising Chikaming goats. Carl Sandburg had achieved that elusive goal for an author—economic success. His six-volume biography of Abraham Lincoln was highly acclaimed. In 1940, he was awarded the Pulitzer Prize for history.

In 1945, the Sandburgs purchased a more than 200-acre farm called "Connemara" in Flat Rock in western North Carolina's Blue Ridge Mountains. The estate had been built in 1838 as a summer home for Christopher Memminger, Confederate secretary of the treasury under Jefferson Davis. The farm was an ideal choice because it combined the solitude needed for a writer with adequate grazing land for Paula's goats, and North Carolina's temperate climate was a welcome change from cold northern winters.

Sandburg lived at Connemara from age sixty-seven until his death in 1967 at age eighty-nine. They were productive years in which he wrote *Remembrance Rock,* his autobiography; *Always the Young Strangers;* and *Complete Poems,* for which he won the Pulitzer Prize in 1951. He often wrote at night on a typewriter on an orange crate in his upstairs study while chewing on a cigar. By the time his family—consisting of his wife, three daughters, and two grandchildren—awakened to tend to the 200 prize-wining dairy goats and other livestock, Sandburg would be going to bed. Later in the day, he would work outside on a chair placed on a granite rock at the edge of the pine forest.

The Sandburgs lived a simple life of family dinners, musical evenings, reading, writing, gardening, and animal raising. Paula Sandburg's goats were national prize-winners. They provided the family with goat milk and cheese, and their milk was sold to local dairies. Paula's genetic breeding program resulted in kids which were sold throughout the United States. Paula also raised the family's vegetables in her garden.

Carl Sandburg died at Connemara on July 22, 1967. Shortly thereafter, the property was acquired by the National Park Service, which established the Carl Sandburg National Historic Site, the first national park to honor a literary figure.

## SITE DESCRIPTION

The **Carl Sandburg Home National Historic Site** is a 264-acre rural property with a large main house, over a dozen outbuildings and barns, a garden, and several hiking trails leading into the hills. The farm is picturesquely set among sweeping pasture land, tall pine trees, ponds, wildflowers, and mountain views in the foothills of western North Carolina.

The **main house**, built in 1838, is a white two-story frame structure over a raised basement. It was the summer home of Charlestonian Christopher G. Memminger, Confederate secretary of the treasury. There are white pillars in front and steps leading up to a broad, comfortable porch that has a view of the Blue Ridge Mountains in the distance. An **information center** is in the basement.

Inside the house, the atmosphere is comfortable, cluttered, sunny, and homey. No interior decorator has left a mark. Although most windows have shades, they have no curtains because the family enjoyed the sunshine and the mountain views. Books and bookshelves are everywhere. Sandburg's collection of manuscripts, letters, and books were sold to the University of Illinois in 1955. However, over ten thousand books and thousands of papers and notes remain at Connemara.

In the **living room** are a grand piano and a guitar, evidence along with record players and records, of the family's love of music. The room is lined with bookshelves, and Edward Steichen photographs are hung on the walls.

Sandburg's book-lined **downstairs study** was the room in which Sandburg worked on his correspondence. His daughter Helga frequently acted as his secretary. The **farm office** was the domain of Paula Sandburg, who handled the family finances, the farm business, and management of the goat herd. It is a tile-floored room with books on plants, bees, and genetics, along with family photos and pictures of her goats.

The **dining room**, with end walls lined with bookshelves from floor to ceiling, also served as a family room. After dinner, the Sandburgs frequently sang, with Carl accompanying them on his guitar, or listened to Carl read from his current work.

**Upstairs** are Sandburg's two small rooms, where the poet, novelist and biographer wore a newspaperman's green eyeshade while pecking at a typewriter with two fingers. Workroom walls are lined with bookcases and filing cabinets. There are a desk, two chairs, a wood stove, and a number of orange crates which are used for furniture. In this atmosphere of comfortable, ordered disarray, Carl Sandburg wrote, starting between eight and ten o'clock at night and finishing around five in the morning. He then went to bed in the adjoining bedroom that has plain, utilitarian furniture, a small sink, and magazine pictures taped on the walls.

Visitors can walk the **grounds** where there are the family garage, the chicken house, the pump house, the springhouse, the woodshed, the goat or donkey house, the Swedish house—a small guest house used for storing papers and books, the tenant house, the farm manager's house, the greenhouse, the barn garage, the buck kid quarters, the main goat barn, the horse barn, the cow shed, storage shed and milk house. A small herd of goats are maintained by the Park Service.

Trails leading from the property include the 1.3-mile **Spring Trail** to Big Glassy Mountain, the 1.3-mile **Memminger Path** (National Recreation Trail) to Big Glassy Mountain, and the .2-mile **Little Glassy Mountain Trail**.

## SIDE TRIPS

Directly across from the Sandburg property is the **Flat Rock Playhouse**, which has been presenting professional summer performances since 1939. Open June through September, the theater presents dramas and musicals Wednesday through Sunday. PO Box 310, Flat Rock NC 28731. (704) 693-0731. Admission is charged.

# TRYON PALACE HISTORIC SITES AND GARDENS

Reconstructed colonial capitol of North Carolina.

**Address:** PO Box 1007, New Bern NC 28563
**Telephone:** (919) 514-4900, 1-800-767-1560
**Location:** New Bern is at the intersection of US 17 and US 70, 1½ hours east of I-95 via US 70. Tryon Palace Historic Sites and Gardens is at the intersection of George and Pollock Street, one block off US 17 (Broad Street).
**Open:** 9:00 A.M.–4:00 P.M. Monday–Saturday, and 1:00 to 4:00 P.M. Sunday. Closed Thanksgiving Day; December 24, 25, 26; and New Year's Day.
**Admission:** All Sites Ticket, which includes all buildings and gardens: adults $12, students $6. Palace and gardens: adults $8, students $4. Stanly and Dixon-Stevenson Houses: adults $8, students $4. Gardens only: adults $4, students $2. New Bern Academy: adults $3, students $1.
**Shops:** Tryon Palace Museum Shop in the Jones House; crafts and garden shop behind the Palace East Wing.
**Facilities:** Visitor center with orientation film, gardens; partially handicapped accessible—phone ahead for assistance.

## WHERE TO STAY

**Inns/Bed & Breakfasts:** The Aerie, 509 Pollock St., New Bern NC 28560, (919) 636-5553, 1-800-849-5553. Harmony House Inn, 215 Pollock St., New Bern NC 28560, (919) 636-3810. King's Arms Inn, 212 Pollock St., New Bern NC 28560, (919) 638-4409, 1-800-872-9306. New Berne House Inn, 709 Broad St., New Bern NC 28560, (919) 636-2250, 1-800-842-7688.
**Motels/Hotels:** Comfort Suites, 218 East Front St., New Bern NC 28560, (919) 636-0022, 1-800-228-5150. Hampton Inn, 200 Hotel Dr., New Bern NC 28562 (919) 637-2111. Ramada Inn Waterfront Marina, 101 Howell Rd., New Bern NC 28562, (919) 636-3637.

Photo by Patricia A. Gutek

## Tryon Palace Historic Sites and Gardens
A view of the reconstructed Tryon Palace through a gate. Tryon Palace served
both as the home of the governors of North Carolina who were appointed by
the British monarch and as the colonial capitol of North Carolina, the seat of
the royal colony's government.

Sheraton Hotel and Marina, One Bicentennial Park, New Bern NC 28560, (919) 638-3585.

**Camping:** Fun Park and Campground, Hwy. 17, New Bern NC 28563, (919) 638-2556, (919) 633-3991.

## OVERVIEW

Tryon Palace, located in New Bern, recounts the story of the British monarch's appointed governor and the palace which served as the seat of the royal colony's government during North Carolina's colonial and revolutionary history. The palace—named for William Tryon, the royal governor who had it built by his architect, John Hawks—has been reconstructed. Tryon Palace Historic Sites and Gardens also includes the John Wright Stanly House, the Dixon-Stevenson House, more than thirteen acres of landscaped gardens, and the New Bern Academy Museum.

Tryon Palace, both the home of North Carolina's royal governors and the colonial capitol, was constructed during the administration of William Tryon. While Tryon and his successor as royal governor lived in the upper story, the council met on the first floor. The palace has been reconstructed based on archaeological and historical research. Travelers to Tryon Palace can experience a time when North Carolina was a royal colony, ruled from England, and learn how the palace became a state capitol in an independent republic.

## HISTORY

North Carolina, Virginia, and South Carolina were royal colonies ruled directly by the British Crown through its appointee, a royal governor. Royal colonies differed from proprietary colonies, such as Pennsylvania, which were governed by a proprietor such as William Penn, who had received a grant of land from the king. They also differed from colonies like Massachusetts, which was a commonwealth governed under its own compact but yet was a British possession.

Even before William Tryon arrived from England to assume his office as the royal governor of North Carolina, New Bern had been founded by Baron Christophe von Graffenried on land between the Neuse and Trent Rivers. Initially a thriving colonial community of Swiss and German settlers, by 1765 New Bern was very much an English and African-American town.

At that time, North Carolina did not have a permanent capitol. The capitol moved with the location of the governor. Tryon's predecessors, the royal governors, Gabriel Johnston and Arthur Dobbs, sought to establish a permanent capitol at New Bern, but failed to gain approval and funding from the privy council in London.

William Tryon, his wife, a daughter, and John Hawks, the architect, arrived on the ship *Friendship*, which had carried them from England to North Carolina in October 1764. King George III had appointed Tryon, former commander of the First Regiment of Footguards and husband of Margaret Wake, a wealthy heiress, as lieutenant governor of North Carolina, though he became royal governor the following year. Tryon's career followed the pattern of other colonial royal governors. They were frequently career army officers who through family connection had gained the patronage of someone close to the king. In Tryon's case, it was Margaret's kinsman Lord Hillsborough, who served as secretary of state for the colonies in 1768.

As the king's personally appointed ruler in the New World, a royal governor such as Tryon left England with elaborate sets of instructions drafted by the Board of Trade, which dealt with political, economic, and religious aspects of colonial life. Although the royal governor had immense power, it was a rare individual who could accomplish all expected of him, especially in the North American political situation.

When the incumbent Governor Dobbs died on March 28, 1765, and Tryon took office, the governor's seat was still in Brunswick. Tryon's tenure as North Carolina's royal governor from 1765 to 1771 occurred when the citizens of England's thirteen North American colonies were growing increasingly resistant to British rule.

Governors in royal colonies were appointed by the king and were responsible to the British government in London. They were aided in governing their colonies by councils, usually a body of twelve to fifteen members who were selected by the Board of Trade from nominees recommended by the governor. However, colonies like North Carolina and Virginia also had elected assemblies. Assemblymen, often wealthy landowners or merchants, were elected by a small number of voters, who were usually white male property-owners. Regarding themselves as colonial "houses of commons," the assemblies frequently challenged the governors who were responsible for implementing laws enacted in England and collecting taxes levied from England. For the members of the assembly, the issue of "no taxation without representation" became a precipitating factor in the American Revolution.

North Carolina's politics were further aggravated by tensions between the governor and the large tidewater-area planters and the small farmers on the backcountry frontier. Tryon would face near insurrection from some of the backcountry farmers, called "Regulators," who resisted colonial officials and taxes. This was the political situation in which Tryon assumed North Carolina's governorship. Tryon wished to maintain British rule in a reasonable manner that would not antagonize the king's subjects in North Carolina.

Tryon took office during the controversy over the Stamp Act, which sparked resistance to taxes imposed, without colonial consent, by Great Britain. The Stamp Act of 1765 required the printing of documents such as deeds, newspapers, wills, and licenses on special stamped paper that was to be purchased from officially appointed tax collectors. The act spurred colonial resistance, provoked speeches such as Patrick Henry's against the British imposition of new taxes, and led to inter-colonial cooperation in the Stamp Act Congress. In North Carolina, Tryon faced a hostile assembly and action by armed militia to force the release of ships impounded by the British. Although Britain still maintained the prerogative of taxing the colonies, the Stamp Act was repealed in 1766.

Once the tension over the Stamp Act had dissipated, on November 8, 1766, Tryon presented his proposal for a permanent capitol at New Bern to the assembly. He requested funds to erect a public building at New Bern which would house the governor and his family, contain meeting rooms for the council and be a repository for government records. The assembly agreed to Tryon's request, and, on December 1, appropriated 5,000 pounds to purchase twelve lots and erect the building. To complete construction, additional appropriations, which reached 12,000 pounds, were made.

John Hawks was named the official architect. On January 9, 1767, Tryon and Hawks signed a contract specifying the architect's responsibilities, his salary of 300 pounds per year, and the specifications for materials and craftsmanship. The two-story palace, to be constructed of brick, was to be 82 by 59 feet, to have the necessary outbuildings, and to be completed by October 1, 1770. Tryon sent two sets of final drawings of the building to England for approval—one to the king and one to the Board of Trade.

By January 1769, both the main building and its two wings were under roof. During the building's construction, Tryon, as did other royal governors, faced mounting colonial opposition to the Townshend Acts, which went into effect in November 1767, by which the crown levied duties on glass, lead, paper, and tea. Crying "no taxation without representation," in October 1769, the North Carolina Assembly passed the Virginia Resolutions, which denied that the British Parliament had the right to tax the American colonies. Tryon responded to the challenge by dissolving the assembly on November 4, 1769. In March 1770, the Townshend Acts, with the exception of the duty on tea, were repealed.

At the end of a difficult year, the palace was opened officially on December 5, 1770, with joint sessions of the council and assembly and a gala celebration.

Tryon continued to face near insurrection from the Regulators, small backcountry farmers who forcefully challenged colonial authorities. At the Battle of Alamance Creek on May 16, 1771, the Regulator movement was crushed.

Tryon left North Carolina in 1771 to become New York's royal governor. His successor in North Carolina was Josiah Martin, who with his wife, Elizabeth, and their six children, arrived at New Bern on August 11, 1771. Martin officially took possession of the Great Seal on August 12. The son of a wealthy sugar-cane planter in Antigua, Martin had pursued a military career and had served in North America during the French and Indian Wars. His wealth enabled him to furnish the palace with fine furniture, carpets, and works of art. More autocratic than Tryon, Martin was locked in continual conflicts with the assembly as relations between Britain and its colonies were reaching a crisis.

On April 18, 1775, the Massachusetts militia at Lexington engaged in a skirmish with the British armies. Martin, fearing armed insurrection and capture by North Carolina militia, abandoned the palace on May 29, 1775, for refuge at Fort Johnston, near Wilmington. During the Revolutionary War, Martin led British and Tory forces against the Continental Army in the state.

The palace was empty until the state governors began to use it as the capitol. The furnishings which Martin had left behind during his hasty departure were confiscated and auctioned off by the state.

On January 16, 1777, Richard Caswell, an experienced politician and wealthy plantation owner, took the oath of office to become North Carolina's first state governor. The oath was administered in the former council chamber. The former royal governor's palace was now the state capitol building where the Council of State met.

In 1794, the state capitol was transferred to Raleigh, and the neglected palace began to deteriorate. On the night of February 27, 1798, a disastrous fire destroyed it.

In 1945, more than 150 years after the fire, the North Carolina legislature authorized the Tryon Palace Commission to supervise the reconstruction and management of the former's governor's palace. William G. Perry, a noted architect, was director of the reconstruction process. The reconstruction historian Alonzo T. Dill conducted research in American and British archives. William Tryon's inventory of 1773 was found, and furnishings were identified and collected by Gregor Norman-Wilcox, the consultant curator. Reconstruction of Tryon Palace was based on John Hawks's original drawings, which were located in the New York Historical Society Library and in the British Public Records Office in London.

The existing gardens were laid out in the 1950s by Morley Jeffers Williams, a landscape architect. A document purporting to be the plan of the original Tryon Palace garden was discovered in Caracas, Venezuela, in 1992.

In the 1940s, Mrs. James Edwin Latham established two trust funds for the Tryon Palace Commission. Tryon Palace is under the supervision of the North Carolina Department of Cultural Resources.

## SITE DESCRIPTION

Tour information is available at the **Tryon Palace Visitor Center**, where you can view the audiovisual orientation program.

The **governor's palace** is a reconstruction of the royal governor's building that burned in 1798. Built according to the plans drawn by John Hawks, the original architect, the brick Georgian-style structure reflects eighteenth-century royal colonial and early republican state government. On the pediment is the coat of arms of King George III.

Based on an inventory of Governor Tryon's possessions made two years after he left New Bern, the palace is furnished with English and American antiques and artifacts from the third quarter of the eighteenth century.

On the first floor are the entrance hall, library, council chamber, drawing room (dining room), parlor, housekeeper's room, steward's or butler's room, and great and lesser staircases. The **entrance hall**, illuminated by a large English glass lantern (ca. 1770), has a floor of white Italian and black Belgian marble. Statues in four niches represent the four continents. Mahogany side chairs bear the arms of Baron Rolls of Stevensone. The **great staircase** of mahogany and pegged walnut steps is illuminated by a skylight roof dome.

The **library**, painted in rich ocher, contains first editions of 400 of the books Tryon owned. Tryon's library contained collections on history, literature, religion, politics, law, military affairs, poetry, agriculture, and navigation. Illuminated by an English brass chandelier, the library is furnished with a mahogany kneehole desk (ca. 1760), a Spanish armorial carpet, a celestial globe, and other period pieces.

The **council chamber**, where the council deliberated on colony affairs and advised the royal governor, was the seat of royal government. After 1776, four state governors were inaugurated in the chamber. The chamber, illuminated by massive cut-glass chandeliers, is hung with full-length portraits of King George III and his consort, Queen Charlotte, in their coronation robes; the portraits flank the Sienna marble mantel supported by two Ionic columns. King George III's coat of arms is displayed over the mantel. Around the mahogany council tables, with stop-fluted legs, are twelve square Gothic Chippendale-style chairs (ca. 1770). The chamber also contains the governor's writing desk and a mechanical tall-case musical clock (ca. 1736) made by Charles Clay, an English clock-maker.

The 26-x-18 feet **drawing room**, also referred to as the dining room, illuminated by an English eight-light chandelier (ca. 1750) has painted woodwork, royal portraits, and a carved wooden fireplace. Its central feature is a formal Adam-Chippendale mahogany dining table (ca. 1770), and a set of six mahogany chairs. The room has an interesting Philadelphia mahogany tall-case clock.

The **parlor**, where musicales were performed, contains a walnut spinet made by Thomas Hitchcock in London (ca. 1720), an elaborately carved Irish table, and eighteenth-century-style walnut chairs with Soho tapestry (ca. 1735). There are a mahogany card table and an English mahogany tea table with a piecrust top (ca. 1760). In the room hangs a portrait of Philip Bowes Broke, which is believed to be one of Thomas Gainsborough's earliest paintings.

The **steward's or butler's room** is where the head male servant would wait to attend on members of the household. The room contains horsehair-bottomed mahogany chairs, a mahogany writing table, and a lantern by which visitors could be escorted from the courtyard. The **housekeeper's room** contains cooking utensils, dishes, glasses, and a very interesting dome-shaped mahogany corner cupboard painted in trompe d'oeil style to resemble a sea shell.

On the second floor is the **governor's bedchamber**, which is furnished with an elaborately carved English canopy bed (ca. 1760), a walnut Queen Anne bonnet-top highboy (ca. 1740), a mahogany night table, and a mahogany kneehole bookcase. There is a portrait of Charles Tryon, father of the governor. Mrs. Tryon's adjoining dressing room contains a Gothic Chippendale mirror, an eighteenth-century painting of Margaret Hamilton, a serpentine commode, and Chelsea-Derby candlesticks. **Miss Tryon's bedchamber** designed for Governor Tryon's daughter, Margaret, contains a four-poster bed, and a rare walnut wing chair. The **family supper room** is appointed with Chinese Chippendale mahogany furniture, a chinoiserie mirror, and colored engravings of Hampton Court Palace in England.

In the cellar area are rooms for the butler and the housekeeper. The **kitchen office, or east wing**, contains a large cooking fireplace, preparing tables, and cooking utensils, as well as the **governor's secretary's office**, with its brick fireplace, large round conference table, and secretary's desk. It is furnished with rare seventeenth- and eighteenth-century North American maps, including one of North Carolina.

The **stable office or west wing** is the one surviving building from the period of Tryon occupancy.

The **Maude Moore Latham Memorial Garden** is planted with tulips in spring and annual beds in summer. The thirteen-acre grounds are planted in ornamental, formal, and vegetable gardens.

The **John Wright Stanly House**, built in the early 1780s, reflects its owner's wealth. During the Revolutionary War, Stanly's merchant ships plied the waters as privateers, capturing British ships to aid the American cause. When President George Washington visited New Bern on his southern tour in 1791, he stayed at the Stanly home.

The **master bedroom** is appointed with fine pieces of Philadelphia-made furniture, a high four-poster bed, a lowboy, period chests and chairs, and an oriental rug. The **parlor**, illuminated by a large chandelier, contains a portrait of two Stanly children with their pet deer. The **library** contains a Massachusetts kettle-base or bombé secretary. In the **dining room** are a portrait of John Wright Stanly's son, John, and a sideboard with family silver. The house's **central passage** has a tall-case clock made by John Seim of Reading Pennsylvania.

The **Dixon-Stevenson House**, built ca. 1830, epitomizes New Bern's life-style in the first half of the nineteenth century when the town, one of North Carolina's largest cities, was a prosperous port. Built for a New Bern mayor, it is a example of neoclassical architecture. Its furnishings reflect the Federal period. At the rear of the home is a **garden** with all white seasonal flowers. When Union troops occupied New Bern during the Civil War, the house was commandeered as a regimental hospital.

The **parlor** contains symbols of the late Federal period—a sunburst on the mantel, lyres in two table bases, an eagle on the mirror, and pineapples on the over-mantel mirror. There are an impressive fireplace and crystal chandelier. The **green bedroom**, appointed in Empire-style that was fashionable in the mid-nineteenth century, has a needlepoint carpet, a sleigh bed, and French wallpaper. There is a **child's bedroom** on the third floor.

The **New Bern Academy Museum** features exhibits on New Bern's history from the early European settlements of 1710 through the Civil War, with a special focus on early education, teaching methods, architecture, and the town's occupation and use as a military hospital by the Union army. The original academy, founded in 1764 with Thomas Thomlinson as schoolmaster, was destroyed by fire in 1795. A new academy was built on New Street in 1809, which makes it among the oldest secondary schools in America.

## FESTIVALS/CRAFTS

Among special annual events are the **Christmas Celebration** in December, the **Decorative Arts Symposium** in March, **Gardener's Weekend** and the **Private Historic Homes and Gardens Tour** in April, the **Independence Day Celebration** in July, and the **Chrysanthemum Festival** in October.

## SIDE TRIPS

**New Bern,** a historic maritime community at the confluence of the Neuse and Trent Rivers, is North Carolina's second oldest town. It was founded in 1710 and named for Bern, Switzerland.

**Attmore-Oliver House,** built in 1790, features eighteenth- and nineteenth-century American furnishings, local photographs, Civil War items, and manuscript collections. 510 Pollock St., New Bern NC 28560. (919) 638-8558. Tuesday–Saturday. Admission is free.

# OLD SALEM

Restoration of an eighteenth-century
Moravian community; NR, NHL.

**Address:** Box F, Winston-Salem NC 27108
**Telephone:** (910) 721-7300
**Location:** Winston-Salem is in northwest North Carolina; Old Salem is near the intersection of I-40 and US 52.
**Open:** 9:30 A.M.–4:30 P.M. Monday–Saturday; 1:30–4:30 P.M. Sunday. Closed Thanksgiving, Christmas Eve, and Christmas Day.
**Admission:** Old Salem: adults $10, children ages 6–14 $5. Old Salem and Museum of Early Southern Decorative Arts: adults $13, children ages 6–14 $6.
**Restaurants:** Old Salem Tavern, Mayberry's.
**Shops:** T. Bagge Merchant, Salem Gift and Book Store, Winkler Bakery.
**Facilities:** Visitor center with orientation film, special events, Museum of Early Southern Decorative Arts.

## WHERE TO STAY

**Inns/Bed & Breakfasts:** Brookstown Inn, 200 Brookstown Ave., Winston-Salem NC 27101, (910) 725-1120, 1-800-845-4262, FAX: (910) 773-0147. Colonel Ludlow, Summit and West Fifth Sts., Winston-Salem NC 27101, (910) 777-1887, FAX: (910) 777-1890, Manor House, Box 1040, Clemmons NC 27012, (910) 766-0591, FAX: (910) 766-8723.
**Motels/Hotels:** Best Western Regency Inn, 128 North Cherry St., Winston-Salem NC 27101, (910) 723-8861, (910) 723-2997. The Marque, 460 North Cherry St., Winston-Salem NC 27101, (910) 725-1234, 1-800-527-2341, FAX: (910) 722-9182. Adam's Mark at Winston Plaza, 425 North Cherry St., Winston-Salem NC 27101, (910) 725-3500, FAX: (910) 722-6475.
**Camping:** Tanglewood Park, PO Box 1040, Clemmons NC 27012, (910) 766-0591. Hanging Rock State Park, Walnut Cove, Danbury NC, (910) 593-8480. Pilot Mountain State Park, Pinnacle NC, (910) 325-2355

## OVERVIEW

Dating from before the American Revolution, Old Salem is a North Carolina planned town founded in 1766 by a pietistical religious group called "Moravians," who were originally from the European province of Moravia (in what is now the Czech Republic). Sometimes called "The Williamsburg of the South," Old Salem includes nine museum buildings that are within a sixteen-block area of Moravian-built eighteenth- and nineteenth-century buildings.

Old Salem's large eighteenth-century buildings show strong European influence. Houses sit flush with the sidewalks and have half-timbered walls, tile roofs, central chimneys, and symmetrically placed windows. The principle structures, which include houses for the single brothers, single sisters, a community store, and a tavern, were built around an open square.

Salem was a congregational community, strictly planned by Moravian church leaders. The site for Salem ("peace" in Hebrew) was chosen because of its good water supply, proper drainage, and southern exposure. Not an agricultural center, Salem was conceived as a trading center for artisans and craftsmen.

The busy industrial city of Winston-Salem has grown up around the colonial town of Salem so that it now is a historic eighteenth-century area in a modern twentieth-century city. To ensure an authentic appearance in the historic area, more than a hundred nonconforming structures within the congregation town limits were demolished when restoration efforts began. As is the case at Williamsburg, many buildings in the historic area are privately owned, but their exteriors have been restored.

The combination of original European-style historic structures, the interesting group that lived in Salem, the beautiful gardens, and the high-quality restoration work makes Old Salem a fine museum village. Even though admission is charged to enter museum buildings, you are free to stroll the brick paths through the restored area at any time, eat at the Salem Tavern, and shop in museum stores.

## HISTORY

The Moravians, who founded Salem in 1766, trace their faith to the Bohemian Protestant martyr Jan Hus, who died at the stake in 1415 because of his unrelenting opposition to corruption in the Roman Catholic Church. A faithful band of his followers known as "Hussites" sought refuge in Moravia, a province in the present-day Czech Republic. In 1457, they formed a society known as *Unitas Fratrum* (Unity of Brethren), renounced the authority of Rome, and began to ordain their own ministers.

Despite persecution, the Unity flourished, spreading across Moravia, Bohemia, and into Poland until the Counter Reformation and Thirty Years' War (1618–1648) destroyed all but a remnant of the group and forced its members into exile. Their "religion of the heart," Pietism, was kept alive by the distinguished educator and Moravian bishop John Amos Komensky (1592–1670), who is also known by his Latin name, Comenius. Moravian brethren believed that the spirit of love should be constantly maintained toward all the children of God, regardless of race or creed.

Like other Protestant denominations, the Moravians, as members of the Unity were commonly called, turned to America as a place where they could practice their beliefs free from persecution. By 1740, the brethren had founded a successful colony at Bethlehem, Pennsylvania. Their reputation as industrious, law-abiding people attracted the attention of a British nobleman, Earl Granville, who approached the Moravian leaders with an offer of land. In 1753, a 98,985-acre tract was purchased in what is now Piedmont, North Carolina. The settlement was known as "Wachovia."

Salem was planned as Wachovia's trade center, a town where economic development and architectural details would be regulated as strictly as people's lives. Construction began in 1766, and by the spring of 1772, most of the major buildings had been completed; early settlers and the government of Wachovia proceeded to move in.

The Moravian beliefs combined pietistic behavior with a zeal for commerce. A person's work and the profit it yielded were considered essential to spiritual growth. Whether a candle-maker or tinsmith, a Moravian craftsman should develop his skills to the utmost in order to glorify the divine taskmaster.

The guild system was the way that the brethren accomplished their many objectives. At about the age of fourteen, Salem youth began their apprenticeship under master craftsmen and, with rare exceptions, remained in that status for a full seven years. Apprentices lived and worked in the Single Brothers' House. After achieving journeyman status, they continued to live with the single brethren until they married. At that time, they moved into their own homes and started their own businesses.

Because the Moravians did not separate church and state, the business of running the town and enforcing the rules of the congregation was vested in three main boards or committees. The duties of the *Aufseher Collegium* (board of overseers) were to superintend trade, enforce zoning laws and building codes, discipline wayward apprentices and masters, control community accounts, and allocate funds for capital-improvement projects. Matters of a strictly spiritual nature were referred to the Elders Conference, while the Congregation Council dealt with issues involving all members of the community.

The Moravian "choir" system arose out of the belief that a close association of persons of like age, sex, or marital status promoted spiritual growth. There were choirs for married people, children, single brothers, single sisters, older boys, older girls, widows, and widowers. Some of the choirs lived in their own choir houses; all choirs worshiped together.

The choir system was closely linked with a sense of shared life and property. The brethren were free to live in their own homes, though the church's leasehold system retained a right to the land on which the house stood and could choose building styles. Moravians were allowed to use alcohol and tobacco in moderation, but dress codes were severe, particularly for women, who wore ankle-length dresses. For a church service, a sister wore the traditional *haube* on her head.

As the area surrounding Wachovia grew more populous, the highly regimented congregation system of Salem lost much of its appeal. Gradually, the old rules were either relaxed or abandoned; and by the middle of the nineteenth century, Salem no longer functioned as a congregation town. Today, only the church, an active Protestant denomination, remains as a Moravian entity.

Although the original Salem ceased to exist, many of its buildings remained standing. Their deterioration was hastened, however, by the founding of a new town, Winston, on Salem's northern border in 1849, together with the growth of Winston's tobacco and textile industries, the merger of Winston and Salem in 1913, and the gradual spreading of that city until it had all but engulfed the old Moravian town.

In the spring of 1950, a broad-based, nonprofit organization known as Old Salem, Inc., brought together Moravians and non-Moravians in an effort to preserve the historic town. More than fifty buildings have now been restored or reconstructed on their original sites, re-creating a former era in the heart of a bustling metropolis.

## SITE DESCRIPTION

After viewing the slide show at the **reception center,** begin your tour at the town square, which was originally farmland but eventually came to resemble a New England commons. The reconstructed **market-fire house** contains an exhibit of early fire-fighting equipment.

The **single brothers' house** is a long, two-story structure with a high basement and two attics. The northern, half-timbered portion dates from 1769; the southern, brick portion was added in 1786. Because lime needed for mortar was scarce in Wachovia, oak timbering was used in 1769 to reinforce the house's brickwork. By 1786, when the addition was built, lime was more plentiful, and the community used brick in all its building projects.

The single brothers' house was not only a residence but also contained the shops of the master craftsmen. The restored building now houses craft shops stocked with appropriate tools, and craftspeople demonstrate and explain their work. Shops include a **tin shop, gun shop, dye shop, weaver's room, tailor's shop, potter's shop, cooper's shop** and **joiner's shop.**

The **boys' school**, a brick building facing Salem's square was built in 1794 by master builder Johannes Gottlob Krause. It is noteworthy for the artistry that appears in the pattern of the brick masonry on the west gable, the covered cornices, and the belt course of brick on the east gable. The school was attended by boys aged six to fourteen, until 1896 when it became the home of the Wachovia Historical Society. Collections of artifacts acquired by Moravian missionaries were displayed here until the 1950s, when Old Salem, Inc., restored the building and assumed management of the collection. Exhibits in the **Wachovia Museum** now relate directly to the history of Wachovia: Moravian pottery, the church's history, Moravian music, ironwork, lighting devices, and Moravian schooling. Moravians placed great emphasis on education, and the boys' curriculum included geometry, Latin and English grammar, geography, history, penmanship, and German.

North of the square is the **Miksch Tobacco Shop**. This 1771 building was the first privately owned house in Salem. Matthew Miksch not only lived in but also operated a tobacco business from this house. The house was built of logs, but because the brethren disapproved of plain log houses on their main street, it (like others) was covered with clapboards. Originally, the house had two rooms, but Miksch added a third room at the back and a loft.

The **Winkler Bakery** was built in 1800 for a baker named Thomas Buttner. In 1808, Christian Winkler acquired the shop. Bread is still being baked in the wood-fired domed brick bake oven attached to the south side of the building. Eighteenth-century baking processes are used to produce European-style breads, cakes, and cookies. The aroma of fresh-baked bread permeates the restored area.

South of the square is the **John Vogler House**, which was built in 1819. This house has many Federal characteristics and thus represents a departure from Salem's Germanic architectural tradition. Vogler was an accomplished silversmith who also dabbled in clock-making, gunsmithing, jewelry-making, and silhouette-making. Seventy percent of the furniture in the house belonged to the Vogler family. One room is used as a Vogler family museum, with their silver, guns, and artwork exhibited. Another room houses **Vogler's silversmithing shop** displaying his spoons, ladles, and snuffboxes.

The **Schultz Shoemaker Shop** was built in 1827. Samuel Schultz originally operated his business from his 1819 home but decided to construct a separate building adjacent to it. The shop displays the tools and products of early-nineteenth-century shoemaking.

The **Vierling House** was built in 1802 and was the last and largest masterwork of Johannes Krause. Unique features of this brick Georgian house are the exposed-stone foundation and the herringbone gable patterns. Krause was commissioned to build the house by Dr. Samuel Benjamin Vierling, the most renowned of Salem's early physicians. It was in this house that Dr. Vierling practiced the professions of the physician, the surgeon, and the apothecary. He is said to have performed mastectomies, skull trepans, and other major operations here.

The **Salem Tavern Museum** (1784) is a plain three-story brick building with a veranda. George Washington spent two days in 1791 at this tavern which had a fine reputation for its food and drink. The first floor has a **publick room**, where the ordinary (a standard meal at a fixed price) was served each day on long tables with benches. Across the hall is a **gentlemen's room** for the more elite clientele, furnished with private tables and Windsor chairs. Cooking was done in the twin fireplaces of the large kitchen. There are several sleeping rooms in addition to the innkeeper's bedroom.

**Salem Tavern** (1816), where today's visitors can stop for a meal, was originally a boarding house built as an adjunct to the main tavern building. The outside is restored to its 1816 appearance, while the inside has been adapted for dining in a tavern atmosphere.

Gardens were part of the early congregational town plan. Each family maintained its own garden to supply vegetables for the table. Gardens that have been restored to various time periods include the **Treibel** and **Miksch Gardens**, 1759–1761; **Eberhardt Garden**, 1814; **Levering Garden**, 1820; **Leinbach Garden**, 1822; **Cape Fear Bank Garden**, 1847; and **Anna**

**Catharina Garden**, 1772. There is also an **arboretum** of native trees near the Museum of Early Southern Decorative Arts.

Operated by Old Salem, Inc., the **Museum of Early Southern Decorative Arts** was founded in 1965 by Frank L. Horton, Old Salem's first director of restoration, who also donated a large part of the collection. Nineteen rooms representative of the early South have been removed from their original locations and reassembled in the museum. They are decorated with furniture, paintings, metal-work, pottery, and glasswork produced by Southern craftsmen. The museum emphasizes the products of craftspeople from the three principal cultural regions of the Old South during the years between 1640 and 1820.

**God's Acre**, founded in 1779, is the graveyard for Salem's Moravian congregation. Long rows of identical gravestones attest to the sect's belief in equality. People were buried with their fellow choir members rather than with their families. A large square is provided for each choir: married women and widows, married men and widowers, single men and boys, and single women and girls.

**Salem Academy and College**, a four-year liberal arts college for women, is an outgrowth of a girls' boarding school operated by the Moravians. The first building for the school was erected in 1805 and has been restored to its 1837 appearance; it now serves as a dormitory. College buildings are not open to tourists.

The **Home Moravian Church** was built in 1800. Although it has undergone many interior renovations, its exterior looks much as it did originally. This church has been occupied continuously by the Moravian congregation since 1800.

Two shops are operated at Old Salem. One is in the southern half of the restored 1775 **T. Bagge Community Store**, and the other, the Salem Gift and Book Store, is in an 1850 addition to the 1810 **Inspector's House**.

## FESTIVALS/CRAFTS

At **Old Salem**, classes or lectures are given on weaving, wool dyeing textiles, candle-making, vegetable and flower gardening, nineteenth-century architecture, rug hooking, beehive-oven baking, and ice cream of the colonial period. Concerts are scheduled throughout the year.

Special events include a **Spring Festival** in April, a **Civil War Encampment** in June, a **Torchlight Procession** on the 4th of July, and **Salem Christmas** in December. An **Easter sunrise service** has been held in **God's Acre** every year since 1772 and now attracts thousands of visitors.

## SIDE TRIPS

**Historic Bethabara** ("house of passage" in Hebrew) is the site of the first Moravian settlement in North Carolina. Archaeological research has uncovered the foundation walls and cellars of many of the original buildings. The 1756 **palisade**, a fort that gave refuge to outlying settlers in times of trouble, has been reconstructed. The 1788 **Gemein Haus** (Congregation House), a fine example of Moravian architecture, the 1782 **potter's house** and the 1803 **brewer's house** have all been restored as exhibit buildings. The **visitors' center** contains exhibits on the early settlers, including many artifacts found on the site. Nature trails lead to the Moravian graveyard called **God's Acre**. Open from Easter to Thanksgiving, 9:30 A.M.–4:30 P.M. Monday–Friday, and 1:30–4:30 P.M. Saturday and Sunday. 2147 Bethabara Road, Winston-Salem NC 27106. (919) 924-8191. Admission is free.

# SOUTH CAROLINA

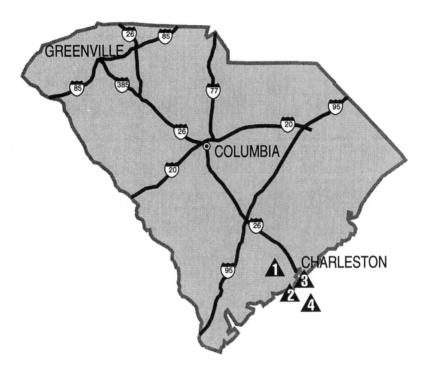

1. Charleston: Drayton Hall
2. Charleston: Middleton Place
3. Mount Pleasant: Boone Hall Plantation
4. Sullivan's Island: Fort Sumter National Monument

# DRAYTON HALL

Mid-eighteenth-century Ashley River plantation house;
example of Georgian Palladian architecture; National
Trust property; NR, NHL.

**Address:** 3380 Ashley River Rd., Charleston SC 29414
**Telephone:** (803) 766-0188
**Location:** In southeastern South Carolina, 9 miles northwest of downtown
Charleston on SC Hwy. 61, Ashley River Rd.
**Open:** March–October, 9:30 A.M.–5:00 P.M. daily; November–February,
9:30 A.M.–4:00 P.M. daily.
**Admission:** Adults $7, children over age 5 $4.
**Shops:** Museum Gift Shop.
**Facilities:** Guided tours, gardens, handicapped accessible, picnic area, na-
ture trails, educational programs for school groups, special events.

## WHERE TO STAY

See entries for other Charleston-area sites.

## OVERVIEW

Drayton Hall is an Ashley River plantation that was built between
1738 and 1742, prior to the American Revolution. A National Trust for
Historic Preservation property, it is prized for its Georgian Palladian architecture and its fine state of preservation. The house was never modernized
with electricity, indoor plumbing, or central heating in the more than 200
years it remained in the Drayton family. Nor was it damaged during the
Revolutionary War, burned during the Civil War, or leveled by any of the
hurricanes that have hit the Charleston area. The National Trust decided
to leave the house unfurnished to highlight the rich handcrafted detailing
found throughout the building.

## HISTORY

Drayton Hall is a historic house museum and a property of the prestigious National Trust for Historic Preservation. The National Trust is a
nonprofit private organization with a mission to encourage preservation of
significant American buildings, sites, and historic districts. National Trust

properties include the homes of presidents or notable Americans, as well as architectural landmarks like Drayton Hall. Built between 1738 and 1742, Drayton Hall is the oldest surviving example of Georgian Palladian architecture in the southern United States.

Located on the Ashley River near Charleston, Drayton Hall was built as a country estate for John Drayton, the son of Thomas Drayton who had immigrated to Carolina from Barbados in 1679. John was a plantation owner, a judge, and a member of the Royal Council to the governor from 1754 until the start of the American Revolution. An owner of several plantations, John Drayton, like many other members of South Carolina's planter class, was a wealthy man. His fortune was based on lucrative rice and indigo crops.

The architecture of the house demonstrates that John Drayton could afford to build a fashionable country estate, and that Charlestonians had access to the latest designs from England and the Continent. In the early 1700s, the Palladian style was popular in England.

Drayton Hall was occupied by seven generations of the Drayton family. It was sold to the National Trust by brothers Charles and Francis Drayton, who inherited the house from their aunt, Charlotta Drayton. The original owner, John Drayton, married four times and had seven children who survived to adulthood. He left the house to his fourth wife, Rebecca Perry Drayton, who was twenty when her husband died in 1779. In 1784, Rebecca passed the house on to Dr. Charles Drayton, her husband's oldest surviving son, and she moved into town. Charles had studied medicine at the University of Edinburgh. He was interested in horticulture and did experimental gardening. The house later passed to Charles's son, Charles, who was also a physician, and then to his grandson, Charles. His great grandson, Charles, was the next owner and the father of Charles and the above-mentioned Charlotta.

In addition to the Drayton family, Drayton Hall plantation was the home of many African-American slaves who worked as house workers, skilled laborers including carpenters and bricklayers, and farm laborers. The number of slaves varied over time. Census records in St. Andrews parish, in which Drayton Hall was located, indicate that in 1790, the first Charles owned 41 slaves. By 1800, he had increased his holdings to 172 slaves, while in 1810, the first and second Charleses together owned 181 slaves. By 1850, the number of slaves had decreased to 45.

Slave housing consisted of small, single-room, wood-frame structures raised on brick piers, often with adjacent space for gardens. Although archeological research has identified the probable locations of Drayton

Hall's slave quarters, none of these structures remain. The old slave cemetery still exists.

Richmond Bowens—a grandson of Caesar Bowens, who was a slave at Drayton Hall—has proven to be a valuable source of oral history. The research staff has recorded many of Bowens's reminiscences for their archives. Mr. Bowens also shares his memories and shows photographs to interested visitors on Mondays, Tuesdays, and Wednesdays. He can be found on the gift shop porch.

## SITE DESCRIPTION

One approaches **Drayton Hall** by driving down a long, shaded avenue of live oak trees. The house is exceptional because none of its owners altered it significantly. Central heating, plumbing, and electricity were never installed. To highlight the well-preserved architectural details and craftsmanship of the building, the National Trust chose not to furnish it.

Drayton Hall was built in the Georgian Palladian style, in which the principal rooms are arranged symmetrically around a spacious hall. The elaborate, handcrafted interior carved-wood decoration is classical. The rectangular, brick, two-story structure has a double-hipped roof, two interior end chimneys, a two-story pedimented entrance portico with two front stairways, and a center rear pediment. A ground-floor utilitarian basement contains the housekeeping and storage rooms. Although the architect is unknown, construction work was done by slaves and colonial craftsmen.

After the ground floor was already completed, John Drayton decided to enlarge the **great hall**. The wall to the **stair hall** was moved forty-two inches off its supporting foundation wall, and the grand staircase was pushed up against the windows of the river front. These changes weakened the whole structure.

Most of the walls of the house are paneled. Rich craftsmanship is displayed in the ornate wooden cornices, ceiling moldings, over mantels, door and window trims, and ceiling decorations. Interior carvings are of yellow poplar and mahogany. Originally, the walls were cream-colored, but they were painted blue about 1875. Original paint can be seen in two passageways.

In the **drawing room** are Ionic pilasters and elaborate cornice moldings. Windows have interior shutters. The **stair hall** has the original elaborately carved mahogany double stairs, mahogany wood-paneling, and a hand-molded, eighteenth-century ornamental ceiling. From the stair hall, you can enter the great hall on the first floor or climb the stairs to the second-floor great hall, both of which were used for entertaining.

At one time, there were flanking wings on either side of the house. There were also outbuildings on the property. Archaeological excavations have discovered much about these structures.

On a stroll along Drayton Hall's **nature trails**, you will see marshes, maritime trees, shrubs, ferns, rice ponds, and a variety of native flora.

## FESTIVALS/CRAFTS

There are the **Candlelight Concert** in March, the **Spring Oyster Roasts** in late March and early April, the **Lecture Series** in October and early November, the **Arts and Crafts Festival** in mid-November, and the **Spirituals Concert** in mid-December.

## SIDE TRIPS

Thomas and Ann Drayton built the first plantation house at **Magnolia Plantation and Gardens** in the 1680s, and, like Drayton Hall, the property remained in the Drayton family. Magnolia Plantation, located one mile north of Drayton Hall, is known for its **world-famous 50-acre gardens**, especially its 900 varieties of camellias and 250 varieties of azaleas. The gardens were planted around 1851 by Reverend John G. Drayton on the advice of his doctor after developing tuberculosis. During Reverend Drayton's lifetime, his gardens were so acclaimed that he opened them to the public in spring. Also on the grounds are an **eighteenth-century herb garden**, a **horticultural maze, large magnolia trees**, a **lawn surrounding an avenue of live oaks**, a **marsh**, a **125-acre wildfowl refuge**, and **walking and bike trails**. The turn-of-the-century plantation house is the third on the site. NR. Ten miles northwest of Charleston on SC Hwy. 61. (803) 571-1266. Open daily. Admission is charged.

# MIDDLETON PLACE

Restored eighteenth-century plantation and stableyards; oldest landscaped gardens in America; NR, NHL, HABS.

**Address:** Ashley River Rd., Charleston SC 29414-7206
**Telephone:** (803) 556-6020, 1-800-782-3608
**Location:** On the Ashley River, 14 miles northwest of Charleston, on SC Hwy. 61.
**Open:** 9:00 A.M.–5:00 P.M. daily.
**Admission:** House: adults $6. Gardens and stableyards: adults $12, children ages 6–12 $6.
**Restaurants:** Middleton Place Restaurant.
**Shops:** Museum Shop.
**Facilities:** 60 acres of formal gardens, limited handicapped accessible, guided house tours, working craftspeople.

## WHERE TO STAY

**Inns/Bed & Breakfasts:** Middleton Inn, SC Hwy. 61 at Ashley River Road, Charleston SC 29414, (803) 556-0500, 1-800-543-4774. Also see entries for other Charleston-area sites.

## OVERVIEW

On the Ashley River, **Middleton Place** is best known for its extraordinary **formal eighteenth-century gardens**. Thought to be the oldest landscaped gardens in America, they were begun by Henry Middleton in 1741, the year that he and Mary Williams were married. Part of Mary Williams's dowry, the plantation has remained in the Middleton family ever since.

The Middletons, who were active politically during the Revolutionary era, can boast of a family member who signed the Declaration of Independence. Later, relatives were active in the Civil War, and a Middleton descendent signed South Carolina's Ordinance of Secession.

During the Civil War, the plantation house and its flankers were burned. The least damaged was the south flanker. That portion of the restored house contains many Middleton family possessions. Living-history demonstrations of life on an eighteenth-century working rice plantation are given in the stableyards.

# HISTORY

Middleton Place was acquired by Henry Middleton in 1741 when he married Mary Williams, the only daughter of John Williams, a wealthy landowner. Mary's dowry included a house and plantation that the couple named "Middleton Place." It was in this home they lived and raised their five sons and seven daughters. Henry was the son of Edward Middleton, who had emigrated from England to Barbados and from there to South Carolina in 1678. On a large grant of land on Goose Creek not far from Charleston, Edward Middleton established a plantation called "The Oaks."

Henry was active politically. He held a variety of offices including Speaker of the Commons and Commissioner for Indian Affairs. He was a member of the governor's council until 1770, when he resigned to join the opposition to British policy. He represented South Carolina in the First Continental Congress and was elected its president in October 1774.

During his life, Henry was a major land holder who owned more than 50,000 acres and 800 slaves. Rice was the major crop grown at Middleton Place, which is located on the Ashley River twelve miles from the port of Charleston. Rice was shipped to Charleston for export to England.

Among Henry's interests was gardening. He was impressed by the formal gardens he had seen in England and other European countries, and began establishing formal gardens at Middleton Place in 1741. Large areas were landscaped in the symmetrical style of André Le Nôtre, who had designed Louis XIV's gardens at the Palace of Versailles. Laying out the gardens initially was a ten-year project labored on by one hundred black slaves.

After his wife Mary's death in 1761, Henry returned to the Oaks and gave Middleton Place to his eldest son, Arthur. Arthur had been educated in England and had studied law there. In 1775, he was elected to succeed his father in the Continental Congress and was a signer of the Declaration of Independence. He served in the defense of Charleston during the Revolution. After Charleston fell to the British in 1780, he was imprisoned for almost a year in St. Augustine.

On Arthur's death, Middleton Place was inherited by his son, Henry, who loved gardening and was a friend of the famous French botanist André Michaux. When Michaux visited Middleton, he brought with him the first camellias to be planted in a American garden.

Photo by Patricia A. Gutek

### Middleton Place, Charleston, South Carolina
The south flanker of the Middleton mansion (1741) became the family residence when, in February of 1865, a fire set by Union troops destroyed the main house and the north flanker. The mansion was built on the Ashley River, twelve miles from the port of Charleston, on a 50,000-acre rice plantation.

Middleton Place was passed next to Williams Middleton, Henry's son. Williams signed South Carolina's Ordinance of Secession. He also supplied the Confederates with laborers and materials for the defense of Charleston and Fort Sumter. Middleton Place was occupied by a detachment of General Sherman's army in 1865. On February 22, 1865, the plantation house was ransacked and burned.

The house at Middleton Place was built before 1741. The two detached flankers were added in 1755, the north designed as a conservatory and library, and the south as plantation offices and gentlemen's guest quarters. The south flanker was the least damaged in the fire. It was roofed over and strengthened, and became the family's residence. The 1886 earthquake reduced the gutted and charred brick walls of the main house and north flanker to rubble.

After years of neglect, the south flanker and the gardens were restored in the 1920s by Mr. and Mrs. J. Pringle Smith, descendants of Henry Middleton. Middleton Place was opened to the public seasonally in the 1930s, and established as a nonprofit organization in 1974.

## Site Description

Allow plenty of time to enjoy the guided tour of the house, and a leisurely self-guided tour of the **stableyards and gardens at Middleton Place**.

The **house at Middleton Place** is a two-story, reddish-brown brick Jacobean manor constructed in 1755 as the south flanker of the main house. It became the family residence after the plantation house was burned in 1865. Now restored, it contains family furniture, paintings, books, and documents dating from the early eighteenth century.

In the **main room** of the house are Benjamin West portraits of Henry Middleton and his son, Arthur, and a Thomas Sully portrait of Susan Pringle Smith. A Charleston-made breakfast table with Chinese Chippendale-style fretwork has been attributed to Thomas Elfe. Family pieces include a lady's workbox which belonged to Hester Middleton, the wife of Charles Drayton of Drayton Hall, eighteenth-century andirons owned by Oliver Hering Middleton, and some family silver.

In the **dining room** is a Sully portrait of his sister, Elizabeth Sully Smith, whose husband was a grandson of Henry Middleton. Over the fireplace is an early-nineteenth-century landscape which had been taken for "safekeeping" by a Massachusetts doctor attached to the Union troops who burned the house. After ten years of correspondence, the doctor agreed to return this and other paintings.

The **front hall** was added to the house after 1865. In it are watercolors and an 1812 archaeology textbook entitled *Grecian Remains in Italy*, by John Izard Middleton, who is considered to be America's first classical archaeologist. Also displayed are bonds and currency showing the Middletons' support of the Confederacy, and a handwritten pass signed by President Abraham Lincoln allowing a Middleton woman safe passage through Union lines.

The second floor has three bedrooms and a library. The **winter bedroom** has a ca. 1800 Charleston rice bed, named for the rice motif carved on the footposts. A leather trunk lined with camphor wood that had been owned by Governor Henry Middleton was found in a plantation barn in the 1930s. It was filled with mid-eighteenth-century garments belonging to the governor's father and grandfather, which are now displayed in a ca. 1800 Charleston clothes press. While heavy bedcovers drape the bed in the winter bedroom, mosquito netting and cotton dimity cover the rice bed in the **summer bedroom**.

Although many of the Middleton family's books burned with the house, the **library** contains rare eighteenth and nineteenth century volumes.

The **plantation stableyards** provide a picture of the day-to-day world of a self-sustaining rice plantation. Barns, sheds, and enclosures were reconstructed in the 1930s and opened to the public in the 1970s. These structures now house working craftspeople, including a blacksmith, potter, carpenter, and weaver, demonstrating their crafts. Horses, mules, sheep, goats, and peacocks wander in the **greensward** and **paddocks**. If visitors are so inclined, they may help with milking, first thing in the morning and again about 4:00 P.M.

An 1870s two-family slave dwelling called **"Eliza's House"** is named for former occupant, Eliza Leach, an African American born in 1891. It had previously been the home of former slaves Ned and Chloe, who remained at Middleton Place after emancipation. The small, rectangular duplex, constructed of mill-sawn weatherboard, has a central, double fireplace.

Middleton Place is famous for its eighteenth-century **landscaped gardens** which were lovingly restored in the 1920s. The Garden Club of America awarded Middleton Place the prestigious Bulkley Metal in 1941 in commemoration of 200 years of enduring beauty.

The gardens were designed to take advantage of the natural beauty of the terrain. On a long curve of the **Ashley River**, a bluff overlooks tidal marshes used as rice fields. The main house was situated on a high point overlooking the water. A succession of gently sculpted, graduated terraces leading to **Butterfly Lakes** are placed between the house and the Ashley River. Butterfly Lakes are a pair of lakes shaped like butterfly wings, separated by a thin bridge of land. The **garden** forms a right triangle lying northwest of the house and is divided by parallel and perpendicular paths and allées.

Tall hedges of azalea, camellia, sweet shrub, and mountain laurel define the small gardens and border the broad lawns. Among the oldest plants are crepe myrtle and the camellias, now small trees which bloom from December through mid-March. The first **camellias** planted in the United States, they were brought to Middleton in the late 1700s by the famous French botanist André Michaux. The 60,000 azaleas at Middleton Gardens are especially dramatic when in bloom from mid-March through mid-April on the **Azalea Hillside**, a bank near the rice millpond. Shaped like a wagon wheel, the **Rose Garden** has a colorful array of eighteenth- and nineteenth-century flowers. Nearby is the 145-foot-wide live oak called the **"Middleton Oak,"** which was on the property when the Middletons arrived and is considered one of the country's oldest oak trees.

## FESTIVALS/CRAFTS

Working craftspeople including a blacksmith, potter, carpenter and weaver demonstrate eighteenth-century crafts on a regular basis. Special events include the **Sheep to Shawl Demonstration** in April, the **Starlight Pops Concert** in May, the **Spoleto Festival Finale** in June, **Plantation Days** in November, and **Christmas activities** in December.

# BOONE HALL PLANTATION

Twentieth-century plantation house and original
mid-nineteenth-century slave cabins; avenue of
live oaks and gardens; NR.

**Address:** PO Box 1554, Mt. Pleasant SC 29465
**Telephone:** (803) 884-4371
**Location:** Mount Pleasant is an island 6 miles north of Charleston, South
Carolina, on US 17.
**Open:** April–Labor Day, 8:30 A.M.–6:30 P.M. Monday–Saturday, 1:00–5:00
P.M. Sunday; Labor Day–March 9:00 A.M.–5:00 P.M. Monday–Satur-
day, 1:00 to 4:00 P.M. Sunday.
**Admission:** Adults $7.50, seniors age 60 and over $6, children ages 6–12
$3.
**Restaurants:** Plantation Kitchen Restaurant.
**Shops:** Gift Shop in Gin House.
**Facilities:** Guided tour, extensive gardens.

## WHERE TO STAY

**Inns/Bed & Breakfasts:** Guilds, 101 Pitt St., Mt. Pleasant SC 29464,
(803) 881-0510.
**Motels/Hotels:** Wild Dunes Resort, Box 20575, Charleston SC 29413,
(803) 886-6000, 1-800-845-8880. Shem Creek Inn, 1401 Shrimp
Boat Lane, Mt. Pleasant SC 29464, 1-800-523-4951, (803)
881-1000.
**Camping:** Campground at James Island County Park, 871 Riverland Dr.,
Charleston SC 29412, (803) 795-9884. Charleston KOA, 9494
Hwy. 78, Ladson SC 29456, (803) 797-1045. Oak Plantation Campground, 3540 Savannah Hwy., Charleston SC 29455, (803)
766-5936.

## OVERVIEW

Every plantation is unique, deviating in some way from the classic
"Gone with the Wind" image. So it is with Boone Hall. Although the history of Boone Hall Plantation goes back to the seventeenth century, its
plantation house dates only to 1935. Yet a magnificent half-mile-long av-

enue of live oaks leading up to the house exceeds expectations. And the truly historical aspect of Boone Hall Plantation is its row of rare, original mid-nineteenth-century slave cabins.

Although the current owners reside in the plantation house, there are guided tours of its first floor. The gardens are especially beautiful.

## HISTORY

Boone Hall Plantation property was part of a series of land grants dating to 1681 from South Carolina's lords proprietors to Major John Boone. Boone came to South Carolina in 1670 with the initial group of English settlers, known as the "First Fleet." He was involved politically, serving as a lord proprietor's deputy, a member of the Grand Council, and a vestry of Christ Church. Boone family members would continue to be politically prominent. Sara Boone, a daughter of John Boone, and her husband, Andrew Rutledge, were the grandparents of Edward Rutledge, a signer of the Declaration of Independence, and John Rutledge, the first governor of South Carolina.

Boone Hall was a cotton plantation which eventually grew to 17,000 acres. When John and Henry Horlbeck became the owners of Boone Hall in 1817, they successfully planted pecan groves. Another industry was the production of handmade bricks and tiles. These bricks were used in many of the plantation's buildings, including the slave cabins built around 1843—nine of which are still standing.

The present house at Boone Hall was built by owner Thomas Stone in 1935, following the floor plan of a previous mid-eighteenth-century house, with the exception of the indoor kitchen. In earlier centuries, particularly in the South, a kitchen was a separate structure built at a distance from the house because of the heat it generated and the constant danger of fire. Six kitchens burned at Boone Hall.

Boone Hall Plantation has been the setting for many television and movie productions including *North and South*, *Queen*, and *Sweet Bird of Youth*. It opened to the public in the 1950s.

## SITE DESCRIPTION

Today, **Boone Hall** is a privately owned 750-acre plantation with still-productive pecan groves. The approach to Boone Hall is through a half-mile drive with a row of live oaks draped with Spanish moss on either side. These trees were planted in 1743 by Captain Thomas Boone, a son of Major John Boone. Although the rows are a considerable distance apart,

Photo by Patricia A. Gutek

**Boone Hall Plantation, Mount Pleasant, South Carolina**
This row of rare, mid-nineteenth-century cabins for house servants is located
near the Boone Hall Plantation House. These nine simple brick dwellings are
among the last remaining original slave quarters in the South.

the 250-year-old trees have intertwined over the road, creating a dramatic
arch.

**Boone Hall Plantation House** was built in 1935 following the design
of its mid-eighteenth-century predecessor. The 1935 house is constructed
of bricks made at Boone Hall, some of which were obtained from the earlier house. The McRae family, the present owners, occupy the second and
third floors of the Greek Revival, two-and-one-half-story plantation
house, while the first floor is open for guided tours. Antique furniture in
the house belongs to the McRaes.

Costumed tour guides take groups through first-floor rooms. Furnishings date from the eighteenth and nineteenth centuries. The **library/music
room** has off-white painted cypress walls, dental molding, and built-in
bookcases. Furniture includes a partners' desk, a 150-year-old Knoble piano, a 1780 marble-top table, and a 1780 piecrust table.

A **free-flying staircase** is in the hall. The **dining room** has an 1840 brass and crystal chandelier, and a long 1700s Hepplewhite mahogany table. The eleven-foot mirror dates to 1841.

The **loggia** is a warm and airy room with vaulted ceilings, brick walls, brick floors, and French doors leading to a large brick patio bordered by a low, serpentine brick wall. Furnished with wicker furniture, it has a charming view of wisteria vine-covered arbors, the gardens, and the creek.

Wooden beams from the original house decorate the ceiling of the wood-paneled **study**, which has several historical pictures of Boone Hall Plantation as well as copies of the Boone land grants.

The nine **slave cabins** are among the last mid-nineteenth-century slave quarters remaining in the South. These small rectangular homes, made from brick produced at Boone Hall Plantation, were built in 1843 near the main house because they were for house servants. Cabins for field workers were located near the cotton fields. The identical one-room cabins have slate roofs, dirt floors, a door, a fireplace, and several shuttered windows. The contrast between the minimal quarters of black slave families and the spacious, well-decorated facilities for the white owner's family is dramatic.

Boone Hall's **formal gardens** are one of its major features. Handmade brick walkways wind through well-tended beds of hundreds of varieties of camellias and azaleas.

# FORT SUMTER NATIONAL MONUMENT

Mid-nineteenth-century seacoast fortification;
site of the first engagement of the Civil War,
April 12–13, 1861; NR, HABS.

**Address:** 1214 Middle St., Sullivan's Island SC 29482

**Telephone:** (803) 883-3123

**Location:** Charleston is in southeast South Carolina, on the Atlantic Ocean. Fort Sumter is in Charleston Harbor and is accessible only by boat. Fort Moultrie, also a part of the National Monument, is located on West Middle St., Sullivan's Island, 10 miles east of Charleston.

**Open:** Fort Sumter: April 1–Labor Day, 10 A.M.–5:30 P.M. daily; hours vary the rest of the year; closed Christmas Day. Fort Moultrie: 9:00 A.M.–5:00 P.M. daily; closed Christmas Day.

**Admission:** Fort Sumter: free. Tour boat to Fort Sumter: adults $9, children ages 6–12 $4.50. Tour boats operated by a National Park Service concessionaire leave from the City Marina on Lockwood Dr., just south of US 17 in Charleston, and from Patriots Point in Mt. Pleasant. For boat schedules, call (803) 722-1691 or write Fort Sumter Tours, Inc., 205 King St., Suite 204, Charleston SC 29401.

**Shops:** Fort Sumter: museum shop. Fort Moultrie: museum shop.

**Facilities:** There is a museum and the whole site is partially handicapped accessible. Fort Moultrie and Battery Jasper on Sullivan's Island have a visitor center.

## WHERE TO STAY

**Inns/Bed & Breakfasts:** Church Street Inn, 177 Church St., Charleston SC 29401, (803) 722-3420, 1-800-552-3777. John Rutledge House, 116 Broad St., Charleston SC 29401, (803) 723-7999, 1-800-476-9741, FAX: (803) 720-2615. The Lodge Alley Inn, 195 East Bay St., Charleston SC 29401, (803) 722-1611, 1-800-845-1004, FAX: (803) 722-1611, ext. 7777.

**Motels/Hotels:** Masters Inn, 300 Wingo Way, Mt. Pleasant SC 29464,

(803) 884-2814, 1-800-633-3434. Hawthorne Suites at the Market, 181 Church St., Charleston SC 29401, (803) 577-2644, FAX: (803) 577-2697. Mills House Hotel, 115 Meeting St., Charleston SC 29401, (803) 577-2400, 1-800-874-9600, FAX: (803) 722-2112. Omni Hotel at Charleston Place, 130 Market St., Charleston SC 29401, (803) 722-4900, FAX: (803) 722-0728.

**Camping:** Edisto Beach State Park, 8377 State Cabin Rd., Edisto Island SC 29438, (803) 869-2756, (803) 869-2156. Francis Marion National Forest, 1835 Assembly St., Columbia SC 29201, (803) 765-5222. James Island County Park, 871 Riverland Dr., Charleston SC 29412, (803) 795-9884. Oak Plantation Campground, 3540 Savannah Hwy., John's Island SC 29455, (803) 766-5936.

## OVERVIEW

A pentagonal seacoast fort built after the War of 1812 was the site of the first conflict of the American Civil War. Possession of the U.S. fort in Charleston Harbor was disputed. South Carolina seceded from the Union in December 1860, after Abraham Lincoln's election as president, and the state considered the unfinished and ungarrisoned fort its territory. When Major Robert Anderson and his Federal troops garrisoned the fort, Charlestonians were outraged and demanded that the Federal government order his evacuation. President Buchanan, who wanted to end his term in office peacefully, refused the request.

When President Lincoln ordered Federal supply ships to bring provisions to Fort Sumter's garrison, who were close to starvation, angry Confederates demanded that Major Anderson surrender the fort immediately. When he refused, Confederate fire on Fort Sumter began on April 12, 1861. It was the first engagement of the Civil War. The thirty-four-hour bombardment ended with a Federal surrender, and the fort remained in Confederate hands until 1865. Federal assaults on the fort during the intervening years severely damaged the brick structure so that today's fort appears substantially different from the original fortification.

## HISTORY

Like Florida's Fort Zachary Taylor (see p. 47), Fort Sumter was one of a series of coastal fortifications built by the United States after the War of 1812. In that conflict, the British successfully blockaded the eastern coast of the United States. British troops took advantage of the poorly defended Chesapeake coast to march into Washington and set fire to the Capitol, the White House, and other government buildings.

Photo by Patricia A. Gutek

**Fort Sumter National Monument, Sullivan's Island, South Carolina**
This 200-pound Parrott rifled cannon was discovered in 1959 during
the excavation of the parade ground at Fort Sumter, the mid-nineteenth-
century pentagonal fortification on the coast of South Carolina where in
1861 the first engagement of the Civil War took place. Federal troops
also used this type of cannon from 1863 to 1865 to bombard Fort Sumter
from Morris Island.

The government's determination to strengthen the seacoast defense
systems resulted in a large-scale fort building program. In 1817, Congress
established a military Board of Engineers for Seacoast Fortifications to survey the coastline of the United States to identify strategic fort locations.

Plans for building Fort Sumter on a shoal in Charleston Harbor were
drawn up in 1827, but construction proceeded very slowly. Operations
were suspended entirely in 1834, when ownership of the fort site became
unclear. In 1841, the federal government received clear title to the 125
acres of underwater land.

Fort Sumter was a pentagonal-shaped fort with five-foot-thick brick
masonry walls built on a granite foundation. It soared fifty feet above low
tide. Situated in the harbor, it was completely surrounded by water.

Fort Sumter was still not completed on December 1860, when Abraham Lincoln was elected U.S. president and South Carolina voted to secede from the Union. Over the next couple of months, Mississippi, Florida, Alabama, Georgia, and Louisiana also seceded. The secessionist states called themselves the Confederate States of America and elected Jefferson Davis as their president in February 1861.

Though U.S. forts and naval yards in most Confederate states were quickly claimed by the South, Fort Sumter was an exception. Because it was still under construction, it was not garrisoned but was occupied by about eighty engineer workmen. Other Federal installations in Charleston Harbor were Fort Moultrie on Sullivan's Island, Castle Pinckney on Shute's Folly Island, Fort Johnson on James Island, and a U.S. arsenal in Charleston. Fort Moultrie was the only garrisoned post.

Six days after South Carolina seceded, Major Robert Anderson transferred the eighty-five men under his command from nearby Fort Moultrie to Fort Sumter because he felt that Moultrie was indefensible. Charlestonians were outraged by what they considered an act of aggression by Anderson. The governor of South Carolina, Francis Pickens, sent commissioners to Washington demanding that the Federal government evacuate Charleston Harbor. On December 28, 1860, President Buchanan denied that request. In fact, the U.S. House of Representatives voted approval of what they termed Anderson's bold and patriotic act.

South Carolina volunteers occupied Fort Moultrie, the U.S. arsenal, Fort Johnson, and Castle Pinckney and began erecting defensive batteries around the harbor. Fort Sumter prepared for attack. In addition to the fifteen guns already mounted when Anderson arrived, forty-five more guns, including forty-two-pounders and Columbiads, were mounted in the first tier of casemates, on the parapet, the parade ground, and around the sally port. The second tier of casemates was bricked up because of the limited number of troops available to man guns. Since the Federal government did not want any aggressive action taken that would spark a civil war, Anderson was under orders to act strictly on the defensive.

Abraham Lincoln was inaugurated as president of the United States on March 4, 1861. In his inaugural address, he stated that national authority must be upheld against the threat of disunion and that the power of the government would be used to hold and occupy Federal forts and property in the seceded states.

Meanwhile, at Fort Sumter, food and supplies were running low. Unless Anderson were resupplied, evacuation of the fort was inevitable. Though most of his cabinet members thought that holding or defending

Fort Sumter was impossible, President Lincoln decided to send ships carrying provisions to Fort Sumter. When this action was announced to the governor of South Carolina, Confederate harbor fortifications were accelerated.

General Beauregard, who was the commander of Confederate military operations in and around Charleston Harbor, was ordered to demand evacuation of the fort, and, if refused, to "reduce the fort." ("Reduce" is a military term which means to take control of or conquer.) On April 11, the request for evacuation was presented to Anderson, who denied it. After a second request, Anderson agreed to evacuate by noon on the 15th of April. Since Federal supply ships were expected by that time, Anderson's answer was rejected by Confederate officers.

The first mortar shell was fired on Fort Sumter by the Confederates at 4:30 A.M. on April 12, 1861. This was the beginning of the Civil War. Though Anderson and his small garrison defended the fort, they were hopelessly outnumbered and outgunned. Surrender terms were offered to Anderson, and after some negotiations, Anderson and his garrison marched out of the fort with drums beating and colors flying on Sunday, April 14. The only fatalities occurred not from the thirty-four-hour bombardment but accidentally just prior to the garrison's departure. On April 14, a misfire during a hundred-gun salute to the United States flag killed Private Daniel Hough and injured Private Edward Galloway, who died several days later. Fort Sumter suffered extensive damage from both the shelling and fire.

Now in Confederate hands, Fort Sumter was garrisoned and repaired. Despite the Federal naval blockade off the Atlantic coast, Confederate ships were able to enter and leave Charleston Harbor with war supplies—much to the chagrin of Union officers. They were determined to re-take Charleston and Fort Sumter. A Federal naval attack on April 7, 1863, was rebuffed. A land and sea attack that commenced the following August and continued until December turned much of the fort to rubble, but the Confederates refused to surrender the fort. In the summer of 1864, a two-month Union bombardment also failed. Eighteen months of bombarding Fort Sumter by the Federals was unsuccessful. However, General William T. Sherman's troops advancing north from Savannah caused the withdrawal of Confederate troops from Fort Sumter. Along with the other Confederate fortifications in Charleston harbor, Fort Sumter was evacuated on February 17, 1865.

After the Civil War, Fort Sumter was a sorry site due to heavy damage from Federal bombardments. In the decade after the war, the army attempted to repair the structure so that it could once again serve as a military facility. From 1876 to 1897, Fort Sumter was not garrisoned and served mainly as a lighthouse station. Improvements—including Battery Huger, a massive concrete emplacement—were made around 1898 because of the impending Spanish-American War. During World War I, a small garrison was stationed at the fort. It again fell into disuse until World War II, when the fort was reactivated. Fort Sumter became a national monument in 1948.

Fort Moultrie is also a part of Fort Sumter National Monument. It is located on Sullivan's Island. This 1809 masonry structure, the third Fort Moultrie on the same site, is structurally intact. The first fort on Sullivan's Island, built in 1776, was constructed of palmetto logs. The second fort was a five-sided structure with earth and timber walls seventeen feet high. Completed in 1798, it was destroyed by a hurricane in 1804.

## SITE DESCRIPTION

Access to **Fort Sumter** is only by boat. Tour boats operated by a National Park Service concessionaire leave from the city marina on Lockwood Drive, just south of US 17 in Charleston, and from Patriots Point in Mount Pleasant.

Fort Sumter today is very different from the red brick, multi-tiered fort that figured so prominently in the onset of the Civil War. Much of the fort was reduced to rubble from continued Federal bombardment during the Civil War. Repairs were made, but the fort was not returned to its original appearance. Fifty-foot walls were reduced to approximately half their original height. A new sally port was constructed. In later years, modifications were added. Battery Huger, a massive concrete emplacement built across the parade ground in 1899, dominates today's fort. The size of the fort still is awesome, and the symmetry of the surviving arched brick casemates is superb.

The **sally port**, or entrance, runs through the center of the fort's **left-flank** wall. When the fort was built, the sally port was on the gorge wall facing Confederate batteries on Morris Island.

Two guns are mounted on casemate, or gunroom, carriages in the left flank. One is a rifled and banded forty-two-pounder while the other is a forty-two-pounder smoothbore. Two tiers of casemates or gunrooms were built on the left-flank wall, right-flank wall, right-face wall, and left-face wall. Each casemate held one gun, which could be moved on a track to adjust the angle of fire through the embrasure. Intact casemates remain on the left-flank and right-face walls.

**Left-face casemates** are in ruins. Holes in the wall still remain from the 1863–1865 siege of Charleston. Near the casemate ruins are two fifteen-inch smoothbore Rodman guns, an eight-inch Columbiad, and a ten-inch mortar.

Displayed in the **right face** are several 100-pounder Parrott rifled cannons, the type used by the Federals on Morris Island to bombard Fort Sumter from 1863 to 1865. They were placed in the lower-tier casemates in the 1870s. When Battery Huger was constructed in 1899, these cannon were buried with the casemates. In 1959, excavation of the parade ground opened the casemates, and eleven Parrott guns were uncovered.

Captain Abner Doubleday fired the first shot from Fort Sumter on April 12, 1861, from a gun in the first-tier casemate of the **right gorge angle**.

Ruins are all that remain of the **officers' quarters** and the **enlisted men's barracks**, each of which had been three-story brick structures.

A plaque in memory of Sumter's Confederate defenders was erected on the left exterior wall of the Sally port in 1929. Another tablet containing a roster of the original garrison that served under Major Anderson was erected in 1932.

When **Battery Huger** was built in 1899 in the parade ground, the remainder of the parade was filled with sand. This was removed by the National Park Service in the 1950s. Flags flying in front of Battery Huger include an 1861 U.S. flag, an 1861 First National Confederate flag, a South Carolina State flag, an 1863 Second National Confederate flag, and an 1865 U.S. flag.

Inside Battery Huger is the fort's **museum**. Until recently, its exhibits concentrated on the fort's 1861–1865 history. Updated exhibits also focus on the constitutional issues that preceded the Civil War, as well as the social, economic, and political events that led up to the conflict.

**Fort Moultrie** has been restored to portray the major periods of its history, which begins in 1776 when it protected Charleston from the British and proceeds to World War II when a Harbor Entrance Control Post was built from which Charleston Harbor defenses were coordinated. There is an audiovisual orientation program in the **visitor center**.

## SIDE TRIPS

**Patriots Point Naval and Maritime Museum**, the world's largest such museum, is located on a point overlooking Charleston Harbor and Fort Sumter. Tours of several famous World War II vessels are fascinating for both children and adults. The enormous aircraft carrier *Yorktown* has historic planes displayed on its hangar and flight decks. The destroyer *Laffey* and the Coast Guard cutter *Ingham* are also World War II vessels. Other ships to tour include the submarine *Clamagore* and the nuclear-powered merchant ship *Savannah*. The museum is located off US 17 on the Mount Pleasant side of the Cooper River Bridge. (803) 884-2727. Open daily. Admission is charged.

# TENNESSEE

1. Gatlinburg: Mountain Farm Museum and Cades Cove
2. Norris: Museum of Appalachia
3. Rugby: Historic Rugby

# MOUNTAIN FARM MUSEUM AND CADES COVE

Re-created 1900 southern Appalachian farmstead and restored rural Tennessee hill country log buildings in the Great Smoky Mountains National Park.

**Address:** Superintendent, Great Smoky Mountains National Park, 107 Park Headquarters Rd., Gatlinburg TN 37738
**Telephone:** (615) 436-1200
**Location:** Great Smoky Mountains National Park is located in southeastern Tennessee and southwestern North Carolina. Mountain Farm Museum is on the North Carolina side, adjacent to the Oconaluftee Visitor Center, 2 miles north of Cherokee, North Carolina. Cades Cove is on the Tennessee side, with the restored buildings located on the 11-mile Cades Cove Loop Road.
**Open:** Daily, sunrise to sunset.
**Admission:** Free.
**Shops:** Bookstores in park's visitor centers.
**Facilities:** Park facilities include three visitor centers, campgrounds, backpacking, bicycling, fishing, trail rides, hiking trails, nature trails, ranger-led walks, ranger lectures.

## WHERE TO STAY

**Inns/Bed & Breakfasts:** Cataloochee Ranch, Rt. 1, Box 500F, Maggie Valley NC 28751, (704) 926-1401, 1-800-868-1401. Hippensteal Inn, Gatlinburg TN 37738, (615) 436-5761, 1-800-527-8110. Buckhorn Inn, 2140 Tudor Mtn. Rd., Gatlinburg TN 37738, (615) 436-4668.
**Motels/Hotels:** Maggie Valley Resort and Country Club, 340 Country Club Road, Maggie Valley NC 28751, 1-800-438-3861, (704) 926-1616. Days Inn, SC Hwy 19 North, Cherokee NC 28719, (704) 497-9171. Holiday Inn-Cherokee, Box 1929, Cherokee NC 28719, (704) 497-9181. Brookside Resort, 463 East Parkway, Gatlinburg TN 37738, 1-800-251-9597, (615) 436-5611. Le Conte View, PO Box

252, 929 Parkway, Gatlinburg TN 37738, (615) 436-5032, 1-800-842-5767.

**Camping:** Great Smoky Mountains National Park, Gatlinburg TN 37738, (615) 436-1200.

## OVERVIEW

Going to the Great Smoky Mountains National Park to see the Mountain Farm Museum and Cades Cove historic sites is definitely putting the cart before the horse. The 800-square-mile southern Appalachian national park known for its flowering plants, half a million acres of forests, mountains covered with mist, and hundreds of miles of hiking trails is definitely the major draw, while its historic structures are the lesser attraction. Still, the focus of this guide book is historic sites, and the setting couldn't be better, so visit the Mountain Farm Museum and Cades Cove during your vacation in the scenic Smoky Mountains.

Mountain Farm Museum, in North Carolina, includes eleven original structures abandoned after land was purchased for the national park. Moved from their original sites and assembled in a clearing surrounded by mountains, they depict a southern Appalachian farmstead.

Cades Cove, Tennessee, was a well-populated rural community of over 600 people in the nineteenth century. Stretched along an eleven-mile loop drive, the remaining structures at Cades Cove include a working gristmill, a variety of barns, three churches, and several log homes and frame homes. The national park has one of the finest collections of log buildings in the country.

## HISTORY

By the late 1700s, white pioneers—mainly people of English, Scotch-Irish, German, and Irish descent—migrated from New York, Pennsylvania, South Carolina, and Georgia to the Oconaluftee River Valley in North Carolina. This area, now occupied by Great Smoky Mountains National Park, straddles the southern Appalachian region. It was inhabited for many centuries by Cherokee Indians, who had constructed permanent towns, cultivated croplands, and laid networks of trails throughout their territory. Land-hungry settlers encroached upon Cherokee land, refusing to recognize the property rights of the tribes. This caused continual friction between whites and Cherokees. Eventually, the whites won.

By 1800, settlers entered the Tennessee side of the Smokies. The terms of a 1819 treaty with the Cherokees made Tennessee the owner of this land. Many individuals acquired state land grants. Also, speculators

Photo by Patricia A. Gutek

## Mountain Farm Museum, Great Smoky Mountains National Park, Gatlinburg, Tennessee

Mountain Farm Museum, a re-created southern Appalachian farmstead set in a small clearing surrounded by heavily wooded mountains, features basic farm machinery and original log structures.

purchased land from the state and then sold it to people who had moved from western North Carolina, southwestern Virginia, and upper east Tennessee. In 1818, John Oliver became the first white settler in Cades Cove. By 1850, Cades Cove had a population of 685 in 132 households.

By the 1835 Treaty of New Echota, all Cherokee lands were ceded to the United States. Cherokees were to be moved beyond the Mississippi River to what is now Oklahoma. Native American resistance to their removal led to their being rounded up by federal troops and forced to march to Oklahoma on the infamous "Trail of Tears." Some members of the Cherokee Nation hid in the mountains and were regarded as fugitives by the United States Army.

Another group who remained behind were the Oconaluftee Indians of North Carolina. On the basis of earlier treaties, they claimed a separate status from the Cherokee Nation, which gave them the right to avoid removal and remain in North Carolina. Since these Qualla or Oconaluftee Cherokees received official permission to stay, they did not hide in the mountains. They are the ancestors of the Eastern Band of the Cherokees who live on a reservation near the national park today.

Life for rural white families in the Oconaluftee River Valley and Cades Cove revolved around subsistence farming supplemented by hunting, trapping, and timbering. Through hard labor, forested areas were gradually turned into field and pastures. Frontier characteristics, including old customs and speech patterns, persisted for a long time.

In the early 1900s, this rural pattern was radically altered by the arrival of logging companies. Sawmills began cutting down one of the finest spreads of timber in the United States. Logging not only altered the beauty of nature but also disrupted the economy of the mountaineers.

A movement to create a national park in the vicinity of the Tennessee-North Carolina border began around the turn of the century but foundered because of the large amount of funding needed to acquire the property. In contrast to some western national parks consisting of unpopulated, government-owned land, fifteen percent of the land to be acquired for the Great Smokies was owned by about 1,400 small farmers, and the other eighty-five percent of the land was owned by approximately eighteen large timber companies. The states of North Carolina and Tennessee raised five million dollars, and that amount in matching funds from the Laura Spellman Rockefeller Memorial Fund facilitated land purchases. By this time, more than sixty percent of the original forest had been lost to the

Photo by Patricia A. Gutek

**Cades Cove, Great Smoky Mountains National Park,
Gatlinburg, Tennessee**
The Primitive Baptist Church was organized in 1827 by the founders of the
rural community called "Cades Cove," who are now buried
in the church's cemetery.

lumber companies, but the remainder was preserved. Most of the forest in
the park today is second growth.

On June 15, 1934, Congress authorized the Great Smoky Mountains
National Park, the largest national park east of the Mississippi River. It
was formally dedicated by President Franklin Roosevelt in September
1940.

Though the mountaineers whose land had been purchased gradually
left the area, their buildings remained. The National Park Service preserved some of these historic structures. Almost a dozen of them were
moved to Mountain Farm Museum, near Oconaluftee Visitors' Center in
Oconaluftee, North Carolina. Another collection of buildings lies just
across the state line in Cades Cove, Tennessee. Other historic buildings
are scattered throughout the park. Of the more than 6,000 structures still

standing when land purchasing began, seventy-seven remain. These buildings help interpret life in the southern Appalachians. Visitors can easily walk through the Mountain Farm Museum; however, the Cades Cove structures are distributed along an eleven-mile loop drive.

## SITE DESCRIPTION

**Mountain Farm Museum**, set in a small clearing surrounded by heavily wooded mountains, consists of eleven historic structures moved from their original locations throughout the half-million-acre park to re-create a southern Appalachian farmstead.

Stop first at the **Oconaluftee Visitors' Center**. Notice the remarkable painting of a local woman at age 100 called *Aunt Winchester, Matriarch of the Smokies*.

Not all buildings at **Pioneer Farmstead** are furnished, and frequently there is no interpretive staff. Tours are self-guided.

The two-story log **John Davis House** with two stone chimneys was built by that craftsman.

A **Meat House** was essential to a winter food supply. Soon after the first frost, usually in November, hogs were butchered. The meat, arranged in layers, was placed in barrels or wooden boxes filled with salt. After the meat was cured, it was hung from poles to keep it dry and inaccessible to rodents. Meat from wild game was also stored in the meat house.

Another food-storage building was the **Apple House**, a two-story wooden structure with a stone base. Summer apples were kept on the upper floor, winter apples on the lower. The thick stone walls prevented freezing.

Corn was stored in the small, one-story **Corncrib**. Corn kept the livestock fed and was the staple of the families' diet.

Chickens, kept in the **Chicken House**, provided meat and eggs as well as feathers for bedding. Other buildings here include a **Corn Crib/ Gear Shed**, where farm implements could be stored; a **Springhouse**, which protected the water source and contained a cooling trough for storing perishables; and a **Blacksmith Shop**.

A **garden**, usually tended by a farm woman and her children, was the family's source of beans, cabbage, lettuce, onions, peppers, potatoes, and turnips. This farmstead also includes a **pigpen**, a **bee gum stand** (sections of hollow black gum trees used as bee hives), and a **sorghum mill** (animal-powered two-roller mill that squeezed the juice from sorghum cane). Molasses was made from the boiled-down sorghum cane juice.

Nearby is the **Mingus Mill**, where corn was ground into meal. The

JOHN OLIVER
1793 ——— 1864
AND WIFE
LURENA FRAZIER
OLIVER
1795 ——— 1888
FIRST PERMANENT
WHITE SETTLERS OF
CADES COVE
1817 ——— 1818

Photo by Patricia A. Gutek

**Cades Cove, Great Smoky Mountains National Park,
Gatlinburg, Tennessee**
In the graveyard of the Primitive Baptist Church in Cades Cove is the
headstone of John and Lurena Frazier Oliver. The inscription indicates that the
Olivers were the first permanent white settlers in this mountain community,
homesteading here in 1817–1818.

mill—named for the Mingus family, believed to be one of the valley's first white settlers—is on its original site.

On the Tennessee side of the park is another collection of nineteenth-century buildings, **Cades Cove**. Follow the eleven-mile loop through what is left of rural Cades Cove. Some of the structures are on their original sites, while others have been moved from other locations in Cades Cove.

The **John Oliver Place**, built in the 1850s, stands on property purchased by John and Lurena Oliver in 1826. The Olivers are buried in the **cemetery** of the **Primitive Baptist Church**, which was organized in 1827.

The small, white frame **Methodist Church** was built by carpenter and blacksmith J. D. McCampbell, who then became its preacher.

A disagreement among members of the Primitive Baptist Church over missionary work resulted in the formation of the **Missionary Baptist Church** in 1839. The white frame church was built in 1894.

At the **Elijah Oliver Homestead**, outbuildings include a **springhouse, barn**, and **meathouse**. The **Elijah Oliver Log House** has a lower kitchen section off the back, which had formerly been the home of the Herron family.

The **John Cable Mill** is on its original site. Cable's corn mill dates to about 1870; it has its original millstones and gears. The large **cantilever barn** was used for livestock, farm equipment, and storage of hay and fodder. The **Gregg-Cable House** was built by Leason Gregg in 1879. It is believed to be the first frame house in the cove. The **blacksmith shop** is a reconstruction.

The craftsmanship of the 1898 **Henry Whitehead Log House** is considered outstanding. Logs were sawn square at a mill, and the interior log faces, ceiling joists, and boards were dressed with a hand plane. The brick chimney was made of brick molded and fired on the property.

Another example of fine craftsmanship can be found at the **Dan Lawson House**, which was built around 1856 by Lawson and his father-in-law, Peter Cable.

At the **Tipton Place** is a frame house built shortly after the Civil War. In 1878, it became the home of James McCaulley, a blacksmith. There are also a **blacksmith shop**, a **bee gum stand**, a **smokehouse**, and a double-pen **corn crib**.

The **Carter Shields Place** is a one-story log house with a loft. Unusual features are the beaded paneling in the living room and a closed-in stairway.

## FESTIVALS/CRAFTS

At Cades Cove, there are **Old Timers' Days** in May and September, a **Storytelling Festival** in late June, a **Quilt Show** at the end of July, and **Molasses Making** in early October. At the **Mountain Farm Museum, Southern Appalachian Women's Day** is in late June, and the **Mountain Life Festival** is held in September.

# MUSEUM OF APPALACHIA

Re-created rural Appalachian mountain village.

**Address:** PO Box 0318, Norris TN 37828
**Telephone:** (615) 494-7680, (615) 494-0514
**Location:** In northeastern Tennessee, 16 miles north of Knoxville, on I-75 exit 122.
**Open:** 8:00 A.M.–5:00 P.M. daily; closed Christmas Day.
**Admission:** Adults $6, children ages 6–15 $4; family rate $16.
**Restaurants:** In museum entrance building.
**Shops:** Craft and gift shop featuring handmade Appalachian crafts, and antique shop in museum entrance building.
**Facilities:** Craft demonstrations, special events.

## WHERE TO STAY

**Motels/Hotels:** Super 8 Motel, Hwy. 61 at I-75 exit 122, Clinton TN 37716 (615) 447-0565. Comfort Inn, 433 South Rutgers Ave., Oak Ridge TN 37830, (615) 481-8200, FAX: (615) 483-6142. Garden Plaza Hotel, 215 South Illinois Ave., Oak Ridge TN 37830, (615) 481-2468, 1-800-342-7336, FAX: (615) 481-2474. Quality Inn North, 6712 Central Ave. Pike, Knoxville TN 37912, (615) 689-6600, 1-800-221-2222.
**Camping:** Norris Dam State Park, Rt. 1, Box 500, Lake City TN 37769, (615) 426-7461. Big Ridge State Rustic Park, Hwy. 61, Maynerdville TN 37807, (615) 992-5523. Fox Inn Campground, Hwy. 61, Norris TN 37828, (615) 494-9386.

## OVERVIEW

Mountain people are what John Rice Irwin likes best to collect—walking, talking Appalachians who tell their life stories in their own words and teach a new generation their ways of life. Unfortunately, people cannot be as easily acquired, restored, cleaned up, and used in museum exhibits as tools, quilts, toys, baskets, furniture, and log houses can. So instead of people, Irwin has collected thousands of examples of eastern Tennessee's Appalachian material culture. That collection and the Appalachian life-style are the focus of this re-created rural village and pioneer-

Photo by Patricia A. Gutek

## Museum of Appalachia, Norris, Tennessee

Contemporary students with backpacks and lunch boxes enter Big Tater Valley
School House at the Museum of Appalachia. It is one of the many
original log buildings which form this re-created rural
Appalachian village in eastern Tennessee.

era working farm on a sixty-five-acre site. John Rice Irwin, the museum's founder, has gathered thirty original log houses and farm buildings, which he has filled with furniture and artifacts. The overflow from his collection of over a quarter million frontier, rural, and mountain artifacts gathered from within a 200-mile radius, is displayed in a large exhibit building.

Irwin is a native of Big Valley in eastern Tennessee, as were his ancestors who settled in the valley in the 1700s. He greatly values the pioneer spirit and self-sufficiency of these mountain folk of Appalachia, who developed a unique culture now threatened with extinction by modernization and the homogenization of American society. His purpose in founding the museum was to preserve the ways and perpetuate the unique crafts, music, and skills of these simple mountain people.

## History

"John Rice Irwin's Museum of Appalachia, a Living Mountain Village," which is the complete name of this outdoor museum, hints strongly at its history. It is indeed John Rice Irwin's museum. It was conceived, implemented, and built by one man, who began collecting artifacts from his native Appalachia in an attempt to preserve aspects of the culture and life-style of his eastern Tennessee forbearers.

Irwin—born in 1930 in Big Valley, Knox County, in eastern Tennessee—was an avid listener of the stories told by his grandparents, great aunts, and great uncles, the descendants of the early pioneers who had settled the area in the 1700s. Irwin's parents, and both sets of grandparents, had farms in Big Valley. In 1934, the building of Norris Dam forced Irwin's parents off their land, which would be flooded. The Norris Dam also brought electricity to the valley. The Irwins moved forty miles down the valley, only to find that a few years later, the government wanted their property for the construction of Oak Ridge, a large nuclear plant. Perhaps these major disruptions in the somewhat isolated and unchanged Big Valley life-style convinced Irwin that the mountain culture of his ancestors would soon disappear forever. He resolved to preserve their material culture, at least.

John Rice Irwin's collecting began with items going back several generations that had been given to him by his Grandfather Rice, who suggested the boy start a museum someday. After his grandparents died, he acquired more of their possessions. He also began buying from local auctions, as well as directly from the mountaineers themselves. He learned and recorded the history of each acquisition. After his collection of antiques outgrew his garage, Irwin, now a school superintendent, purchased a mountain cabin which he furnished with the furniture and artifacts he had amassed. More cabins followed, as well as land. People began stopping to see Irwin's collection, which continued to grow. By 1969, there were 600 visitors a year. Formal establishment of the Museum of Appalachia soon followed.

## SITE DESCRIPTION

Those aren't museum interpreters you see at the **Museum of Appalachia**; those are the mountain folk of Appalachia practicing skills and crafts handed down from generation to generation. They are part of the folksy charm of this unique outdoor museum, which mixes history with a hands-on, family-style approach to the past. Since most museum buildings are small and of log construction, there is not the architectural variety seen at other outdoor museums.

The **Museum of Appalachia Hall of Fame** is housed in a three-story antebellum structure. Members of the Hall of Fame are both famous and locally known individuals who are connected with the Southern Appalachian Mountains. Personal items belonging to these people are displayed. The members include Seargent Alvin C. York and Cordell Hull—as well as Aunt Mary Foust, who lived to be 115, and Tater Hole Joe, who lived in a hole in the ground.

The **main display building** houses over 200,000 locally obtained pioneer artifacts, and provides information about the people who made or owned them. Displayed are tools, leather shoes and saddles, barrels, metal containers, locks, scales, yokes, animal traps, and folk art. In the building are a fully stocked country store, a watch-repair shop, and a woodworking shop, together with equipment used in spinning and weaving, bee keeping, and dairy operations.

The **General Bunch House**, built in western Anderson County in 1898, was the first dwelling erected at the museum. The two-room log house, built by Pryor Bunch, was home to a family of twelve children. It was dismantled and brought sixty miles to the museum. The adjacent **smokehouse** came from Liberty Hill.

The **Arnwine Cabin**, which is listed on the National Register, was built by Wes Arnwine about 1800 on Clinch River near Liberty Hill in Grainger County. The one-story log cabin has one room and a loft, and an exterior end stick-and-mud chimney. The **McClung House** (ca. 1790) is a dogtrot-style cabin from Turkey Creek, near Knoxville. Cooking is done in the large fireplace on the kitchen side of the cabin; the other side was used for sleeping.

The **"Dan'l Boone" Cabin** is a one-room dirt-floored log structure built in the early 1800s. Its name comes from the fact that it was used as the frontier home of Daniel Boone in the CBS TV series called *Young Dan'l Boone*.

Other village buildings include the **Big Tater Valley School House**, a **ca. 1840 church** with log benches, **a broom and rope house, a leather shop, a blacksmith shop, a mill house and wheelwright shop**, and **a loom house**.

On the pioneer farm is the **Old Peters' Homestead**, which was built in 1838 near Luttrell by Nathaniel Peters. This two-story log house has a large central chimney. The homestead's outbuildings include the **privy, the underground dairy, the corn crib, the smokehouse and granary, the chicken house, the cantilever barn, and the Parkey Blacksmith Shop**. Animals at the farm include Highland cattle, oxen, horses, mules, goats, sheep, turkeys, ducks, and chickens.

## FESTIVALS/CRAFTS

Special events include a **July 4th Celebration and Anvil Shoot** and the **Tennessee Fall Homecoming** held the second full weekend in October. The Homecoming is a four-day celebration of Appalachian culture with over 200 musicians and singers performing mountain, folk, hymn, and traditional music. Craftspeople and artists display and sell their wares. Interpreters demonstrate cane grinding with a mule-powered mill, molasses boiling, lye soap-making, yarn spinning, quilt-making, rail splitting, and sheep herding. **Christmas in Old Appalachia** features traditional Christmas decorations, music, and food.

# HISTORIC RUGBY

Restored nineteenth-century Victorian English village; NR.

**Address:** PO Box 8, Hwy. 52, Rugby TN 37733
**Telephone:** (615) 628-2441, (615) 628-2430
**Location:** In northeastern Tennessee, about 125 miles northeast of Nashville and about 70 miles northwest of Knoxville; 35 miles from both I-75 exit 141 and I-40 exit 300, on TN Hwy. 52.
**Open:** February–December, 9:30 A.M.–5:00 P.M. Monday–Saturday; 12:00 noon–5:00 P.M. Sunday. Tours by appointment in January.
**Admission:** Adults $4, senior citizens $3.50, students $2.
**Restaurants:** The Harrow Road Café.
**Shops:** Rugby Craft Commissary, Board of Aid Bookshop.
**Facilities:** Visitor center, guided tours, archive and research centre, craft workshops, special events.

## WHERE TO STAY

**Inns/Bed & Breakfasts:** Newbury House, 1880 Pioneer Cottage, and Percy Cottage, PO Box 8, Hwy. 52, Rugby TN 37733, (615) 628-2441, (615) 628-2430.
**Camping:** Big South Fork National River and Recreation Area, PO Drawer 630, Oneida TN 37841, (615) 879-4890.

## OVERVIEW

Nestled among the lush vegetation of Tennessee's Cumberland Plateau is a restored village of English Victorian cottages, vestiges of a planned experimental community for the younger sons of England's landed gentry. Founded by Thomas Hughes, the late-nineteenth-century town was designed as a haven for well-educated but discontented second-, third-, and fourth-born sons who could establish a new life, own land, and work at careers of their choice without the traditional constraints imposed by England's rigid social structure.

Rugby's location, as much as anything, makes this museum village outstanding. Travelers have no clue that Tennessee's Cumberland Plateau has a charming English Victorian village hidden in its backwoods. The village is adjacent to the southern portion of the 105,000-acre Big South Fork

National River and Recreation Area. A winding road from the interstate passes through scenic but sparsely populated rural and mining hamlets so remote that electricity arrived only in the 1950s.

More than twenty original or reconstructed buildings remain in the Victorian village, about half of which are privately owned. Rugby's wooded setting is isolated, so make sure you have enough toothpaste, aspirin, and batteries for your camera.

Overnight accommodations are available in two restored buildings, the Newbury House Inn and the Pioneer Cottage, and in the reconstructed Percy Cottage.

## HISTORY

Thomas Hughes, a second son of a English upper-class family, deplored the idle, useless life-style assigned to many young Englishmen. Primogeniture—wherein only the first-born sons could inherit their fathers' titles and estates—was the traditional inheritance pattern in England. Younger sons, who were not heirs, were educated at elite public schools, really prestigious private schools, like their older brothers, yet second sons would never own their own land. They were encouraged to earn their living by entering the professions of ministry, law, medicine, public service, or the military.

In fact, many younger sons did not enter these overcrowded professions and were left with a life of unemployment, an inadequate allowance their only source of income. Hughes condemned the aristocracy, who would rather see their children starve like gentlemen than thrive in a trade or profession considered beneath them. "Yes; of the many sad sights in our England," wrote Hughes in the book he titled *Rugby*, "there is none sadder than this, of first-rate human material going helplessly to waste. . . ."

A prolific writer, Hughes's most famous book is *Tom Brown's School Days*, a fictional account of his own education at Rugby, one of England's most prestigious public schools. Hughes attended Rugby from 1833 to 1841, and was influenced by the ideas of Thomas Arnold, who advocated reform of the public schools. English public schools, contrary to their name, were highly selective, prestigious boarding schools that prepared the scions of upper-class families to be English gentlemen who would be comfortable on the playing field as well as in the drawing room. Their curricula emphasized the classics, literature, and history, but ignored science, the professions, and technical study. Public-school education stressed the inappropriateness and the social stigma attached to engaging in business, trades, or the manual arts.

Hughes studied law at Oxford, practiced law in London, and was a member of the House of Commons from 1865 to 1874. He was a social reformer who championed Christian socialism, supported the co-operative movement and the trade-union movement, and was involved in founding and running the Working Men's College in London. After visiting the more socially open United States in 1870, Thomas Hughes proposed founding a community there of English gentlemen farmers.

While in the United States, Hughes met Franklin W. Smith, a Boston capitalist who headed a company known as the Board of Aid to Land Ownership. The company had an option on 100,000 acres of east Tennessee land, which was offered to Hughes. After obtaining financial backing from Henry Kimber and John Boyle of London, Hughes became the official spokesman for the land company, which retained the original name. The property was beautifully situated on a heavily wooded high plain between two deep river gorges.

Because the Board of Aid to Land Ownership, Ltd., was a commercial venture, land was made available to all buyers, not just English second sons. Hughes believed that the settlement should be open to all who subscribed to his principles and ways, whether Englishmen or Americans. According to Hughes, participants would lead a peasant's life during working hours but find themselves in a cultivated society when their work was done. Hughes named the community "Rugby," after the school he had attended, and the town officially opened in October 1880. Three weeks later, Rugby's population was 120, and by the following January, it had grown to 200 English and Scottish people, with a good percentage of Americans, some of whom were natives of the Tennessee mountains. Despite the emphasis on sons, the population was almost evenly divided between men and women.

By the summer of 1881, Rugby had a café, a boarding house, a three-story hotel, private homes, and a co-operative commissary. Because many of the British residents were well-educated members of a leisure class, recreational and cultural pursuits were important considerations. The community had tennis courts, bowling greens, bridle paths, and a gentlemen's swimming hole. Croquet, hunting, and musical events were popular. A number of clubs were formed—the Lawn Tennis Club, the Rugby Social Club, Rugby Musical and Dramatic Club, the Philharmonic Society, the Masonic Lodge, the Ladies Church Working Society, and the Cornet Band. A weekly newspaper, the *Rugbeian*, began publication in 1880. The Rugby Schoolhouse was constructed in 1880, and in 1882, a public library was built. Religious services were held in the school; Christ Church was not built until 1887. Colonists dressed for afternoon tea at four o'clock. Since Hughes was a temperance advocate, liquor was prohibited in the village.

The population of Rugby fluctuated as residents faced arduous weather, a typhoid epidemic, leadership problems, and the burdens of manual labor. Although John Boyle, who had been sent by Hughes to survey the suitability of the Cumberland Plateau land, had raved about the pure and genial atmosphere and the temperature which had at once attracted him favorably towards the climate, the first winter in Rugby was harsh and very cold, the worst winter in that part of Tennessee in twenty-five years. When typhoid broke out in August 1881, twenty cases were reported, and seven people died. The contamination was traced to one of the earliest buildings constructed in Rugby, a three-story hotel called the Tabard Inn. Though the inn was closed, frightened residents fled the community, and the population plunged from 300 to 60 by December.

Despite this inauspicious beginning, Hughes was determined to make the colony succeed—though he was not himself a resident of Rugby. He visited the community for a few months annually. His brother Hastings did live there, and in 1881, Thomas and Hastings's mother, Margaret Hughes, moved to Rugby, where she lived until her death in 1887 at the age of ninety. Her presence had a steadying effect on the shaky community.

Gradually, the population increased. By 1884, there were between 400 and 450 residents, and some sixty-five buildings in Rugby. Commercial activities included farming, a canning company, a sawmill, boarding houses, public stables, a drug store, blacksmith shops, and summer tourism with guests accommodated at the Tabard Inn. Unfortunately, the Tabard Inn was destroyed in a fire in October 1884. A new Tabard was opened in summer of 1887, the year that Christ Church was built.

Rugby survived from 1880 to 1887 with various successes and setbacks, but from 1887 on, it gradually declined—partly because very few of the English pioneers had brought any kind of manual skill, business ability, or agricultural knowledge to the community.

Thomas Hughes's last visit to Rugby was in 1887, the year his mother died. Hastings Hughes moved to Massachusetts. Thomas Hughes died in 1896 having lost a great deal of money in the Rugby venture, as had the other stockholders of the Board of Aid to Land Ownership. In the early 1900s, that company sold its remaining 25,000 acres to American investors. Most of the original colonists had already left Rugby.

Rugby, Tennessee, overlooked and neglected for the following half-century, existed as a small farming community. As it happens with many historic sites, progress in terms of urban sprawl and highway construction destroys, while neglect preserves. Rugby's remote location helped much of the Victorian village remain intact. In 1966, a sixteen-year-old boy, Brian Stagg, led a Rugby restoration movement. Tours of historic buildings began in 1967, and in 1972, the village was placed on the National Register of Historic Places. Historic Rugby, Inc., has restored several buildings and reconstructed several others. A master plan for the historic site includes restoration and rebuilding of even more buildings.

## SITE DESCRIPTION

Tours begin at the **Schoolhouse Visitor Centre**, a two-story frame structure built in 1907 and used as a school until 1951. It replaced a three-story schoolhouse built in 1880 that was destroyed by fire in 1906. Exhibits in the **Schoolhouse** focus on Thomas Hughes, Rugby, cottage Victorian architecture, and the Cumberland Mountains, and include photographs and documents. Guided tours leave from the Schoolhouse.

Rugby's pièce de résistance is the **Thomas Hughes Free Public Library**, housed in its original 1882 one-story frame building with a cupola. Gold lettering on the arched frosted glass panels on the front doors announces that the Hughes Public Library was opened October 5, 1882. The collection of 7,000 rare books includes 2,000 volumes brought from England and 5,000 donated books—one of the finest collections of Victorian literature in the United States. No volume on its shelves was published after 1899, its oldest book having been printed in 1687. Though the building has no electricity and is unheated, the books are in remarkably good condition. Floor-to-ceiling bookshelves line the walls. In addition to free-standing bookcases, there are wooden tables and chairs.

**Christ Church Episcopal** was built in 1887, and Sunday services are still held there. The Carpenter Gothic church, designed by Cornelius Onderdonk, has board-and-batten siding with maroon and gray trim. Its interior is paneled with native yellow pine, which was not painted or stained but has darkened naturally. The stained-glass window above the altar was dedicated to Margaret Hughes and Mary Blacklock. Other windows, which are original, are clear—although they had previously been covered with rice paper to give the illusion of stained glass. The original oil lamps were electrified in the 1950s. The rosewood, harmonium reed organ was made in London in 1849 and is still in use.

**Kingstone Lisle** is the house that was built in 1884 for Thomas Hughes, who made annual visits to Rugby. The wooden walls, ceilings, and floors of the interior are yellow pine. Furnishings were either made in Rugby or brought from England by Rugby colonists. The parlor has a Weber piano and a silver plate for calling cards. Windows have long puddling drapes. In the bedroom is Thomas Hughes's green felt-covered writing desk as well as his trunk.

The reconstructed **Harrow Road Café** is a flourishing restaurant. Another reconstruction, the **Rugby Craft Commissary** is a craft store. This co-operative commissary once supplied all the needs of the town's residents. Today it is a craft shop featuring Appalachian crafts such as quilts, baskets, and dulcimers. The **Board of Aid Land Office** is a bookshop.

Overnight accommodations are available in the simple one-story frame **Pioneer Cottage**. Built in 1880, it served as a temporary haven for early colonists until their houses were built. Thomas Hughes stayed at Pioneer Cottage during his first visit to Rugby. Another bed-and-breakfast, the **Newbury House** (1880) was Rugby's first boarding house. The two-story, mansard-roofed inn has been restored, and its five bedrooms are furnished in the Victorian period. A third lodging facility is **Percy Cottage**, a Victorian building reconstructed on its original foundation. The original Percy Cottage was built in 1884 for Sir Henry Kimber.

Colonists are buried in the **Laurel Dale Cemetery** on Donnington Road. From there, an 1880s trail leads to the **gentlemen's swimming hole** one-half mile away. This trail continues for one mile to the **Meeting of the Waters**, where **Clear Fork River** and **White Oak Creek** intersect.

## FESTIVALS/CRAFTS

Many of the privately owned houses in Rugby have also been restored, and can be seen from the outside. They are open for touring during the annual **Rugby Pilgrimage**, held the first weekend in October. Another annual event is the **Spring Music and Crafts Festival**, held in mid-May. The festival features craftspeople selling and demonstrating their crafts, as well as British and Appalachian music and dancing. Crafts are also available at the **Thanksgiving Marketplace** held Thanksgiving weekend. The **Christmas at Rugby** celebration, held in early December, features candlelight tours and a Victorian dinner.

Workshops are taught in a variety of crafts such as cane seating, hand-spinning, tatting, and basketry.

## SIDE TRIPS

**Big South Fork National River and Recreation Area**, just north of Historic Rugby, is a 105,000-acre park managed by the National Park Service. It is situated in a rugged gorge area of the Cumberland Plateau in southwestern Kentucky and northeastern Tennessee. Activities include hiking, camping, hunting, horseback riding, canoeing, kayaking, whitewater rafting, fishing. Superintendent, PO Drawer 630, Oneida TN 37841.

**Cumberland Gap National Historical Park** commemorates the significance of the Cumberland Gap, a natural doorway across the Appalachian Mountains that allowed easterners to settle Kentucky territory west of the mountains. **Wilderness Trail** in the Cumberland Gap was marked out by Daniel Boone in 1775, and trans-Allegheny migration began immediately. Kentucky was admitted to the Union in 1792. By 1800, over 300,000 people had traveled across the gap.

The national park contains over 20,000 unspoiled acres of hiking trails and campgrounds in Kentucky, Virginia, and Tennessee, as well as a restored pioneer community. **Hensley Settlement** in Cumberland Gap's Brush Mountain was founded in 1903 by several members of the Hensley family who established farmsteads. After the settlement was abandoned around 1951, buildings decayed until the National Park Service began its restoration. Three farmsteads with their houses, barns, and fences as well as the schoolhouse and cemetery have been restored; seventy acres have been returned to farming and pasture. Hensley Settlement can be accessed only on foot, on the three-and-one-half-mile Chadwell Gap trail. Open daily, 8:00 A.M.–5:00 P.M. Cumberland Gap NHP, Box 1848, Middlesboro KY 40965. (606) 248-2817.

# VIRGINIA

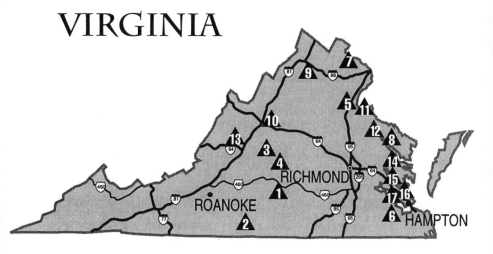

1. Appomattox: Appomattox Court House National Historical Park
2. Brookneal: Red Hill, the Patrick Henry National Memorial
3. Charlottesville: Ash Lawn-Highland
4. Charlottesville: Monticello
5. Fredericksburg: Kenmore
6. James River Plantations
   Charles City: Berkeley Plantation
                 Sherwood Forest Plantation
                 Shirley Plantation
   Surry: Chippokes Plantation State Park
7. Leesburg: Oatlands
8. Lorton: Gunston Hall Plantation
9. McLean: Arlington House, the Robert E. Lee Memorial
10. Montpelier Station: Montpelier
11. Mount Vernon: Mount Vernon
12. Mount Vernon: Woodlawn Plantation and Pope-Leighey House
13. Staunton: Museum of American Frontier Culture
14. Stratford: Stratford Hall Plantation
15. Williamsburg: Carter's Grove
16. Williamsburg: Colonial Williamsburg
17. Yorktown: Colonial National Historical Park,
    Jamestown and Yorktown

# APPOMATTOX COURT HOUSE NATIONAL HISTORICAL PARK

Restored village of Appomattox Court House,
site of surrender of General Robert E. Lee's
Army of Northern Virginia to Union armies of
General Ulysses S. Grant, April 9, 1865; NR, HABS.

**Address:** Superintendent, Appomattox Court House National Historical
Park, PO Box 218, Appomattox VA 24522

**Telephone:** (804) 352-8987

**Location:** The town of Appomattox is in south central Virginia, 92 miles
west of Richmond and 18 miles east of Lynchburg. Appomattox
Court House National Historical Park is on VA Hwy. 24, 3 miles
northeast of Appomattox on US 460.

**Open:** 9:00 A.M.–5 P.M. daily; closed President's Day, Martin Luther King
Jr.'s Birthday, and Thanksgiving, Christmas, and New Year's Days.

**Admission:** Adults, ages 17 and over, $2.

**Shops:** Bookstore with large selection of Civil War books and gift shop.

**Facilities:** Handicapped accessible.

## WHERE TO STAY

**Motels/Hotels:** Super 8 Motel, Hwy. 460 West, Appomattox VA 24522,
(804)352-2339. Budget Inn Motel, 714 West Confederate Ave., Appomattox VA 24552, (804) 352-7451. Lee-Grant Motel, Hwy. 460,
Appomattox VA 24522, (804) 352-5234. Holiday Inn Crowne
Plaza, 601 Main St., Lynchburg VA 24504, (804) 528-2500, FAX:
(804) 528-0062.

**Camping:** Holliday Lake State Park, Rt. 2, Box 230, Appomattox VA
24522, (804) 248-6308. Jellystone Park Campground, Hwy. 460
West, Appomattox VA 24522, (804) 993-3332.

## OVERVIEW

On April 9, 1865, General Robert E. Lee, commander of the Army of Northern Virginia—the Confederacy's largest field force—surrendered his troops to Ulysses S. Grant, General in Chief of the United States armies, at the village of Appomattox Court House. The actual meeting between Lee and Grant took place in the parlor of the McLean House, not in the courthouse building. Appomattox Court House is the name of the village that was the county seat. Today, the village, a National Historical Park, has been restored as it appeared when Lee surrendered. Visitors to Appomattox Court House can experience the Confederacy's last days and the surrender that ended the Civil War.

## HISTORY

Although several very weakened Confederate armies were still in the field, Lee's surrender marked the effective end of hostilities between the North and South, as well as the end of the Confederacy's struggle for independence. On April 12, three days after Lee's surrender, 22,349 Confederate officers and men laid down their weapons and furled their battle flags along the Richmond-Lynchburg Stage Road and began returning to their homes. General Lee then left for Richmond. Grant had already returned to Washington.

The country crossroads town of Appomattox Court House, where the Civil War ended, was originally called "Clover Hill." A small settlement with a few houses and a tavern, Clover Hill was originally a stopping-off point on the Richmond-Lynchburg Stage Road. When Appomattox was organized as a county in 1845, Clover Hill, renamed Appomattox Court House, became the county seat. The courthouse building was erected in 1846.

The county seat in an agricultural region, Appomattox Court House prospered and grew. When the Civil War began in 1861, the town—with a population of 125—was the center of the county's commercial and political life. The town's stores and businesses filled the needs of the county's rural population of 8,895—fifty-four percent of whom were black.

In April 1865, the nation's Civil War reached its dramatic conclusion in the small Southern town of Appomattox Court House with Lee's historic surrender to Grant. The two generals who faced each other in McLean's parlor, though markedly different in bearing and temperament, were well-matched opponents.

Photo by Patricia A. Gutek

## Appomattox Court House National Historical Park, Appomattox, Virginia

The restored village of Appomattox Court House is the site of the surrender of
General Robert E. Lee's Army of Northern Virginia to the Union armies of
General Ulysses S. Grant, April 9, 1865. This ended the Civil War.

Throughout the war, Lee, commanding the Army of Northern Virginia, successfully defended the Confederacy's eastern borders. He had even carried the war into the North, reaching as far as Pennsylvania's Gettysburg before being turned back southward. A courtly officer of the old school, Lee was an astute military strategist who used to great advantage his aggressiveness and his uncanny ability to find his opponents' weaknesses. Although he had held a larger Union army at bay for four years, Lee's time was running out. His once proud army was in tatters, worn out by war's attrition.

Unlike Lee, who was the South's leading general throughout the war, Ulysses S. Grant had slowly emerged as the man for whom Lincoln had been searching to bring the struggle to an end. Grant's dogged but successful siege of Vicksburg caused Lincoln to give Grant overall command of the Union army. A relentless opponent who knew how to wear his enemies down and exploit their weaknesses, Grant was closing in on Lee's beleaguered Confederates.

By the end of 1864, the futility of continued Confederate resistance was becoming apparent. General Sherman led a Union army though Georgia, marching from Atlanta to the sea, destroying everything in his path that was of economic or military value. Sherman then turned north, through the Carolinas, to link his troops with those of Grant, who had been besieging Lee at Petersburg for ten months.

On April 2, 1865, Grant, in a concerted attack, forced Lee's troops to abandon Petersburg and Richmond, the Confederate capital. Grant's army then pursued Lee's starving and exhausted troops. The fierce battle that took place on April 6 further decimated Lee's army. Having arrived in Appomattox County, Lee's army was cut off from aid and without hope of reinforcements. Recognizing the senselessness of further resistance, Lee knew that surrender was now inevitable.

The signing of the surrender took place in the parlor of Wilmer McLean's house in Appomattox Court House. McLean had relocated his family from Manassas in northern Virginia to Appomattox so that his family might escape the battles taking place on the northern Virginia front.

The unassuming Grant, generous in victory, required only that the Confederates pledge not to take up arms against the United States. Officers were allowed to keep their side arms, and any man who owned a horse was allowed to take it home with him.

Although Lee's surrender took the Army of Northern Virginia out of the war, several other Confederate forces remained in the field, namely General Joseph E. Johnston's army in North Carolina and General Edmund Kirby Smith's in Texas. With Johnston's surrender to General William T. Sherman on April 26, and Smith's surrender on June 2, the Confederacy's army ceased to exist and hostilities ended.

After its brief moment in history, the fame of Appomattox Court House quickly declined. Greater public attention was paid to sites such as Gettysburg, where major battles had been fought. Lacking a railroad connection, Appomattox Court House's business activity shifted to Appomattox Station, which was on the rail line. After the courthouse building burned down in 1892, the county seat was transferred to Appomattox, formerly known as Appomattox Station.

In 1893, the McLean House was dismantled for a projected relocation to Washington DC. The actual move of the house never occurred, however, and the building remained a neglected pile of bricks and lumber.

In 1930, Congress passed a bill to erect a monument at the site of the old courthouse. However, the monument was never erected. In 1934–1935, the National Park Service developed a proposal to restore the entire village, and legislation to create the historical park passed in 1936. Interrupted by the Depression and World War II, work finally began in 1947 in the area designated Appomattox Court House National Historical Monument—changed to Appomattox Court House National Historical Park in April 1954. Today, the village looks much as it did on that historic day in April 1865, when Lee and Grant met to end the Civil War.

## SITE DESCRIPTION

Begin your tour at the **visitor center** in the **courthouse**, which is a reconstruction of the original 1846 building. None of the surrender events took place here. The information desk is located on the ground floor; upstairs are a museum and an auditorium, where interpretive slide shows present the events of the surrender. Photographs of the prelude to Lee's surrender and civil war weapons are exhibited.

**Clover Hill Tavern**, built in 1819, is the village's oldest structure. It was a travelers' stop on the Richmond-Lynchburg stagecoach line. At one time, the tavern included two frame additions—one for the dining room and one for the bar. Today, one room is appointed as a tavern, while the other has exhibits of photographs and illustrations of the surrender. Many of the illustrations show the reactions of Confederate and Union soldiers, especially a very moving painting of defeated Confederate troops furling the Confederate flag. Behind the tavern are the kitchen, now a bookstore, and the slave quarters, now containing restrooms. Beside the tavern is the **tavern guest house**, where people were accommodated when the tavern was full.

**Woodson Law Office**, a beige frame building, was purchased in 1856 by John W. Woodson, an attorney who practiced law in Appomattox Court House until his death eight years later. Appointed as a typical small town lawyer's office of the mid-nineteenth century, it contains an attorney's desk, a safe, and a large portrait of George Washington.

The gray frame **Meeks' Store** was built in 1852 by John Plunkett. At the time of the surrender, it was owned by Albert Francis Meeks, the village storekeeper, postmaster, and druggist. The first floor houses the store, stocked with period merchandise, and the village post office. Meeks's son, Lafayette, who is buried behind the store, contracted typhoid fever while serving in the Confederate army and died at age nineteen. The store was later used as a private residence and the Presbyterian Church parsonage.

A key building on your tour is the red brick **McLean House,** where Lee surrendered to Grant on April 9, 1865. The present house is a reconstruction of the original home built in 1848. It was purchased in 1862 by sugar speculator Wilmer McLean, who moved his family to Appomattox Court House to escape the heavy fighting taking place in the Manassas area. The three-story house contains a parlor and dining room on the second floor and bedrooms on the third floor. The **parlor,** where Lee and Grant negotiated the surrender terms, contains the original sofa and vases. Other furnishings are copies of the originals.

Behind the main house are the **slaves' quarters** and a **kitchen** which contains a large fireplace cooking area. Food could be carried directly from the kitchen to the dining room. An **icehouse** is located east of the front entrance. The well is inside the **gazebo.** All of these buildings are reconstructions.

The **jail,** completed in 1870, served for twenty-two years as the sheriff's office and county jail. Until 1940, it was used as a voting station.

The **Mariah Wright House,** a frame house constructed in the mid-1820s, is one of the village's older buildings. Its stone and brick chimneys are architecturally representative of the region.

**Isbell House** was built by Thomas S. Bocock, who was the speaker of the Confederate Congress. In 1865, it was owned by Commonwealth Attorney Lewis D. Isbell. **Peers House,** built in the early 1850s, was the home of George Peers, clerk of the court for Appomattox County for forty years. Neither Isbell House nor Peers House is open to the public.

Outside of the village, several locations associated with the Confederate surrender are connected by a six-mile walking trail. The site of **Lee's headquarters** is northeast of the village. In the opposite direction is the site of **Grant's headquarters.** A small **Confederate cemetery** west of the village contains the graves of eighteen Confederate soliders and one Union soldier who were killed on April 9.

## FESTIVALS/CRAFTS

A **Living History Interpretive Program** is conducted by modern-day soldiers at Clover Hill Tavern, June through August.

## SIDE TRIPS

**Holliday Lake State Park** is located 17 miles from the town of Appomattox. The 250-acre park provides wooded campgrounds, a swimming beach, a fishing lake, and nature trails. Rt. 2, Box 230, Appomattox VA 24522. (804) 248-6308.

# RED HILL, THE PATRICK HENRY NATIONAL MEMORIAL

### Reconstructed plantation house and burial place of patriot Patrick Henry; NR.

**Address:** Rt. 2, Box 127, Brookneal VA 24528-9302
**Telephone:** (804) 376-2044
**Location:** In south central Virginia, 35 miles south of Lynchburg; on VA Hwy. 600, 5 miles southeast of Brookneal.
**Open:** April–October, 9:00 A.M.–5:00 P.M. daily; November–March, 9:00 A.M.–4:00 P.M. daily. Closed Thanksgiving, Christmas, and New Year's Days.
**Admission:** Adults $3, children $1.

## WHERE TO STAY

**Inns/Bed & Breakfasts:** Staunton Hill, Rt. 2, Box 44, Bookneal VA 24528, (804) 376-2718, FAX: (804) 376-5929.
**Motels/Hotels:** Sheldon's, Rt. 2, Box 189, Keysville VA 23947, (804) 736-8434. Innkeeper, 2901 Candler's Mountain Rd., Lynchburg VA 24502, (804) 237-7771, 1-800-822-9899, FAX: (804) 239-0659.
**Camping:** Staunton River State Park, VA Hwy. 344, South Boston VA 24592, (804) 572-4623. Twin Lakes State Park, VA Hwy. 613, Keysville VA 23947, (804) 392-3435. Yogi Bear Campground, Rt. 1, Box 220, Keeling VA 24566, (804) 836-4880.

## OVERVIEW

**Red Hill Plantation** is the home of Patrick Henry, the eloquent spokesman for American independence, in Virginia. It contains the reconstructed main house, which was Henry's residence, as well as dependency buildings which have been either reconstructed or restored to their appearance at the time Henry lived at Red Hill.

# HISTORY

Patrick Henry (1736–1799), famous for his ringing challenge to British rule, "Give me liberty or give me death," was a forceful leader in colonial America's movement to independence. At Red Hill, visitors can gain insights into Henry's private life.

Patrick Henry was born on May 29, 1736, at Studley in Hanover County, Virginia. In 1754, he married Sarah Shelton at Rural Plains. Admitted to the bar, he began his legal practice in 1760. For Henry, the law led to politics. A young lawyer of twenty-seven, Henry gained notoriety in 1763 from his victory in the "Parson's Case," which arose from King George III's nullification of an Act of Virginia's assembly, the House of Burgesses.

Two years later in 1765, Henry, now twenty-nine, was elected to the House of Burgesses. On May 29, 1765, he eloquently denounced the British-imposed Stamp Act, which taxed every newspaper, pamphlet, will, deed, and document in the colonies. Henry introduced five resolutions, called the "Virginia Resolves," in the House of Burgesses. Protesting taxation without representation, Henry asserted that only Virginians could tax themselves. An impassioned Henry, condemning the Stamp Act, warned that as "Caesar had his Brutus, Charles I his Cromwell," so George III might profit by their example. Henry's Virginia Resolves, circulated to the other colonies, provoked a similar response from their assemblies. Although the British government repealed the Stamp Act, momentum in the colonies mounted for independence from Great Britain.

Great Britain continued to impose taxes on the colonials. The Townshend Revenue Acts, which imposed duties on glass, lead, paper, paint, and tea, provoked the Boston Tea Party and caused anti-British demonstrations in Williamsburg, Virginia's capital.

The royal governor dissolved the Virginia legislature but Patrick Henry, Thomas Jefferson, George Mason, Richard Henry Lee, Francis Lightfoot Lee, Peyton Randolph, and Dabny Carr met at Raleigh Tavern and issued a call for representatives from all of the colonies to meet in Philadelphia. In September 1774, Patrick Henry, George Washington, Richard Henry Lee, and Peyton Randolph were named as Virginia's delegates to the First Continental Congress.

As tension mounted, Patrick Henry, at St. John's Church in Richmond, delivered an oration which included the stirring line, "I know not what course others may take, but as for me, give me liberty or give me death!"

In 1776, Patrick Henry was elected the first governor of the independent Commonwealth of Virginia. He served for five one-year terms; the first three were consecutive.

Henry lived in a dozen locations in Virginia during his lifetime. But to him, his last home, Red Hill, was "the garden spot of Virginia." Henry was very much of a family man. His first wife, Sarah Shelton, died in 1775. He married Dorothea Dandridge, the granddaughter of the former Royal Governor Alexander Spotswood, on October 9, 1777. Henry was the father of seventeen children, eleven of whom were born to Dorothea. Dorothea survived him by thirty-two years.

At age fifty-seven, Henry wanted to leave public life to enjoy the peace of rural Virginia. He declined requests from President Washington to serve as secretary of state and as chief justice of the Supreme Court. In 1793, he and Dorothea moved to Red Hill in the Staunton River Valley. For the next three years, Henry divided his time between his two plantations, one at Red Hill and the other at Long Island, eighteen miles up river from Red Hill. In 1796, he placed Long Island under an agent's management and made Red Hill his permanent residence.

Red Hill Plantation consisted of 2,920 acres of land, a one-and-one-half-story frame dwelling, a detached kitchen, a smokehouse, an icehouse, an overseer's cottage, and Henry's law office.

Henry died on June 6, 1799, and was buried in the family cemetery at Red Hill. After Patrick Henry's death, his son John inherited the plantation. He built a two-story addition to the original house. John Henry's son, William Wirt Henry, who next inherited the estate, used it as a summer home. In the early 1900s, Patrick Henry's two great-granddaughters, Lucy Harrison and Elizabeth Lyons, made extensive additions which enlarged the original Henry main house into an eighteen-room mansion. In 1919, fire destroyed the mansion.

The nonprofit Patrick Henry Memorial Foundation was established in 1944 to reconstruct Red Hill as a memorial to Patrick Henry. In 1978, the U.S. Department of the Interior officially recognized Red Hill as a historic landmark and it was entered in the National Register of Historic Places.

## SITE DESCRIPTION

Begin your tour at the **Patrick Henry Visitors' Center and Museum**, and see the orientation video program, "Patrick Henry's Red Hill." The museum exhibits many personal items and artifacts associated with Patrick Henry and his descendants. A focal point of the museum is P. H. Rothermel's painting *Patrick Henry before the Virginia House of Burgesses,* which portrays Henry's speech denouncing the Stamp Act.

The **main house**, destroyed by fire in 1919, has been authentically reconstructed on its original foundations. The one-and-one-half-story house was re-created as it was during Henry's residency and does not include additions made by his descendants. After purchasing Red Hill from Richard Marot Booker in 1794, Henry added a room on the left side of the house. There are three rooms on the first floor and two bedrooms upstairs. The house is furnished with eighteenth-century period pieces; some are original, and others are reproductions.

The **kitchen**, reconstructed on its original foundations, is a frame building that retains its original brick floor and stone hearth. The kitchen, like those on many other plantations, was built separately from the house to avoid fire. A unique feature is its Virginia chimney, which has a warming oven and large cooking fireplace. The kitchen is furnished with eighteenth-century utensils and cooking ware. The meat-cutting block and beaten-biscuit box are original to Red Hill. The **smokehouse**, reconstructed on its original foundation, was used to cure meat. Its stone floor contains a stone-lined fire pit.

The **servant's cabin**, rebuilt from original logs, was the home of Harrison and Milly, slaves who were the coachman and cook for the Henry family. Harrison, who was born at Red Hill, continued to work on the plantation after emancipation. On display are a large spinning wheel, a wool wheel, and a clock reel, or weasel.

A garden walk leads to the **graveyard**, which is surrounded by a box hedge and a stone wall. Here are the graves of Patrick and Dorothea Henry. On Henry's gravestone are the words "His fame his best epitaph." The **garden** has been restored.

**Patrick Henry's Law Office**, a restored original building, has been relocated near its original site. When Henry lived at Red Hill, his law practice was greatly restricted, but it is likely that his sons, nephews, and a grandson "read law" in the office under his tutelage. Among its furnishings are a document press, a stand-up desk, and an eighteenth-century writing desk.

The **stables and carriage house** were reconstructed on their original sites to represent the plantation as it was during Henry's lifetime. The top level contains a hay loft and the lower level a tack room, horse stalls, and feed bins.

The **Big Tree**, the largest Osage orange tree in the world, stands more than sixty-four feet tall with a spread of more than ninety-six feet. The tree is registered in the Hall of Fame of American Forestry.

# ASH LAWN-HIGHLAND

## Plantation home of President James Monroe; NR.

**Address:** James Monroe Parkway, Charlottesville VA 22902-8722
**Telephone:** (804) 293-9539
**Location:** Near I-64 and US 250; 2 miles beyond Monticello on County Rd. 795 (James Monroe Parkway).
**Open:** March–October, 9:00 A.M.–6:00 P.M. daily; November–February, 10:00 A.M.–5:00 P.M. daily. Closed Thanksgiving, Christmas and New Year's Days.
**Admission:** Adults $6, seniors $5.50, children ages 6–11 $3. Group rates and tour packages available.
**Shops:** Museum Gift Shop.
**Facilities:** Picnic area, handicapped accessible.

### WHERE TO STAY

**Inns/Bed & Breakfasts:** The Inn at Monticello, Rt. 19, Box 112, Charlottesville VA 22902, (804) 979-3593. The Inn at the Crossroads, Rt. 2, Box 6, RR 692, North Garden VA 22959, (804) 979-6452. High Meadows Vineyard Inn, Rt. 4, Box 6 (VA Hwy. 20 South), Scottsville VA 24590, (804) 286-2218. Prospect Hill Plantation Inn, Rt. 3, Box 430 (VA Hwy. 613 at Zion Crossroads), Trevilians VA 23093, 1-800-277-0844.
**Motels/Hotels:** Best Western-Mount Vernon, 1613 Emmet St. (Jct. US 29 and US 250 Bypass) Charlottesville VA 22906, (804) 296-5501. Boar's Head Inn, PO Box 5307, US 250 West, Charlottesville VA 22905, 1-800-476-1988, (804) 296-2181. Comfort Inn-Charlottesville, 1807 Emmet St. (US 29 North at US 250 Bypass, I-64 exit 118), Charlottesville VA 22901, (804) 293-6188. Omni, 235 West Main St. (at McIntire Rd.), Charlottesville VA 22901, (804) 977-5500.
**Camping:** Charlottesville KOA, Rt. 1, Box 144 (I-64 exit 121), Charlottesville VA 22903, (804) 296-9881, (804) 336-9881.

## Overview

Ash Lawn-Highland, situated on a 535-acre estate in a range of mountains near Charlottesville, was the home of James Monroe, the fifth president of the United States (1817–1825). The home, which Monroe called his "cabin-castle," was situated to be near to Jefferson's Monticello. A visit provides the traveler with an interesting insight into the life and career of Monroe. Ash Lawn-Highland also re-creates the atmosphere of an early-nineteenth-century small Southern plantation.

## History

James Monroe's Ash Lawn-Highland recalls the history of America's fifth president and the Virginia dynasty of presidents. Monroe (1758–1831), president from 1817 to 1825, was a key player in Virginia's legacy of leadership to the nation. Preceded in the presidency by Thomas Jefferson and James Madison, Monroe saw that office occupied without interruption by Virginians from 1801 to 1825. Jefferson, Madison, and Monroe enjoyed a special political kinship as leaders of the Democratic-Republic Party.

Monroe was well-prepared to be president. He had served as a lieutenant in the Third Virginia Regiment during the Revolutionary War, was named to the U.S. Senate in 1790, and was governor of Virginia from 1799 to 1803 and again in 1811. Skilled in foreign affairs and diplomacy, he served as minister plenipotentiary to England, Spain, and France. He successfully negotiated the Louisiana Purchase with the French Emperor Napoleon. He served in President Madison's cabinet as secretary of state from 1811 to 1817.

Monroe's presidency has been termed the "era of good feelings" in that he encountered only nominal opposition from the Federalists. In his re-election to the presidency in 1820, Monroe received all but one of the 232 electoral votes. During his second administration, Spain's colonies in the Western Hemisphere revolted and gained their independence. To oppose intervention by the European powers in the Western Hemisphere, Monroe issued his famous "Monroe Doctrine," which firmly declared the United States' opposition to any further European colonization in the Americas or any effort to extend their political systems outside of their own hemisphere.

Monroe's choice of Ash Lawn-Highland as his home was motivated by his long friendship with his legal and political mentor, Thomas Jefferson. Monroe purchased acreage adjacent to Monticello in 1793 in order to live near Jefferson in what Jefferson had called "a society to our taste." It is believed that Jefferson advised Monroe on the location of the house site and sent gardeners to prepare the gardens and orchards. However, before Monroe could begin the work on his estate, President George Washington called him into diplomatic service as minister to France.

It was not until November 23, 1799, that Monroe and his wife moved to his estate, named "Highland." He may have selected that name because his ancestors had immigrated from the Scottish highlands or because the plantation was located in Virginia's upland country. Monroe and his wife, Elizabeth Kortright Monroe, had two daughters, Eliza and Maria, and a son, James.

At Highland, the Monroes entertained Jefferson and the man who would immediately precede him in the presidency, James Madison, and his wife, Dolley. Although its owner's primary profession was politics and diplomacy, Monroe intended Highland to be a working plantation. Some thirty slaves, directed by an overseer, cultivated tobacco on the plantation's 3,500 acres. After growing tobacco for several years, Monroe realized that it was rapidly depleting the soil, leaching it of nutrients. He then turned to grain cultivation and raising cattle and sheep. Monroe also planted Bordeaux grapes, brought from France, for wine.

Although he had planned to retire to Ash Lawn-Highland, Monroe, indebted by his public service, sold it in 1826 for financial reasons.

Renamed "Ash Lawn" in 1838, the house had several different owners in the nineteenth century. In 1882, Parson John Massey, who then owned the property, added a large wing. He also conducted a school for the area's freed slaves.

In 1930, Jay Winston Johns, a wealthy industrialist from Pittsburgh, purchased Ash Lawn from Massey's descendants. Johns, who appreciated the house's historical significance, sought to maintain it and began furnishing it with Monroe furniture and artifacts. He opened it to the public in 1931. Upon his death in 1974, Johns bequeathed Ash Lawn, its furnishings, and 535 acres to the College of William and Mary, which Monroe had attended from 1774 to 1776.

The college began an on-going process of historical restoration and preservation in January 1975. Based upon archeological and historical research, the house has been carefully restored. In April 1975, it was reopened to the public, and in 1985 it became known officially as Ash Lawn-Highland.

## SITE DESCRIPTION

Visitors to **Ash Lawn-Highland** can experience what it was like to live on a small nineteenth-century Southern plantation owned by an illustrious Virginian who was president of the United States. Tour tickets can be purchased in the **museum gift shop**. Led by trained historical interpreters, the house tour requires from thirty to forty-five minutes.

The house, which Monroe called his "cabin-castle," is accessed through an **entrance hall** which leads to the **drawing room** and **study**. The **dining room** is furnished with an elegant mahogany dining room suite. The **master bedroom** contains a highly polished four-poster bed, a foot warmer, and a copper bed warmer. The **girl's bedroom** has a hand-carved crib. There is a **basement kitchen** with period utensils, pots, and pans. Here, food was cooked over a open fire.

On the grounds are the two-room **overseer's cottage**, the **smokehouse**, and reconstructed **slave quarters**.

Ash Lawn-Highland **grounds** are of special interest for their careful planting and landscaping, especially the boxwood hedges. Peacocks walk about the lawns. On the grounds are the **flower, vegetable, and herb gardens**. While walking through the gardens, see the **statue of James Monroe** and enjoy the view of **Jefferson's Monticello**. The pastures with grazing cattle, horses, and sheep recapture an earlier time.

**James Monroe Historical Trail**, a three-mile nature and ecology hiking path, begins at the **museum gift shop** and leads to the top of **Carter's Mountain**. It is a self-guiding tour along a trail with nature and ecology markers.

## FESTIVALS/CRAFTS

Ash Lawn-Highland offers special tours, workshops, and events, including the **Extended Tour of the Monroe Plantation**, the **Dairy Products Workshop**, the **Candle-making Workshop**, and **overnight camp-ins**.

The **Summer Festival** features musical, dance, and operatic performances, June through mid-August. Rt. 6, Box 37, Charlottesville VA 22902. (804) 293-4500.

# MONTICELLO

Restored late-eighteenth-century home, gardens, and grave of Thomas Jefferson; house designed by Jefferson; NR, NHL, HABS.

**Address:** Thomas Jefferson Memorial Foundation, PO Box 316, Charlottesville VA 22902
**Telephone:** (804) 295-8181, (804) 295-2657
**Location:** In north central Virginia, on VA Hwy. 53, 3 miles southeast of Charlottesville near the intersection of VA Hwy. 20 and I-64; Charlottesville is 125 miles southwest of Washington DC.
**Open:** March–October, 8:00 A.M.–5:00 P.M. daily; November–February, 9:00 A.M.–4:30 P.M. daily. Closed Christmas Day.
**Admission:** Adults $8, seniors $7, children ages 6–11 $4. Group rates and student rates available.
**Restaurants:** Refreshments at shuttle station.
**Shops:** Museum shops, garden shop.
**Facilities:** Thomas Jefferson Visitor Center with orientation film, permanent exhibits, a museum shop, and an education department; guided tours; foreign-language tours; accessible to handicapped; archaeological excavations; Thomas Jefferson Center for Historic Plants; Monticello Research Center; picnic area; shuttle service from parking lot.

## WHERE TO STAY

**Inns/Bed & Breakfasts:** The Inn at Monticello, Rt. 19, Box 112, Charlottesville VA 22902, (804) 979-3593. The Inn at the Crossroads, Rt. 2, Box 6, Rt. 692, North Garden VA 22959, (804) 979-6452. High Meadows Vineyard Inn, Rt. 4, Box 6 (VA Hwy. 20 South), Scottsville VA 24590, (804) 286-2218. Prospect Hill Plantation Inn, Hwy. 613 at Zion Crossroads, Trevilians VA 23093, 1-800-277-0844.
**Motels/Hotels:** Best Western-Mount Vernon, 1613 Emmet St. (Jct. US 29 and US 250 Bypass), Charlottesville VA 22906, (804) 296-5501. Boar's Head Inn, PO Box 5307, US 250 West, Charlottesville VA 22905, 1-800-476-1988, (804) 296-2181. Comfort Inn-Charlottes-

ville, 1807 Emmet St. (US 29 North at US 250 Bypass, I-64 exit 118), Charlottesville VA 22901, (804) 293-6188. Holiday Inn-Charlottesville/Monticello, 1200 5th St., Charlottesville VA 22901, (804) 977-5100.

**Camping:** Charlottesville KOA, Rt. 1, Box 144, Charlottesville VA 22903 (I-64, Exit 121), (804) 296-9881, (804) 336-9881.

## OVERVIEW

Genius is the word that springs to mind when one visits Monticello, the thirty-three room residence designed and remodeled from 1769 to 1809 by Thomas Jefferson. Placed on a mountaintop to take advantage of the views, Monticello was the home of Jefferson—the nation's third and one of its most famous presidents—his wife, children, grandchildren, white workers, and African-American slaves. Jefferson's 5,000-acre estate consisted of farms, gardens, orchards, slave dwellings, and workshops. Monticello is a historical site not only because it is associated with Jefferson, but also because it is an architectural showplace in and of itself. Monticello has been restored to its state in 1809, the year Jefferson retired there after completing his second term as U.S. president.

## HISTORY

Monticello is the estate of Thomas Jefferson (1743–1826), the third president of the United States. When he was fourteen years old, Thomas—the son of Peter Jefferson, a successful planter and surveyor, and Jane Randolph, a member of one of Virginia's most distinguished families—inherited 5,000 acres of land along the Rivanna River from his father. Eight years later, young Jefferson began constructing a home of his own design on the property. Over the next forty years, Jefferson remodeled and enlarged this house.

Thomas Jefferson was a multi-talented man. We know from history that he was a student at William and Mary, practiced law in the general court at Williamsburg, was a member of the House of Burgesses, attended Philadelphia's Continental Congress, drafted the Declaration of Independence, was governor of Virginia, minister to France, first secretary of state under President George Washington, vice president under President John Adams, and a two-term U.S. president who negotiated the purchase of the Louisiana Territory from France and arranged the Lewis and Clark expedition to the northwest. In his free time, Jefferson designed, built, furnished, re-designed, and re-built Monticello.

Jefferson was a self-taught architect. He, like Frank Lloyd Wright, saw architecture as a process rather than the creation of a final product. Both men continually rebuilt and remodeled their own homes. In 1809, Jefferson said to Margaret Bayard Smith, "Architecture is my delight and putting up, and pulling down, one of my favorite amusements."

Jefferson chose to build his home on a mountaintop that had been cleared and leveled in 1768. The eight-room house—which Jefferson designed in 1769 when he was twenty-six years old—consisted of a center block with flanking wings in a modified neoclassical style. Jefferson named his house "Monticello," which means "little mountain" in Italian.

Monticello was built on Jefferson's 5,000-acre, largely self-sufficient plantation. Tobacco, wheat, corn, potatoes, and small grains were grown on four farms. Cattle, hogs, and sheep were raised. Also on the plantation were a blacksmith shop, a nailery, a joiner, a utility shed, a dairy, a smokehouse, slave quarters, worker's quarters, and an icehouse. The plantation had a residential labor force composed of free white workers and about sixty adult African-American slaves who had been inherited from both Jefferson's father and father-in-law. About eighty of the 200 slaves owned by Jefferson lived at Monticello at any one time.

Much of the building material for Monticello, including bricks and nails, was made on the property. Structural timber came from Jefferson's land, and the stone and limestone were quarried there.

Many of the plantation's white workers and African-American slaves took part in the construction. Stone and brick work was done by local masons. Carpenters assisted by Monticello slave carpenters provided the rough structural woodwork. Floors, cornices, and other moldings were finished by skilled joiners and their slave assistants.

In 1772, a few years after Jefferson began building Monticello, he married Martha Wayles Skelton. Although the Jeffersons had six children, only two survived childhood—Martha, born in 1772, and Mary, born in 1778. Their mother died in 1782, after only ten years of marriage. Jefferson never remarried. His daughter Martha served as his hostess and housekeeper. She had married her cousin, Thomas Mann Randolph, Jr., and their eleven children grew up at Monticello. Mary Jefferson—who married another cousin, John W. Eppes, and had a son, Francis—died at age twenty-five. Francis Eppes also spent much of his childhood at Monticello.

After living in France from 1784 until 1789 while serving as minister to France, Jefferson decided to redesign and enlarge Monticello based on French architecture. Remodeling began in 1796. He removed the upper story and enlarged the house from eight to twenty-one rooms. A dome was erected over the center portion of the building. Piazzas or arched loggias were placed on the north and south ends of the building. Following a Parisian design, the house appeared to be one story, though steep, narrow stairs led to second and third floors, where bedrooms were tucked under the eaves.

Jefferson selected the furnishings of his home. He acquired a large collection of art and furnishings in Paris and purchased furniture from cabinetmakers in Williamsburg, London, New York, and Philadelphia. Jefferson also designed furniture, which he had made by his own cabinetmakers.

Landscape designs done by Jefferson at Monticello include ornamental flower gardens near the house, fruit orchards, and a 1,000-foot-long garden where Jefferson experimented with hundreds of varieties of vegetables. Jefferson had also laid out the family burial ground by 1773, and he is buried in it.

Monticello is owned and operated by the Thomas Jefferson Memorial Foundation, Inc., a private, nonprofit organization formed in 1923.

## SITE DESCRIPTION

Visitors take the shuttle up the mountain to **Monticello** after parking their cars and buses at the bottom of the hill.

On 2,000 acres of Jefferson's original 5,000-acre site is the remarkable home designed by the third president of the United States on a low mountain site. To the east can be seen **Virginia Piedmont farmlands**, while to the west are the city of **Charlottesville** and the **University of Virginia**, founded by Jefferson. In the distance are the **Blue Ridge Mountains**.

Monticello has been restored to 1809. Nearly all of the furniture and artifacts in the house were owned by Jefferson or his family. A 1993 exhibit called "The Worlds of Thomas Jefferson at Monticello" to commemorate the 250th anniversary of Jefferson's birth re-united Monticello and over 150 Jefferson artifacts, some of which were sold soon after Jefferson's death to pay his debts. Unfortunately, many of these items were returned to their collections after the exhibit ended.

Monticello has eleven rooms on the first floor and six bedrooms on the second floor, which is reached by two, steep, narrow stairways. On the third floor are three bedrooms with skylights and a large octagonal room below the dome called the "dome room." Only the first floor is open to the public. There are also rooms in the cellar and in the attached dependency wings.

On the first floor are the **entrance hall**, which served as a reception hall, and a **museum** containing items of **art, natural history, and Native**

**American culture**. There are American Indian artifacts from the Lewis and Clark expedition, a buffalo skull, moose and elk antlers, and mastodon bones, engraved wall maps, and busts of Turgot, Voltaire, Alexander Hamilton and Jefferson. The entrance hall, which has a grass-green floor, has twenty-eight reproduction Windsor chairs constructed according to Jefferson's specifications. An unusual calendar clock designed by Jefferson has faces on both the inside and outside of the house and tells the days of the week.

Jefferson's private suite of rooms for sleeping, reading, writing, and conducting scientific experiments are the bedroom, the book room, the cabinet, and the greenhouse. Jefferson's **bedroom** in the south portion of the house is a two-story room with a skylight and an alcove bed. Jefferson died here on July 4, 1826.

His **cabinet or study**, south of his bedroom, includes five presses used to store papers, a revolving chair, a table, book stand, and a polygraph—a two-pen, letter-duplicating devise. An adjacent **book room** contains hundreds of his books. In 1815, Jefferson sold the bulk of his 6,700-volume library to the federal government; they formed the nucleus of the Library of Congress. Other Jefferson pieces in the book room are a tall-backed Sheraton chair, a Virginia-made architect's table with Chinese fretwork, and an octagonal filing table. The **greenhouse** is a glassed-in piazza which Jefferson used for horticultural experiments.

In the **south square room**, which was used as a sitting room, is a portrait by James Ford of Martha Randolph, Jefferson's daughter. There is also a table made by a slave craftsman.

The **parlor**, a large, elegant room with a semi-octagonal bay, is separated from the entrance hall by single-acting double glass doors. Jefferson was intrigued by gadgetry and incorporated some unique things in the house, like the parlor doors and the dining room's dumb waiters. Both family members and guests used the parlor for socializing, music, games, and reading. There are a harpsichord, a pianoforte, a cittern, and a violin. Three tiers of paintings and engravings hang on the wall.

The **dining room**, like Jefferson's bedroom, is a two-story room with a skylight. Breakfast and dinner were served there each day. In the **tea room** are busts of Adams, Washington, Franklin, and Lafayette.

The **north octagonal room, or Madison Bedroom**, a guest bedroom, has hand-blocked wall paper. The **north square room, or Abbe Correia Bedroom**, was another guest bedroom.

After thirty-three months of research and a year and a half of construction, Monticello's complex **roof system** was restored in 1992. The house has L-shaped wings connected to the cellars of the house by an all-weather passageway which contained dependencies. Their roofs formed terraces which extended from the main floor of the house. Beneath the north terrace were stables, carriage bays, and an icehouse. Beneath the south terrace were the kitchen, cook's room, house servants' rooms, a smokehouse, and the dairy.

In addition to the house tour, a tour of **Mulberry Row** and of **house dependencies** is given daily at 12:00 noon and 1:20 P.M., April through October. The tour focuses on the lives of the plantation's slaves, as well as their labor systems and activities. "Mulberry Row" refers to the shops and free-worker and slave dwellings along a plantation road that is lined with mulberry trees. The structures along Mulberry Row have disappeared, with the exception of the foundations and chimney of the **joinery**, part of a **stone stable**, and a **stone workman's house** that is now attached to a modern gift ship and office. Archaeological excavations along Mulberry Row have uncovered thousands of discarded artifacts, some of which can be seen at the **Thomas Jefferson Visitor Center**. The **kitchen** and **cook's room** in the dependency are also visited.

**Garden tours** are offered daily from mid-April through October. Self-guided tours of the gardens can be taken all year. Jefferson's **flower gardens** consisted of twenty oval-shaped flower beds at the four corners of the house, a graveled "roundabout" walk with a flower border on the west side of the house, and a flower border along a winding walk before the house. In the flower beds are a variety of plants, including Columbian lilies, cardinal flowers, tulips, sweet williams, Maltese crosses, and Jeffersonia diphyllas. In 1939, the Garden Club of Virginia restored these gardens. The **fruit and vegetable gardens** were replanted in the 1980s. In 1977, a project was started to re-create the **grove of deciduous trees** planted by Jefferson.

Your last stop at Monticello is the **graveyard** laid out by Jefferson in 1773. He is buried there.

The **Thomas Jefferson Visitor Center**, which has exhibits, a film, a museum shop, and a visitors information bureau is located on VA Hwy. 20 South at I-64, approximately two miles west of Monticello.

## FESTIVALS/CRAFTS

Special events occur on **Jefferson's birthday, April 13**, and the **4th of July**. The **Holiday Candlelight Open House** in early December gives visitors a chance to visit Monticello after dark. A series of workshops called **"Saturdays in the Garden,"** which is offered mid-April through October, features natural-history walks and lectures.

## SIDE TRIPS

**Historic Michie Tavern Museum** combines a museum of pre-revolutionary furniture and artifacts and a restaurant serving Southern colonial fare at lunch in **The Ordinary**, a converted log cabin which was used as a slave cabin 200 years ago. One of the oldest homesteads remaining in Virginia, the original property owner was Major John Henry, father of patriot Patrick Henry, who was granted the land in 1735. In 1746, Major Henry sold his 3,000 acres to John Michie, and by 1784, the Michie family operated a tavern offering food and shelter to travelers. The Michie Tavern was originally located on a stage coach road seventeen miles northeast of its present location until 1927. It remained in the Michie family until 1910. The museum is open 9:00 A.M.–5:00 P.M. daily; lunch is served from 11:30 A.M. to 3:00 P.M. daily. Admission is charged. Thomas Jefferson Parkway, Charlottesville VA 22902. (804) 977-1234.

Jefferson designed two homes for himself. The other one, which he used as his personal retreat at his Bedford County plantation, is **Poplar Forest**, near Lynchburg. Built in 1806, the octagonal house was privately owned until 1984, when it was acquired by the Corporation for Jefferson's Poplar Forest, a nonprofit organization. Although restoration is in its infant stages as archaeologists and restoration architects study the site, Poplar Forest is open to visitors 10:00 A.M.–4:00 P.M., Wednesday–Sunday, from April through October. Poplar Forest is just southwest of Lynchburg on Rt. 661, one mile from Rt. 221. Admission is charged. PO Box 419, Forest VA 24551-0419. (804) 525-1806.

# KENMORE

Restored eighteenth-century manor house,
home of Betty Washington Lewis,
sister of George Washington; NR, NHL, HABS.

**Address:** 1201 Washington Ave., Fredericksburg VA 22401
**Telephone:** (703) 373-3381
**Location:** In northern Virginia.
**Open:** March–November, 9:00 A.M.–5:00 P.M. daily; December–February, 10:00 A.M.–4:00 P.M. daily. Closed Thanksgiving, Christmas Eve and Day, and New Year's Eve and Day.
**Admission:** Adults $5, children ages 6–18 $2.50.
**Restaurants:** Tea and gingerbread in the kitchen.
**Shops:** Gift Shop.
**Facilities:** Crowinshield Gallery with changing exhibits and a diorama of early Fredericksburg, educational and artistic programs, tours for visually and hearing-impaired visitors.

## WHERE TO STAY

**Inns/Bed & Breakfasts:** Fredericksburg Colonial, 1707 Princess Anne St., Fredericksburg VA 22401, (703) 371-5666, FAX: (703) 373-7557.
**Motels/Hotels:** Sheraton Inn, PO Box 618, 2801 Plank Rd., Fredericksburg VA 22404, (703) 786-8321, FAX: (703) 786-3957. Hampton Inn, 2310 William St., Fredericksburg 22401, (703) 371-0330, FAX: (703) 371-1753.
**Camping:** KOA Fredericksburg, 4100 Guinea Station Rd., Fredericksburg VA 22408, 1-800-443-7887, (703) 898-7252.

## OVERVIEW

Kenmore is a beautifully restored eighteenth-century house that was once the centerpiece of a plantation of over 1,000 acres. It now occupies one city block in the town of Fredericksburg. Kenmore is historically important because it was the home of George Washington's only sister, Betty, and her husband, Fielding Lewis; Washington was a frequent guest. The house is famous for its rich interior decoration, especially its elaborate plasterwork ceilings.

# HISTORY

In 1750, Fielding Lewis, a young widower with one son, married seventeen-year-old Betty Washington, the only sister of George Washington. Lewis was from a Virginia family that was related to the Washingtons. The grandmothers of Fielding Lewis and Betty Washington were sisters, daughters of Augustine Warner. Fielding Lewis's first wife was another cousin, Catherine Washington.

Lewis was a prominent person who served in the House of Burgesses and was a landowner, a county militia commander, and a trading and shipping merchant. In 1752, he purchased 861 acres on the Rappahannock River near Fredericksburg which had been surveyed the previous month by nineteen-year-old George Washington. In the early 1770s, the Lewis house was constructed, it is believed, by John Ariss.

George Washington was a frequent visitor to both the Lewises, and his mother, Mary Washington, who lived in an adjacent house.

Fielding Lewis was committed to Revolutionary causes. He was commissioned to build a gunnery in Fredericksburg during the third Virginia Convention in July, 1775. Revolutionary leaders were particularly concerned by the shortage of firearms. Patriotic zeal caused Lewis to advance large amounts of his own money for the Fredericksburg Gunnery. He also lent money for outfitting ships. By 1781, Lewis's distress at his inability to pay his taxes and continue his business caused him to appeal to the state of Virginia for repayment. Fielding Lewis died that year, and Betty and their five sons and one daughter operated the plantation until 1796.

After Betty Washington Lewis died in 1797, the plantation, which had grown to 1,100 acres, was sold by its heir, John Lewis, Fielding's son by his first wife. It passed through the hands of a number of owners before it was purchased in 1819 by Samuel Gordon of Scotland, who named it "Kenmore." The Gordons sold Kenmore in 1859, just before the Civil War—during which the house was turned into a field hospital. Later, the property was subdivided and sold off until all that was left was the small parcel of land on which the house stood.

Plans to demolish the historic house or remodel it into apartments angered local preservationists, who formed a group to save Kenmore in 1922. The Kenmore Association purchased and restored the house to its original eighteenth-century appearance. Furnishings that either belonged to the Lewises or were appropriate to the period were gradually acquired for the house.

## SITE DESCRIPTION

**Kenmore** is a solid two-story house, fifty-three feet wide and forty-one feet deep, with a basement and an attic. Brick walls, laid in Flemish bond, are two feet thick. The plain, symmetrical exterior has two windows on each side of a center door on the first floor, and five windows on the second floor.

On the first floor are a **dining room, drawing room, chamber, small room**, and **entrance hall**. On the second floor are the **gentlemen's room**, the **blue chamber**, the **children's room**, and **Mary Washington's bedroom**. Furniture throughout the mansion has been chosen based on a detailed inventory of each room made on Fielding Lewis's death. Although some pieces belonged to the Lewises, most did not. However, meticulous research has resulted in an extraordinary collection of Colonial furniture at Kenmore.

Although the exterior of the house is plain, its interior is heavily embellished with outstanding decorative plasterwork on the ceilings and overmantels of the dining room, drawing room and chamber, the work of an unknown plasterer who also worked at Mount Vernon. Most of the paneling and woodwork is original.

The **dining-room ceiling** is considered to have the most exceptional plasterwork. Decorative elements include festoons, rosettes, cornucopias, flowers, stylized leaves and trailing vines. The overmantel in this room contains a plaster bas-relief of a scene from Aesop's *Fables*. Portraits of Betty and Fielding Lewis by John Wollaston are on the wall. Eighteenth-century English creamware rests on the 1745 dining table from Williamsburg.

The **drawing room**, the largest room in the house, has a paneled wall, and wainscoting. Plaster decorations on the ceiling include the Mask of Apollo, the Sun God.

The **ceiling in the chamber**, called the "**Four Seasons Ceiling**," displays plants symbolic of each season in its four corners. There are palm fronds for spring, grapes for summer, acorns for fall, and mistletoe for winter. This ceiling was repaired in 1881, by twenty-one-year-old William Key Howard, Jr., whose family owned the house. The bed and windows are hung with white dimity.

The **small room** is decorated as if it were Fielding Lewis's plantation office. The walnut desk-bookcase was probably made by Anthony Hay in Williamsburg in 1780. The corner chair and side chairs are eighteenth-century Virginia pieces.

In the **entrance hall** are Windsor chairs and a 1750 tall-case clock from London.

In the **blue chamber** upstairs are a 1760–1780 desk and bed that belonged to the Lewises.

The **kitchen** and the **south dependency** were reconstructed in the 1930s to replace structures that had disappeared. In the kitchen is a collection of cooking and serving wares. There, visitors can have tea and gingerbread.

The **grounds** at Kenmore are planted with dogwood, holly, and boxwood. A low brick wall separates the lawn from the cutting garden.

## SIDE TRIPS

On Washington Avenue, a short distance from Kenmore, is the **Mary Washington Monument.** This obelisk marks the grave of Mary Ball Washington, mother of George Washington and Betty Washington Lewis.

**Fredericksburg and Spotsylvania County Battlefields Memorial National Military Park** preserves, on a 5,900-acre site, portions of four major Civil War battlefields: Fredericksburg, Chancellorsville, the Wilderness, and Spotsylvania Court House (1862–1864). More than 15,000 Federal interments, of which 13,000 are unknown, are in **Fredericksburg National Cemetery.** Open 9:00 A.M.–5:00 P.M. daily. PO Box 679, Fredericksburg VA 22404. (703) 373-4461. Admission is free.

# JAMES RIVER PLANTATIONS

Seventeenth-century colonial plantations with restored
eighteenth-century houses situated on the James River.

## WHERE TO STAY

**Inns/Bed & Breakfasts:** North Bend Plantation, 12200 Weyanoke Rd.,
Charles City VA 23030, (804) 829-5176, 1-800-841-1479. Edge-
wood Plantation, Rt. 5, Charles City VA 23030, (804) 829-2962.
Piney Grove at Southall's Plantation, 16920 Southall Plantation
Lane, Charles City VA 23030, (804) 829-2480. Seward House Inn,
PO Box 352, Surry VA 23883, (804) 294-3810.

**Motels/Hotels:** The Jefferson Grand Heritage, Franklin and Adams Sts.,
Richmond VA 23220, (804) 788-8000, 1-800-424-8014, FAX: (804)
344-5162. Hilton Airport, 5501 Euband Rd., Sandston VA 23150,
(804) 226-6400, FAX: (804) 226-1269. Also see entry for Colonial
Williamsburg.

**Camping:** Anvil Campground, 5243 Mooretown Rd., Williamsburg VA
23188, (804) 563-2300, 1-800-633-4442. Colonial Campgrounds,
4712 Lightfoot Rd., Williamsburg VA 23188, (804) 565-2734. Williamsburg KOA Campground, 5210 Lightfoot Rd., Williamsburg VA
23188.

## OVERVIEW

Along Virginia's James River, between Richmond and Williamsburg,
is a stretch of plantation country that has connections with American
Revolutionary figures as well as later prominent politicians. Like other regions in Louisiana and South Carolina, this area is one of beautifully restored mansions and well-landscaped grounds that shed light on the life-
style of plantation families in the antebellum South. The fact that the
James River plantations are associated with prominent American politicians adds yet another dimension to their allure.

Historical homes are commonplace in Virginia—the first, largest,
and wealthiest of the British colonies in America. The state, not overrun
by industry and growing populations, has retained its rural character. Active preservation groups protect hundreds of structures related to the nation's past. The tidewater region that includes Jamestown, Yorktown,
Williamsburg, and Richmond is particularly rich historically.

Some James River plantation houses are open only during Historic Garden Week at the end of April. Others permit tours of their gardens and grounds, but not of their houses, year-round. However, four James River sites—Berkeley, Sherwood Forest, Shirley, and Chippokes Plantations—are open to the public, and they're definitely worth a visit.

Berkeley Plantation was the birthplace of Benjamin Harrison, a signer of the Declaration of Independence, and of William Henry Harrison, president of the United States. Sherwood Forest Plantation was the home of President John Tyler from 1842 to 1862 and is still owned by his direct descendants. Shirley Plantation, established in 1613, is the oldest plantation in Virginia and has remained in the prominent Hill-Carter family for over 300 years. Ann Hill Carter was the mother of General Robert E. Lee. Chippokes Plantation has been a working farm since the 1600s.

# BERKELEY PLANTATION

Restored early-eighteenth-century mansion;
birthplace of Benjamin Harrison and
William Henry Harrison; NR, NHL, HABS.

**Address:** 12602 Harrison Landing Rd., Charles City VA 23030
**Telephone:** (804) 829-6018
**Location:** 22 miles east of Richmond, 27 miles west of Williamsburg; on
VA Hwy. 5, 5 miles east of Benjamin Harrison Bridge.
**Open:** 8:00 A.M.–5:00 P.M. daily.
**Admission:** Adults $8.50, children $4.
**Restaurants:** Coach House Tavern.
**Facilities:** Picnic area, gardens.

## HISTORY

Thirty-eight Gloucestershire men sailed from England on the *Margaret*, landing in Virginia December 4, 1619. Led by Captain John Woodlief, these members of the Berkeley Company settled on an 8,000-acre grant from the London Company called Berkeley Hundred. In 1622, the entire Berkeley Hundred colony was wiped out in a attack by hostile American Indians.

In 1691, Berkeley was acquired by Benjamin Harrison III, who was descended from Surry County planters on the opposite shore of the James River. Harrison established a prosperous tobacco export business. His shipyard built vessels for transporting tobacco from his warehouse to the Caribbean and England. Three Revolutionary War eighteen-gun warships were also built here. His busy ship landing was dubbed "Harrison's Landing."

Benjamin Harrison IV built a house in 1726 for himself and his wife, Anne Carter, the daughter of a leading Virginia entrepreneur, Robert "King" Carter. Their son, Benjamin Harrison V, was a signer of the Declaration of Independence, a three-time governor of Virginia, a member of the House of Burgesses, and its speaker during the Revolution. He represented Virginia at the Continental Congress in Philadelphia and was a friend of George Washington, who was entertained at Berkeley.

In 1781, Benedict Arnold brought British troops to Berkeley. They burned its furnishings, shot the cattle, and carried off forty slaves.

Benjamin V married Elizabeth Bassett, and they had seven children.

Their son William Henry was a soldier and politician who was elected president of the United States in 1840. He returned to Berkeley to write his inaugural address in the room in which he was born.

Previously, William Henry Harrison had risen to the rank of major general in the U.S. Army, served as governor of the Indiana Territory, fought in the Battle of Tippecanoe, was secretary of the Northwest Territory, U.S. representative, superintendent of Indian Affairs, Ohio state senator, U.S. senator, and minister to Columbia. Harrison died one month after being inaugurated president.

The first ten presidents of the United States all visited the prominent Harrison family at Berkeley Plantation.

During the Civil War, Berkeley Plantation became the temporary headquarters of Union General George B. McClellan and his 140,000 troops. After McClellan's seven-day Peninsula Campaign failed to capture the Confederate capital of Richmond in July, 1862, the Union's Army of the Potomac moved back to the James River, which was protected by Federal gunboats at Harrison's Landing. While at Berkeley, President Lincoln sailed down the Chesapeake to confer with his commanding general.

While camped at Berkeley, a member of McClellan's staff, General Daniel Butterfield, composed the melody called "Taps." It was first played by bugler Over W. Norton. Adopted by both the Union and Confederate armies, "Taps" is now the official bugle call of the United States Army.

Berkeley changed hands several times after the Civil War and fell into a state of decline. In 1907, the plantation was purchased by John Jamieson of Scotland, who had been a drummer boy in McClellan's army. Jamieson's son, Malcolm, and his wife, Grace, restored the house in the 1930s. It is furnished with Colonial antiques.

## SITE DESCRIPTION

**Berkeley** is a classic, early Georgian two-story brick building with two tall chimneys and six dormers. A circular date-stone on the west end of the house bears the inscription "H," for Harrison, "B," for Benjamin, "A" for Anne Carter, a heart, and the date 1726.

The interior features notable woodwork and tinted plaster walls. The **entrance hall** is forty-five feet long.

There are two drawing rooms separated by double arches. A French desk and a chest-on-chest in the **north drawing room** came from Westover Plantation. There is a portrait of Benjamin Harrison V over the mantel.

In the **south drawing room** is an English secretary desk with diamond back mirrors. Hung over its mantel is a portrait of Thomas Jefferson's niece, who was the great-great-grandmother of Mrs. Jamieson. Hand-carved cornices and chair moldings were added to the drawing rooms by Benjamin VI in 1790.

Between the house and the James River lie the five-level, ten-acre terraced **boxwood gardens** designed by Benjamin IV. Cockscomb and chrysanthemums bloom in the **ladies winter garden**.

# SHERWOOD FOREST PLANTATION

Restored home of President John Tyler; eighteenth-century plantation house and grounds; NR, NHL, HABS.

**Address:** PO Box 8, 14501 John Tyler Memorial Highway, Charles City VA 23030
**Telephone:** (804) 829-5377, FAX: (804) 829-2947
**Location:** 18 miles west of Williamsburg and 35 miles east of Richmond on VA Hwy. 5; 3 miles east of the Charles City County Courthouse.
**Open:** 9:00 A.M.–5:00 P.M. daily; closed Thanksgiving, Christmas, and New Year's Days.
**Admission:** Adults $7.50, seniors $7, students (kindergarten-through college-age) $4.50.
**Restaurants:** Refreshments and box lunches by reservation in Tippecanoe Room.
**Shops:** Gift Shop.
**Facilities:** Picnic area.

## HISTORY

Sherwood Forest Plantation was the last home of John Tyler, tenth president of the United States, from 1842 until his death in 1862. The plantation has remained in the Tyler family, and the house is currently owned by Harrison Tyler, a grandson, who is responsible for its restoration. The plantation had also been owned by the ninth president of the United States, William Henry Harrison, who inherited it from his sister in 1789. It is not known whether Harrison actually lived there.

John Tyler became president April 6, 1841, when as vice-president, he attained the office after the death of William Henry Harrison, who had served only thirty days as president.

John Tyler was born March 29, 1790, in Charles City County, Virginia. He was the son of Virginians, John Tyler and Mary Marot Armistead Tyler. Educated in local Virginia schools, he graduated from the College of William and Mary in 1807. A lawyer and a politician, he served in the Virginia House of Delegates, the Virginia senate, the U.S. House of Representatives, and the U.S. Senate. He was the governor of Virginia, and the vice-presidential running mate of Whig candidate William Henry Harrison in the presidential election of 1840. Tyler served out Harrison's term until 1845 and did not seek re-election.

John Tyler married Letitia Christian in 1813; they had eight children. Letitia Tyler died in the White House in 1842. Tyler married Julia Gardiner in 1844; he and Julia had seven children.

In 1842, Tyler purchased Walnut Grove plantation in Charles County, Virginia. He and his bride moved there in 1845. A political foe, Henry Clay, said that, like Robin Hood, Tyler was going off to his Sherwood Forest. Amused by the comment, Tyler changed the name of the 1,600-acre plantation to Sherwood Forest.

John and Julia Tyler operated the large plantation and extensively renovated the house. The plantation, originally named "Smith's Hundred," dates back to a 1616 land grant. A house was built around 1660 but was destroyed between 1700 and 1730. A second house, built over the original basement, was constructed around 1730. Wings were added to the house in 1780 and in the years from 1800 to 1830. John and Julia Tyler added to the house in 1844 and 1845.

The plantation has remained in the Tyler family. The house and fifty acres were purchased by a grandson, Harrison Tyler and his wife, Payne, from other family members in 1975. Although the house survived the Civil War, it had suffered damage. Time and neglect had also taken their toll. The couple began the daunting job of restoration aided by Julia's letters and plates from an 1835 architectural book by Minard LaFever, whose drawings were used by Julia Tyler to style the doors and door frames.

## SITE DESCRIPTION

Architecturally, **Sherwood Forest** is quite unique. At 300 feet, it is considered the longest wood manor house in the country. Called "Virginia Tidewater style," the white frame house has twenty-four rooms and sixteen fireplaces.

The 1730 house, positioned over the basement of the 1660 house, was a three-story English Georgian townhouse. A detached dependency was also erected at that time. Around 1780, a three-story wing connecting the main house and the dependency was added. In the early 1800s, an addition was placed on the other side of the house for balance and symmetry. Around that time, a *garçonnièr*, or separate living quarters for the planter's sons, was built. John Tyler added a 68-x-12 foot ballroom which connected the house and the garconnier on one side, and a colonnade between the house and a seventeenth-century kitchen/laundry on the other side. The result, indeed, is a long, narrow house.

When John and Julia Tyler remodeled the house, they were influenced by the then-popular Greek Revival style. The features of that style which they incorporated were porches, pilasters, cornices, and ornate medallions.

Most of the eighteenth-century furniture, paintings, and artifacts now in Sherwood Forest belonged either to the Tyler family or the family of Payne Bouknight Tyler, Harrison Tyler's wife and the house's primary restorer, who grew up at Mulberry Hill Plantation in South Carolina.

Portraits of Julia and John Tyler hang in the **entry hall**, which also contains a French pier table that had been in the White House. In the **dining room** is a 1840s Hepplewhite table from Virginia with a set of china used by the president at the White House, along with a gilded mirror and a marble-top table. President Tyler's books, thought to have been hidden during the Civil War, were found in a hay-covered box in the barn. They are in the **gray room**. The very long and narrow **ballroom**, designed for the Virginia reel, has floor to ceiling windows and a unique vaulted ceiling designed by Julia Tyler. In the **drawing room** is a Rose Medallion tea set from China that is part of a collection given to Tyler by Caleb Cushing, the ambassador to China during the Tyler administration.

The twenty-five-acre site includes several outbuildings normally found on a working plantation. They include an 1820 two-room **overseer's house**, a 1745 **smokehouse**, a 1660 **wine house**, an 1845 **garden house, or privy**, a 1745 **milk house**, and a ca. 1790–1830 **slave house**. More than eighty varieties of trees over one hundred years old are on the grounds.

# SHIRLEY PLANTATION

Oldest plantation in Virginia, established in 1613;
early-eighteenth-century house, in the Hill-Carter
family since 1660; NR, NHL, HABS.

**Address:** 501 Shirley Plantation Rd., Charles City VA 23030
**Telephone:** (804) 829-5121, 1-800-232-1613, FAX: (804) 829-6322
**Location:** 35 miles west of Williamsburg, 18 miles east of Richmond, 10
 miles east of the I-295 and VA Hwy. 5 intersection.
**Open:** 9:00 A.M.–5:00 P.M. daily.
**Admission:** Adults $7, military and seniors $6, youths ages 13–21 $5, chil-
 dren ages 6–12 $3.50.
**Shops:** Gift shop.
**Facilities:** Guided tours.

## HISTORY

Shirley Plantation was settled by Sir Thomas West in 1613, just six
years after the English colonists arrived at Jamestown. West named the plantation for his wife, Cecily Shirley. The property was located on the James
River, which was a main artery of commercial activity. One of the earliest tobacco plantations in Virginia, Shirley was exporting that crop by 1616.

In 1660, Colonel Edward Hill II acquired the property, and it is still
owned by the Hill-Carter family today. Edward Hill III, a member of the
House of Burgesses, built the present house around 1723 for his daughter
Elizabeth, who married John Carter, son of Robert "King" Carter, considered the richest man in colonial Virginia.

Prominent Virginians who visited Shirley Plantation included
Washington, Jefferson, and members of the Byrd and Harrison families.
During the American Revolution, Shirley was a supply center for the Con-
tinental Army.

Ann Hill Carter, a great-granddaughter of Edward Hill III, who was
born at Shirley Plantation, was married in its parlor to Henry "Light-Horse
Harry" Lee, a Revolutionary War calvary officer. They are the parents of
Confederate General Robert E. Lee.

By the early 1800s, the plantation had been expanded to 170,000
acres with more than 200 African-American slaves. Today, still operated
by the Hills and the Carters, it is an 800-acre working plantation.

## SITE DESCRIPTION

The **Shirley Plantation House** is Georgian with two-story porticos on both main facades. It has a double-hipped roof with a single pineapple finial. The pineapple was a colonial symbol of hospitality. Pineapples can also be seen in the hand-carved woodwork in the house. There are gabled dormers on all four sides of the roof.

In the unusually large **entrance hall**, a hanging stair without visible means of support rises three flights. The walnut staircase is squared rather than curved. The house is known for its superb paneling and elegant carved woodwork. Full paneling can be seen in several rooms, and there are ornate broken pediments over interior doorways. Most of the furnishings and silver are original family pieces. Portraits of prominent members of the Carter family are hung throughout the house.

The fully paneled **parlor** has dental molding and interior window shutters. It is the room in which Robert E. Lee's parents were married.

Brick outbuildings constructed in 1723 form a **Georgian forecourt** that is a unique and impressive aspect of Shirley Plantation. Built in this handsome architectural style is a large two-story **kitchen** with a stone floor, a fireplace, and an oven. There are also a **laundry house**, two **barns**, one of which has an icehouse under it, a **stable**, a **smokehouse**, and a **dove cote**.

# CHIPPOKES PLANTATION STATE PARK

## 1854 mansion on 1619 plantation; NR.

**Address:** 695 Chippokes Park Rd., Surry VA 23883
**Telephone:** Park, (804) 294-3625; museum, (804) 294-3439
**Location:** On the south bank of the James River, 5 miles east of Surry and 65 miles southeast of Richmond; on Rt. 634, just off VA Hwy. 10.
**Open:** Park: 8:00 A.M.—dusk, daily. Mansion: Memorial Day through Labor Day and during Garden Week in late April and the Christmas season, 10:00 A.M.–6:00 P.M. Wednesday–Sunday. Farm and Forestry Museum: Memorial Day through Labor Day, 10:00 A.M.–6:00 P.M. Wednesday–Sunday; March through May and September through November, 10:00 A.M.–4:00 P.M. Saturday, 1:00–4:00 P.M. Sunday.
**Admission:** Park: $1 per vehicle; mansion: adults $2, children, ages 12 and under, $1.
**Restaurants:** Snack bar.
**Facilities:** Visitor center with audiovisual program, Farm and Forestry Museum, swimming pool, fishing, handicapped accessible; picnic area, hiking and bicycling trails, conference shelter.

### HISTORY

Captain William Powell, who came to Virginia from England in 1610, was the first owner of the Chippokes Plantation property. Powell was a native of the County of Surrey and a shareholder in the Virginia Company of London in the Charter of 1609. He received a grant for 550 acres of river frontage on Chippokes Creek in 1619. Both the plantation and creek were named for a local Indian chief, Choapoke, who was friendly to the English settlers.

Powell was a captain of the Governor's Guards and Company, lieutenant governor and commander of Jamestown, and a member for James City of the first assembly of 1619. He participated in the 1622 Indian massacre at Jamestown and was killed while leading an expedition against the Chickahominy Indians in February 1623.

After William Powell's death, the property was inherited by his son, George Powell, who died without a legal heir in 1643. The property reverted to the crown and was then granted to Governor Sir William Berkeley. In 1646, Berkeley granted a patent of 1,200 acres, including Powell's acreage, to Colonel Henry Bishop, who came from Henfield, Sussex, England in 1640. The property passed through many hands and had grown to 1,334 acres when it was purchased in 1837 for $12,000 by Albert Carroll Jones, who built the mansion in 1854.

After Albert Jones's death in 1882, the property was owned by several Jones family members. In 1911, Chippokes Plantation was purchased by Isabella H. Cuthbert, a Jones in-law, who was forced by creditors to sell in 1918. The 1,403-acre estate was purchased by Victor Stewart for $47,000 and given to the Commonwealth of Virginia by his widow in 1967.

Chippokes Plantation has been continuously farmed since the 1600s and is one of the oldest working farms in the nation. It is now a Virginia State Park which offers recreational facilities in addition to tours of the mid-nineteenth-century mansion. Recently, a Farm and Forestry Museum which focuses on the development of agriculture and forestry in Virginia has been established.

## SITE DESCRIPTION

**Chippokes Plantation State Park** preserves the 1,403-acre plantation as a historical and recreational site. In addition to the mansion house which may be toured during the summer, there are a **visitor center** with historical exhibits, a **Farm and Forestry Museum**, and a **sawmill**. **Recreational facilities** include a swimming pool; fishing in the James River, College Run Creek, and Lower Chippokes Creek; hiking trails; bike trails; and picnic areas.

The **plantation house** is a 1854 brick two-story Greek Revival-style dwelling. It was stuccoed and painted white. There are a separate brick kitchen and carriage house, as well as other outbuildings. An earlier structure, the **River House**, built in 1829, overlooks the James River. It has two dependencies, a kitchen-laundry, and a slave quarter. The **formal gardens** surrounding the mansion are accented by azaleas, crepe myrtle, boxwood, and seasonal flowers.

The **Farm and Forestry Museum** displays hundreds of agricultural implements and exhibits that tell the story of agricultural development from colonial times to the present.

## FESTIVALS/CRAFTS

The **Pork, Peanut and Pine Festival**, held in mid-July, celebrates the main industries of Surry County—two locally grown products and lumbering. The **Chippokes Steam and Gas Engine Show**, held in early June, features demonstrations of antique engines and farm machinery.

## SIDE TRIPS

**Brandon Plantation**, part of a 7,000-acre 1616 land grant to John Martin, is a National Historic Landmark. It is known for its superb gardens, which retain their original design. The main house was designed by Thomas Jefferson. Although the Brandon Plantation gardens are open daily from 9:00 A.M. to 5:00 P.M., the house is open only during **Historic Garden Week** in late April to group tours by appointment. 23500 Brandon Rd., Spring Grove VA 23881. (804) 866-8416, (804) 866-8486, (804) 866-0506. Admission is charged.

**Westover** has a outstanding Georgian colonial home built by William Byrd II in 1730 on a plantation that dates to 1619. The mansion consists of a two-story central section and two attached wings, one of which is a post-Civil War replacement for a wing that was burned. Grounds, outbuildings, and gardens are open daily, 9:00 A.M.–6:00 P.M. The house is open only during annual Historic Garden Week in late April. 7000 Westover Rd., Charles City VA 23030. (804) 829-2882. Admission is charged.

Climb aboard the *Annabel Lee* for a three-and-one-half-hour **river-boat cruise** from Richmond to Westover Plantation on the James River. The boat docks at Westover Plantation, and passengers take a guided tour of **Westover, Berkeley,** and **Evelynton Plantations.** (804) 222-5700, 1-800-752-7093.

**Evelynton Plantation** was originally part of William Byrd's Westover Plantation. In 1847, it was purchased by the Ruffin family, and it remains in that family today. Edmund Ruffin fired the first shot of the Civil War on Fort Sumter. During that war, the original mansion and outbuildings burned. The current house—built by Augustine Ruffin, Jr.—dates to 1937. Conferences, private luncheons, brunches, teas, cocktail parties, dinners, and weddings can be arranged. Guided tours of the house, grounds, and gardens are given daily, 9:00 A.M.–5:00 P.M. 6701 John Tyler Memorial Highway, Charles City VA 23030. (804) 829-5075, 1-800-473-5075. Admission is charged.

**Smith's Fort Plantation** is located on the south side of the James River in Surry County on Gray's Creek, on land that was a wedding gift from Chief Powhatan to his daughter, Pocahontas, and her husband, John Rolfe, in 1614. Its name derives from a nearby early-seventeenth-century fort built by Capt. John Smith during the first two years of the Jamestown colony. The eighteenth-century, one-and-one-half-story brick house has most of its original pine woodwork. On Rt. 31 between Surry and the Jamestown Ferry Landing. (804) 294-3872. Administered by the Association for the Preservation of Virginia Antiquities, it is open April through October, and on weekends in March and November, 10:00 A.M.–4:00 P.M. Tuesday–Saturday, and 12:00 noon–4:00 P.M. Sunday. Admission is charged.

**Bacon's Castle**, built by Arthur Allen in 1665, is a brick Jacobean-style, two-and-one-half-story structure in a cruciform design. The main body of the house is joined by a porch tower on the front and a stair tower to the rear.

In 1676, the colony of Virgina rebelled against Royal Governor William Berkeley. The rebellion was led by Nathaniel Bacon. Major Arthur Allen's home was occupied for four months by the rebels, which is how Bacon's Castle got its name. A large addition to the house was built by John Henry Hankins in 1844. The house and forty acres were purchased by the Association for the Preservation of Virginia Antiquities in 1973. Archaeological excavation has revealed gardens from the seventeenth, eighteenth, and nineteenth centuries. There are nineteenth-

and twentieth-century outbuildings. NR, NHL. Off Rt. 10 in Surry Country. Open April through October, and on weekends in March and November, 10:00 A.M.–4:00 P.M. Tuesday–Saturday, and 12:00 noon–4:00 P.M. Sunday. PO Box 364, Surry VA 23883. (804) 357-5976. Admission is charged.

# OATLANDS

Early-nineteenth-century plantation home and
gardens built by George Carter;
early-twentieth-century furnishings of Eustis family;
National Trust property; NR, NHL.

**Address:** Route 2, Box 352, Leesburg VA 22075
**Telephone:** (703) 777-3174
**Location:** In northeastern Virginia, 40 miles northwest of Washington
DC; on US 15, midway between US 7 (Leesburg) and US 50 (Gilbert's Corner) in Loudoun County.
**Open:** April–late December, 10:00 A.M.–4:00 P.M. Tuesday–Saturday, and
1:00–4:00 P.M. Sunday. Group tours by reservation in January, February, and March.
**Admission:** House tour: adults $6, children under age 12 free. Special rates
for seniors and groups.
**Shops:** Carriage House Gift Shop.
**Facilities:** Available for weddings and meetings; with prior notice, special
assistance for persons with handicaps.

## WHERE TO STAY

**Inns/Bed & Breakfasts:** The Norris House Inn, 108 Loudoun St. SW,
Leesburg VA 22075, 703-777-1806, FAX: (703) 771-8051. Colonial
Inn of Leesburg, 19 South King St., Leesburg VA 22075, (703) 777-5000. Laurel Brigade Inn, 20 West Market St., Leesburg VA 22075,
(703) 777-1010.
**Motels/Hotels:** Lansdowne Conference Resort, 44050 Woodridge Parkway, Leesburg VA 22075, (703) 729-8400. Marriott, 333 West Service Rd., Dulles Airport VA 22021, (703) 471-9500. Marriott Suites
Washington-Dulles, 13101 Worldgate Dr., Herndon VA 22070,
(703) 709-0400.
**Camping:** Hillwood Camping Park, 14222 Lee Highway, Gainesville VA
22065, (703) 754-4611. Yogi Bear's Jellystone Park, 14004 Shelter
Lane, Haymarket VA 22069, (703) 754-7944.

## OVERVIEW

Oatlands, a property of the National Trust for Historic Preservation, was built between 1803 and 1810 by George Carter, a member of one of Virginia's leading families, on a 3,400-acre plantation in Loudoun County that had been in the Carter family since 1728.

Located between Washington DC and Virginia's Shenandoah Valley, Oatlands represents two historic periods and styles of life. The plantation mansion reflects the early-nineteenth-century Virginia planter lifestyle of the Carters. After its putchase by William Eustis in 1903, Oatlands took on the appearance of an English country estate of the era between World Wars I and II. The house appears as it did when the Eustises were in residence. Neglected and overgrown historic gardens have been lovingly restored and are one of the most attractive features of Oatland.

## HISTORY

The early history of Oatlands is intimately related to the Carters, one of Virginia's most prestigious families. The Carter family history in Virginia began when two brothers, Thomas and John, arrived from England in 1635. John, who received a grant of 1,300 acres on the Rappahannock River, became an important colonial personage. He was elected to the House of Burgesses and served on the colonial governor's council.

John Carter's son, Robert, born in 1663, continued to augment the family's power, prestige, and land. Called "King Carter" because of his wealth and status, Robert Carter profited from his interests in banking, commerce, farming, land acquisition, copper mining, and the slave trade. A member of Virginia's colonial elite, he held several public offices and served as a trustee of the College of William and Mary. By the time of his death in 1732, Carter owned 330,000 acres of prime Virginia farm land.

Robert Carter's son, Robert Carter II, died as a young man. His infant son, Robert III, born in 1728, inherited the 11,357 acres on Goose Creek in Loudoun county that later became the site of Oatlands. Robert III was educated at the College of William and Mary and in England. In 1754, he married Frances Anne Tasker, the daughter of a wealthy Baltimore family. Robert, a member of the governor's council, earned the name of "Councillor" because of his service as advisor to Virginia's royal governors. Like his grandfather, Councillor Carter continued to build the family's land and economic fortunes. He also came to oppose slavery and began to free his slaves.

The fifteenth child of Robert and Frances Carter, George, who was to build Oatlands, was born in 1777. In 1786, George Carter was sent with his brother, John Tasker Carter, to a Baptist college in Providence, Rhode Island, which later became Brown University. George studied law at the University of Pennsylvania, where he completed his legal education in 1796.

Since Councillor Carter disagreed with primogeniture, by which the eldest son inherited his father's entire estate, Robert divided his vast land holdings equally among his children, having them draw lots which entitled them to specific properties. George drew lot number seven, which entitled him to the 3,400 acres of land in Loudoun and Fairfax counties on which he built Oatlands. Much of the mansion was constructed in 1803 from bricks molded and fired on the property. Over the next ten to fifteen years, George constantly modified the mansion.

By 1816, Carter had constructed a gristmill on nearby Goose Creek. In the early nineteenth century, gristmills and sawmills often formed the hub of small communities. Oatlands Mill became the center of a thriving community that included the miller's residence, a blacksmith shop, a school, a church, and a store.

At age fifty-nine, George Carter married Elizabeth Osborn Lewis; they had four children. George Carter died in 1846, and his son, George II, inherited Oatlands. Although the house was spared during the Civil War, the Carters, like other planter families, faced declining economic fortunes after the war. To add income, George II and his wife, Katherine Whiting Powell, operated the mansion as a summer rural vacation retreat for city people during the 1870s.

In 1897, the Carters sold Oatlands to Stilson Hutchins, a founder of the *Washington Post*. Hutchins, however, never lived at Oatlands, and the property deteriorated.

Mr. and Mrs. William Corcoran Eustis purchased Oatlands in 1903. William Eustis was the grandson of William Wilson Corcoran, a Washington banker and art patron. Mrs. Eustis was Edith Livingston Morton, the daughter of Levi Parsons Morton, who had served as ambassador to France, governor of New York, and vice-president under Benjamin Harrison from 1889 to 1893. Under the Eustises ownership, Oatlands was furnished as an English-style country house. Between World Wars I and II, it was a center of Washington social life, especially for long summer weekends and the fox hunting season.

Recognizing the house's historic significance, the Eustises restored the house rather than making major structural changes. The addition of hardwood floors, central heating, plumbing, gaslight, and electricity modernized the house. An half-octagonal porch off of the octagonal drawing room was also added. The vibrant post-World War I era of the 1920s and 1930s is reflected in the Eustises' decor.

Mr. Eustis, an enthusiastic sportsman, constructed the frame carriage house at Oatlands. Mrs. Eustis expanded the gardens and added a reflecting pool, bowling green, and gazebo.

After William Eustis's death in 1921, Mrs. Eustis continued to spend much of her time at Oatlands. She died in 1964. Their daughters, Margaret Eustis Finley and Anne Eustis Emmet, presented the 261-acre estate to the National Trust for Historic Preservation in 1966. Oatlands, designated a National Historic Landmark in 1972, is a co-stewardship property of the National Trust for Historic Preservation, administered by Oatlands, Inc.

## SITE DESCRIPTION

Although nearly two hundred years old, **Oatlands** has been lived in by only two families—the Carters from 1803 to 1897, and the Eustises from 1903 to 1964. The museum house reflects the Eustis years from the turn of the century until after World War II.

The original house built by George Carter between 1803 and 1810 was a simple rectangle of red brick surmounted by a cupola. Until the 1830s, though, Carter continued to make architectural changes to the mansion. He added the two-story portico with its delicate Corinthian columns and converted the drawing room to octagonal form. Half-octagonal stair wings, with grand stairways, were added on either side of the house. Today, Oatlands is a twenty-two room Federal building with pale yellow stucco walls, green flower-boxes and shutters, white columns and window trim, and the elaborate interior neoclassical plasterwork added by George Carter.

During the 1830s, the house's interior was decorated in the popular Greek Revival style, but furnishings now reflect the country-house style of the 1920s and 1930s.

The **entrance hall** contains full-length portraits of George and Louise Corcoran Eustis, William Eustis's parents, painted in Rome in 1859. An Italian brass lantern is suspended from a huge ceiling rose of molded plaster. Furnishings include a tooled-leather-top Louis XV table, Hepplewhite shield-back side chairs, and a pair of mahogany card tables.

The **dining room** has a black marble fireplace, an eighteenth-century English pedestal dining table, and a massive mid-nineteenth-century sideboard. An 1825 portrait of Commander Charles Morris, the grandfather of Mrs. George Eustis, and an eighteenth-century portrait of Governor William Eustis of Massachusetts hang on the walls.

The octagonal **drawing room** has a pillared fireplace of Pennsylvania marble, while the library fireplace is black-veined white marble. Over the mantel is a portrait of William Wilson Corcoran, Mr. Eustis's grandfather, who gave the Corcoran Gallery of Art to the city of Washington.

The **gardens** at Oatlands were designed and planted by George Carter in the early 1800s in a series of connecting terraces built on a hill near the house. Two stone staircases lead from the entrance gate into the four-and-one-half-acre, walled and terraced English-style garden of boxwood parterres and allées. Based on research and historical documents, the gardens were restored by horticulturist Alfredo Siani. Dramatic, sweeping vistas can be seen from the terraces, which drop about 200 feet through six levels. The lush gardens have a **wisteria arbor**, a **Victorian garden** with cleomes, lilies, irises, and petunias, and an **herb garden** with more than one hundred varieties of herbs. A **rose garden** contains more than one hundred kinds of roses. Three terraces of boxwood parterres are planted with hostas and lilies. In the 1920s, a classic **tea house** was added along with a **bowling green**.

Among the structures within the garden walls are the **Carter family tomb** and a former **smokehouse**. The brick building adjoining the cutting garden is the "Carter Barn," originally used as a **granary**.

The brick garden wall and all of the brick buildings were built by George Carter in the nineteenth century. The wood buildings, including the carriage house, were built by the Eustis family after 1900.

## Festivals/Crafts

Among special events at Oatlands are **Loudoun County Day** in April, **Sheep Dog Trials** in May, **Antiques Fair** and **Draft Horse and Mule Day** in September, **Needlework Exhibition** and **Middleburg Dog Show** in October, and **Christmas at Oatlands** from mid-November through December.

## Side Trips

**Waterford, Virginia**, a village founded by Quakers in 1733 is now a National Historic Landmark. Special events are the **May Art Mart and Garden Tour** and the **October Homes Tour and Crafts Exhibit**. Architectural **walking tours** are available, and craft shops are open throughout the year. Waterford is west of Leesburg VA, off of Route 9. Waterford Foundation, PO Box 142, Waterford VA 22190. 703-882-3018.

# GUNSTON HALL PLANTATION

Restored eighteenth-century home of George Mason, author of the Virginia Declaration of Rights; NR, NHL.

**Address:** Mason Neck, Lorton VA 22079
**Telephone:** (703) 550-9220
**Location:** In northeastern Virginia, on the Potomac River, about 17 miles south of Washington DC; I-95 North, exit 161, or I-95 South, exit 163, to US 1.
**Open:** 9:30 A.M.–5:00 P.M. daily; closed Thanksgiving, Christmas, and New Year's Days.
**Admission:** Adults $5, seniors $4, children ages 12 and under $1.50.
**Shops:** Museum shop.
**Facilities:** Formal gardens, picnic area, museum, guided tours, nature trail, educational programs, research library and archives available by appointment.

## WHERE TO STAY

**Inns/Bed & Breakfasts:** The Bailiwick Inn, 4023 Chain Bridge Rd., Fairfax VA 22030, (703) 691-2266, 1-800-366-7666. B&B Alexandria, 819 Prince St., Alexandria VA 22314, (703) 683-2159.
**Motels/Hotels:** Days Inn, 14619 Potomac Mills Rd., Woodbridge VA 22192, (703) 494-4433. Springfield Hilton, 6550 Loisdale Rd., Springfield VA 22150, (703) 971-8900. Morrison House, 116 South Alfred St., Alexandria VA 22314, (703) 683-8000.
**Camping:** Pohick Bay Regional Park, 6501 Gunston Rd., Lorton VA 22079, (703) 339-6104.

## OVERVIEW

**Gunston Hall** is a plantation remarkable both for the prominence of its architecture and for the quality of its restoration. George Mason, who built Gunston Hall in the late 1750s, was an influential Revolutionary patriot. He was the principal author of Virginia's Declaration of Rights, a document that probably influenced Thomas Jefferson's Declaration of Independence as well as the Bill of Rights, the first ten amendments to the U.S. Constitution.

Thorough, careful research has gone into the restoration of Gunston Hall. Many of the Georgian house's secrets were uncovered in the process and have been used to replace missing features and woodwork. A fine collection of eighteenth-century furniture can be seen throughout. The gardens, restored in the 1950s, add to the beauty of the tidewater Virginia plantation.

## HISTORY

Gunston Hall was built ca. 1755–1759 by George Mason IV, author of the Virginia Declaration of Rights. He was the great-grandson of George Mason I, who settled in Westmoreland County, Virginia, about 1651. Both George Mason I and George Mason II left a legacy of public service. Each was the Stafford County sheriff, served in the militia, and was a member of the Virginia legislature. The Masons owned property near the Potomac River in Virginia and Maryland which was passed on to George Mason III.

When George IV took over the management of the family property in 1746, over 5,000 acres were on Doeg's Neck, a peninsula in the Potomac River now known as "Mason Neck." During his lifetime, George Mason IV raised corn, wheat, and tobacco, as well as leasing a number of fisheries where shad and herring were salted and packed.

George Mason IV, probably born December 11, 1725, was one of three children of Ann Thomson and George Mason III. His father drowned in the Potomac River when young George was ten years old, and his mother operated the estate until he came of age. He married sixteen-year-old Ann Eilbeck in 1750, and they had twelve children, nine of whom survived. Mason was a trustee of the towns of Alexandria and Dumfies, and served in the Fairfax militia and on the vestry of Pohick Church. He was the justice of the peace in Fairfax County and a delegate to the House of Burgesses from 1759 to 1761.

Mason was a member of the Virginia Convention in Richmond in July 1775 and the Virginia Convention of 1776 in Williamsburg. He was the chief author of the Virginia Declaration of Rights which was adopted on June 12, 1776. The introduction to the Declaration of Independence, written by Thomas Jefferson, bears a striking resemblance to Mason's Declaration of Rights.

Mason was a delegate to the Philadelphia Constitutional Convention in 1787, but he refused to sign the constitution because it lacked a Bill of Rights. Among a number of other objections, Mason did not approve of the decision to continue importing slaves until 1807. Although the Constitution was ratified in 1788, the movement to add a Bill of Rights continued until it became part of the United States Constitution on December 15, 1791.

George and Ann probably began building their home at Doeg's Neck about 1755. Mason was involved in its design, as was William Buckland, an indentured carpenter-joiner from England. The plantation house was a Georgian-style, one-and-one-half-story brick structure facing the river.

After George Mason IV's death in 1792, Gunston Hall was owned by two more generations of George Masons, and it stayed in the Mason family until 1866. The house and 1,000 acres were then sold to William Merrill and William Dawson and later to four more owners. In 1932, the last owner, Louis Hertle, who did some restoration work on both the house and garden, donated the house to the state of Virginia. After his death in 1949, the house opened as a museum under the administration of a Board of Regents of the National Society of the Colonial Dames of America.

Fiske Kimball, an architectural historian from Philadelphia, directed the restoration of Gunston Hall during the 1950s. Architectural research initiated in 1982 by Charles Phillips and Paul Buchanan provided a wealth of additional information about the original character of the house. The house has been carefully restored and decorated based on this research. Furnishings predate 1792, the year of George Mason's death. Some Mason family pieces are in the house.

## SITE DESCRIPTION

Begin your tour with the orientation film in the **visitor center**. The **museum** contains exhibits on George Mason's role in American government and on life at Gunston Hall—including the house's construction, social and family life, horticulture, and husbandry. A diorama of the eighteenth-century working plantation is displayed.

**Gunston Hall** is a 1755 Georgian-style house on a 550-acre site surrounded by formal gardens and several outbuildings. The one-and-one-half-story brick house has five dormers, an attic, and a full English basement, and originally contained a wine cellar. The brick work is Flemish bond with corner quoins of local Aquia sandstone. On the riverfront entrance is a portico with "Gothic" arches. Mason added a Palladian-styled portico to the land-front facade around 1780.

On the first floor is a central hall with a parlor and dining room on the west side, and a bedchamber and a little parlor on the east. Seven bedrooms and a storage room are upstairs.

The **entrance hall**, extending from the front to the back door, is papered in a vivid Prussian blue. Much of the woodwork, including twelve pilasters and a frieze with medallions beneath the original cornice, has been replaced as a result of recent architectural research.

Elegance and formality characterize the **Palladian Parlor**, which was used for entertaining guests. Cards and board games were played there. In the **dining room**, also used for guests, is a small drop-leaf table which belonged to the Mason family.

The **little parlor** was the family room, used for meals and as an office for George Mason. Built-in cupboards with doors flank the restored fireplace. According to family tradition, the pole ladder, used to reach objects on higher shelves, was a gift of Thomas Jefferson. Family history also relates that the small writing table in front of the desk and bookcase was in constant use by George Mason.

The first-floor **chamber** served as a bedroom and office for Ann Mason. She stored rare spices and other expensive commodities in a cupboard next to the fireplace.

The children and their governess undoubtedly slept in **upstairs bedrooms**. The four bedrooms on the east and west walls were heated by fireplaces while the others were unheated. Simply furnished rooms contain beds, chairs, chests and desks.

Gunston Hall has a strong **educational program**. Two rooms of its basement are filled with touchable household, agricultural, and textile objects available to school groups.

Mason was an avid gardener who planted boxwood gardens on the river side of the mansion. Gunston Hall's **formal gardens** are composed of four parterres outlined by English box with a central allée of boxwood on the upper level and small beds in the lower parterre. Each north parterre has a topiary tree in the center, with hollies, fringe trees, and chaste trees in the corner beds. The south parterres have grass centers surrounded by rectangular flower beds. The gardens, restored by the Garden Club of Virginia in the early 1950s, retain the central allée's original boxwood, now twelve feet high.

At one time, the 5,000-acre plantation had as many as thirty outbuildings near the house. Some were homes of slaves who lived and worked at Gunston Hall, while others were service buildings. Although all of these structures have disappeared, the **chicken house, kitchen, dairy, laundry, smokehouse**, and **schoolhouse** have been reconstructed.

Exhibits in the domestic yard and kitchen relate to the lives of the African Americans at Gunston Hall, particularly the cooks. During special events, docents demonstrate cooking methods over an open hearth. Eighteenth-century education is the topic emphasized in the schoolhouse.

At the end of a long **cedar-lined walkway** is the **graveyard** in which Mason family members were buried until 1870. George and Ann Mason are buried there.

# ARLINGTON HOUSE, THE ROBERT E. LEE MEMORIAL

**1818 plantation home of Mary Custis Lee and her husband, Confederate General Robert E. Lee; restored to Lee family's occupancy, 1831–1861; NR, HABS.**

**Address:** Superintendent, George Washington Memorial Parkway, Turkey Run Park, McLean VA 22101

**Telephone:** (703) 557-0613

**Location:** In Arlington National Cemetery, Arlington VA; at the west end of Memorial Bridge.

**Open:** April–September, 9:30 A.M.–6:00 P.M. daily; October–March, 9:30 A.M.–4:30 P.M. daily.

**Admission:** Free.

**Shops:** Book store.

**Facilities:** Self-guided tours, Robert E. Lee Museum.

## WHERE TO STAY

**Motels/Hotels:** Hyatt Arlington, 1325 Wilson Blvd., Arlington VA 22209, (703) 525-1234, FAX: (703) 875-3393. Marriott Key Bridge, 1401 Lee Hwy., Arlington VA 22209, (703) 524-6400, FAX: (703) 524-8964.

**Camping:** Burke Lake Park, VA Hwy. 123, Fairfax VA 22030, (703) 323-6601. Lake Fairfax Park, VA Hwy. 606, Fairfax VA 22030, (703) 471-5415.

## OVERVIEW

Robert E. Lee, the great Confederate general, is memorialized at Arlington House, a plantation house in Arlington National Cemetery. Lee lived in Arlington House after marrying Mary Custis, the daughter of its builder, George Washington Parke Custis, who was the adopted grandson of George Washington. Lee was a military man who had a thirty-two-year career in the U.S. Army. When tensions in the North and South resulted in the secession of Southern states including Virginia, Lee, a native son of

Virginia, resigned from the army and became the commander of the military forces of Virginia and eventually the general in chief of the armies of the Confederate states. Ironically, the home of the Confederate general, Arlington House, was quickly occupied and used as a headquarters by the Union army. Later, it was sold at auction for non-payment of taxes and purchased by the government. A portion of the plantation was used as a military cemetery. In the 1930s, the mansion, under the auspices of the National Park Service, was restored to the years when Mary and Robert E. Lee and their children lived there, 1831–1861.

## HISTORY

Robert E. Lee, the general in chief of the armies of the Confederate states during the Civil War, was born January 19, 1807, at Stratford Hall (see p. 376). He was a member of the prominent Lee family of Virginia, and the son of the soldier and scholar "Light-Horse Harry" Lee. Young Lee was appointed to the U.S. Military Academy at West Point in 1825. He graduated second in his class in 1829 and began a long, successful career in the army.

Throughout his childhood, Robert E. Lee visited his cousin Mary Custis of Arlington House. Mary Anna Randolph Custis was the daughter of Mary Lee Fitzhugh and George Washington Parke Custis, the grandson of Martha Washington and the adopted grandson of George Washington. On June 30, 1831, Robert E. Lee and Mary Custis were married in the family parlor at Arlington House. When not living at a military site, they made their home at Arlington House with Mary's parents. Six of their seven children were born there.

Arlington House was built by George Washington Parke Custis between 1802 and 1818 on a 1,100-acre estate purchased by Custis's father, John Parke Custis, in 1778. The imposing Greek Revival house was designed by English architect George Hadfield. Situated on a hill above the Potomac River, the mansion was filled with Washington heirlooms.

Lee served in the army's engineer corps, an elite group of officers engaged in engineering work on harbor defenses in the east. Since many of these projects closed down during the winter, Robert and his family were able to spend that time at Arlington House.

In 1846, Lee served at the front during the Mexican War. He was decorated for bravery three times and promoted to a brevet colonel. He then returned to his engineering duties until 1852, when he was appointed superintendent of the U.S. Military Academy at West Point. In 1855, he was ordered to join the Second U.S. Cavalry in Texas, where for the first time he commanded troops in the field. His family remained at Arlington House with his father-in-law. When Mr. Custis died in 1857, Lee, who was the executor of Custis's estate, returned home. Finding the estate heavily in debt, he spent the next three years putting the plantation on a sound financial basis. In 1860, he returned to his regiment in Texas.

Meanwhile, the political tensions that had been mounting throughout the country were accelerated by the November 1860 election of Abraham Lincoln. When Texas seceded from the Union in February, 1861, Lee returned to Arlington. After Fort Sumter's fall to the South on April 14, 1861, President Lincoln pledged to preserve the Union. A few days later, Lee was offered a high Union command; at the same time, the Virginia legislature was meeting in secret session to consider secession. Although Lee opposed a divided country, he declined the U.S. Army command because he refused to take part in an invasion of the Southern states. When Virginia seceded from the Union, Colonel Lee resigned his United States Army commission, thus ending a thirty-two-year career.

Lee's services were immediately solicited by his home state, where he was given command of the defense forces of Virginia. When the Virginia militia was absorbed by the Confederate army, he became a Confederate officer and later served as military advisor to President Jefferson Davis. He was given command of the Army of Northern Virginia in May, 1862. Victorious at Fredericksburg and Chancellorsville, he was defeated at Gettysburg, Pennsylvania. Lee was named general in chief of the armies of the Confederate states February 6, 1865. Union forces under the command of General Ulysses S. Grant took Richmond in 1865, and Lee surrendered his Army of Northern Virginia on April 9, 1865 at Appomattox Court House (see p. 295).

At the urging of her husband, Mary Lee left Arlington House in May 1861, just days before the Union army occupied it. Ironically, the home of Confederate General Lee became a headquarters for the U.S. Army. In January 1864, the estate was seized for unpaid taxes and sold at auction to the government under questionable circumstances. Mrs. Lee had attempted to pay the taxes in Alexandria through her agent, but they were refused because she was not physically present. In June 1864, a 200-acre section of the Arlington Estate was set aside as a military cemetery.

The Lee family lost not only their property but also the furnishings that had remained in their house. After Mrs. Lee's death in 1873, her son, Custis Lee, entered suit against the United States to regain title to Arlington. In 1883, Congress paid $150,000 for title to Arlington House and its

1,100 acres. By an executive order of the president of the United States, the Custis furnishings were returned to the family.

Initially used as cemetery headquarters, a law established the house and a small amount of land as the Lee Mansion National Memorial in 1925. Now administered by the National Park Service, Arlington House is restored to the time when the Lee family was in residence, 1831–1861. Restoration is ongoing.

## SITE DESCRIPTION

The twenty-six room Greek Revival-style house was built by George Washington Parke Custis and designed by George Hadfield, an English architect who was, for a time, in charge of the construction of the U.S. Capitol. Located on a hill above the Potomac River, **Arlington House** has a marvelous view of Washington DC. Construction began in 1802 with the north wing, followed by the 1804 south wing. The center section and the large portico with its eight Doric columns were completed in 1818.

Tours of the house are self-guided with costumed park rangers available to answer questions. Early-nineteenth-century furnishings including many Lee family pieces decorate the house.

The **center hall** has a ceiling lantern that is a copy of the Mount Vernon lantern brought to Arlington by Mr. Custis. Several hunting scenes painted by Custis on plaster are at the west end of the hall. Robert E. Lee and Mary Custis were married in the **family parlor** on June 30, 1831. In the **family dining room** are Custis and Lee family china, silver, glassware, and serving tables. The Victorian furniture in the **white parlor** was selected by Robert E. Lee. The **morning room** served as an auxiliary painting studio for George Washington Parke Custis, and his painting of the Revolutionary War Battle of Monmouth, New Jersey, is exhibited there. The **conservatory** was originally an open porch which was enclosed to protect Mrs. Lee's plants in winter. The **office and studio** was used by both Custis and Lee to manage the estate.

On the second floor are **five bed chambers** and the **girls' dressing room**. One chamber and dressing closet belonged to Colonel and Mrs. Lee, while their sons, Custis, William, and Robert, Jr., shared another. Their oldest daughter, Mary, shared a room with her cousin, Markie Williams, and another room was shared by daughters Annie, Agnes, and Mildred. The girls' dressing room was also used as a playroom.

In the first floor's **north wing** are the **outer hall pantry**, a **bath** installed by Lee in the 1840s, a **school and sewing room**, where the Lee children were tutored by their grandmother and mother, **Mr. and Mrs. Custis's chamber**, and a **guest chamber**.

In the cellar are the **winter kitchen** and the **wine cellar**. After touring the mansion, visit the **servants' quarters**, the **Lee Museum**, and the restored **garden**.

## FESTIVALS/CRAFTS

Special events include celebrations of **Robert E. Lee's birthday** in January, **George Washington's birthday** in February, **St. Patrick's Day** in March, and the **wedding anniversary of Robert and Mary Lee** in June. There are also the **Arlington County Heritage Day** evening open house in October and the **Christmas activities** in December.

## SIDE TRIPS

**Arlington National Cemetery**, the location of Arlington House, is a military cemetery and an American shrine that inspires awe and sadness. Headstones on over 200,000 graves of military personnel from the Civil War to the present seem to go on forever. Two presidents, William Howard Taft and John F. Kennedy, are buried there. In 1994, Jacqueline Kennedy Onassis was buried in the Kennedy plot. At the Tomb of the Unknowns are soldiers from World War I, World War II, the Korean Conflict, and the Vietnam War. Open daily. Admission is free, but there is a fee for parking and for the tourmobile. Located at the west end of Memorial Bridge, off George Washington Memorial Parkway, in Arlington VA. (703) 979-0690.

# MONTPELIER

1760 plantation home of President James Madison, extensively remodeled into a 55-room house in the twentieth century by the du Pont family; NR, NHL.

**Address:** PO Box 67, Montpelier Station VA 22957
**Telephone:** (703) 672-2728
**Location:** Montpelier is 4 miles southwest of Orange on VA Hwy. 20; approximately 25 miles north of Charlottesville and 70 miles south of Washington DC.
**Open:** March 16–December 31, 10:00 A.M.–4:00 P.M. daily; January 2–March 15, weekends only. Closed Thanksgiving, Christmas, and New Year's Days, and the first Saturday in November.
**Admission:** Adults $6, children ages 6–12 $1.
**Shops:** Museum shop.
**Facilities:** Shuttle bus, picnic areas, gardens, tree walk.

## WHERE TO STAY

**Inns/Bed & Breakfasts:** Hidden Inn, 249 Caroline St., Orange VA 22960, (703) 672-3625. The Holladay House, 155 W. Main St., Orange VA 22960, (703) 672-4893. The Shadows, 14291 Constitution Hwy., Orange VA 22960, (703) 672-5057. Willow Grove Inn, 14079 Plantation Way, Orange VA 22960, (703) 672-5982, 800-WGN-1778.
**Motels/Hotels:** Days Inn, 332 Caroline St., Orange VA 22960, (703) 672-4855, FAX: (703) 672-4886.
**Camping:** Lake Anna State Park, VA Hwy. 208, Spotsylvania VA 22553, (703) 854-5503. Christopher Run Campground, Rt. 1, Box 326, Mineral VA 23117, (703) 894-4744, 1-800-582-1707.

## OVERVIEW

Montpelier was the plantation home of James Madison, "Father of the U.S. Constitution," chief proponent of the Bill of Rights, and fourth U.S. president. James Madison was the third generation of his family to live on this extensive plantation in Virginia's Piedmont.

Montpelier's history—a complex web of persons, ideas, and events—began in the colonial period, moved through the revolutionary

Photo courtesy of Montpelier

**Montpelier, Montpelier Station, Virginia**
Montpelier is the 1760 plantation house that was the home of James Madison,
fourth president of the United States. It was remodeled into a 55-room
residence in the twentieth century.

and early national eras, and reached the twentieth century. In 1900, Montpelier was purchased by William and Anna du Pont, and extensively remodeled into a fifty-five-room mansion. In 1984, the property was bequeathed to the National Trust for Historic Preservation. The main house, with its numerous additions and renovations, poses fascinating questions of preservation, restoration, and historic interpretation. Visitors can tour the architectural areas identified with the Madisons in the larger context of the fifty-five-room former du Pont mansion.

## HISTORY

Montpelier was the home of one of America's leading statesmen, James Madison, Jr., the fourth president of the United States. The Madison family owned the plantation for more than a century.

The family's origins in America begin with John Madison, a settler from England who was granted land in Gloucester County, Virginia, in 1653. His son, also named John, married Isabella Minor Todd and served as sheriff of King and Queen County, Virginia. John and Isabella were the parents of Ambrose Madison (1700–1732), the future president's grandfather.

In 1721, Ambrose married Frances Taylor (1700–1761), and in 1723, they moved to Virginia's Piedmont, where he had acquired several large land tracts, including the site of Montpelier on which Ambrose built a house. Though the origins of the name "Montpelier" are uncertain, the plantation may have been named for Montpellier, a French resort area. Archaeologists are still searching for the location of Montpelier's first house.

Ambrose's son, James (1723–1801), was the next owner of Montpelier. In 1749, James married Nelly Rose Conway (1732–1829), and around 1760, he built the earliest portion of Montpelier's main house. In addition to being an enterprising plantation owner, James constructed an extensive and profitable iron foundry on the property. Montpelier prospered under the care of James, Sr., a public official, justice of the peace, and vestryman.

James Madison, Jr. (1751–1836), the eldest of James and Nelly's twelve children, was born on March 16, 1751. Destined to be a chief executive of a yet-to-be-established republic, Madison—with Washington, Jefferson, and Monroe—would be one of the Virginia dynasty of presidents. Madison graduated from the College of New Jersey, later named Princeton, entered the law, and was drawn to Jefferson's political circle. He enjoyed a life-long, nearly half-century, friendship with Thomas Jefferson, his mentor. Jefferson and Madison began their association in Virginia politics on the eve of the American Revolution. In 1779, when Jefferson was Virginia's governor, Madison served on his official advisory council. Possessing wide ranging interests, the two corresponded frequently. During Jefferson's presidency, from 1801 to 1809, Madison served as secretary of state.

In 1794, Madison, a forty-three-year-old bachelor, met and fell in love with Dolley Dandridge Payne Todd (1768–1849), a twenty-six-year-old widow and mother. After their marriage on September 15, 1794, Dolley, her son, John Payne Todd, and her youngest sister, Anna, came to live at Montpelier. When her husband was secretary of state, Dolley Madison often acted as hostess at official functions for Jefferson, the widowed chief executive. When Madison was president, Dolley, a charming and vivacious first lady, hosted popular dinners and entertainments at the White House. She set the style for future first ladies.

Between 1797 and 1800, James Madison, Jr., doubled the size of the main house at Montpelier, extending it thirty feet to the north. He and his family occupied one part of the house while his parents lived in the other part. After his father's death in 1801, James Madison, Jr., inherited Montpelier.

Montpelier provided a quiet haven, a retreat, for the reserved and unassuming Madison during his fifty-three years of public life. Madison served in the Virginia legislature from 1776 to 1777, was a Virginia delegate to the Continental Congress from 1780 to 1783, a member of the U.S. House of Representatives from 1789 to 1797, Jefferson's secretary of state from 1801 to 1809, and U.S. president from 1809 to 1817.

One of the new republic's most intelligent political theorists, Madison had a special ability to translate abstract political philosophy into practice. His political acumen was tested by his service as a leading delegate from Virginia to the Constitutional Convention, which met in Philadelphia in 1787. Recognizing the weaknesses of the confederation of states that had been established after the Revolution, Madison proposed a federal system of checks and balances that equalized interests and regions. His famous essay "The Federalist" argued that the popular will, expressed through representative government, could overcome narrowly prescribed special interests.

Madison was a key mover in developing the "Virginia Plan," which proposed a federal system with power divided between legislative, judicial, and executive branches. In 1789, he introduced the amendments to the Constitution that are known as the Bill of Rights, stipulations designed to protect from government interference the individual right to freedom of speech, the freedom of the press, and freedom of assembly and of religion, and the right to a speedy and impartial jury trial, and the right to bear arms.

Madison served two presidential terms, from 1809 to 1817. His administration faced serious foreign policy tests from France, ambitiously aggressive under Napoleon, and from Great Britain, which sought revenge for losing its American colonies. Anglo-American relations had reached an impasse over the impressment of American seamen into the British navy, the violation of U.S. maritime rights, and the suspicion that the British were provoking Indian attacks on frontier settlements. Madison presented Congress with a declaration of war against Britain on June 1, 1812. He was pressured into hostilities by a strong congressional faction known as the "war hawks," who wanted to extend America's territory and annex Canada to the United States.

The War of 1812 against England entailed see-sawing battles in Canada, New York, on the Great Lakes, and on the Atlantic. The results were inconclusive for both combatants. Among the noteworthy events of the war was the British burning of the Capitol at Washington DC on August 24, 1814, Francis Scott Key's writing of the "Star-Spangled Banner" during the British bombardment of Fort McHenry at Baltimore, and Andrew Jackson's defeat of the British at New Orleans, on January 8, 1815, two weeks after the signing of a peace treaty at Ghent on December 24, 1814.

After completing his second presidential term in 1817, Madison retired to Montpelier. He added symmetrical one-story wings to the mansion. The house was furnished with an assortment of Quaker, rural Virginian, and stylish English and French furniture. Madison also acquired an extensive collection of paintings and other works of art. Madison died in 1836 and was buried on the estate.

Because of financial indebtedness, Dolley Madison was forced to sell the house and auction its furnishings. She moved to Washington DC, where she lived until her death in 1849. Her body was brought to rest next to that of her husband in the Madison family cemetery at Montpelier.

After leaving Madison family ownership, Montpelier experienced a series of owners until its purchase in 1900 by William and Anna Rogers du Pont. The owners between Madison and the du Ponts made numerous alterations to the house, many of which are undocumented. The front portico's pillars were extended to the ground, the roof was replaced, and the interior was remodeled.

William du Pont, a grandson of industrialist E. I. du Pont, purchased Montpelier for his children, William, Jr., and Marion. The du Ponts substantially enlarged the house to its present fifty-five rooms. The added rooms were wrapped onto and around the Madison rooms. Marion du Pont Scott, the wife of actor Randolph Scott, acquired the property in 1928. A dedicated sportsperson, she added a racetrack, a steeplechase course, and assorted horse stables to the property.

The National Trust for Historic Preservation received the property following Mrs. Scott's death in 1983. One of the last homes of the Founding Fathers to pass into public hands, Montpelier posed significant problems of historic preservation and interpretation for the Trust. The main house, which had been radically altered over the years, was located on acreage much larger than any administered by the Trust. After extensive research, the property was opened for public tours in 1987 as part of the bicentennial celebration of the U.S. Constitution.

## SITE DESCRIPTION

Visitors to **Montpelier** have a rare and exciting opportunity to learn about Madison, one of America's greatest statesmen, and to experience the process of historic preservation.

The **visitor center**, located near the **museum gift shop**, is across from the railroad station. Here, you can see the orientation film about

Madison's life and the program of archaeological research and preservation at Montpelier. A shuttle bus takes visitors to the fifty-five-room mansion for a **guided tour**. You can then take a **self-guided tour** of the 2,700-acre estate's gardens and more than forty species of trees.

Tours of Montpelier are different from most of those described in our book. Because of its architectural history, Montpelier differs from older and more conventional house museums such as George Washington's Mount Vernon or Jefferson's Monticello, which have been restored and furnished as they were during their famous owner's residence. Rather than a tour of a restored building, your visit to Montpelier will be a foray into the ongoing process of archaeological research and historic preservation.

The National Trust for Historic Preservation has owned Montpelier since 1983 and the **Montpelier mansion** has been open to the public only since 1987. In fact, in 1991 and 1992, the National Trust placed the mansion on its list of America's eleven most endangered historic places because the building had many additions through the years, was in poor structural condition, and was virtually empty of original furnishings.

After a great deal of research, debate, and consideration of reports by experts on preservation, restoration, archaeology, and history, the National Trust decided to preserve the grounds and the exterior of the mansion as it was when owned by the du Ponts. The du Pont additions to the Madison main house would not be removed. The Trust would focus on the Madison period by identifying and restoring those interior areas that were part of the original Madison main house. It was also decided not to embark on the highly difficult, if not impossible, task of trying to locate and purchase the furniture which Dolley Madison had sold.

Site interpretation focuses on both a historically significant property and a historically important political figure, James Madison, and his contribution to American culture and politics. Visitors find themselves involved in the highly intriguing archaeological puzzle of locating the Madisonian portions of the house within the structural framework of later additions.

James Madison, Sr., who built the central portion of the Montpelier main house around 1760, probably designed his own house and supervised its construction by a workforce of enslaved African Americans. From 1797 to 1800, there were additions to the main house, including the front portico and a dining room on the northeast end of the house.

Further additions occurred between 1809 and 1812. The interior was renovated, and one-story wings were added to each end of the house. The central, or main, section of the house remained plain brick, while the wings were painted white. During these renovations, the kitchens, located in the basements of the wings, were brought into the main house for the first time. After an involved correspondence between Madison and Jefferson concerning materials and techniques for applying stucco, the entire structure was stuccoed in 1813.

Owners after the Madisons made numerous alterations in the house, such as enlarging the portico. After the du Ponts bought the house, additions between 1901 and 1903 doubled its size. Marion du Pont Scott made still more additions and renovations between 1928 and 1937.

Since its acquisition by the National Trust for Historic Preservation, the Montpelier Research Center has been involved in an exploration called "The Search for James Madison" that involves archaeology, historical research, and materials analysis. On the basis of "structural archaeology"—a method involving the partial removal of areas of plaster, technical and chemical analysis, and documentary research—the main house has been explored to determine its configuration during President Madison's life. The findings of this research have produced some important reinterpretations about the house's construction and appearance.

The first phase of archaeological research was designed to determine the main house's interior when it was built in 1760. The second phase involved surveying all available primary source documents such as visitor accounts, letters, and bills pertaining to the main house. The third phase involved sub-surface examinations of the various techniques and materials used during construction episodes from 1760 to the present. Results include the discovery that a doorway believed to be part of a later renovation was actually part of the 1760 house. Research also suggests that James Madison, Sr., may have had an office in the house.

The **center hallway**, unfurnished today, was once the Madison's lavishly appointed drawing room. The **library** is where James Madison must have considered problems of state and defined his political philosophy. Although it once housed a vast collection of books and documents, most of them were either sold or donated to the University of Virginia. Researchers continue their efforts to re-create a catalogue of books that were once in Madison's library. The **Madison Dining Room**, the only room with Madison belongings, contains three Windsor chairs owned by the Madisons. The **dining room**, used for formal dining and entertaining, was one of Madison's four art galleries. The **kitchen** is located in the basement of the south wing.

Three rooms furnished by the du Ponts bring the visitor into the twentieth century. Two first-floor rooms added to the rear of the house—the **morning room** and the **drawing room**, with its Adamesque ceiling—reflect the du Pont period. The **red room**, furnished by Marion du

Pont Scott in the Art Deco style highlights her interest in horses, which is portrayed in prints and photographs.

The **Montpelier garden** was originally planted as a large, four-acre terraced garden containing vegetables, fruit trees, flowers, and ornamental shrubs in the landscape style of the early nineteenth century. After William du Pont purchased the property in 1900, his wife, Anna Rogers du Pont, reconfigured the neglected garden into a formal garden. Profiles of terraces were restored, and brick garden walls, statuary, and ornamental iron gates were added. Restoration of the present two-acre formal garden began in 1990 with support from the Garden Club of Virginia. Near the garden are buildings of the du Pont period such as the one-lane **bowling alley** and the **pony barn**.

The **garden temple**, 110 feet from the main house's north corner, is the only unaltered building remaining from the Madison period. The temple was built over remnants of an icehouse that had been built over the ironworks operated by James Madison, Sr. Archaeological investigation has determined the dimensions of the ironworks. It is believed that iron products constituted a large part of the senior Madison's income.

The **tree walk** includes over forty species of trees from all over the world, including many native to Virginia.

## Festivals/Crafts

There are special events on **President Madison's birthday**, March 16, and on **Dolley Madison's birthday**, May 20. Also held are the **Virginia Garden Week** tours in late April, **Orange Country Fair** in late July, **Constitution Day** on September 17, and **Montpelier Hunt Races** on the first weekend in November.

## Side Trips

**Wilderness Civil War Battlefield**, where the armies of Lee and Grant clashed May 5–6, 1864, marked Grant's first approach to Appomattox. The **battlefield tour** begins at the National Park Service Wilderness Exhibit shelter on Route 20, one mile west of the Route 3 intersection. Open daily. (703) 373-4461.

**James Madison Museum**, 129 Caroline St., Orange VA, is open March 1–November 30, 9:00 A.M.–4:00 P.M. weekdays, and 1:00–4:00 P.M. weekends. Closed Memorial Day, July 4, Labor Day, Thanksgiving and Christmas Days and New Year's Eve. (703) 672-1776. Admission is charged.

# MOUNT VERNON

## Home of George Washington, first president of the United States; NR, NHL.

**Address:** Mount Vernon Ladies' Association, Mount Vernon VA 22121
**Telephone:** (703) 780-2000, TDD: (703) 799-8121
**Location:** 16 miles south of Washington DC, and 8 miles south of Alexandria, at the southern terminus of the George Washington Memorial Parkway.
**Open:** April–August, 8:00 A.M.–5:00 P.M. daily; September–March, 9:00 A.M.–5:00 P.M. daily.
**Admission:** Adults $7; seniors, over age 62, $6; children, 6–11, $3.
**Restaurants:** Mount Vernon Inn, A Quick Bite to Eat.
**Shops:** Museum Shop, Mount Vernon Inn Gift Shop, Christmas Corner.
**Facilities:** Museum and Museum Annex, library, post office.

### WHERE TO STAY

**Inns/Bed & Breakfasts:** Morrison House, 116 South Alfred St., Alexandria VA 22314, (703) 838-8000, 1-800-367-0800, FAX: (703) 684-6283.
**Motels/Hotels:** Comfort Inn-Mt. Vernon, 7212 Richmond Hwy., Alexandria VA 22306, (703) 765-9000, FAX: (703) 765-2325. Hampton Inn, 4800 Leesburg Pike, Alexandria VA 22302, (703) 671-4800, FAX: (703) 671-2442. Best Western Old Colony Inn, 625 First St., Alexandria VA 22314, (703) 548-6300, FAX: (703) 548-8032. Radisson Plaza at Mark Center, 5000 Seminary Rd., Alexandria VA 22311, (703) 845-1010, FAX: (703) 820-6425.

### OVERVIEW

Mount Vernon, the home of George Washington, the first president of the United States, is an American national shrine. Even before President Washington died in 1799, people were curious about where and how this legendary historic figure lived. Thanks to a private preservation group, Mount Vernon has been beautifully preserved and restored. The property belonged to the Washington family from 1674 to 1858 when it was purchased by the Mount Vernon Ladies' Association, the first such organiza-

**Mount Vernon, Mount Vernon, Virginia**

The Mount Vernon mansion, home of the nation's first president, was built by
Augustine Washington in the late 1730s and expanded by both Lawrence and
George Washington. A cross between a Southern planation and a national
shrine, Mount Vernon is a heavily visited site, even on a rainy day.

tion in America. In addition to being the dwelling of a famous American
historic figure, Mount Vernon re-creates the life-style of a late-eighteenth-
century Southern plantation. The restoration includes Washington's mansion; ten plantation outbuildings; flower, kitchen, and botanical gardens;
George and Martha Washington's tomb; and a museum with Washington
family memorabilia.

## HISTORY

In 1674, the Mount Vernon homesite was granted to George Washington's great-grandfather, who was a pioneer settler in the area between
the Potomac and the Rappahannock Rivers referred to as the "Northern
Neck." It was part of a 5,000-acre site along the upper Potomac River
granted to John Washington and Nicholas Spencer by Lord Culpeper, proprietor of the Northern Neck under King Charles II.

In 1690, this tract of land was divided between Lawrence Washington,
John Washington's son, and the Spencer heirs. The Washington half of

the property, which became known as Hunting Creek Plantation, was next inherited by Lawrence's daughter, Mildred, who sold it to her brother, Augustine, in 1726. Augustine Washington was George Washington's father.

George Washington's birth in 1732 took place at Popes Creek Plantation in Westmoreland County, Virginia. When George was three years old, Augustine moved his family to Hunting Creek Plantation but left after four years to live at Ferry Farm, near Fredericksburg. In 1740, Augustine Washington deeded the Hunting Creek Plantation to his son, Lawrence, who renamed the estate "Mount Vernon," in honor of Admiral Edward Vernon under whom he had served in the Caribbean. Young George spent part of his youth at Mount Vernon with Lawrence. Two years after Lawrence died in 1752, George Washington leased Mount Vernon from his brother's widow. When she died in 1761, Washington inherited the 2,126-acre estate, which would increase under his ownership to 8,000 acres.

In 1759, twenty-seven-year-old George Washington married Martha Dandridge Custis, the widow of Daniel Parke Custis and the mother of a five-year-old son and a three-year-old daughter. The family settled at Mount Vernon. Although George Washington would live at Mount Vernon until his death in 1799, his residency was interrupted by his extended periods of service to his country during the turbulent revolutionary years.

In 1775, he was appointed commander in chief of the Continental forces. After resigning his commission in 1783, General Washington retired to Mount Vernon until 1787, when he presided over the Constitutional Convention in Philadelphia. From 1789 to 1797, he served as the first president of the United States.

After Martha Washington's death in 1802, the plantation was divided among a number of heirs. The mansion property was inherited by Washington's nephew Bushrod Washington who left it to his nephew, John Augustine Washington. His son, John Augustine Washington, Jr., who was a great-grandnephew of General Washington, was the last Washington-family owner of Mount Vernon. He sold the mansion, outbuildings, and 200 acres to the Mount Vernon Ladies' Association in 1858. Restoration began immediately, and the estate was opened to the public. 300 additional acres have been added to the Mount Vernon site.

The house at Mount Vernon was built by Augustine Washington between 1735 and 1739 and was expanded by both Lawrence and George Washington. The 500 acres surrounding the mansion, called "Mansion House Farm," was not farmed but landscaped in the style of an English gentlemen's country seat—arranged to provide open vistas to the Potomac

River and beyond to the Maryland shore. There were rolling meadows, groves of trees, a vineyard, a bowling green, lawns, a formal flower garden, botanical and kitchen gardens, and a greenhouse.

On Washington's 8,000 acres were five farms, each a complete unit with its own overseer, more than 200 slaves, livestock, equipment, and buildings. General Washington was a progressive farmer who experimented with new crops and agricultural techniques. Although he initially raised tobacco, wheat became his principal crop. He experimented with crop-rotation systems, tested sixty different crops and many fertilizers, and personally supervised farm activities when in residence. Farm managers reported to him on a weekly basis, even during the presidential years when reports were sent and responded to by post.

As it was on other Southern plantations, African-American slaves constituted the bulk of the work force in this self-contained community. Living and working in simple outbuildings at Mount Vernon, slaves were blacksmiths, carpenters, gardeners, shoemakers, painters, brick-makers, herdsmen, house servants, coachmen, spinners, weavers, seamstresses, cooks, dairy maids, millers, coopers, and farm workers.

George Washington was a Virginian, a Southern plantation owner, and a slave owner. However, during his lifetime and most intensely after the Revolution, General Washington's attitude toward slavery changed until he had become an advocate of emancipation. According to his will, his 124 slaves were freed one year after his death, and provisions were made for the care and support of the newly freed people.

## SITE DESCRIPTION

**Mount Vernon** has been restored to 1799, the year of George Washington's death. At this late-eighteenth-century Southern plantation site, the focus is on Washington's domestic and agricultural life rather than his military or political careers.

The **mansion** was built by Augustine Washington, George's father, in the 1730s. Originally, it was one and one-half stories high with a central hall and four small rooms on the first floor. In the late 1750s, the house was raised to two and one-half stories. George Washington further enlarged the house, beginning in 1774. Additions were made to both the south and north ends of the house; wing buildings and connecting colonnades were also constructed. A high-columned piazza extending the full length of the side of the house facing the Potomac River was erected in 1777.

Harmony and balance are characteristics of the mansion, which is built in the Colonial architectural style. Fourteen rooms are open for viewing, with costumed interpreters in each room. Many of the furnishings are original. Room settings are based on a 1799 fifty-page inventory prepared after President Washington's death. Paint colors throughout the house, which also date to 1799, were determined through scientific analysis.

The **large dining room** in the north addition is a two-story room which extends the width of the house. A well-balanced room, its palladian window faces the fireplace; a door faces a door, and a window faces a window. The room was used for social functions including dining, but there is no table. Instead, when dining tables were needed, trestles and boards were moved into the room and covered with linen tablecloths. Nine of the twenty-four chairs are original to the room; they were made by John Aitken of Philadelphia, as was one of the Hepplewhite mahogany sideboards. The dining room is painted in two shades of verdigris green, colors selected by Washington. Woodwork and ceiling decorations are elaborate. After George Washington's death and according to his wishes, he lay in state in this room for three days.

The **passage**, or central hall, which also runs the width of the house, is a paneled room which contains the stairway to the second floor. All of the wood in the passage has been grained to resemble mahogany as it appeared in 1797. A key to the Bastille, a gift to Washington from General Lafayette in 1790, hangs in here. President George Bush took the key to France in 1990 for the 200th anniversary of the French Revolution, then returned it to Mount Vernon.

Also on the first floor are the **little parlor**, the **west parlor**, the **small dining room**, and the **downstairs bedroom**.

There are five bedchambers on the second floor. Of greatest interest is **General and Mrs. Washington's bedchamber** in the south addition from which General Washington's first-floor **study** was accessed by a narrow stairway. These rooms were designed and added by George Washington to provide privacy for himself and Martha in a house filled with family members, including Martha's two children and two grandchildren, whom the couple raised, as well as guests and servants.

It is a moving experience to enter the private bedroom of the first president of the United States and see the bed made in Philadelphia about 1794 in which George Washington died December 14, 1799. Also in the bedchamber is Martha Washington's French desk, which she used for correspondence and household management.

From his **study**, George Washington directed the management of his estate. He wrote letters, posted accounts, and received overseers' reports at the tambour secretary desk made by John Aitken. Other original furnishings in the study are the presidential chair, a terrestrial globe, a gold-headed walking staff, a large ducking gun, a barometer, a portrait of Lawrence Washington, and seventy-five books. There are a library book-press and a dressing table; Washington also used the study as his dressing room.

The Washingtons had numerous visitors, who stayed in the mansion for varying lengths of time. Washington remarked in a letter—which is now in the museum—that unless someone should appear in the next few hours, it would be the first time in twenty years that he and Martha dined alone. In addition to the guest bedroom on the first floor, there are three bedrooms on the third floor.

Black slaves and white employees lived and worked at Mount Vernon. Ten outbuildings have been restored including the **white servants' hall, kitchen, storehouse and clerk's quarters, smokehouse, washhouse, coachhouse, stable, overseer's quarters and spinning room, garden house,** and **salthouse.**

A 1785 **greenhouse** with adjoining **slave quarters** that were destroyed by fire in 1835 has been reconstructed on its original site. The slave quarters are outfitted like an early military barracks with three tiers of beds built into the walls; tables and chairs are the only other furnishings. There is a nineteenth-century **icehouse.**

Many personal and household possessions of George and Martha Washington are in the **museum** while the **museum annex** contains restoration and archaeological exhibits.

The **grounds and gardens** at Mount Vernon, designed by George Washington, have been restored to their eighteenth-century appearance. The mansion opens onto an **oval courtyard**. Beyond it is a **bowling green**, a broad expanse of lawn bordered by shrubs and trees. Some of the trees planted by Washington remain. Symmetrically placed on each side of the bowling green are the **upper garden**, a flower garden with annuals and perennials known to have grown in Virginia gardens of the period, and the **lower garden**, a kitchen garden of fruits, vegetables, and herbs. A **grove of locust trees** has been replanted at the north end of the Mansion.

George and Martha Washington are buried at Mount Vernon in the brick **family tomb** that was built in 1831 according to the wishes expressed in George Washington's will. Nearby is a burial ground for the slaves who died at Mount Vernon.

# WOODLAWN PLANTATION AND POPE-LEIGHEY HOUSE

Woodlawn is a ca. 1800 Federal mansion,
home of Lawrence Lewis, nephew of George Washington,
and Nelly Custis Lewis, granddaughter of Martha
Washington. Pope-Leighey is a 1940s Usonian home
designed by Frank Lloyd Wright; NR, HABS.

**Address:** 9000 Richmond Hwy., Alexandria VA 22309
**Telephone:** (703) 780-4000, FAX: (703) 780-8509
**Location:** In northern Virginia, 14 miles south of Washington DC on US 1, 3 miles southwest of Mount Vernon.
**Open:** March–December, 9:30 A.M.–4:30 P.M. daily; closed Thanksgiving, Christmas, and New Year's Days.
**Admission:** Woodlawn: adults $6. Pope-Leighey: adults $5.
**Restaurant:** Pub.
**Shops:** Museum shop.
**Facilities:** 126-acre site with landscaping and gardens, 1800 mansion, and 1940s Usonian house.

## WHERE TO STAY

**Motels/Hotels:** Executive Club Suites, 619 Bashford Lane, Alexandria VA 22314, (703) 642-3422, 1-800-535-2582, FAX: (703) 548-0266. Holiday Inn Old Town, 480 King St., Alexandria VA 22314, (703) 549-6080, FAX: (703) 684-6508.
**Camping:** Burke Lake Park, VA Hwy. 123, Fairfax Station VA 22170, (703) 323-6601.

## OVERVIEW

This unusual site combines an early-nineteenth-century plantation mansion owned by a family related to our first president with a mid-twentieth-century middle-class dwelling designed by America's preeminent architect, Frank Lloyd Wright. This curious combination offers the opportunity to compare and contrast this country's architectural heritage.

Overlooking the Potomac River is the 1800–1805 plantation mansion built by Nelly Custis Lewis, granddaughter of Martha Washington, and Lawrence Lewis, nephew of George Washington. Two thousand acres of Mount Vernon property was part of the former president's wedding gift to the couple. The house and a 126-acre parcel of the original land are now the property of the National Trust for Historic Preservation.

A second National Trust acquisition has been relocated to Woodlawn Plantation. The Pope-Leighey House is a 1940 Frank Lloyd Wright Usonian house that was built in Falls Church, Virginia, and was threatened with demolition because of highway construction. The Usonian house is an example of Wright's Depression-era quest for well-designed, affordable housing.

## HISTORY

In 1799, George Washington gave 2,000 acres of his Mount Vernon property as part of a wedding present to Eleanor Parke Custis, called "Nelly," and Lawrence Lewis. Lewis was a nephew of George Washington, and Nelly was a granddaughter of Martha Washington. Nelly and her brother, George Washington Parke Custis, were raised by George and Martha after the death of their father, John Parke Custis, who was Martha's son. The Lewises were married February 22, 1799, on George Washington's sixty-seventh and last birthday; he died the following December.

The newlyweds named their farm property "Woodlawn" and raised grain crops and cattle and bred merino sheep and blooded horses. Between 1800 and 1805, they built a Federal neoclassical brick house designed by Dr. William Thornton, first designer of the U.S. Capitol building and a family friend. It was situated on a hill ninety-two feet above sea level in a grove of oak trees and commanded a view of the Potomac River. Many of the furnishings used at Woodlawn came from Mount Vernon.

Nelly Custis, who was tall and beautiful, grew up as the daughter of the founding father of the nation. As a young woman, she was a belle of Philadelphia society. She and Lawrence had eight children, four of whom died in infancy. The Lewises were prominent in the social world of Alexandria, Virginia, and Washington DC, largely because of their relationship to George Washington.

In 1824, the Marquis de Lafayette took a triumphal tour of the United States, renewing acquaintances with many old friends from the revolutionary days. He and his party—including his son, George Washington Lafayette—visited the Lewises at Woodlawn. As a boy, George Washington Lafayette had escaped from the revolution in France and lived with the Washingtons at Mount Vernon. It had been George Washington's hope that Nelly and young Lafayette would marry, thus joining the two prominent families.

Both Lawrence Lewis and his daughter, Angela Lewis Conrad, died in the fall of 1839—she, of childbirth complications. Nelly, along with her slaves, went to live with her son Lorenzo at Audley in Clarke County, Virginia. After the house had stood empty for seven years, Nelly Custis Lewis put Woodlawn—along with its 2,030 acres and its barns, sheds, stables, corn house, and stone mill—on the market in 1846.

Woodlawn was bought by a group of Quakers from New Jersey and Pennsylvania led by Jacob Troth, who opened the first free public school for blacks and whites in Virginia on the grounds. Much to Nelly Lewis's distress, the new owners cut trees in the thousand-acre woodlands and even in the park around the house. Subdivision of the property began.

The next owners of Woodlawn were John Mason and his wife, Rachel, who was a cousin of Abraham Lincoln. Services of the Woodlawn Baptist Church, to which the Masons belonged, were occasionally held there. Woodlawn was occupied by Federal forces as soon as the Civil War began. It is believed that Woodlawn was a stop on the Underground Railroad.

In 1901, Paul Kester, a playwright, paid $8,000 for Woodlawn, which had been vacant for the previous thirteen years. One wing had been severely damaged in a storm. Kester rebuilt and enlarged the damaged wing; then, because of the imbalance this created, he enlarged the other wing.

In 1905, Kester sold Woodlawn for $25,000 to Elizabeth Sharpe, a coal heiress who immediately began making the much-needed repairs to the house. When Sharpe died in 1924, Woodlawn was purchased by Senator Oscar Underwood of Alabama and his wife, Bertha. They also purchased some of Elizabeth Sharpe's furnishings. Senator Underwood died in 1929. In 1948, Bertha was ill and living in a nursing home in Philadelphia under the guardianship of her children. Woodlawn and its 130 acres were sold to a Belgian religious order, the Immaculate Heart of Mary Mission Society, for use as an international headquarters. The Woodlawn Public Foundation was formed by local people to block the purchase and turn Woodlawn into a house museum. Winning a legal battle, the foundation was allowed to purchase Woodlawn for $170,000 on May 21, 1949. The newly formed National Trust took a fifty-year lease on Woodlawn in 1951, and in 1957, the Trust became the owners of Woodlawn.

Also on the Woodlawn Plantation property is the Pope-Leighey House, a Usonian house built in 1940 by Frank Lloyd Wright. During the

Depression, Wright became interested in designing inexpensive housing for the middle class. He developed what he dubbed the "Usonian" house, a residence that was affordable, designed with style, and built of natural material like wood and modern building material like concrete.

The Pope-Leighey House was built for Charlotte and Loren Pope at a cost of $6,000 on a one-and-one-half-acre wooded lot in Falls Church, Virginia. Facing demolition in 1964 because of highway construction, the house was donated to the National Trust by its second owner, Marjorie Leighey. It was dismantled in sections and reassembled and relocated to the Trust's Woodlawn Plantation property. Although opened to the public in 1965, Marjorie Leighey retained the right to live in the house, which she did from 1969 until her death in 1983.

## SITE DESCRIPTION

**Woodlawn**, a ca. 1800 red brick two-and-one-half-story late Georgian mansion trimmed in Aquia sandstone, stands on a 126-acre site of forests and meadows on the banks of the Potomac River. The imposing structure, designed by Dr. William Thornton, is a central block with two one-and-one-half-story end pavilions and two one-story hyphens. The west facade was the carriage entrance; the east facade faced the Potomac River. The house, constructed of locally made brick and native pine with Carolina yellow pine floors, has two pairs of interior end chimneys, large rooms, and tall windows.

Rooms are decorated with furniture of the period as well as furniture and art owned by the Lewises. Nelly was an accomplished needlewoman and artist. Examples of her work, including footstool covers, fire screens, and drawings, are displayed.

A winding, circular **staircase** is an outstanding feature of the long hall that extends from the front door to the back door. A marble bust of George Washington sculpted in 1846 by Hiram Powers from a work by Jean Antoine Houdon stands on a pedestal in the hall.

In the **Music Room** on the main floor is a portrait of Lawrence and Nelly Custis Lewis in old age, painted by John Beale Bordley. A portrait of Nelly Custis Lewis above the fireplace in the family parlor is the work of John Trumbull.

In the **upstairs bedroom** believed to have been occupied by Lafayette is a fire-screen desk. In **Lorenzo Lewis's bedroom** are original stuffed birds; the boy was a naturalist interested in ornithology. In the **girls' room** is an early dollhouse as well as other toys.

Woodlawn's **grounds** were landscaped by the Garden Club of Virginia under the direction of Alden Hopkins in the 1950s. The early-nineteenth-century carriage circle was re-created in its original location. Features include **extensive lawns, 200-year old oak trees, boxwood plantings, and a Heritage Rose garden**.

On a slope north of Woodlawn's mansion is the **Pope-Leighey House**, a 1940 **Usonian house** designed by Frank Lloyd Wright. It is a one-story, modified L-shaped structure of cypress wood, brick, and glass with a brick chimney core and a carport. Following Wright's usual horizontal design, there is a flat roof with a broad overhang. The interior is divided into overlapping spaces with much **built-in furniture**. Features included by Wright are recessed lighting and heated concrete-slab floors. The two-bedroom house contains all of the original Wright-designed furnishings.

Not all of the house is original; neither the brickwork nor the cement floor survived the relocation. Because of damage done during the relocation and further deterioration related to problems with marine clay, the National Trust is planning to reposition the house west of its present site. Necessary repairs will be made, and the setting will be changed to conform to Wright's original intentions.

# MUSEUM OF AMERICAN FRONTIER CULTURE

**Re-created German, English, Ulster, and Shenandoah Valley farmsteads.**

**Address:** PO Box 810, Staunton VA 24402-0810
**Telephone:** (703) 332-7850
**Location:** In west central Virginia, in the Shenandoah Valley; 10 miles from the Blue Ridge Parkway and Skyline Dr., 1 mile from I-81 exit 222, on US 250 West.
**Open:** Mid-March–November, 9:00 A.M.–5:00 P.M. daily; December–mid-March, 10:00 A.M.–4:00 P.M. daily. Closed Thanksgiving, Christmas, and New Year's Days.
**Admission:** Adults $7, seniors $6.50, children ages 6–12 $3.
**Shops:** Museum Store.
**Facilities:** Visitor center, special events, workshops, Education and Research Center, octagonal barn activities center; partially handicapped accessible.

## WHERE TO STAY

**Inns/Bed & Breakfasts:** Belle Grae, 515 West Frederick St., Staunton VA 24401, (703) 886-5151. Ashton Country House, 1205 Middlebrook Rd., Staunton VA 24401, (703) 885-7819. Frederick House, 18 East Frederick St., Staunton VA 24401, (703) 885-4220, 1-800-334-5575. Kenwood, 235 East Beverly St., Staunton VA 24401, (703) 886-0524. Sampson Eagon Inn, 238 East Beverly St., Staunton VA 24401, (703) 886-8200.
**Motels/Hotels:** Holiday Inn, PO Box 2526 (I-81 at Woodrow Wilson Pkwy.), Staunton VA 24401, (703) 248-6020. Best Western Staunton Inn, 260 Rowe Rd. (I-81 exit 222 at US 250), Staunton VA 24401, (703) 885-1112. Econo Lodge, 1031 Richmond Ave., Staunton VA 24401, (703) 885-5158. Shoney's Inn, I-81 at US 250, Staunton VA 24401, (703) 885-3117, FAX: (703) 885-3117. Super 8, 1015 Richmond Ave., Staunton VA 24401, (703) 886-2888.

**Camping:** Shenandoah National Park, Rt. 4, Box 348, Luray VA 22835, (703) 999-3483. Shenandoah Acres Resort, PO Box 300, Stuarts Draft VA 24477, (703) 337-1911. Walnut Hills Campground, 391 Walnut Hills Rd., Staunton VA 24401, (703) 337-3920. Shenandoah Valley KOA, Box 98, Verona VA 24482, (703) 248-2746, 1-800-562-9949. Natural Chimneys Regional Park, Rt. 1, Box 286, Mt. Solon VA 22843, (703) 350-2510.

## OVERVIEW

Discover a little bit of Europe's countryside in Virginia's Shenandoah Valley. Without having to show your passport, you can visit an eighteenth-century German farm, a seventeenth-century English farm, and an eighteenth-century Ulster farm. Travelers are whisked not only back in time but across the ocean, too, at this unique outdoor museum.

The Museum of American Frontier Culture is a living-history museum designed around an unusual concept. To emphasize the heritage of seventeenth- and eighteenth-century European immigrants to Virginia, the museum has re-created farmsteads using actual farmhouses and agricultural buildings moved from their homelands. The life-style and culture built by Virginia's early settlers are also a focus of the museum. German, English, Ulster Scots, and American Valley of Virginia farmsteads complete with restored historic buildings, furnishings, fences, animals, and plants are exhibited.

This is a young museum, having been open only since 1988. Some farmstead buildings are still under restoration and are not yet ready for touring. Still, they provide visitors with the opportunity to observe the restoration process.

## HISTORY

The Museum of American Frontier Culture is a living-history museum highlighting the roots of Virginia's eighteenth-century European immigrants by re-creating farmsteads from their native countries. Historic European houses and agricultural buildings have been transported to the museum and re-assembled to create historic farms. The idea is to illustrate the cultures and life-styles of the early settlers in their homelands of Germany, Ireland, and England. In addition, an American farm focuses on the settlers' adaptation to the Appalachian region.

The concept behind the Museum of American Frontier Culture is unique among outdoor museums. Most museums that bring together a collection of historic buildings on a site use the European, particularly Scan-

Photo by Patricia A. Gutek

## Museum of American Frontier Culture, Staunton, Virginia
This whitewashed sandstone two-room cottage with a thatched roof was moved
to Virginia from its original site on a farm in Ulster, Northern Ireland, where it
was built between 1800 and 1825.

dinavian, model of open-air museums. Historic buildings are moved and restored to preserve vernacular architecture that has become obsolete and in danger of decay. Old World Wisconsin also re-creates ethnic farmsteads, but it has gathered local farm buildings constructed by European immigrants who used architectural models from their homelands when building their Wisconsin farmhouses and barns. The fact that this Virginia museum has brought together structures from Europe to illustrate the heritage of their early settlers is an innovation.

The proposal for this new museum emerged during America's bicentennial. In 1978, the Commonwealth of Virginia set aside seventy-eight acres of land in Staunton and authorized preliminary planning and further study. A 1981 feasibility study prepared by Virginia Polytechnic Institute and State University recommended the project. Funds were raised by the American Frontier Culture Foundation, and construction began in 1985. The Frontier Culture Museum of Virginia opened to the public in September, 1988.

## SITE DESCRIPTION

An orientation film is shown in the **visitor center**.

The **Museum of American Frontier Culture** not only displays historic European structures but also replicates the original layout of the farm buildings and the landscape in which they originally stood. Trees, flowers, shrubs, plants, crops, farm animals, and fences have been selected on the basis of research on seventeenth-, eighteenth-, and nineteenth-century farms in the same areas. Interpreters dressed in period costumes engage in seasonal agricultural activities.

The **Ulster Farm** was located near the village of Drumquin, County Tyrone, Northern Ireland. Called the "Goan Farm," it was home to the Goan family from at least 1860 until the 1970s. Presbyterian Scots were among the people who colonized Ulster after England gained control of Ireland in 1603. These Ulster Scots engaged in constant struggles with the English monarch over issues of religious tolerance and civil liberty. Economic conditions in Ulster were also difficult. Because of these problems, the Ulster Scots began emigrating to America around 1710.

The **Ulster Farmhouse**, built between 1800 and 1825, is a one-story building with two-foot-thick whitewashed sandstone walls, a thatched roof of long-stem rye straw, and flagstone and clay floors. Its two rooms are a kitchen and a bedroom, with the parents' bed tucked into the outshot near the fireplace. An attached barn was a later addition.

The long whitewashed sandstone **outbuilding**, built between 1830 and 1860, has a thatched roof. It is divided into a four-cow barn, turf store, cart shed, and stable. There is also a small 1850 stone **pig craw/hen house** with a thatched roof. Fields on the Ulster Farm are divided by thorn hedges and ditches, or stone fences. The Ulster farm is complete and can be toured.

Presently under restoration on the Ulster site is an eighteenth-century blacksmith forge complete with original tools.

The **German Farm** represents a typical eighteenth-century farm from Germany's Rhineland-Palatinate region. This locality experienced heavy eighteenth-century emigration to America due to the devastating economic impact of the Thirty Years' War in the seventeenth century, and a series of regional wars in the early eighteenth century. Intolerance of all who did not adhere to the Catholic Church also made life in the Palatinate unbearable for religious dissenters. The prospect of religious freedom and improved economic conditions stimulated mass migrations to America beginning in 1709.

On the German Farm are a house, a barn with a wagon shed addition, and a tobacco barn originally from the village of Hordt, located near the Rhine River in the Rhineland-Palatinate region. Traditionally, farmers built their farmhouses and barns in small villages and went out into the countryside to farm their fields.

The house and barn are examples of traditional *fachwerk*, or half-timbered construction. The heavy timber frame was filled with wattle-and-daub panels composed of woven pieces of wood covered with a mixture of clay, sand, lime, and straw. A thin coat of plaster or stucco was applied over the panels, but the frame was left exposed.

The original portion of the **house** dates to the late seventeenth century and contained a four-room plan consisting of a *stube,* **or living room**; a *kammer,* **or bedroom**; a *kuche,* **or kitchen**; and a *flur,* **or hall**. A second floor provided sleeping space for children and servants, and a third level was used for agricultural storage. Fritz and Berta Schweikert were the last residents of the house.

The **barn** is also of fachwerk construction, with a clay-tile gable roof. A **wagon shed** was added to one end of the barn in the early nineteenth century. A **tobacco barn**, which connects the house and barn, was added around 1900. Only the **house, gardens**, and **activity shed** are open while reconstruction of the barns is in progress.

At the **English Site**, which is restored to the 1680–1695 era, are two seventeenth-century **barns** that are awaiting restoration and a late-eighteenth-century **cattle shed** from the Garlands Farm in Petworth in West Sussex, England. The buildings are of English timber-framed construction, with weatherboards covering the framing on the barns. The two main barns had thatched roofs, while the cattle shed had a clay tile roof. The Garlands farmhouse cannot be removed from England because it is protected by English preservation laws. The **cattle shed** is open for touring.

Adjacent to the Garlands Farm is a **seventeenth-century house** from Worcestershire, England. This house, whose oldest sections date to the 1630s, was located in Norchard, near the village of Hartlebury, in what is now the county of Hereford and Worcester. The museum was permitted to transport this house from England because it was dismantled in 1972, prior to the 1976 English preservation laws regarding ancient houses and buildings.

The 350-year-old building is a typical West Midlands timber-frame farmhouse. It is L-shaped and, characteristic of English Jacobean architecture, has a large central sandstone and brick chimney with three flues that terminate in massive brick cannons. Walls are a combination of wattle and daub. The house has seven windows, made up of small rectangular panes of glass that are set inside casement-style wrought-iron frames. On the ground floor of the two-story house are a hall, a kitchen, and a parlor, while upstairs are three chamber rooms used for sleeping and storage.

During dismantling of the house, a gold coin of the reign of Charles I was found in the fireplace, and many Georgian coins were discovered under the floor. The first recorded owner was John Smyth, who died in 1671.

The **American Farm**, which is open for touring, represents the intermingling of the European heritage with the American frontier experience. Whatever their old-country traditions had been, immigrants to America now had neighbors from a variety of countries. People were forced to adapt rather quickly to their new circumstances, which included differences in weather conditions, soil, crops, animals, and building materials.

The American Farm came from Botetourt County, near the town of Eagle Rock in the Valley of Virginia. John Barger, who purchased the land in 1832, was the first permanent settler on the original 187-acre site. He was descended from an eighteenth-century German immigrant family. The farm contains a mid-nineteenth-century **house, barn, and tobacco barn**, along with a **springhouse, smokehouse, bee house, washhouse**, and **produce building**—which date from the late nineteenth and early twentieth centuries. The house and two barns display the European tradition of log construction, while the outbuildings reflect a variety of construction techniques.

The original part of the 1830s two-story rectangular log house contained one room on each floor. Each floor was later partitioned into two rooms. A log **kitchen** with a large cooking fireplace, a **root cellar**, and an unfinished **attic** were added to the house in the late 1840s. The house was then covered with weatherboards and front and back porches were added. Interior features include whitewashed log walls, exposed and beaded ceiling joists, molded chair railings, and enclosed corner stairwells.

The square-log **tobacco barn** was used for curing tobacco. Fires in the stone hearths once sent smoke into the airtight barn. The double-pen log **barn** has a central threshing floor, with horse stalls and a sheep pen on one side, and a cattle pen and granary on the other. Hay storage was on the upper level.

An **Education and Research Center**, housed in a converted 1950s dairy barn, has a **public library and seminar/lecture hall** on the upper level, and **educational facilities and a children's discovery area** on the lower level. The **Octagonal Barn Activities Center**, reconstructed from a 1915 barn, is used for traveling exhibitions, cultural presentations, and public functions.

## FESTIVALS/CRAFTS

The **Museum of American Frontier Culture** has an extensive list of special events, workshops, and educational programs. Special events include **African-American History Month** in February, the **Heritage Lecture Series** in March, **Easter Traditions** in April, **Wool Days** in May, **Summer on the Farms** children's program in June, **Celebrate Your Independence** in July, **Traditional Frontier Festival** in September, **Halloween** and **Cornhusking** in October, **Guy Fawkes Day** and **Threshing** in November, and **Holiday Traditions** and **Holiday Lantern Tours** in December.

# STRATFORD HALL PLANTATION

1738 boyhood home of Richard Henry and
Francis Lightfoot Lee, the only brothers to sign the
Declaration of Independence; birthplace of General
Robert E. Lee; NR, NHL, HABS.

**Address:** Stratford VA 22558
**Telephone:** (804) 493-8038, (804) 493-8371
**Location:** On the Potomac River, 42 miles east of Fredericksburg, off VA
Hwy. 3
**Open:** 9:00 A.M.–4:30 P.M. daily; closed Christmas Day.
**Admission:** Adults $5, seniors $4, children ages 6–18 $2.50.
**Restaurants:** Dining room in reception center.
**Shops:** Gift shop.
**Facilities:** Reception center with orientation program, 1,675-acre working
plantation, guided tours, operating gristmill, Jesse Ball du Pont Me-
morial Library, nature trail, special events, teacher seminars, handi-
capped accessible, meeting facilities.

## WHERE TO STAY

**Inns/Bed & Breakfasts:** Montross Inn, PO Box 908, Courthouse Square,
Montross VA 22520, (804) 493-9097, 1-800-321-0979.
**Motels/Hotels:** Days Inn, PO Box 1356, Tappahannock VA 22560, (804)
443-9200. Super 8, PO Box 1748, Tappahannock VA 22560, (804)
443-3888, FAX: (804) 443-3888.
**Camping:** Westmoreland State Park, VA Hwy. 347, Montross VA 22520,
(804) 493-8821. Chesapeake Bay/Smith Island KOA, Rt. 1, Box
1910, Reedville VA 22539, (804) 453-3430, (804) 453-3854.

### OVERVIEW

Stratford Hall is the beautifully restored eighteenth-century ancestral home of the Lees, one of the most prominent political and military
families in the history of America. Members of the family include Revo-

lutionary heroes, brothers who signed the Declaration of Independence, and brothers who became diplomats from the new republic to Europe. It is also the birthplace of Confederate General Robert E. Lee.

In addition to the restored mansion, there are two gardens, several eighteenth-century dependencies, and an operating gristmill.

## HISTORY

Stratford Hall was built around 1738 by Thomas Lee, who had purchased the property along the Potomac River in 1716. Lee was a grandson of Richard Lee, who came to Jamestown from England in the 1630s. Thomas Lee was Justice of Westmoreland, a member of the House of Burgesses, Naval Officer of the Potomac, and, like his father and grandfather, a member of His Majesty's Council and later its president. He married Hannah Harrison Ludwell in 1722, and they had eight children, two of whom signed the Declaration of Independence. The remarkable Lee family can boast of numerous American patriots, diplomats, and soldiers. In addition to Thomas Lee's family of eight children, their cousin "Light-Horse Harry" Lee lived at Stratford for twenty years, and his son, the outstanding Confederate General Robert Edward Lee, was born there.

The house, constructed in 1738 of brick fired on the property and lumber from its woods, is located on a bluff over the Potomac River. The architect of the imposing two-story brick Georgian structure is unknown.

After Thomas Lee's death in 1750, Stratford Hall went to his oldest son, twenty-four-year-old Philip Ludwell, who was reading law at the Inner Temple in London. Philip, too, became a member of the House of Burgesses and the Council of Virginia. He successfully managed the plantation, built a gristmill, began a shipbuilding business, and raised race horses. Philip, who was not sympathetic to revolutionary causes, died on the eve of the Revolution in 1775.

Philip's five younger brothers—Thomas Ludwell, Richard Henry, Francis Lightfoot, William, and Arthur—were singled out for praise by John Adams for their important role in leading the colonies to independence from Great Britain. Richard was a delegate to the First Continental Congress in 1774, and Francis was a delegate to the Second Continental Congress in 1775. There, in Philadelphia, on June 7, 1776, Richard was accorded the honor of introducing the resolution severing the political connection between the American colonies and Great Britain. Both Richard Henry and Francis Lightfoot signed the Declaration of Independence.

After Philip's death, Stratford Hall passed to his older daughter, Matilda, who, in 1782, married Henry "Light-Horse Harry" Lee, her cousin. Henry was a Princeton graduate and a captain in the Virginia Light Dragoons in the Continental Army. He attracted the attention of General Washington by leading his men in lightning raids on enemy supply trains, thus earning the moniker "Light-Horse Harry." After the British surrender, he resigned his commission and, having ended a brilliant military career, began a political career which included serving in the Virginia House of Delegates and the Continental Congress. He and Matilda had three children.

Matilda died in 1790, and Henry, then governor of Virginia, married Ann Hill Carter of Shirley Plantation (see p. 328) in 1792. The couple had six children, the fifth of whom, Robert Edward Lee, was born in the Mother's Room at Stratford on January 19, 1807. He became the distinguished general in chief of the Confederate armies during the Civil War.

Although an outstanding soldier and legislator, Henry did not enjoy farming. He lost money in land speculation, and his financial situation declined so badly that he was put in debtor's prison. While there, he wrote his *Memoirs of the War in the Southern Department of the United States.* On his release in 1810, the family moved to Alexandria and Henry Lee IV, son of Matilda and Henry, took over Stratford.

Like his father, Henry IV was a legislator and soldier. He married Anne McCarty, and they repaired and refurbished the neglected mansion. Tragedy befell the couple when their only child died in an accident at Stratford Hall. In 1822, to discharge a debt, Henry was forced to sell Stratford Hall, thus ending over eighty years of ownership of Stratford by the Lee family.

Henry's sister-in-law, Elizabeth McCarty Stroke, and her husband, Henry Storke, acquired the house in 1826. Elizabeth lived there until her death in 1879. In 1929, the Robert E. Lee Memorial Association, founded by May Field Lanier, purchased the mansion. After being repaired, restored, and furnished, Stratford Hall was opened to the public in 1935. Work, aided by archeologists and architectural historians, continues on the historic Lee estate.

## SITE DESCRIPTION

**Stratford Hall Plantation** is a working farm on 1,675 of its original 30,000 acres. Its elegant brick Georgian mansion is built on a H-shaped plan with two symmetrical wings jutting out on either side of a recessed ninety-foot-wide central block. The 200-foot-wide house is one story elevated over a raised basement. The central doorway is approached by stairs that narrow as they ascend. A notable feature are the chimneys, which consist of two clusters of four interlocked but independent flues bound together by arches enclosing balustraded platforms.

The house has been restored to the years of residence by the Lee family, approximately 1738–1822. Decorated to reflect a variety of time periods, the **dining room** and **great hall** indicate Thomas Lee's era, while the **parlor** shows Light-Horse Harry Lee's era. Over two hundred high-quality pieces of eighteenth-century American and English furniture donated to Stratford by Caroline Clendenin Ryan Foulke are used throughout the mansion and outbuildings along with a few Lee belongings.

On the mansion's first floor is the spectacular **great hall**, which is twenty-eight feet square, with seventeen-foot ceilings. This room is considered one of the finest American Colonial rooms extant. It has double doors on both sides of the room, four tall windows with window seats, paneled walls, and four book-closets. Furnishings include an eight-foot American Chippendale sofa, English eagle console tables, a spinet, and a harp.

On the west side of the great hall are the **library**, which Thomas Lee used as an office, the **library closet**, the **parlor** which contains a secretary-bookcase that was owned by the Lees, and the **parlor closet**.

On the east side are the **nursery**, the **dining room**, and the **dining room closet**, as well as the famous **"Mother's Room,"** which was used for Lee family births. Six of Thomas Lee's children—including the sons who signed the Declaration of Independence, as well as General Lee—were born in this large airy room overlooking the garden. General Lee's cradle stands by a window. A Sully portrait of Julia Calvert Stuart hangs over the mantel.

In the **dining room** are Queen Anne chairs with leather seats, a seventeenth-century single-hand clock, marble-topped serving tables, and a portrait of King George III. A portrait of Queen Caroline hangs in the adjoining **dining room closet**.

On the ground floor are the bedrooms including the **red room, green room, boys' room**, and **blue room**. In the **counting room**, Thomas Lee collected rent from tenants and taxes from sea captains on goods shipped. **Wet and dry stores** were used for the storage of wine, vinegar, molasses, lumber, and iron. There were also a **housekeeper's room** and a **winter kitchen**.

In addition to the plantation house, remaining original brick outbuildings include the **stables** and the **Southwest Dependency**, which houses a small museum, kitchen, smokehouse, and schoolhouse.

Two gardens have been restored by the Garden Club of Virginia. The **East Garden**, restored in the 1930s sports English boxwood, crape myrtle, and dogwood, together with an orchard and a grape arbor. The **West Garden** was laid out in 1942 by Umberto Innocenti and combines flowers, fruits, and vegetables.

The stone and frame **gristmill** has been reconstructed on the foundation of the original mill. Flour, cornmeal, and a pancake mixture are ground there and sold in the Stratford Store.

## FESTIVALS/CRAFTS

Annual special events include **Robert E. Lee's birthday celebration** in January, **African-American Heritage Day** in late February, **Kite Day** in late March, the **Easter Egg Hunt** in April, the **Civil War Encampment and Re-enactment** in early June, the **4th of July celebration**, and **Christmas Candlelight** tours. **Children's Days** and **Summer Seminar for Teachers** are held in the summer. Every third year, **Coaching Day** is held in April.

# CARTER'S GROVE

Mid-eighteenth-century Georgian mansion with
twentieth-century additions; archaeological site of
seventeenth-century English colonial town; re-created
slave quarters; NR, HABS.

**Address:** The Colonial Williamsburg Foundation, PO Box 1776, Williamsburg VA 23187-1776

**Telephone:** (804) 229-1000

**Location:** On US 60 East, 8 miles east of Colonial Williamsburg.

**Open:** Mid-March through October, 9:00 A.M.–5:00 P.M. Tuesday–Sunday; November and December, 9:00 A.M.–4:00 P.M. Tuesday–Sunday.

**Admission:** Adults $13, children ages 6–12 $8. Colonial Williamsburg's Patriot's Pass, which includes Carter's Grove: adults $29, children ages 6–12 $17.

**Restaurants:** Bake Shop at the Stable.

**Shops:** Gift Shop in the reception center.

**Facilities:** Reception center with audiovisual orientation program, picnic area, handicapped accessible, Winthrop Rockefeller Archaeology Museum.

## WHERE TO STAY

See entry for Colonial Williamsburg, Virginia.

## OVERVIEW

Carter's Grove, owned by Colonial Williamsburg though located eight miles away, is an eighty-acre plantation tract with an outstanding eighteenth-century Georgian mansion. The main house was built in 1750 by Carter Burwell, grandson of Virginia entrepreneur Robert "King" Carter. In the 1930s, additions connecting the main house to dependencies on either side were built. The house is restored to the Colonial Revival style of the 1930s.

Also on the property is an excavated seventeenth-century English town. In 1619, English people settled a large plantation called "Martin's Hundred" and built a town called "Wolstenholme Towne." This settlement disappeared after many of its residents were killed or kidnapped by hostile American Indians in 1622. Archaeologists have recently discovered and excavated the site of this early English colonial village. Wolstenholme Towne has been partially reconstructed, and the Winthrop Rockefeller Archaeology Museum now exhibits the artifacts that have been found there.

Another feature of Carter's Grove is the slave quarter of the 1700s, which focuses on the lives of the enslaved African Americans who constituted the workforce at Carter's Grove. Half the population of eighteenth-century Williamsburg was black.

## HISTORY

In 1619, English settlers arrived at a plantation along Virginia's James River, where Carter's Grove Plantation is today. For shelter and security, they erected Wolstenholme Towne, which became the administrative seat of 21,500-acre Martin's Hundred, a subsidiary joint-stock plantation of the Virginia Company of London. When American Indians massacred English settlers in 1622, the town disappeared. Archaeologists rediscovered the site in 1976. The 7,000-square-foot Winthrop Rockefeller Archaeology Museum portrays the history and archaeology of the settlement.

Carter's Grove was part of the huge holdings of Robert "King" Carter. His royal designation derived from his massive property holdings in Virginia totaling 300,000 acres. Carter—a merchant, planter, fur-trader, and agent for Lord Fairfax—is said to have also owned a thousand slaves and ten thousand pounds sterling when he died in 1732. He donated the funds to build Christ's Church in Irvington, Virginia, where he and other members of the Carter family are buried.

Robert Carter, who had fifteen children by his two wives, purchased Carter's Grove, a 1,400-acre tract, early in the eighteenth century for his eldest daughter, Elizabeth, and her son Carter Burwell. Robert stipulated in his will that the plantation always be named "Carter's Grove."

Carter Burwell built the Georgian mansion in 1754. David Minitree was the contractor-builder, while Richard Taliaferro may have had a hand in its overall design. Though Burwell died months after its completion, the plantation remained in his family for five generations, until 1838.

After a series of owners, it was purchased by Mr. and Mrs. Archibald McCrea in 1928. The McCreas embarked on an ambitious remodeling program that included raising the roof to allow for rooms on the third floor, enlarging the flanking kitchen and laundry dependencies, and building connectors between the main house and its dependencies. The remodeled house, which is over 200 feet long, has been restored to the Colonial Revival style of the 1930s.

The property was purchased in 1963 by the Sealantic Fund, Inc., upon the death of Mrs. McCrea. Late in 1969, the house was given to the nearby Colonial Williamsburg Foundation, which doubled the acreage to preserve the estate from intrusion.

Colonial Williamsburg undertook extensive archaeological research on the property and happily discovered, below the bluff on which Carter's Grove mansion stands, the seventeenth-century site of Wolstenholme Towne.

## SITE DESCRIPTION

An architectural historian, Samuel Chamberlain, once called **Carter's Grove's mansion** the most beautiful house in America. Built in 1754 and restored to the 1930s, the Georgian-style brick mansion now consists of five connected sections. When originally constructed, the house was a two-story, seventy-two-foot-long central block separated from flanking story-and-a-half dependencies that antedated the main house. The **kitchen dependency** is the oldest part of the structure, its back section possibly dating from the end of the seventeenth century.

In 1927–1928, **hyphens** were built that connected the three detached buildings, changing it to a single 201-foot-long mansion. Additionally, rows of **dormers** were installed on the main roof, which was raised eleven feet to accommodate new rooms on the third floor.

The house is noted for its outstanding woodwork, which was done by Richard Baylis, an English artisan brought by Burwell to Virginia. Original ornate paneling can be seen in the entry as well as nine other rooms. The entry and hall are paneled in locally cut heart pine, which was painted when the house was built; stairs and balusters are of walnut. The **entry and stair hall**, with its broad elliptical arch, is regarded as one of the finest rooms in Georgian architecture.

Furnishings, most of which belonged to the McCrea's, range from the seventeenth to the twentieth centuries.

The **terraced gardens**—called "falling terraces" in the eighteenth century—which originally stepped down to the James River, have been reconstructed based on eighteenth-century designs uncovered by archaeologists.

Nearby, a **slave quarter** of the 1700s has been reconstructed on its original site as determined archaeologically. Half the population of eighteenth-century Williamsburg was of African descent. The 1770s slave quarter, which would have housed field laborers, includes three log dwellings, a corn crib, chicken enclosures and garden plots. Adjacent to the slave quarter are fields planted with wheat, and corn, and apple orchards. Animals from Williamsburg's rare breed program graze in the fields.

Also at Carter's Grove is the **Winthrop Rockefeller Archaeology Museum**, a subterranean museum built under a hillside so as not to intrude upon the historic landscape. Exhibits in ten galleries narrate the story of Martin's Hundred, the 1619 plantation on the James River whose principal settlement, Wolstenholme Towne, was lost in 1622. The discovery of the site of the colonial village in the 1970s was headed by archaeologist Ivor Noel Hume. Some of the most prized items were discovered in a well and a pond: the first intact face-covering helmets from a suit of armor ever found in North America. The museum exits directly onto the **Wolstenholme Town site**, where fences and buildings have been partially reconstructed.

To return to Williamsburg, take the eight-mile, one-way Country Road that passes marshes, tidal creeks, wooded hills, and open fields.

# COLONIAL WILLIAMSBURG

Restoration of the eighteenth-century capital of the
English colony of Virginia; NR, NHL, HABS.

**Address:** PO Box 1776, Williamsburg VA 23187-1776
**Telephone:** (804) 229-1000, 1-800-HISTORY
**Location:** In southeast Virginia, midway between Richmond and Norfolk
on I-64.
**Open:** 9:00 A.M.–5:00 P.M. daily.
**Admission:** Patriot's Pass (admission to all major exhibits in Colonial Williamsburg for one year): adults $29, children ages 6–12 $17.50. Royal
Governor's Pass (admission to all major exhibits in the Historic Area
plus Governor's Palace, the Abby Aldrich Rockefeller Folk Art Cen-
ter, and the DeWitt Wallace Decorative Arts Gallery during current
visit): adults $26.50, children ages 6–12 $16. Basic Admission
Ticket (admission to exhibits in the Historic Area, valid only for
that day): adults $24, children ages 6–12 $14.50. Separate admission
tickets available for Governor's Palace, Carter's Grove, Wallace Gal-
lery, and Folk Art Center.
**Restaurants:** Christiana Campbell's Tavern, King's Arms Tavern, Shields
Tavern, Chowning's Tavern, Regency Dining Room, Bay Room,
Cascades Restaurant, Wallace Gallery Café, Golden Horseshoe
Clubhouse Grills, Woodlands Grill.
**Shops:** Tarpley's Store, Raleigh Tavern Bake Shop, Hunter's Store, Prentis
Store, Mary Dickinson Store, John Greenhow Store, Post Office,
Golden Ball, McKenzie Apothecary, Craft House, Visitor Center
Bookstore, Merchants Square, Everything Williamsburg, Sign of the
Rooster (at the Folk Art Center), Wallace Gallery Gift Shop.
**Facilities:** Visitor center with orientation film, craft demonstrations, Cen-
tral Library, golf courses, bus transportation, special events, educa-
tional forums, handicapped accessible, DeWitt Wallace Decorative
Arts Gallery, Winthrop Rockefeller Archaeology Museum, Abby
Aldrich Rockefeller Folk Art Center, Carter's Grove, Basset Hall.

## WHERE TO STAY

**Inns/Bed & Breakfasts:** For information and reservations, call Colonial Houses and Taverns, Williamsburg, 1-800-HISTORY.

**Motels/Hotels:** In Colonial Williamsburg: Williamsburg Inn, Williamsburg Lodge, Williamsburg Woodlands, Governor's Inn, and Providence Hall, 1-800-HISTORY. Fort Magruder Inn, 6945 Pocahontas Trail, Williamsburg VA 23187, (804) 220-2250, 1-800-582-1010.

**Camping:** Jamestown Beach Campsites, PO Box CB, Williamsburg VA 23187, (804) 229-7609, (804) 229-3300. Williamsburg KOA, 5210 Lightfoot Rd., Williamsburg VA 23188, 1-800-635-2717, (804) 565-2907. Colonial Campgrounds, 4712 Lightfoot Rd., Williamsburg VA 23188, 1-800-336-2734, (804) 565-2734.

## OVERVIEW

In an atmosphere that combines history and romance, Williamsburg is the museum village that virtually everyone has heard of, and it is usually their favorite. It has everything—a huge restored area that takes several days to see; original eighteenth-century buildings on their original sites; an important historical connection to the American Revolution; 225 period rooms decorated with original American antiques; well-informed costumed guides; expert craft demonstrations; a park-like, well-landscaped site; exceptional museum collections of folk art and decorative art; restaurants in romantic colonial taverns; shops loaded with books, reproduction furniture, and craft items—as well as all the facilities found at resorts, including fine hotels, tennis courts, and golf courses.

Without doubt, Williamsburg is the crown jewel of America's restored museum villages. Indeed, many of the other restored villages and communities that are described in this book owe their inspiration and design to Colonial Williamsburg. The quality and breadth of its restoration and its programs attract about a million visitors each year—which means you need to plan in advance for accommodations during the busiest seasons at Colonial Williamsburg.

Today, the Historic Area of Williamsburg covers 173 acres of the original 220-acre town, based on the 1781 street plan. It is a mile long, with the Wren Building of the College of William and Mary at the western boundary and the Capitol at the eastern end; the average width is one-half mile. Within or adjacent to this area are eighty-eight restored houses, shops, taverns, public buildings, and dependencies. In addition to the Governor's Palace and the Capitol, more than fifty structures have been rebuilt on their original sites. Ninety acres of gardens have been planted in eighteenth-century style, and the Colonial Williamsburg area is surrounded by 3,000 acres of greenbelt.

## HISTORY

Williamsburg has been both an outpost of the powerful British Empire in the New World and an ideological training ground for those who would help to lead America to independence. Virginia was a royal colony, and the 1720 Royal Governor's Palace was the official residence of the king's representative in Virginia. The College of William and Mary, founded in Williamsburg in 1693, is named in honor of British sovereigns.

In 1699, Williamsburg became Virginia's second capital, replacing Jamestown, the first permanent English settlement in the New World. Activity in the House of Burgesses, composed of elected representatives of Virginia's counties, centered on the fledgling efforts of Americans to govern themselves.

In Williamsburg, George Washington, Patrick Henry, George Wythe, Thomas Jefferson, and other Virginians began the struggle that would lead to the birth of a new nation. At Williamsburg on May 15, 1776, the Virginia Convention passed a resolution urging the Continental Congress to declare the colonies free and independent of Great Britain and to create a national confederation. Acting on that resolution, Richard Henry Lee proposed in Philadelphia that Congress declare the colonies "absolved from all allegiance to the British Crown." Congress adopted Lee's resolution on July 2 and approved the amended Declaration of Independence on July 4.

On June 12, 1776, the Virginia Convention at Williamsburg adopted George Mason's Virginia Declaration of Rights, which later became the basis for the first ten amendments of the Constitution of the United States.

In 1781, Williamsburg surrendered its role as Virginia's capital when the offices of the new commonwealth were moved to Richmond to be more convenient to the state's growing population and to be better protected from enemy attacks.

Williamsburg is also significant in the field of historic restoration in the United States. Colonial Williamsburg represents one of the finest outdoor museum villages not just in the United States but in the world.

Colonial Williamsburg is the name identifying all the activities of the Colonial Williamsburg Foundation, a nonprofit educational organization. Among its activities are the restoration and interpretation of the historic sections of Williamsburg, the development of an extensive educational and cultural program based on Williamsburg's historical significance, the management of visitor accommodations and services, and the operation and maintenance of the DeWitt Wallace Decorative Arts Gallery, the Winthrop Rockefeller Archaeology Museum, the Abby Aldrich Rockefeller Folk Art Center, Carter's Grove Plantation, and Bassett Hall, the home of Mr. and Mrs. John D. Rockefeller, Jr.

The concept of restoring the colonial capital originated with the Reverend Dr. W. A. R. Goodwin, rector of the Bruton Parish Church. In 1926, Goodwin discussed the idea with John D. Rockefeller, Jr., who agreed to provide financial support. It was decided to restore the extant buildings to their appearance during the colonial era. Important buildings such as the Governor's Palace and the Capitol, which no longer existed, were painstakingly researched and re-created.

## SITE DESCRIPTION

Because Colonial Williamsburg is large and complex, begin your tour at the official **Colonial Williamsburg Visitor Center,** a scene of much activity. Here you will find ticket sales, an orientation film, cultural and historical exhibits, information on accommodations and dining, activities and programs of the day, and guides for handicapped visitors. Historic area buses provide transportation for ticket holders.

Because of the size of the Williamsburg restoration, the site description follows the major streets and comments only on the buildings open to the public. Buildings front on the three major streets of the city: **Duke of Gloucester, Francis, and Nicholson Streets,** each of which has a number of privately owned restored buildings.

The **Capitol,** one of the major landmarks, is a careful re-creation of the first building that served as Virginia's capitol from 1704 until it was destroyed by fire in 1747. A second capitol was completed in 1753, which incorporated the surviving walls of the first capitol but was a different architectural style. In 1781, Virginia's government moved to Richmond.

Under the supervision of Henry Cary, a leading colonial architect, the foundations of the capitol were laid in 1701, and construction was completed in 1705. The architecture is a simplified version of the Renaissance style. Note the round and arched windows and cupola. Since the capitol was built during Queen Anne's reign, her coat of arms is emblazoned on its tower.

The building's H-shaped design reflects the composition of the colonial government, which was headed by a royal governor appointed by the British crown. One wing housed the elected House of Burgesses on the first floor and their committee rooms on the second. Among the distinguished Americans who served as burgesses are George Washington, Patrick Henry, Richard Henry Lee, and Thomas Jefferson. The capitol's other wing housed the general court room and the council chamber. The council consisted of the governor and his appointees.

Be sure to see the **portraits** of Edmund Pendleton, John Robinson, and Patrick Henry in the conference room and the large painting of George Washington by the famous American artist Charles Wilson Peale that hangs in the hallway.

The **Pasteur and Galt Apothecary Shop**, built in 1760, is marked with the mortar-and-pestle sign of the apothecary and the snake-entwined staff of the physician. It was the office of physicians Dr. William Pasteur and his partner, Dr. John Galt. The shop contains exhibits of ointments, herbs, medicines, and elixirs of the colonial period. The room at the rear contains the doctors' apparatus and surgical instruments. Behind the shop is an **herb garden**.

The **Raleigh Tavern**, a reconstruction on the north side of Duke of Gloucester Street, was named for Sir Walter Raleigh, who encouraged English settlement in North America and popularized the use of tobacco in Europe. Colonial taverns were places of public receptions, meetings, and dining. Among the prominent persons who dined or met at the Raleigh are George Washington, Peyton Randolph, John Marshall, Thomas Jefferson, and the Marquis de Lafayette. At the **Raleigh Tavern Bakery**, bread and cakes made according to colonial recipes are sold.

The **Golden Ball** is a reconstruction of the jeweler's shop that stood on the site from 1727 to 1907 and was first owned by James Craig. Displays feature eighteenth-century jewelry and silver, and a costumed artisan is at work.

**Wetherburn's Tavern** is located on property purchased by Henry Wetherburn in 1738. The restored white frame building, used continuously for the past 200 years, has been variously a tavern, store, girls' school, guesthouse, and inn. A detailed inventory of Wetherburn's estate was used as a guide in furnishing the tavern. Added information came from archaeological excavations of the site, which uncovered 192,000 artifacts such as glass, pottery, porcelain, and bottles. In addition to the Wetherburn family, twelve slaves lived and worked at the tavern. A **kitchen, dairy, and garden** are behind the tavern.

The **Printing Office** was owned in the eighteenth century by William Parks, publisher of the *Virginia Gazette*, which first appeared in 1736.

Site excavations unearthed pieces of type, bookbinder's ornaments, and other artifacts related to printing. The site is the location of the **Printing Office, Post Office**, and **Bookbindery**, which are craft shops. Of particular interest are the demonstrations of the printing press and bookbinding.

The **Market Square Tavern**, at the intersection of Queen and Duke of Gloucester Streets, is operated as a hostelry of the Williamsburg Inn. Among the tavern's famous guests are Thomas Jefferson and Patrick Henry. The tavern has an attractive **garden** planted with the trees, flowers, and herbs that were popular in the eighteenth century.

**Chowning's Tavern**, which was opened in 1766 by Josiah Chowning, is a reconstruction operated as an tavern, or ordinary. It serves **luncheons and dinners** featuring such popular period fare as Brunswick stew, Welsh rabbit, oysters, clams, and draft ale. Behind the tavern is a delightful **garden** shaded by an arbor of scuppernong grape vines.

The **Magazine**, a substantial red brick, octagonal building, was erected in 1715 by Governor Alexander Spotswood. It was used as an arsenal for the weapons, powder, and ammunition needed to defend the colony, and now houses a display of weapons of the French and Indian Wars, including flintlock muskets, the standard arms of British and colonial troops.

The **Courthouse**, built in 1770, was used by Williamsburg and James City County until 1932. The restored red brick T-shaped building features arched windows, a white octagonal cupola, and overhanging pediments. Inside, costumed interpreters take the roles of judges, clerks, lawyers, and citizens as they reenact eighteenth-century legal proceedings.

The **James Geddy House and Foundry**, a two-story L-shaped structure, was built in 1760. From 1760 to 1777, it was home to James Geddy, one of Williamsburg's leading silversmiths, and it includes a collection of watches and watchmaker's tools. In the foundry behind the house, skilled craftsmen cast objects of bronze, brass, pewter, and silver.

The **Bruton Parish Church**, at the corner of Duke of Gloucester Street and Palace Green, has been used as a place of worship since 1715. During the colonial era, the Church of England, or the Anglican church, was established as the official religion. Today, the Bruton Parish Church functions as an Episcopal church, the contemporary American descendant of the Anglican church. The churchyard contains **tombstones** marking the graves of colonial members of the congregation.

The **College of William and Mary**, located at the western end of Duke of Gloucester Street, is one of America's oldest institutions of higher learning. Among its famous graduates are Thomas Jefferson and John Marshall. Through the efforts of the Reverend James Blair, Episcopal commissary for Virginia, a royal charter issued in 1693 authorized the establishment of the college.

**Bassett Hall**, an eighteenth-century house that was the Williamsburg home of Mr. and Mrs. John D. Rockefeller, Jr., looks as it did when the Rockefellers restored and furnished the house in the mid-twentieth century.

The **DeWitt Wallace Decorative Arts Gallery**, on Nassau Street, displays high-quality art objects, furniture, silver, ceramics, textiles, and paintings. The modern, 62,000-square-foot museum is entered through the lobby of the reconstructed **public hospital** of 1773, the last major public building of eighteenth-century Williamsburg to have been reconstructed. The original hospital burned in 1885. Heartrending exhibits focus on the evolution of beliefs about and treatment of mentally ill people. Both an eighteenth-century prison-like cell and a nineteenth-century patient's apartment can be viewed.

The restored 1704 **public gaol** is located on the north side of Nicholson Street. Debtors' cells were added in 1711, and the keeper's quarters were added in 1722. It was used by the colony until 1780 and served as the city jail of Williamsburg until 1910.

**Anthony Hay's Cabinetmaking Shop** was purchased by Anthony Hay in 1756; the shop's addition was built around 1770. The reconstructed building houses an operating craft shop. Today's cabinetmakers use the cherry, walnut, and mahogany woods so popular in the eighteenth century to produce handmade furniture and musical instruments, including harpsichords and guitars.

The **Peyton Randolph House** is the imposing home of the distinguished statesman who served both colonial Virginia and the early American Republic. From 1766 to 1775, Randolph was the speaker of Virginia's House of Burgesses. He was elected president of the Continental Congress in 1774. The western section of the house was built by Sir John Randolph, Peyton Randolph's father, in 1715. In 1724, the one-and-one-half-story house next door was purchased; a middle two-story addition was then built to join the two houses.

**Robertson's Windmill** has been reconstructed. The mill's lower chamber contained machinery to screen and sack flour and meal; the upper chamber held the shaft and millstones that ground the grain. The mill was wind-powered by sails lashed to wooden frames.

The **Brush-Everard House**, a restored frame town house, was built in 1717 by John Brush, a gunsmith and armorer, as his residence and shop.

It was also owned by Thomas Everard, a politician who was auditor of Virginia and mayor of Williamsburg. Everard enlarged the house by adding two wings that formed a U-shaped design.

The reconstructed **Governor's Palace**, which resembles a Georgian-style English country manor, is a splendid structure that recalls the power and majesty of the British Empire. Designed by Henry Cary and completed in 1720, it was the residence and official headquarters of seven royal governors of Virginia until the outbreak of the American Revolution in 1775. It then served as the official mansion of the Commonwealth of Virginia's first two governors, Patrick Henry and Thomas Jefferson.

The palace was destroyed by fire in 1781. Reconstruction of the building, begun in 1931, was based on archaeological excavations, which unearthed the foundations, and research that included the use of Thomas Jefferson's 1779 floor plan, records of the House of Burgesses, and a copper plate of the palace found in the Bodleian Library at Oxford University. Of particular interest is the first-floor **entry hall**, with its collection of firearms and swords.

The formally designed palace **garden** features both native American and European trees and plants, including boxwood and holly. Behind the palace are a **kitchen** and a **stable** with a working wheelwright.

The restored **George Wythe House** is a handsome brick house that has four rooms and a wide central passage on each floor. Two chimneys are between the paired rooms so that all eight rooms have fireplaces. The garden and yard area is the location of an **orchard** and several reconstructed frame dependencies including a **kitchen, laundry, smokehouse, stable,** and **chicken house.**

George Wythe (1726–1806) was a scholar, a lawyer, a member of the House of Burgesses, the colony's attorney general, a signer of the Declaration of Independence, and a professor of law at the College of William and Mary.

The **Abby Aldrich Rockefeller Folk Art Center** is a museum and gallery housing an outstanding folk art collection given to Colonial Williamsburg in 1939 by Mrs. John D. Rockefeller, Jr. Built in 1957, the museum expanded in 1992 into a new 19,000-square-foot building, which tripled the exhibition space. With 3,000 folk art objects dating from the colonial period to the present, it is the nation's leading folk art collection. Included are portraits, landscapes, fraktur drawings, still-life paintings, shop signs, weather vanes, pottery, metalware, quilts and coverlets, carvings, furniture, and toys.

## Festivals/Crafts

Williamsburg's living-history program includes thirty-six colonial craftsmen and tradesmen including bakers, printers, bookbinders, tailors, housewrights, jewelers, engravers, carpenters, millers, milliners, spinners, weavers, silversmiths, ironsmiths, wheelwrights, and makers of shoes, baskets, furniture, wigs, cloth, harnesses, and musical instruments.

Annual educational forums include an **Energy Management Conference** in mid-January, **Colonial Weekends** held on four weekends in January and February, an **Antiques Forum** in early February, a **Learning Weekend** in early March, a **Garden Symposium** in early April, and the **History Forum** in early November.

Interpretive programs include topical escorted walking tours, special events, and evening entertainment. There are so many events at Colonial Williamsburg that a brochure listing them is published each week and is given to ticket holders.

Colonial Williamsburg is especially beautiful during the **Christmas season**. Ornaments are made of pheasant feathers, fragrant lemons, evergreens, fruits, and berries. Wreaths hang on doorways, lanterns and candles shine in the windows, and carolers stroll the streets.

# COLONIAL NATIONAL HISTORICAL PARK, JAMESTOWN AND YORKTOWN

Jamestown was the first permanent English settlement in North America; Yorktown is the site of last major battle of the American Revolution; Colonial Parkway is a 23-mile scenic roadway which connects Jamestown, Williamsburg, and Yorktown; NR, HABS.

**Address:** Colonial National Historical Park, PO Box 210, Yorktown VA 23690

**Telephone:** (804) 898-3400

**Location:** In southeastern Virginia; Jamestown and Yorktown are located on the Virginia Peninsula, between the James and York Rivers; Colonial Parkway is reached from I-64 exits 242A and B.

**Open:** Jamestown Visitor Center: mid-June–late August, 9:00 A.M.–6:00 P.M. daily; April–mid-June and late August–September, 9:00 A.M.–5:30 P.M. daily; October–March, 9:00 A.M.–5:00 P.M. daily. Yorktown Visitor Center: mid-June–late August, 8:30 A.M.–6:00 P.M. daily; April–mid-June and late August–September, 8:30 A.M.–5:30 P.M. daily; October–March, 8:30 A.M.–5:00 P.M. daily.

**Admission:** Jamestown: $8 per car, $2 per person for bicyclists and pedestrians. Yorktown: free.

**Restaurants:** Cafeteria at Jamestown Settlement Museum near Jamestown Island.

**Shops:** Gift shops in Jamestown Visitor Center and in Yorktown Visitor Center.

**Facilities:** Visitor centers with orientation films, guided tours, picnic areas on the Colonial Parkway and in Yorktown, partially handicapped accessible, glassblowing demonstrations at Jamestown, special events.

Photo by Patricia A. Gutek

**Jamestown, Colonial National Historical Park, Yorktown, Virginia**
At Jamestown, the first permanent English settlement in North America, a
craftsman demonstrates seventeenth-century glassblowing techniques in a
reconstructed glasshouse.

## WHERE TO STAY

**Inns/Bed and Breakfasts:** For accommodations operated by Colonial Williamsburg, call 1-800-HISTORY..

**Motels/Hotels:** Duke of York, PO Box E, 508 Water St., Yorktown VA 23690, (804) 898-3232. Kingsmill Resort, 1010 Kingsmill Rd., Williamsburg VA 23185, (804) 253-1703, 1-800-832-5665, FAX: (804) 253-3993. Williamsburg Hospitality House, 415 Richmond Rd., Williamsburg VA 23185, (804) 229-4020, 1-800-932-9192, FAX: (804) 220-1560. Hotel/Motel Association, 1-800-446-9244.

**Camping:** Newport News Park Campsites, 13564 Jefferson Ave., Newport News VA 23603, (804) 888-3333. Jamestown Beach Campsites, PO Box CB, Williamsburg VA 23187, (804) 229-7609, 1-800-446-9228.

## OVERVIEW

Colonial National Park, established by Congress in 1930, includes Jamestown, Yorktown Battlefield, and the Colonial Parkway. The park, which includes the sites where British rule began and ended, presents travelers with a unique opportunity to experience two hundred years of early American colonial and Revolutionary War history. Colonial Parkway is a twenty-three-mile scenic drive that links Jamestown, Williamsburg, and Yorktown.

On May 13, 1607, 104 English men and boys landed at Jamestown Island to plant the beginning of the British Empire in the New World. Jamestown was Virginia's capital from 1607 until its relocation to Williamsburg in 1699. The combined research of archaeologists, architects, and historians illuminate the events of Jamestown's founding and its settlers' struggle to survive on the tidewater's untamed frontier. Excavations have uncovered foundations, artifacts, and burial grounds.

On October 19, 1781, 174 years after the landing at Jamestown, the British lost their thirteen North American colonies when Lord Cornwallis surrendered his troops to General George Washington's American and French forces at Yorktown. Using eighteenth-century military maps and archeological excavations, the National Park Service has been able to shape an account of Washington's successful siege of the British army, the Revolution's last major battle: original and reconstructed earthworks as well as excavated siege lines help tell the story.

## HISTORY

Jamestown, located on the Virginia Peninsula along the James River, was the site of the first permanent English settlement in North America. On April 10, 1606, King James I granted a charter to the London Company, a joint stock company, to establish plantations in Virginia. The Company's investors hoped to earn a profit from the discovery of gold and from the projected silk and glass industries.

In December 1606, three small ships—the *Susan Constant,* the *Godspeed,* and the *Discovery*—sailed for North America, carrying 104 men and boys charged with establishing an English fort on a large navigable river. Reaching Virginia's coast in late April 1607, the colonists determined to construct their fortified outpost on a marshy peninsula fifty-seven miles from the mouth of the James River. Here, they eventually built a timber fortification, triangular in shape. Although the site offered a deep-water port and an easily defended position, disease, mosquitos, and contaminated brackish water caused a high death rate among the settlers.

The colonists' ignorance of frontier realities produced a series of calamities that also threatened the settlement's existence. An ill-sorted and undisciplined collection of fortune hunters, the settlers were completely unprepared for the trials of surviving in the wilderness. Rather than establishing a firm footing for the new colony by planting crops, they ran off in all directions on elusive searches for gold, diamonds, and rubies. The unruly settlers dissipated their energies in quarrels and fell victim to disease, starvation, and hostile American Indians.

The presence of Captain John Smith—an intrepid explorer, author, and soldier—helped to save Jamestown from extinction. He secured food by trading with Native Americans and drew a useful and accurate map of Chesapeake Bay. In the well-known dramatic event, Pocahontas, the American Indian princess, persuaded her father, the Chief Powhatan, to spare Smith's life. Pocahontas, who later married John Rolfe, eventually traveled to England and appeared at Court. As president of the Virginia Council from 1608 to 1609, Smith imposed strict discipline to promote the small colony's survival. He admonished, "He who will not work, will not eat." Unfortunately for the colony, a serious accident forced Smith's return to England.

With Smith's absence, the sense of order and discipline eroded. The colonists suffered famine during the "Starving Time" in 1609–1610, when over 400 of Jamestown's estimated 500 inhabitants died. The desperate survivors were on the verge of abandoning the colony when a relief ship arrived from England. The new governor, Lord De La Warr, and his successors, Thomas Gates and Thomas Dale, ruled by martial law and restored some order and stability to the colony.

Despite King James I's aversion to the noxious weed, tobacco, which he wrote was "lothsome to the eye, hatefull to the nose, harmefull to the braine, and dangerous to the lungs," the colonists began to raise tobacco for export. As smoking became fashionable in London, the market for tobacco accelerated. To cultivate the profitable cash crop, large tobacco plantations were established in the Virginia colony from the James to the other river valleys.

Increasing numbers of settlers were now attracted to economically prosperous Virginia. Sir Edwin Sandys, leading the revitalized stockholders, encouraged migration to Virginia. Between 1619 and 1622, 3,570 additional settlers immigrated to Virginia. Many of them were indentured servants. In 1619, the first forcible importation of Africans to Virginia occurred. It is believed these first blacks were treated as indentured servants. However, by the 1640s, the ugly institution of black slavery was being born.

In 1625, King Charles I made Virginia a royal colony, ending the Company's rule. The crown now directly appointed the governor and the council. Although not recognized officially by the crown, the House of Burgesses, Virginia's representative assembly which first met in 1619, continued to hold sessions. In 1639, King Charles officially recognized the House of Burgesses.

Even before the statehouse was burned during Bacon's rebellion in 1676, there were plans to move the capital inland from the coast, which was regarded as an unhealthy location. Jamestown had been Virginia's capital for ninety-two years, from 1607 to 1699, when it was relocated to Williamsburg.

While Britain's empire in America began at Jamestown, it ended at Yorktown, scene of the last major battle of the American War for Independence. Here, the American army, aided by French army and naval units under Rochambeau and Grasse, defeated the British army.

Lord Cornwallis, the British commander, had selected Yorktown, a tobacco market port located on the York River, as his headquarters. Washington, commander of the American army and a native Virginian, benefitted from his intimate knowledge of the area's topography. Washington quickly determined to capitalize on Cornwallis's serious strategic blunder. The heights above the York River, which Cornwallis had chosen for tactical reasons, proved to be a trap. Aided by his French allies, Washington completed his encirclement of the British. While Admiral Grasse's French fleet, controlling Chesapeake Bay, cut Cornwallis off from the sea, Washington's American forces, supported by French troops under the command of Rochambeau, surrounded the British on land. On October 19, 1781, Cornwallis surrendered his entire army of 8,300 men. It is rumored that as they surrendered, the British prisoners of war marched to their own military band's playing of "The World Turned Upside Down."

## SITE DESCRIPTION

Access to both **Jamestown** and **Yorktown** is via the twenty-three-mile Colonial Parkway, which links Jamestown, Yorktown, and Williamsburg—three of the most important sites relating to colonial Virginia and to the British Empire in North America.

Although Jamestown's original buildings no longer exist, visitors, aided by museum and archeological exhibits, can visualize life in Britain's first permanent North American colony.

Exciting archeological research and debate still continue over the precise location of the original fort at Jamestown. Local archaeologists and the Association for the Preservation of Virginia Antiquities are excavating the James River shoreline in search of traces of the fort. Their goal is to find and authenticate the fort's original site by the year 2007, which will mark the 400th anniversary of Jamestown's founding. At one time, the National Park Service concluded that the fort's site was located in the river; that opinion was based on historical research and the fact that the shoreline has receded more than 100 yards since Jamestown was founded.

Begin your visit at the **Jamestown Visitor Center and Museum** by seeing the fifteen-minute orientation film. Using archeological research and its extensive collection of seventeenth-century artifacts, the Jamestown Museum has informative exhibits on the colonists' housing, industries, crafts, and food. Artifacts exhibited include serving dishes, utensils, coins, weapons, glassware, tools, and pottery. There are a diorama of the original triangular-shaped fort and models of the three ships—the *Discovery*, the *Godspeed*, and *Susan Constant*.

Self-guided or guided walking tours lead through the site of "James Cittie," or **Jamestown Townsite**. Excavated ruins of the early homes and public buildings may be seen.

The **Tercentenary Monument**, a 103-foot shaft of New Hampshire granite erected in 1907, commemorates the 300th anniversary of

Jamestown's settlement. From the monument's terrace, you can survey the townsite.

The **Old Church Tower**, an addition to the first brick church built in 1639, is the only surviving seventeenth-century structure. The official religion in the colony was Church of England, or Anglicanism, which was administered by the Diocese of London. The Reverend Robert Hunt, a minister, accompanied the first colonists. The first church was built of timbers within the fort. After it burned in January 1608, the colonists erected another frame church. In 1617, a third frame church was built on the site of the present church. The church was the meeting place for the first representative assembly on July 30, 1619.

In 1639, a brick church replaced the frame church. The brick church tower, which was added in 1647, is approximately eighteen feet square, with walls three feet thick at the base. Originally, the tower, which is all that remains of the brick church, was forty-six feet high and had two upper floors. In 1907, a memorial church was built over the foundation of the brick church by the National Society of Colonial Dames of America. In the **Memorial Church** can be seen the brick and cobblestone foundation of the 1617 frame church and the brick foundation of the 1639 church.

Twentieth-century bricks have been placed over the original seventeenth-century foundations of the **Long House**, the **Jaquelin Ambler House**, the **Country House**, the **Mary Hartwell House**, and the **Third and Fourth Statehouses**. The third statehouse was burned by Nathaniel Bacon or his sympathizers during the rebellion in 1676 against Governor William Berkeley's colonial administration. The fourth statehouse, which replaced it, burned in 1698.

Of special interest is the **Memorial Cross**, which commemorates the colonists who died during the "Starving Time" of 1609–1610. There are also a shrine to Robert Hunt, the colony's first Anglican minister, and statues of Captain John Smith and Pocahontas.

Near the entrance gate leading to Jamestown Island, stop and see the reconstructed **glasshouse**. Here costumed craftspeople demonstrate seventeenth-century glassblowing, one of Virginia's early industries. Nearby are the ruins of the original glass furnaces, built in 1608.

Jamestown Island may be explored on the three- and five-mile-loop drives, which contain markers telling the island's history. Trails lead from the tour road to **Travis Graveyard** and **Black Point**.

Jamestown is jointly administered by the U.S. Department of the Interior's National Park Service and the Association for the Preservation of Virginia Antiquities.

Just below the entrance station is the **Jamestown Settlement Museum**, a state-operated facility. Here, you can see replicas of the fort, an American Indian lodge, and the conjectural reconstructions of the three ships *Susan Constant*, *Godspeed*, and *Discovery*. An admission fee is charged.

Situated at the Colonial Parkway's eastern terminus, **Yorktown**, scene of the Revolutionary War's last major battle, is a small living town in which several colonial homes and structures survive. At the town's western edge, on VA Hwy. 238, is the **Yorktown Victory Center**, administered by the Jamestown-Yorktown Foundation for the Commonwealth of Virginia. The center offers a film, *The Road to Yorktown*, and museum exhibits. The **Yorktown Victory Monument**, erected by the United States to commemorate the French alliance and the victory over Cornwallis, stands near Main Street's east end. The monument's cornerstone, laid in 1881, commemorates the surrender's centenary.

**Yorktown Battlefield**, administered by the National Park Service, U.S. Department of the Interior, has a **visitor center**. The center's sixteen-minute multimedia theater program, *Siege at Yorktown*, and its exhibits recount the naval and land events of the siege of Yorktown. An illuminated map illustrates British, American, and French troop movements during the siege. You can walk through a full-size replica of a quarter deck on the reconstructed British frigate, which contains artifacts recovered from the York River. Among the center's exhibits are parts of General Washington's tents as well as dioramas depicting aspects of the siege. The **Siege Line Overlook** on the center's upper level provides a panoramic overview of the battlefield.

Close to Yorktown are remnants of the **British earthworks** of 1781, which were later modified and reinforced by the Confederate army during the Civil War. A few hundred yards beyond them are reconstructed parts of the French and American siege lines. Although these siege lines were leveled on orders of General Washington, their more significant parts have been reconstructed according to archeological and documentary research.

An easy, 30-minute **walking tour** covering 500 yards near the visitor center, the **"British Inner Defense Line"** recounts the events of the siege. Stops include the bluffs overlooking the York River, the British inner defense line, and a view of the Allies' siege lines and Redoubts 9 and 10.

Two self-guided auto tours, the 7-mile-long **Battlefield Tour** (marked with red arrows) and 9-mile-long **Encampment Tour** (marked with yellow arrows) begin at the visitor center. These tours feature markers, field displays, and other aids which help visitors to interpret the siege and surrender. (A taped battlefield tour can be rented for $2 at the visitor center gift shop.) Stops on the **Battlefield Tour** are the **British Inner Defense Line**, which extended 1½ miles around Yorktown, where Lord Cornwallis withdrew his troops to consolidate his position; the **Grand French Battery**, the largest gun emplacement on the Allies' siege line which contains both original and reproduction artillery pieces; the **Second Siege Line**, dug as the Allies moved closer to the British positions; and **Redoubts 9 and 10**, two small fortified British positions which were overrun after fierce fighting by the Allies. The tour continues to the **Augustine Moore House**, where on October 18, 1781, peace commissioners drafted the conditions by which Cornwallis's British army surrendered to Washington's allied American and French forces. The Moore House has been restored to its eighteenth-century appearance. The tour concludes at **Surrender Field**, where the British forces officially laid down their arms. The surrender of Cornwallis's forces, constituting one-third of Britain's forces in the North American colonies, was the Revolutionary War's last major battle. With the signing of the Treaty of Paris two years later, Great Britain officially recognized American independence.

The **Encampment Tour**, which begins at the **Surrender Field**, illustrates the behind-the-lines military strategy that gave the Allies their victory. The tour features stops at the sites of the **Pigeon Hill Redoubt**, the **Untouched Redoubt**, the **French Artillery Park**, the **French Cemetery**, **Washington's Headquarters**, **Rochambeau's Headquarters**, and **Stueben's Division**. Revolutionary War cannons are mounted in several reconstructed redoubts and batteries.

Also in the town of Yorktown, see the **Thomas Nelson House**, the eighteenth-century residence of Thomas Nelson, Jr., a signer of the Declaration of Independence, a governor of Virginia, and commander of the Virginia Militia during the siege of Yorktown. Built in 1711, it is an excellent example of early Georgian architecture in Virginia. During the Civil War, the house was commandeered as a field hospital by both Confederate and Union armies.

## FESTIVALS/CRAFTS

At Jamestown, programs especially for children are the **Young Settler's Program**, the **Pinch Pot Program**, and the **Colonial Junior Ranger Program** for children up to twelve years old, in family groups only.

Special events at Jamestown include **Jamestown Weekend**, celebrating Jamestown's founding, and **First Assembly Day**, which marks the anniversary of the first representative government in the New World.

Special events at Yorktown include the **Revolutionary War Weekend, Civil War Weekend**, and **Yorktown Day**, October 19.

## SIDE TRIPS

The **Jamestown Settlement** uses a film program and indoor gallery and outdoor living-history exhibits to tell the story of Jamestown's settlement. Exhibits include a re-created **Powhatan Indian Village**, full-size replicas of the **ships**—the *Susan Constant, Godspeed*, and *Discovery*—that carried the colonists to Virginia, and the re-created palisaded **Fort James**. Jamestown Settlement is located off VA Hwy. 31, six miles from Williamsburg. Open 9:00 A.M.–5:00 P.M. daily, except Christmas and New Year's Days. PO Box JF, Williamsburg VA 23187. (804) 229-1607.

In the town of **Yorktown** are historic buildings, many of which are privately owned. On the western side of Yorktown, the **Yorktown Victory Center**, a **multi-media museum**, and an **outdoor encampment area** tell the story of the Revolutionary War. Open 9:00 A.M.–5:00 P.M. daily, except Christmas and New Year's Days. Yorktown Victory Center, PO Box 1776, Yorktown VA 23690. (804) 887-1776.

# WEST VIRGINIA

Harpers Ferry: Harpers Ferry National Historical Park

# HARPERS FERRY NATIONAL HISTORICAL PARK

Restoration of a mid-nineteenth-century village;
site of John Brown's raid; NR.

**Address:** PO Box 65, Harpers Ferry WV 25425
**Telephone:** (304) 535-6298
**Location:** In eastern West Virginia, at the Maryland, West Virginia, Virginia borders; 65 miles northwest of Washington DC, 20 miles southwest of Frederick MD via US 340.
**Open:** Visitor center: 8:00 A.M.–5:00 P.M. daily; closed Christmas Day. Historic buildings are open only during summer months
**Admission:** Vehicles $5, walk-ins $3 per person.
**Shops:** Bookstore in information center.
**Facilities:** Visitor center, information center, shuttle buses, audiovisual presentation, guided tours, picnic areas.

## WHERE TO STAY

**Inns/Bed & Breakfasts:** Hillbrook, Rt. 2, Box 152, Summit Point Rd., Charles Town WV 25414, (304) 725-4223. Bavarian Inn and Lodge, Rt. 1, Box 30, Shepherdstown WV 25443, (304) 876-2551, FAX: (304) 876-9355. Thomas Shepherd Inn, PO Box 1162, 300 W. German St., Shepherdstown WV 25443, (304) 876-3715.
**Motels/Hotels:** Cliffside Inn, PO Box 786, Harpers Ferry WV 25425, (304) 535-6302, 1-800-782-9437. Comfort Inn, PO Box 980, Union St. and WV Hwy. 340, Harpers Ferry WV 25425, (304) 535-6391, FAX: (304) 535-6395. Sheraton Inn, 301 Foxcroft Ave., Martinsburg WV 25401, (304) 267-5500, FAX: (304) 264-9157.
**Camping:** Harpers Ferry Camp Resort, Rt. 3, Box 1300, Harpers Ferry WV 25425, (304) 535-6895, 1-800-323-8899. Gambrill State Park, Frederick MD 21701, (301) 791-4767. Sharpsburg campground of Chesapeake and Ohio Canal National Historical Park, PO Box 4, Sharpsburg MD 21782, (301) 739-4200.

## Overview

A place of natural beauty as well as history, Thomas Jefferson described the scene at Harpers Ferry as being "worth a voyage across the Atlantic." Harpers Ferry gained national prominence because of its connection with John Brown, the abolitionist who seized the U.S. arsenal at Harpers Ferry in 1859.

In 1859, Harpers Ferry was a thriving industrial center. Many factories, powered by water, lined the river banks. Later, because of lack of economic opportunity and repeated flooding, the town did not grow and prosper, and thus retained much of its mid-nineteenth-century appearance. Now restored by the National Park Service as a National Historical Park, the buildings are typically three-story brick or stone structures grouped closely together on the river banks and rising picturesquely up steep High Street. The restoration is to 1859, the year of John Brown's raid. Exhibits and interpretive presentations are organized around the themes of industry, John Brown, the Civil War, African-American history, and natural history.

## History

Harpers Ferry's location—at the confluence of the Shenandoah and Potomac Rivers on a point of land where Virginia, Maryland, and West Virginia meet in the Blue Ridge Mountains—has contributed to its role in history. Noted for its beauty, the scene is one in which early-nineteenth-century buildings climb the hills from the river banks and steep, tree-covered cliffs look down on the town.

It was not the beauty of the town but economic opportunity that lured Peter Stephens, the area's first white settler, in 1733. He operated a ferry across the river. In 1747, Stephen's ferry operation was purchased by Robert Harper. In 1763, the Virginia General Assembly established the town of "Shenandoah Falls at Mr. Harper's Ferry" and gave Harper the exclusive right to maintain a ferry across the Potomac River. The ferry ceased operations in 1824, when a double wooden span bridge was built across the river by Harper's descendants, who operated it as a toll bridge until 1839.

George Washington chose Harpers Ferry for the site of a second national armory. In 1796, the federal government purchased 118 acres, and construction of the U.S. armory and arsenal began in 1799. Muskets, rifles, and pistols were manufactured in the twenty workshops and offices located along the Potomac that made up the U.S. musket factory. A privately owned company, Hall's Rifle Works, produced breech-loading rifles for the government in nine buildings along the Shenandoah River.

It was the U.S. armory that drew John Brown to Harpers Ferry. Brown, a fifty-nine-year-old abolitionist, decided to arm an uprising of slaves. At midnight on Sunday, October 16, 1859, John Brown, leading eighteen men who called themselves the "Provisional Army of the United States," captured the bridge watchman and crossed the covered bridge into Harpers Ferry. Without resistance, the raiders seized the Shenandoah bridge, Hall's Rifle Works, and the Federal arsenal, barricaded the Baltimore and Ohio bridge across the Potomac, cut telegraph wires, and took prisoners—all in the space of two hours.

John Brown needed the armaments because he intended to set up a stronghold for freed slaves in the mountains of Maryland and Virginia and create an army of liberated African Americans who would forcibly end slavery.

Brown's initial success at Harpers Ferry was short-lived. His raiders stopped the 1:20 A.M.-Baltimore train but decided to allow it to go through. News of the raid spread quickly. Militia companies from Virginia and Maryland entered Harpers Ferry, capturing or killing several raiders. U.S. Marines, commanded by Colonel Robert E. Lee and Lieutenant J. E. B. Stuart, recaptured the Federal armory on Tuesday, October 18. Brown, his remaining raiders, and their hostages, who had barricaded themselves in the armory's fire-engine house, were soon captured.

When it was all over, ten raiders had been killed, five were captured, and four escaped. Four townspeople, one marine, and a free African American named Heyward Shephard also died. Ironically, the first victim of John Brown's violent attempt to liberate slaves was a free black man. When Shephard, who was the baggagemaster on duty at the train station the night of the raid, tried to investigate the commotion outside, he was shot and killed.

John Brown was tried and found guilty of murder, treason, and conspiring with slaves to cause insurrection. He was hanged at nearby Charles Town on December 2, 1859. Brown's unsuccessful raid, a widely publicized event, dramatized the strong and divergent positions on the slavery issue that culminated in the Civil War.

On the day of his execution, Brown wrote, "I, John Brown, am now quite certain that the crimes of the guilty land will never be purged away but with blood." Less than a year and a half later, the Civil War began. Union armies marched off to face their Confederate adversaries singing the verse "John Brown's body lies a-moldering in the grave, but his soul goes marching on."

When the Civil War began, Harpers Ferry was in Virginia; West Virginia seceded from Virginia and became a state in 1863. On the day that Virginia seceded from the Union—April 17, 1861—the armory became an immediate military target. With several companies of Virginia Militia marching toward the 100 Union troops guarding the armory, Lieutenant Roger Jones decided to torch the facility, burning some 15,000 arms. Confederate troops were able to confiscate and ship to Richmond the armory's ordinance stock, machinery, and tools. When they withdrew in June, the Confederates burned the remaining armory buildings.

Constant military occupation and the loss of employment at the arsenal left Harpers Ferry in physical and economic ruins. Devastating floods in the late 1800s added to the decline of the once-flourishing industrial town.

Harpers Ferry is now part of a national historical park operated by the National Park Service. The town has been restored to 1859, when John Brown made his midnight raid.

## SITE DESCRIPTION

A new **visitor center** has been built outside the historic area. From there, you can board a shuttle bus into the lower town.

The **Stagecoach Inn** on Shenandoah Street is an 1826 two-and-one-half-story structure that was operated as an inn from 1830 to 1837 by Major James Stephenson. During the Civil War, the building was used by the Federal government as a military warehouse and quarters for troops. It is now used as an **information center** and a **bookstore**.

**Shenandoah Street** had been part of the Charles Town and Smithfield Turnpike Company's toll road in the 1830s. The street has been restored to its 1833 macadamized finish, which consists of small broken stones compacted into a solid layer.

On Shenandoah Street are the **provost office** and a **dry goods store** in an 1812 building that was used as quarters for the master armorer until 1858. The 1858 brick building next door was to be the new quarters for the master armorer. However, it was occupied by John E. P. Daingerfield, the paymaster's clerk at the time of the raid, and Daingerfield was taken hostage. The building is now a **gun museum** with exhibits on the history of gun-making.

The **John Brown Museum** in an 1839 building focuses on the story of John Brown and his raiders. A movie on the raid is shown here.

Across from the museums is **Arsenal Square**, where the foundations of two of the original buildings have been excavated. The buildings were burned in 1861, at the start of the Civil War.

**"John Brown's Fort"** is the ironic name given to the small, one-story 1848 armory fire-engine house and watchman's office. During the raid, Brown originally held hostages here. Later, he and his followers barricaded themselves there. When the marines' demand for surrender was turned down by Brown, they battered down the engine-house door and took the raiders captive. The engine house was the only armory building to survive the Civil War. In 1891, it was displayed at the Chicago World's Fair, where it generated little interest. It was returned to Harpers Ferry and placed at various locations until 1968, when the National Park Service moved it to its present location on Shenandoah Street, not far from its original site on Potomac Street.

Armory employees relaxed over a drink in the **1839 Whitehall Tavern** on Potomac Street. In the **confectionery** on High Street, built in 1845 and enlarged later, townspeople could buy Frederick A. Roeder's breads, cakes, and rolls.

The **Civil War Museum** focuses on the war's impact on Harpers Ferry. Constant troop movements, battles to occupy the strategic town, shellings from the bulwarks on nearby cliffs, and occupation or burning of buildings combined to wreak havoc on the once-prosperous town.

The **Black History Exhibit** focuses on the African-American struggle to gain freedom.

**Harper House**, a stone house built on the side of a hill, is the oldest house in town. Robert Harper began building it in 1775, but the Revolutionary War delayed completion until 1782. Unfortunately, Harper died that year without ever occupying it. The house was used as the town's tavern until 1803 and served such prominent guests as George Washington and Thomas Jefferson. It is restored as a tenant house of the 1850s with families living in crowded conditions on each level.

Stone steps, cut out of rock at the turn of the nineteenth century, lead to **St. Peter's Catholic Church**, which was built in the 1830s, and the ruins of **St. John's Episcopal Church**, which was built in 1852 and served as both a Confederate barracks and as a hospital during the Civil War.

At Harpers Ferry, the restoration and the town flow into each other. Most of the restored buildings are in the **lower town**. Buildings along **High Street** are historically and architecturally similar to restored buildings but are privately owned and used as businesses.

In the **upper town** near **Filmore Street** are a cluster of restored brick buildings built in the mid-1850s for armory officials, including the superintendent and the paymaster, and the clerks. Unused armory dwellings became campus buildings of **Storer College**, a normal school for the education of free African Americans. The college remained in operation until 1955. Now the buildings are used as a training center for National Park Service employees.

**Harpers Ferry National Historical Park** includes large tracts of land along the rivers. There are marked hiking trails in all areas. **Civil War ruins and batteries** can be viewed along the **Maryland Heights Trail**.

**Loudoun Heights**, another part of the park, also figured in Civil War battles. The 2,000-mile Appalachian Trail, which extends from Maine to Georgia, runs through Loudoun Heights.

## SIDE TRIPS

**Antietam Battlefield**, maintained by the National Park Service, is just across the state line in Sharpsburg, Maryland. It was the site of a major Civil War battle. On September 17, 1862, General Robert E. Lee invaded the North, pitting 41,000 Confederate troops against 87,000 Union troops under General George B. McClellan. The intense battle resulted in Union losses of 12,410 and Confederate losses of 10,700; it has been called the bloodiest day of the Civil War. The **visitor center** is open daily, 8:30 A.M.–6:00 P.M. June–August, and 8:30 A.M.–5:00 P.M. the rest of the year. On Rt. 65, north of Sharpsburg. PO Box 158, Sharpsburg MD 21782. (301) 432-5124. Admission is charged.

Hikers and cyclists can take the **Chesapeake and Ohio towpath** along the banks of the canal in the **Chesapeake and Ohio Canal National Historical Park**. The construction of the **Chesapeake and Ohio Canal**, which was supposed to provide an economical shipping route from Georgetown to Pittsburgh, was begun in 1828 and ended in the 1850s, when it had reached Cumberland, Maryland, a distance of 185 miles. The National Park Service maintains the towpath and walk-in campgrounds along the route. PO Box 4, Sharpsburg MD 21782. (301) 739-4200.

# INDEX